D0881151

BRITISH ANALYTICAL PHILOSOPHY

International Library of Philosophy
and Scientific Method

EDITOR: TED HONDERICH
ADVISORY EDITOR: BERNARD WILLIAMS

A Catalogue of books already published in the
International Library of Philosophy and Scientific Method
will be found at the end of this volume.

BRITISH
ANALYTICAL
PHILOSOPHY

Edited by
Bernard Williams
and
Alan Montefiore

LONDON
ROUTLEDGE & KEGAN PAUL
NEW YORK : THE HUMANITIES PRESS

THE COLLEGE AND SEMINARY LIBRARY
NAPERVILLE, ILLINOIS

First published 1966
by Routledge & Kegan Paul Ltd
Broadway House, 68–74 Carter Lane
London, E.C.4

Printed in Great Britain
by Richard Clay (The Chaucer Press), Ltd
Bungay, Suffolk

© *Routledge & Kegan Paul Ltd 1966*

No part of this book may be reproduced
in any form without permission from
the publisher, except for the quotation
of brief passages in criticism

Second impression 1967

192
W67b

CONTENTS

8-26-68 B&T 7.21 Phil.

v

98976

INTRODUCTORY NOTE TO THE
ENGLISH EDITION

THIS BOOK was originally planned and written with a Continental audience in mind—in the first instance a specifically Italian one. In presenting these essays to a British audience, we have nevertheless thought it best to leave them, as well as our own Introduction, exactly as they were first written.

INTRODUCTION

WHAT constitutes a philosophical movement? The movements or schools of the past had their unity—or were given it by the historian of philosophy—most often in one of two ways. Either there was some great philosopher to whom the movement owed its leading ideas and its name, as when a group of philosophers were styled in antiquity 'Epicureans', or, more recently, 'Kantians' or 'Hegelians'; or, alternatively, it was more directly the terms of some broad agreement of philosophical doctrine and conclusion that provided the unity, as with the 'Stoicism' of antiquity or the 'Logical Positivism' of the twenties and thirties of this century. In this sort of sense, it is not easy to identify 'schools' of philosophy in contemporary Western thought. Leaving on one side the extremely special case of Marxism, even those movements in Europe that have a self-conscious title, notably the 'existentialist' and 'phenomenological' movements, do not display straightforwardly the unity either of allegiance or of doctrine that is to be found at earlier times in the history of philosophy. While the figure of Husserl stands behind phenomenology, it is certainly not as 'Husserlians' that phenomenologists go forth; again, to recognize some philosophical writings as 'existentialist' is to recognize rather a style and a type of concern rather than a readily isolable body of doctrine.

If this is true of movements such as these, it is still more evidently true of the kind of philosophy represented by the essays in this book. In some part, no doubt, this difference between the philosophy of the present day and some philosophy of the past is due merely to its being *the present day*: the comforting unities in past schools appear only as the falsifying effect of distance and the inevitable over-simplifications of history. But even when allowance has been made for this, a contrast remains, a contrast that has its roots in the historical development of philosophy in the last hundred years and, more particularly, in this century. This is most conspicuously true of the sort of philosophy presented here, but it also has some application to the Continental movements. The kind of unity that rested on a group of philosophers sharing the same doctrines and conclusions presupposes, of course, that there are characteristic philosophical conclusions to be shared; while the allegiance to a great philosophical figure—at least that sort of allegiance that gives his name to a school, unlike, for instance, the allegiance to Socrates—characteristically demands that the followers suppose their master to have discovered, at least in outline, the final truth. The notion of 'final truths' in philosophy is one that the modern temper tends to treat with scepticism; and indeed, more radically than this, even the idea of there being doctrines or conclusions at all in philosophy (whether final or not) is open to question. Such doctrines have usually offered themselves in the past as contributions to theoretical knowledge, while yet being characteristically different from the theoretical knowledge embodied in the natural and mathematical sciences; and the overwhelming practical and intellectual achievements of those sciences in the present time have inevitably reinforced in a powerful way a certain doubt that has been lurking in philosophy at least from the time of Kant, and indeed earlier: the doubt that all genuine theoretical knowledge is scientific, and that it cannot be as a contribution to such knowledge that philosophy has its peculiar, non-scientific, role to play.

Whatever the justice of such a doubt, it certainly appears as no accident that the characteristic agreements and disagreements between philosophers of the same and different schools at this time should not express themselves so much in doctrine, as in method. It is in certain styles and methods of thought, certain types of questions and certain sets of terms and ideas for discussing them, that the unity of existentialist thought, for example, most obviously appears; and similarly with the essays collected in this book. They are all examples of methods of philosophical discussion that have been most influential and important in Great Britain and elsewhere in the English-speaking world since the war, and which (it is fair to say) remain so. The range of styles and subject matter to be found even in this collection, limited as it necessarily is, illustrate the fact that a certain definite unity in this philosophical style is compatible with considerable variety in both philosophical interests, and in general belief. It is perhaps worth remarking in particular, as something more readily taken for granted in this style of philosophy than in many European styles, that the authors (who represent, incidentally, the younger age-group among English-speaking philosophers, being mostly in their thirties or early forties) include both Christians and non-Christians. This variety is further witnessed in the movement's not having any agreed name: 'linguistic philosophy', 'linguistic analysis', even 'Oxford philosophy' (with reference to the university where these methods have been, not so much originated, as most influentially practised), are all titles which have been applied to these ways of philosophical discussion. It is notable that these titles have been more enthusiastically employed by critics or expositors of these ideas than by the philosophers in question themselves, who prefer in general to describe their activity merely as 'doing philosophy'. To some people, this description might seem to embody the claim that these were the only ways of doing philosophy. To some extent, the rejection of labels is more connected with a dislike of 'taking sides in philosophy' (to use a phrase of Professor Gilbert Ryle's), a wholesale rejection of programmatic aspirations and zealotry, than it is with an exclusive claim to have *the* programme of philosophy; however, it is also true that many of these philosophers would claim that their way of approaching philosophical problems was better—more illuminating, more realistic, and more rational—than others. Such a claim is a proper consequence of their believing in what they are doing. Though the 'English-speaking' style of philosophy is an academic style—a point that we shall come back to—it does not suffer from that particularly barren form of academicism which blankly accords equal respect to any activity that calls itself 'philosophy'.

It is not an aim of this Introduction to attempt a general account of this type of philosophizing. On the contrary, we have assembled the essays that follow precisely in the belief that no purely expository survey of this type of philosophy is fruitful or even, in the end, really possible; but that the only effective way to present a style of philosophy is to present it in action, with philosophers writing about philosophical problems that concern them. The essays in this book are thus, in the first instance, *examples* of philosophy in the contemporary British, or rather

'English-speaking', style. However, there is clearly a danger that such a collection, just by itself, would not serve the purpose, which we hope this book will serve, of effectively introducing this type of philosophy to Continental readers to whom it is unfamiliar, because the various contributions will be too particular and discontinuous, and will not relate in any clear way either to one another, or to any historical background. This difficulty we have sought to overcome in two ways. First, we have asked our contributors, all of whom have written specially for this volume, to set the problem that they are discussing so far as possible in a broader framework, and to make clear how their problem arises as a real problem for them in the structure of philosophical activity in which they find themselves. In some cases, an opportunity has arisen to show how the problems are conditioned by certain traditional concerns of British philosophy as opposed to others more influential on the continent of Europe. We hope that these discussions of particular philosophical issues conducted in the consciousness of their wider connections and of their origins will serve to illuminate the methods of discussion themselves.

Secondly, we have provided a bibliography at the end containing all the works referred to by the various contributors, and also some more of general interest, including some which offer historical accounts of recent philosophical developments. This bibliography, while it has no pretensions to being a full selection of important works, we nevertheless hope will provide a substantial and representative guide to interesting writings in the philosophical mode which this book presents; and the fact that it is in good part connected with the essays may give it an advantage over a blank assemblage of leading works, in that it provides a natural direction of exploration from the issues discussed in the essays. We must acknowledge, however, that the bibliography has one obvious and substantial disadvantage from the point of view of the Continental reader—that almost all the works listed in it are in English, and many or most of them have not been translated. This is a difficulty which a book like the present one is bound to meet, since, if many of the works in the bibliography had been translated, this book would not need to exist; or at least, not to exist in the form which we have tried to give it. The comparative lack of translations is one symptom of a certain gap between the British and the European philosophical traditions, which we hope

4

that this collection of essays may do something to bridge. We can only hope that the desire to build bridges is shared by others on both sides of the gap, and that one result of this may be that more works in English will become available in other languages, and conversely.

This is, at least, our hope. But it would be idle merely to voice this hope without facing the difficulties that lie in the way of its being realized. It is important to see where these difficulties really lie. There is a well-known textbook contrast between the traditions of British and of Continental philosophy; that British philosophy is empirical, down-to-earth, and sober in expression, while that of the Continent tends to be speculative, metaphysical, and either obscure in utterance or, if not, to have the special sort of clarity that goes with an ambitious rationalism. This contrast is, of course, an absurd caricature. It does, like many caricatures, make a gesture towards something true; in particular, so far as the present situation is concerned, there is a genuine divergence between a rather matter-of-fact tone in the British style, and the darker and more intense note that is struck by much writing on the Continent. The cause is neither banal superficiality on the part of the British philosopher, nor pretentious obscurity on the part of the Continental one—though the divergence is itself marked by the fact that when they succumb to their characteristic vices, these are the vices that each succumbs to. The divergence is rather connected with a genuine disagreement about what constitutes seriousness in philosophy; this, again, is a point that we shall come back to later in this Introduction.

In other respects, the caricature that we have just referred to is extremely misleading. It particularly misleads in suggesting that British philosophy is empirical, if what this means is that it is the *philosophy of empiricism*, directly in the tradition of Locke, Berkeley and Hume. Such a philosophy certainly has had in recent times distinguished exponents: notably Bertrand Russell, and—in a rather different manner—A. J. Ayer, though Ayer has modified his position considerably from the extreme empiricism of *Language, Truth and Logic* (1936) and *The Foundations of Empirical Knowledge* (1940). It is also true that British philosophy retains certain empiricist interests (see, for instance, Mr Quinton's contribution to this book), and even certain empiricist (though not necessarily exclusively empiricist) principles and attitudes, notably a scepticism about large-scale metaphysical conclusions sup-posedly founded on the deliverances of reason or intuition. But more generally it is certainly not in any allegiance to traditional empiricism that this philosophy is distinguished from the philo-sophies of the Continent. Indeed, in so far as British philosophy is sceptical of large-scale metaphysical conclusions, it will be as suspicious of the metaphysics of empiricism—the attempt to establish the basic constituents of the universe as experiences—as of any other.

There is a further point. Traditionally, empiricism has been expressed in psychological terms; it was as a theory of the human mind that it typically appeared, and its vocabulary was that of ideas, impressions and the powers of association. The appearance of being a kind of *a priori* psychology is not, however, essential to empiricism; it has been characteristic of many sorts of philosophy in the twentieth century to try to shake off the idiom of psycholo-gism; this it has done under such diverse influences as those of Frege, Husserl and G. E. Moore, in some part because of the new birth in the last hundred years of logic as a non-psychological science, and also in some part because of the growth of psychology itself as a natural science independent of philosophy. Empiricism was able to respond to this change, and what was essentially the empiricism of Hume, though with many refinements, was pre-sented, particularly by the logical positivists of the Vienna Circle, not in a psychological, but in a logical and linguistic form: as a doctrine not about the powers and nature of the mind, but as a theory of language and the limits of meaning. But while this was a possible expression of empiricism, its linguistic emphasis has proved more powerfully influential than its empiricist content. The concern with meaning, with what can be sensibly and point-fully said in what circumstances, and more generally with the conditions of meaningful discourse, has in a sense turned against empiricism itself, particularly against its characteristic doctrine of the primacy of the 'data' of immediate sense-experience.

This has led—by what some philosophers (but perhaps not these philosophers) might regard as a typically dialectic movement —to the development of a certain underlying tension in contem-porary British philosophy. On the one hand, the mood and intent are still predominantly empiricist; on the other hand, the impli-cations of many of the methods used and of the insights attained are not. This tension, too, is to be felt in the collection of essays of this book; in some cases, perhaps, within the individual essays themselves, but certainly within the collection taken as a whole. How this tension is to be resolved may be seen as one of the most general of the questions facing British philosophy at the present time.

All this may suggest that the present gap between British and Continental philosophy may lie in a rather different place than the emphasis on empiricism would indicate. It does, however, at the same time suggest a new and real kind of difficulty in bridging the gap. For it may be wondered whether there are not certain objections *in principle* to this linguistic philosophy ever moving outside the English-speaking world by the medium of translation. The concern with language in this philosophy is not merely abstract and general as it is in the general science of linguistics and in communication theory and such studies. It is rather that particular features of the use of language, particularly in the most ordinary concerns of everyday life, are thought both to give rise to some philosophical problems, and to provide at least clues to their solution. The language whose uses are studied by these philosophers is, not surprisingly, their own—English. It may well be suggested that this sort of concern with the everyday workings of a natural language must inevitably defy satisfactory translation: if English-speaking philosophy is linguistic, then it must inevitably remain the philosophy of English speakers.

If we did not think that this objection could be answered, we should clearly not have asked our contributors to write essays to be translated—we should not have embarked on assembling this book at all. In fact, we believe that there is a number of answers to this objection relating to different aspects of so-called 'linguistic' philosophy. First, for a good deal of the work which recognizably belongs to this type of philosophy, it is not true that its arguments make any direct appeal to features of the English, or any other, language. It is 'linguistic' only in being constantly aware of the presence of language, not merely in the negative sense of being sensitive to the dangers of being misled by words and trapped into empty verbal argument if we do not ask 'what is the point of using language in this way?', but also in the more positive sense of an awareness that in discussing, as philosophy always has, the relations between concepts and the nature of various ideas, one always comes back to the expression of such things in the human activity of thinking and talking about the world. A good number of essays in this book are examples of 'linguistic' philosophy only in this limiting sense, such as, for instance, those of Mr Gardiner, Professor Wollheim and Mr Kenny.

A special case of this type of philosophy whose linguistic interests do not raise the problem of translation from a natural language is that of those more precise and formal subjects which admit of treatment with the use of a *non-natural* language, that is to say, a formalized language of logical symbolism. There has been some discussion and disagreement in the past years about the question of to what extent formalized languages can fruitfully be applied to philosophical problems. All would agree that there were certain subjects, most obviously the philosophy of mathematics, to which the application of formalized languages was valuable, perhaps essential; their wider application, however, is more favoured by some philosophers (notably in the United States, such as Quine) than by others (notably certain Oxford philosophers, such as Strawson). One essay in this book offers to some extent such a formal treatment of its problems, Mr Harré's on the philosophy of science.

Thus a good deal of so-called 'linguistic' philosophy is not so linguistic as all that, in the sense at least of its arguments referring to particular features of some natural language such as English. Some of it, however, does undoubtedly proceed by making explicit references to distinctions embodied in the English language. Nevertheless, even in these cases, translation is not necessarily a hopeless task. For in very many cases, the distinctions that are being made are of a general and important kind which it is highly probable will also be reflected in very similar distinctions made in other natural languages. In these respects, the problem of translating English 'linguistic' philosophy will be no more radical than that of translating, for instance, Aristotle or other philosophers who have claimed to discover important distinctions which they have explained by reference to structures in their own languages. The linguistic interest in such cases is not peculiar to the philosopher's own language, although it is in that language, and by reference to it, that his points are made. A striking example of this type of philosophy in the recent tradition is the work of Professor

Gilbert Ryle. His *Concept of Mind* (1949) is a work that uses very many examples drawn from English forms of speech; his points, however, are of a sufficiently general kind for the book to have been successfully translated into Italian by F. Rossi-Landi (under the title *Lo Spirito come Comportamento*). In so far as essays in the present book do use explicitly linguistic arguments, we can only ask the reader to judge for himself whether they have been successfully translated by seeing whether they make their point.

It must be admitted, however, that there is one sort of work in recent British philosophy which presents a problem to a translator of a kind more radical than, for instance, Ryle's work presents, or the essays in this book. This is work of a type practised and advocated by the late Professor J. L. Austin (whose work is described by Mr Pears in this book, and in one respect criticized by Mr Searle). Austin's concern was with extremely fine distinctions in the meaning and use of certain English expressions, and it differed from Ryle's interests, for example, in not being concerned only with distinctions of a rather broad and general kind such as we have argued are very probably to be found also in other languages. Ryle's concentration on some fairly broad distinctions at the expense of others is connected with his willingness to accept from the philosophical tradition some large-scale distinctions of category, such as that between an event, a process, a disposition, etc., in terms of which he handles his philosophical problems. Austin's approach was in a sense more radical; he, like others before him, sought 'new beginnings' in philosophy, and was unwilling to accept traditional categorial structures, or even traditional philosophical problems. Accordingly, he felt that no distinction embodied in everyday speech could safely be overlooked, and was prepared to consider nuances of meaning which other philosophers would probably dismiss as trivial or of no philosophical significance. Some of his writings in this manner and those of his followers might well prove, as they stand, untranslatable, since the shades of meaning for which Austin had a peculiarly fine ear, often lie at a level at which one is certainly concerned with idiosyncracies of the English language.

While this is so, it does not follow that Austin's *philosophy* could not be practised by non-English speakers. This would be to assume that only English had fruitfully distinguishable nuances.

It is rather that some of his work, instead of being translated from English, would need to be carried on as a fresh enterprise in terms of another language; indeed, there has been at least one attempt at such an activity, by Professor Leon Apostel, which won Austin's commendation.[1] How far it may be worth while to pursue Austin's style of analysis in any pure form, in English or another language, it is perhaps too early to judge. It is arguable that there is a certain ambiguity about its relevance to what have traditionally been regarded as philosophical problems, an ambiguity that existed in Austin's own mind. On the one hand, he sometimes spoke as though the aim of his activity was to get away from philosophy as traditionally understood, and rather lay the foundations for a systematic and empirical study of language; and some of the concepts that he developed for the description of language, such as that of a 'speech-act', may well come to play an important part in the developing science of linguistics.[2] On the other hand, Austin clearly thought that many of the distinctions to which he drew attention were highly relevant to the issues which (in his view) philosophers had in the past wildly over-simplified in their discussions; and his discussions of the language of perception, or again of the ways in which we describe human actions, were certainly intended to undercut much of what has in the past gone on in the philosophical treatment of those issues. In this connection, Austin's concern with nice distinctions of English usage appears at once as more philosophical and, in a sense, less essential. For the use of the distinctions there was essentially to *recall one to the facts*; the immensely complex facts of perception and action which the philosophers have traditionally treated in such a cavalier fashion. The aim was essentially to make one realize in a concrete way the complex variety of situations to which the language of perception and action applies, and in this respect there are analogies between Austin and the later work of Wittgenstein (some of which Mr Pears explores in the paper already referred to). Both wished to recall philosophy to the world, and in this attempt the concern with our ordinary speech, the ways in which we unreflectively describe the world in our ordinary

[1] *Cahiers de Royaumont*, pp. 188–247. In general this book—the proceedings of a conference on Analytical Philosophy held at Royaumont in 1959—throws much valuable light on the relations between the analytic and other schools of philosophy.

[2] For a highly programmatic sketch of some such developments, see P. Ziff, *Semantic Analysis*, Cornell University Press, U.S.A., 1960.

concerns, has a double role. First, it was the *means* of recall: reflection on ordinary language could realize for one the distinctions
in the world; this was so for Austin more than for Wittgenstein,
and it is a significant fact that Wittgenstein's works were written
not in English, but in German, being published in each case together with an English translation. Secondly, the language was
itself part of the world, of the human world which philosophy
had to understand instead of embarking on the vast and over-
simplified theories which have always been its bane—not merely,
it should be said, in the form of the ambitious speculative metaphysics which has often been mistrusted, but even in the form of
less ambitious empiricist theories which were not to be trusted
any the more because they were not obviously high-flown.

This concern with the return to the facts was something that in
their different ways Austin and Wittgenstein seem to have had in
common. By this phrase one is, of course, immediately reminded
of Husserl: and indeed Austin was prepared to call his studies by
the name of 'linguistic phenomenology'. But the resemblance
does not go all that deep. For the facts to which both Austin and
Wittgenstein wished to recall philosophy were very common-
place and everyday facts of ordinary life, not construed as data of
consciousness; nor themselves products of any particular supposed insight into phenomena: just facts of the common world,
shared with the least philosophical human observer. In this respect
Austin and Wittgenstein resembled each other. But their ways
were very different; their temperament and approach almost
diametrically opposed. For Wittgenstein, a man of strongly metaphysical temper, philosophy was an agonizing activity, which
aimed at depth of insight. Austin's outlook was more that of a
scholarly man who had also a great respect for the world of
affairs; he felt that what philosophy needed was principally a lot
more unvarnished *truth*, to be secured by hard work, patience and
accuracy. Those were characteristics and aims which to a considerable extent were shared by a powerfully influential figure in the
British philosophy of this century, G. E. Moore.

These differences of temperament between these philosophers
are of more than biographical interest. For they are connected
with certain features of British philosophy which certainly contribute strongly to the existing lack of *rapport* between it and most
contemporary philosophy on the continent of Europe; features

which range from a fairly superficial difference of tone to a more fundamental difference in their basic concern. These are the sorts of difference which can make a less familiar way of philosophizing seem unsympathetic at the outset, and discourage one from ever coming to grips with what it has to offer; accordingly, we should like to end this Introduction with some general remarks on these kinds of difference.

If Wittgenstein had been as powerful an influence on the *spirit* of British philosophy as he has been on its content, European philosophers would have been readier perhaps than they have been to grant the seriousness of that philosophy. Wittgenstein's deep personal commitment to philosophy, the powerfully individual and pungent quality of his writing, which some have compared to Nietzsche, and the peculiar affinity which, despite all the obvious oppositions, some aspects of his thought bear to some nineteenth-century German philosophy, notably that of Schopenhauer: all these features carry a kind of conviction which, one would have thought, would be instantly recognizable in the European tradition. If, as has perhaps been the case, even the writings of Wittgenstein himself have not received the attention elsewhere that they have in the English-speaking world, this can only be for a reason that we shall return to below—the fact that in most of his later work his concern is with philosophy itself, in particular, with the philosophy of logic and language, and does not express itself in any explicit way on moral or political topics.

But, in any case, the truth is that in spirit and tone, it is not so much the Wittgensteinian mode that prevails in contemporary British writing, as that which earlier we identified with Austin and Moore: it is a certain academic dryness, a deliberate rejection of the literary and dramatic, that is for the most part the style of this philosophy. Critics who are oppressed by these characteristics tend to ascribe them to some sort of intellectual cowardice, a failure of nerve in face of the more challenging aspects of experience. But this is certainly a superficial criticism, and there is more than one reason why the prevailing British style should be as it is. First, there are undoubtedly factors of straightforward historical tradition, which can almost, if not totally—be summed up in the fact that British philosophy responded to Kant in ways quite different from those in which Continental philosophy did: in particular it has never fundamentally been influenced by Hegel, and therefore not by the manifold post-Hegelian developments and reactions which constitute the mainstream of the German, and indeed other Continental, subsequent tradition. To state this fact, is not, of course, to explain anything; the fact itself invites explanation. Nevertheless, it is to the point that it is not a unique feature of *contemporary* British philosophy that a divergence should exist from the Continental style—it dates back to the end of the eighteenth century.

To come to more particular points: it is an important feature of British philosophy that it is self-consciously academic, in the sense that its exponents are aware of being engaged jointly with others in a subject which is taught to undergraduates and is a subject of research in universities. It is not, of course, alone in this —all this is equally true of philosophy on the continent of Europe. What is perhaps peculiar, however, is certain consequences that are felt to follow from the philosopher's academic standing, about both the responsibilities and the limitations of his position; connected, perhaps, with certain differences in the structure of academic life. The adoption of a relatively sober and undramatic style and an objective form of argument responds to the demands, not just (as some critics urge) of academic respectability, but of a professional conscience. This point raises, in fact, the whole question of how philosophy can honestly be taught at all—*philosophy*, that is to say, as opposed to the mere history of philosophy on the one hand, or a sterile dogmatic system on the other; and this is a puzzling enough question. The nature of the 'British style' in philosophy is certainly connected with one view on this question: a view that emphasizes the availability of the subject in objective instruction and rational discussion. It is a view whose emphasis is on *the colleague* rather than on *the master*.

However, these are perhaps not points of the first importance. The rejection of the dramatic style goes deeper than this; and we would suggest that there is a genuine difference between much British and much Continental philosophy in this respect, which causes genuine misunderstanding. It comes out in the different role or treatment of examples in the two cases. It is a characteristic of much Continental writing that if a concept or idea is under discussion, the examples that are given to make it come to life, to illustrate its application, are either themselves of a striking or intense kind, or, if not, are described in a striking and intense manner. A literary perception is brought to bear on the example which seeks to elicit the force of the example in terms which have an emotional impact. A very striking example of this is, of course, Sartre: a typical case would be the well-known passage in *L'Etre et le Néant* in which, seeking the fundamental basis of negation, he gives a powerfully realized description of a man's consciousness of a café *not* containing someone whom he expected to see there. This is not the only sort of negative judgement he admits, of course; but the significant point is that it is such examples that he regards as centrally important, as not being 'merely abstract', and as having 'a real foundation'. Sartre is, perhaps, an untypical example, being as distinguished a creative writer as philosopher; the point, however, applies more generally—Merleau-Ponty's *Phénoménologie de la Perception*, for instance, contains many phenomenological descriptions whose aim is clearly to heighten the intensity of our awareness of what we see and feel in certain situations by description of what is in fact an intense awareness of such things. Common to both, and to many other writers, one might say, is this: that reflection on our ordinary consciousness takes the path of the description of a reflective consciousness, where a reflective consciousness is precisely marked by a certain emotional intensity and single-mindedness.

A British philosopher will tend to say, on the other hand: if you want to understand the notion of negation, you must see it in its most humdrum applications; not those in which the recognition that someone is not there is intensified by a personal sense of disappointment, but just the case where, for instance, one finds that one's shoes are not under the bed, and so forth. And of those occasions, one must give descriptions that match precisely the unexciting everyday character of such incidents. The aim is indeed to reflect on everyday consciousness, but it will be a falsification of that to represent it, in reflective description, as intense: for everyday consciousness is not intense. The *essence* of ordinary experience emerges in its ordinariness, and ordinary experience—it is a simple tautology to say—is where most of our concepts most typically do their work.

This deliberate rejection of the idea that situations of heightened consciousness are those that reveal the most important features of our thought is very fundamental to British philosophy, and is one of the particular influences of Wittgenstein—the dramatic intensity of whose approach to *the subject* revealed this idea with an impact lacking in Moore, who in a quiet transfixed sort of way took it for granted. We suggested earlier that there was a genuine disagreement between the British school and many Continental ones about what constituted seriousness in philosophy; and this disagreement comes to a focus at this point. Seriousness and intensity are for the British outlook certainly different: for while a serious study may itself have to be an intense study, a serious representation of the world is not the representation of a world of intensity. On the contrary, it is a representation of the world which takes seriously the way that the world presents itself to ordinary, practical concerns of common life.

For many of the concepts and features of human thought studied by philosophy, this general attitude of the British philosopher must surely be correct. Yet it obviously has its dangers. For there are other aspects of human experience in which intensity of consciousness is itself, one might say, part of the issue, and where it will be a contrary falsification to suppose that the most everyday styles of thought were the most revealing. Such may well be the case with moral and aesthetic experience, and to some extent with politics. Politics is necessarily a special case, since the intensity of political experience in a society is so evidently a function of history; and the lack of political philosophy in the recent British tradition (commented on by Professor Wollheim in his essay in this book), and most obviously, of course, the lack of a Marxist tradition (discussed by Mr Taylor) are clearly connected with the freedom from disruptive change in British history, the sort of change that demands fundamental political reflection on questions that *have* to be answered. It is interesting that in recent years there has been a strong indication of dissatisfaction with these aspects of British philosophy among younger students in particular, which comes very probably from a sense of fundamental political issues which now face the British in common with everyone else. There are some signs of a growing recognition of such issues, and a corresponding revival in significant political philosophy.

Moral issues present a more complex problem, since the role of intensity of consciousness can itself be, in a sense, a moral issue. To illustrate this very crudely: it is possible for a moral philosopher to see a rather settled structure of rights, duties and human aims (something which is often—and, he may even think, *rightly*—taken for granted), as constituting the basic fabric of moral thought, and to concentrate on trying to systematize and explain this; while another sees this only as a background to creative acts of moral imagination, born of intense moral reflection, which he regards as the most important element to be considered in reflecting on moral thought and action. The difference between these two is scarcely just a theoretical difference. It is a familiar enough picture that regards the first as dead and the second alive; or the first unfree, and the second free; or the first in bad faith, and the second an honest man; but these, in their turn, are scarcely theoretical descriptions. Thus, there is no simple or uncommitted position from which to evaluate, in these sorts of respects, the contributions of a style of moral philosophy. The contributions of recent British philosophy to moral issues have primarily been to the study of morality as, one might say, an anthropological concept: how moral principles are to be distinguished from other rules or institutions in society, and similar questions. In part, this emphasis has been conditioned by a certain theoretical belief about philosophical morality, the so-called distinction between fact and value; but—as Mr Montefiore's discussion of this in his essay tries to show—this is not a pure theoretical belief itself, and the peculiar role it has played in structuring a style of moral philosophy which, while often illuminating, has undoubtedly been rather formal, demure and unadventurous, itself requires explanation, perhaps of a sociological kind, which we shall not attempt here. This, again, is an aspect of British philosophical thought that shows signs of awakening to a more vital kind of life than it has often achieved recently.

As we said earlier, it was not the intention of this Introduction to attempt any general exposition of the origins or nature of the prevailing philosophical movement in the English-speaking world. We have tried merely to put into context a few of its features, and to remove perhaps one or two initial misunderstandings. We hope that the essays that follow will, in their own right, do more.

1. WITTGENSTEIN AND AUSTIN

DAVID PEARS

WITTGENSTEIN'S philosophy is very unlike Austin's, so that it is difficult at first to see what they could have in common. Wittgenstein is always imaginative, and his early work, before his view of philosophy changed, is sometimes speculative: in fact, there is a strong affinity between his first book, the *Tractatus Logico-Philosophicus* [WITTGENSTEIN (2)], and the work of the seventeenth-century Continental Rationalists. Austin, on the other hand, keeps down to earth and distrusts the flights of pure reason, and his style of thinking (but not his doctrine) is like that of the British Empiricists. However, underneath this difference there are many similarities. Perhaps the two most important ones are these: they both thought that there was something wrong with the methods of earlier philosophers, and they both thought that the right method would involve the study of language. These two points of similarity are apt to cause misunderstanding. For any philosopher who uses a new method is likely to give the impression that he is not really doing philosophy at all, but some other subject, which has somehow taken the place of philosophy in his mind. And people are particularly likely to get this impression when the other subject is language. For how could something as superficial as the study of language lead to the solution of any of the profound problems of philosophy? It is this question that I shall try to answer in this article—or rather I shall try to explain how Austin and Wittgenstein thought that it should be answered.

It will be best to try to elicit Austin's answer first, because his view of philosophy is simpler and more unvarying than Wittgenstein's. For Wittgenstein's view underwent a great change: his first rebellion against traditional philosophy was incomplete, since the theory of language on which it was based was the sort of thing that his adversaries might well have produced; it was simple, general and contemptuous of recalcitrant facts. But Austin mistrusted that kind of theory from the beginning, so that his critique of traditional philosophy was never tempered by imitation.

Austin only published seven papers in his lifetime. They are all included in *Philosophical Papers* [AUSTIN (2)], which is the first of his posthumous works. The earliest of them, 'A Priori Concepts', appeared in 1939, and the latest, 'Pretending', in 1958, two years before his death. There are also three papers that he did not publish, one of which, 'Performative Utterances', was given as a broadcast talk in 1956. His other two posthumously published books are both sets of lectures given in Oxford University on various occasions in the last fifteen years. *Sense and Sensibilia* [AUSTIN (3)], which is about perception, was first given in 1947, and was subsequently revised many times. *How to Do Things with Words* [AUSTIN (4)], which is about the different things that speakers do with their utterances, is a version of the William James Lectures delivered in Harvard University in 1955. It, too, went through various vicissitudes, since it was based on a set of lectures first given in Oxford University in 1952, and it had further revisions after 1955.

In the earliest of the papers his mistrust of the terminology of philosophers is already conspicuous. He thought that one of the reasons why so many philosophical controversies are protracted and indecisive is that both sides have accepted an unrealistic terminology. If two people invented a game and then discovered in the course of play that the rules did not cover certain contingencies that inevitably arose, or that they were contradictory, neither of them could hope for victory, and the only reasonable thing for them to do would be to go back and make the rules more realistic. Similarly, in philosophy a lot of co-operative work has to be done before the competitive stage, which most people find more enjoyable, can begin.

Sometimes technical terminology loses contact with reality because meanings are not precisely fixed, so that two philosophers, who think that they are disputing about a matter of substance, are really only using a term in two different ways. It would be absurd if this happened often in science. But in philosophy new terms are introduced at moments of great but ill-defined need, so that even this simple kind of lack of realism is frequent. And there are other, more complex kinds. For instance, two technical terms can live a life of official incompatibility for centuries, although all the time there were perfectly familiar examples to which they both apply, if only someone had noticed them. Alternatively, the official view may be that together they cover everything, although there are examples to which neither of them applies. Or a technical term may be ambiguous, or it may combine two ideas that are sufficiently important to be kept apart, or it may introduce confusion into the principles of classification.

Austin has been credited with the view, or at least with an inclination towards the view, that in philosophy technical terminology is necessarily unrealistic because the maximum number of valid distinctions has already been drawn and marked in nontechnical language. But he repudiated this view on several occasions, and in any case he himself introduced so much new technical terminology into philosophy that he could not have held it. What he believed was that technical terminology is unrealistic if it is introduced hastily, and that in philosophy its introduction nearly always is hasty. That cannot be represented even as an inclination towards the view that it is necessarily unrealistic.

However, there are several things that explain why this misunderstanding occurred. First, though his philosophy never changed direction, it was more critical at the beginning and more constructive at the end; and the relentless way in which he undermines traditional terminology in some of his early work might suggest that he believed that no such apparatus could be well founded.

But the misunderstanding also has another, more important source. Many philosophical problems first arose at a time when the areas of human experience with which they are concerned had not been touched by science or by any other exact discipline; many have remained in this state, and perhaps some will continue in it. However, that did not mean that the philosopher was confronted by completely unclassified material. On the contrary, the ordinary, non-technical ways in which people thought about a particular area of their experience, like sense-perception, and in which they described it, would provide him with many well-founded distinctions from which he could start; Aristotle's work often begins in this way. Now even if technical distinctions are added later—Wittgenstein compared them to suburbs built around the old city—the central mass of ordinary distinctions still remains important, and it is reasonable to require, as Austin did, that, when a philosopher introduces some new technical terms of his own, they should at least be founded on these ordinary distinctions. But that requirement is easily misconstrued. For the rejection of all technical terminology to which philosophers have not given a non-technical foundation creates the illusion that all technical terminology whatsoever is being eliminated, and this total elimination is taken to apply not only to philosophy but also to science.

The idea that Austin regarded terminological innovations in science as inadmissible is, of course, the more bizarre of the two misunderstandings. But there is something about Austin's method that explains even this misinterpretation of his work. He made two assumptions, neither of them new: the first was that language reveals the structure of thought; and the second was that, if a system of thought has been functioning successfully for a long time, the distinctions underlying its classifications of its objects will be well founded. Given these two assumptions, it was natural to concentrate on non-scientific language. But though this reason for concentrating on non-scientific language might seem to imply mistrust of scientific language, all that it really implies is that the former possesses a credential that guarantees realism—its long service—whereas the latter often lacks that credential. But recent enrolment does not necessarily mean lack of realism, and if a scientific term is introduced carefully to meet a definite need, it will last. This kind of introduction will also ensure a long life for a philosophical term. But it is, of course, the cause of longevity that is important, rather than the longevity itself. A long life of what Wittgenstein called 'running idle' would be worthless.

It is particularly necessary to understand the nature of Austin's critique of the technical terminology of philosophy, not only because it is important in itself but also because of the way in which his constructive work grew out of it. For his critical work and his positive contributions to philosophy were closely connected. The connection between them is complex, but it is not difficult to trace one main line of development. Suppose that Austin wished to get rid of a piece of unrealistic technical terminology. Then it was sometimes enough merely to cite familiar examples, described in non-technical language, which philosophers had simply overlooked. But there were also many cases where it was necessary to penetrate below the level of non-technical language and thought, and to try to discover what lies beneath it. For the structure of the non-technical system often needs to be explored thoroughly before it is possible to say whether or not the technical philosophical system fits on to it properly.

However, there were other reasons why he undertook this exploration, which, in fact, occupied most of his time. One was that he wanted to correct another fault which, according to him, often vitiated philosophical writing, the unrealistic use of non-technical terminology; the lectures on perception contain good examples of this kind of criticism, which is as important as his criticism of technical terminology. But the most important result of the exploration was his own constructive work. The transition was a natural one, since the facts that he used in criticizing others deserved to be investigated for their own sake. In general, what he wanted to stop was philosophical thinking without understanding. If that aim were realized, the negative consequence would be that unrealistic technical terminology and the unrealistic use of non-technical terminology would both be eliminated from philosophy, and the positive consequence would be an understanding of the realities with which philosophy ought to be concerned.

His constructive procedure was usually to take a familiar word or group of words, and to describe those features of their use that reveal their meaning. Given the first of his two assumptions, the result would be an account of the conceptual scheme that underlies the part of language that was being examined. The simplest example of this kind of work is the paper 'Pretending'. But even here one learns a lot; and that might be found surprising, because the concept is so familiar. Yet this phenomenon was noted long ago by Socrates: the analysis of a familiar concept only has to go a little deeper than usual, and it produces a result about which people do not feel able to say whether they are learning it for the first time or are merely being reminded of it.

There are more complicated pieces of work of this kind in the lectures on perception. Here Austin attacks the traditional theory that there are only two kinds of objects of perception, material objects and sense-data; sense-data, of course, have been given various names in different periods, and the distinction between the two kinds of thing has been presented in this century as a distinction between two languages. So the general plan of these lectures is polemical, the most frequently criticized text being Professor A. J. Ayer's *Foundations of Empirical Knowledge* [AYER (2)]. But at many points Austin abandons criticism, in order to develop his own ideas independently. Whether he is working in a constructive or a critical way, his procedure in these lectures is always the same; patiently to try to understand the complex system of non-technical language and thought whose evolution has been conditioned by the complex facts of sense perception.

This book raises a controversial question about philosophical method. Is it enough to understand the system of non-technical thought and language, and, if it is not enough, what more is needed? Many who believe that the philosophy of perception ought to be a linguistic investigation would consider Austin's procedure too restrictive. For the arguments for the existence of sense-data that he examines are not the only ones. There is also the causal argument, which relies on scientific facts. Russell, for instance, puts great weight on this argument, as his predecessors, the British Empiricists of the seventeenth and eighteenth centuries, did before him. So there is a strong case for extending the investigation and including in its scope some scientific thought and language.

A similar doubt might be felt about the paper 'A Plea for Excuses' [AUSTIN (2), Ch. 6]. Here Austin examines the various ways in which what at first sight seems to be a person's action can fail to be his action in the full sense of those words. Each of these ways is marked by an appropriate adverb or qualifying phrase, and some of them are held to diminish responsibility. Now it is clear that these qualifications are relevant to the traditional problem of freedom of the will. But when Austin suggests that, if philosophers investigated them thoroughly, they might completely dispose of that problem, he seems to be claiming too much. For this is surely a field in which scientific discovery might prove the inadequacy of non-technical language and thought.

But not all of Austin's constructive work was of this kind. For he was also prepared to introduce new philosophical terminology of his own when he discovered distinctions for which no words existed. The phenomena that he classified in new ways were always linguistic. He produced more and more of this kind of work towards the end of his life. The set of lectures, *How to Do Things with Words* [AUSTIN (4)], is largely devoted to a triple classification of the ways in which to say something is to do something. To utter a certain sentence with a certain sense and reference is to perform a locutionary act: to do this with a certain force, such as informing, warning, ordering, etc., is to perform an illocutionary act; and to achieve thereby something like convincing, deterring, etc., is to perform a perlocutionary act.

This is a brief and rough account of his classification. He develops it very gradually, and with the circumspection that one would expect in a philosopher who was so aware of the dangers of this kind of work. It is a contribution to the new science of language which, according to him, would take over part of the field that is now covered by philosophy. He did not believe in the special kind of grammar and syntax that Wittgenstein and others have called 'logical'. His idea was that, if only ordinary grammar and syntax could be made more general and more empirical, they would coincide with much of philosophy, and at the same time become scientific. This explains the impartiality with which he examines linguistic phenomena in this book. It is a piece of science, and all the phenomena deserve attention and not merely those that are connected with familiar philosophical problems. Indeed, when he applies his results to these problems, he is deliberately brief.

In all his work, critical and constructive, his paramount purpose was to keep philosophy in close contact with human experience. The result is that his positive achievements have a firmness and solidity that are rare in the history of the subject. It is as if the way to represent the third dimension on a plane surface had just been discovered—or, rather, rediscovered, because Austin's realism was not entirely new. The particular way in which it relied on language was new, and so, too, were the meticulousness and devotion with which he practised it. But other philosophers in other periods have preached a return to realism and practised it. The practice is exceedingly hard, but those who follow it win their intellectual freedom by using only what they understand of the apparatus offered to them by tradition. They are not preoccupied with the history of philosophy. They look out on the world, and what they write is unmistakably about it. Perhaps if philosophy, or at least parts of it, became rather more like science, philosophers might confront their subject more and one another less.

Philosophy done by Austin looks so different from philosophy done by others that its novelty has been exaggerated by both admirers and detractors. It is true that he made use of the evidence of language in a new way, but what he was trying to win from it was the kind of understanding that other philosophers had sought in other ways. So the goal was the same even if the method was different. But even the method is not entirely modern. In fact, it has affinities with the Socratic method. For when Socrates was asked some large and exciting question, it was characteristic of him to find some other question that would have to be answered first. For example, when he was asked whether virtue could be taught, he said that he was unable to answer the question because he did not know what virtue was. He meant, of course, that he did not know exactly what it was. It is understandable that many people found his way of doing philosophy maddening. For consecutive thought is such a difficult achievement that it is natural to feel resentment when someone takes up the first word and questions its exact application. He is not playing the game. But of course he is not. That is his whole point.

However, Austin's way of making thought more realistic differed from Socrates's way. When Socrates tried to find out what virtue was, or what anything else was, he always looked for a definition which would tie the term down to its object in a straightforward way. But when Austin analysed a term, he did not look for such a simple connection with reality. He believed that it would often turn out to be applicable to a variety of different cases, which could not be brought under any general formula. This was why he always collected such a wide range of examples and paid such close attention to detail. He never had the feeling that Wittgenstein stigmatized as 'the craving for generality' or 'the contemptuous attitude towards the particular case'. It is curious that some people have thought that when Austin made philosophy more empirical he made it easier. If anything, he made it more difficult. But, of course, what he really did was to show how difficult it is.

Austin's philosophy suggests various questions about the nature of the subject. There is, first, the very general question, whether all philosophy is or ought to be the study of language. Whatever the answer to this question, it is clear that the two alternatives, the investigation of language and the investigation of reality, are not exclusive. Nor is their overlap a recent discovery. It was familiar to the Greeks.

There are also more specific questions, some of which have already been mentioned. Even his meticulousness has caused misgivings. Do philosophers really have to cover the ground as thoroughly as he did? For when he thought about something he kept very close to it, and used every detail as a foothold. But possibly the dangers of generalization are not as great as he thought, so that his sure-footed style was not really necessary.

But the most difficult question about his particular form of linguistic philosophy is this. To what extent was he working in the same field as earlier philosophers? This is partly a question of historical fact and partly a question of value. Even the historical question is hard to answer, because the originality of Austin's philosophy and the novelty of its form make it hard to see the underlying continuities. The question of value, which is difficult to answer for other reasons, arises in two ways: some believe that the perennial problems of philosophy are the important ones, so that their neglect is a fault; and others believe that much of traditional philosophy is ill founded, so that its elimination is a virtue. Both beliefs are debatable, and it is obvious that neither of them is likely to be wholly true or wholly false.

There is not the same difficulty in understanding the relationship between Wittgenstein's work and traditional philosophy. For Wittgenstein never appeared to have strayed into some other subject. Even the detailed linguistic investigations of his later period have a detectable connection with the questions that have exercised other philosophers. And it is very clear how his earlier work is related to the past. For the *Tractatus Logico-Philosophicus* is a critique of language, which is, by implication, a critique of traditional philosophy, designed to show that many of its questions are unanswerable because they transgress the limits of language, so that neither they nor their answers have any meaning. This critique is Kantian in its general conception and purpose. It is true that for Wittgenstein the boundary is fixed not by the possibility of experience but by the possibility of meaningful language. But this difference is not necessarily a very great one.

Another, general way in which Wittgenstein's critique resembles Kant's is that it is founded on a philosophical theory of a traditional kind, whose status is, therefore, precarious. If Kant's theory had been based on experience in a straightforward way it would have been a piece of psychology, but it is not a piece of psychology; on what, then, is it based? There is a parallel question for Wittgenstein: given that his theory is not an ordinary theory about language, how does it achieve the meaningfulness which it would have to achieve in order to be true?

But though Wittgenstein's theory of language makes its own status difficult to understand, there is no doubt that everything else in the *Tractatus* is meant to follow from it. According to the theory propositions are pictures, and from this point deductions flow out in many directions. First, he deduced an ontology from it, because he believed that the structure of propositions reflects the structure of reality. Then it led him to one of the most important things in the book, the thesis that logical propositions are tautologies. But there are also many other philosophical problems to which he applies it. Some of them are transformed into questions about language, and answered as such, while others are dismissed as meaningless because they transgress the limits of language.

The *Tractatus* is the only book of Wittgenstein's that was published in his lifetime. It first appeared in Ostwald's *Annalen der Naturphilosophie* in 1921. It was translated into English in 1922, and into Italian in 1954. It is extremely difficult reading. This is partly explained by the method of composition. For it was compiled from earlier sets of notes, most of which have now been published under the title *Wittgenstein's Notebooks 1914–16* [WITTGENSTEIN (1)]. This method of preparing the book for publication produces a curious effect, an overloading of its structure which makes it difficult to understand, or even to know when one has not understood it. There are so many connections between its propositions that they cannot all be brought out by simple serial order. He used an ingenious system of numbering the propositions, which does something to remedy the inadequacy of an arrangement in one dimension, but not enough.

The *Notebooks* often make it easier to understand the *Tractatus*. For the *Tractatus* is very aloof and enigmatic, like some of the great architectural achievements of the past. We see the results, but we do not see how they have been reached. But the *Notebooks* often contain a more complete and continuous discussion of difficult points. For example, Wittgenstein's ontological theory, that the ultimate constituents of the world are simple objects, is very briefly and inadequately presented in the *Tractatus*. But in the *Notebooks* it is developed in a long, tormented dialectical discussion, which not only makes his reasons for maintaining it clearer but also reveals some of the difficulties, in spite of which he still maintained it. The stresses and strains are made visible, and the illusion of effortlessness and inevitability which is conveyed by the final version is dispelled.

This is the most extreme example of contrasting treatments. But something similar happens to the other main theories of the *Tractatus*. When they are being developed, it is easier to understand them, because it is possible to see in greater detail the ways in which they are adapted to the situations that produced them. They are alive and mutable, conditioned by one set of considerations and threatened by another. Of course, there is always such a difference between the preliminary, exploratory stage of a piece of work and its finished state. But Wittgenstein evidently felt a special difficulty in casting his work into a final form. This was not merely a matter of choosing an appropriate literary convention —a problem which philosophers have often recognized, and solved in different ways. His difficulty seems to have been that from the beginning he felt the tension between fact and theory, between the multifariousness of the facts and the simplicity of theory, which, at that time, was his ideal. He later abandoned this ideal, but, while he still held to it, the very difficulty of realizing it made him exaggerate its demands. There are moments of despair in the *Notebooks*. Yet the *Tractatus* announces definitive results. The change of mood does not seem to be explained by progress made between the two times of writing. The definitiveness of the *Tractatus* is partly an achievement of the will.

The *Tractatus* begins with a statement of the ontological theory, and then moves on to the theory that propositions are pictures. This is, in one way, a natural order of exposition, since propositions are only a part of the world and exist in it. But it is not the logical order of development. For the theory of propositions is the premise from which the ontology is deduced. The deduction rests on the assumption that language is a mirror held up to the world.

This is not just because what we say is sometimes true but because, even when it is false, its structure reflects the structure of reality. Now according to the pictorial theory a proposition is composed of names, which by convention denote certain things in the world. Another kind of convention is needed in order to determine what a particular arrangement of names—i.e. a particular proposition—says about the things that the names denote. Then the proposition will show how the things are arranged if it is true, and, of course, it says that they are so arranged. It is, in fact, a sort of picture.

At first sight this theory seems to be merely an over-simplified account of fact-stating discourse, which has been generalized to cover all discourse. However, it has several remarkable features. One, which has been mentioned, is that it puts great weight on denoting. But there are two others which have not yet been mentioned. Wittgenstein held that the sense of a proposition could always be unfolded in an analysis that would be equivalent to it; and that it offers to reality two precisely determined alternatives, one of which would make it true, and the other of which would make it false, there being no third alternative.

These two theses are connected with the deduction of the theory of simple objects. The first is used in the following way. In an ordinary proposition a word may denote a complex thing. But this complex thing does not have to exist in order to give the proposition its sense. On the contrary, the existence of the complex thing is one of the facts in the set of facts that make the proposition true, if it is true; for the analysis of the proposition will begin with the assertion that the complex thing exists, and that it is composed of certain elements. Now these elements may themselves be complex. But could the process of division and subdivision go on to infinity? Here Wittgenstein seems to have invoked the second thesis, and claimed that, if the process did go on to infinity, there would be no precise determination of what each of the two alternatives, truth and falsity, involved. Therefore the analysis cannot be infinite, and its terminus is marked by elementary propositions in which names denote simple objects.

It is no coincidence that this ontology is very like Russell's logical atomism. For Wittgenstein had been Russell's pupil before the war, and the lectures in which Russell expounded his theory in 1918 [RUSSELL (4)] owed much to earlier discussions between the two philosophers. Perhaps the main difference between their theories is that, whereas Russell makes it clear that his logical atoms include universals as well as particulars, Wittgenstein leaves it obscure in the *Tractatus* whether all his simple objects are particulars or some of them are universals. It is really extraordinary that he left this question without a clear answer. The explanation is probably that when he compiled the *Tractatus* he turned away from the difficulties inherent in logical atomism, and concentrated on the corollaries of his theory of language, many of which would not be affected by those difficulties.

His theory of language is like much of traditional philosophy. For it is a very general and abstract theory which takes no account of the differences between various types of proposition. Those that are obviously not covered by the theory are said to lack sense, which does not mean that they are nonsensical; and those that are covered by it are treated without enough respect for their individual characteristics. For what Wittgenstein was trying to do was to penetrate to the essential nature of propositions, and he regarded their accidental characteristics not as aids to understanding but as impediments which the philosopher must push aside. The result is a very unempirical theory of language. It is not that a detailed investigation has shown that the facts are so but rather that from a very distant vantage point it looks as if they must be so. But when a philosopher speaks in this way, what are his credentials? This is precisely the question that Wittgenstein put to the philosophers whom he himself criticized.

The inquiry which ended in the formulation of the theory of language was started by discussions with Russell about the nature of logic, and the thesis that the propositions of logic are tautologies is one of its most important corollaries. This thesis is often understood as a piece of pure conventionalism because its connection with the pictorial theory of propositions is overlooked. But the connection is essential, since Wittgenstein thought that propositions can be combined to form tautologies only because they offer reality two precisely determined alternatives, and that they can do this only because the structure of reality is logically atomic. So tautologies have a certain connection with the world; they do not say anything about it, like contingent propositions, but they show its essential structure. This tempers the conventionalism of Wittgenstein's theory. He thought that the propositions of logic disclose something about the world in somewhat the same way that Kant thought that the propositions of Newtonian physics disclose something about all possible experience. He allows that we have some choice in the development of logic. But our freedom extends only to the accidental features of symbolism; the ground plan is fixed by reality. So we certainly do not choose axioms and rules of inference arbitrarily. There is not even any need for a logical calculus. The whole of logic grows spontaneously out of the essential nature of propositions, and so out of the essential nature of reality.

Perhaps the most important consequence of the pictorial theory of propositions is the most general one, that it sets a limit to meaningful language. Wittgenstein's method of fixing the limit is, in theory, very simple. He maintains that all propositions that have a sense—this excludes, among others, logical propositions—are truth-functions of elementary propositions. If this thesis is added to the pictorial theory of propositions, the consequence is that the limit of language depends on what objects there are in the world. But the simplicity of this method of fixing the limit is really illusory. For the theory that all propositions are truth-functions of elementary propositions is difficult to reconcile with the facts. And, even if this theory and the pictorial theory were both true, how would the method work in practice?

If people were acquainted with objects, and if there were general agreement about what counted and what did not count as an object, then Wittgenstein's method of tracing the boundary, whether it was valid or not—and its validity would depend on the truth of the two theories—would work very smoothly in practice. Now in Russell's version of logical atomism all simple entities are particulars, qualities and relations given by the five senses. If Wittgenstein's version is interpreted in this way, the basis that he uses for fixing the limit of meaningful language is an empiricist's basis. This is how the philosophers of the Vienna Circle read the *Tractatus*, and certainly it is written in a way that not only always allows but also often supports this interpretation. However, it would be incorrect to say that the verification principle is implied by the *Tractatus*. For Wittgenstein's theory of simple objects is entirely general and does not rely on any empirical identification of them. According to him their existence is proved by his theory of language, but the analysis that would terminate with them has never been completed. We know that when we utter an ordinary proposition we mean something precise, but we do not know precisely what it is. So how can Wittgenstein's method of fixing the limit be used?

It is an essential part of Wittgenstein's theory that the limit cannot be reported in a contingent proposition, like a boundary between two countries, but can only be shown. Similarly, the propositions of logic can only show the structure of reality. For Wittgenstein thought that it was the general predicament of philosophers that many of the things that they have tried to say cannot be said but only shown. In a letter which he wrote to Russell about the *Tractatus* in 1919 he says that this is his main contention, and he calls it the cardinal problem of philosophy.

This is not an exaggeration. A critique, which, like Kant's or Wittgenstein's, questions the status of philosophical propositions, necessarily raises the question of its own status. If it is not a piece of science, what is it? Wittgenstein believed that the essential nature of propositions cannot be a subject for empirical investigation because all empirical knowledge presupposes it. So philosophy is not a science but a critique of language that precedes science. But there are difficulties in this view. One conspicuous difference between Wittgenstein's theory of language and science is that it does not take account of the complexity of the facts, and this looks like a fault. It is not enough for Wittgenstein to reply that it is not intended as a piece of science because one of its consequences is that its own status is different. For this reply leaves its status entirely mysterious, and, in any case, it could not save the theory from confrontation with the facts. Certainly its status is different, and, in general, those who think that linguistic philosophy is simply a science seem to be wrong. But the difference cannot be that a philosophical theory need not be concerned about the facts. It must lie elsewhere.

After the publication of the *Tractatus* Wittgenstein changed his view of philosophy. Some lectures which he dictated to pupils in Cambridge between 1933 and 1935 are the earliest of his published works in which the effects of the change may be seen. They were brought out in 1958 after his death under the title *The Blue and Brown Books* [WITTGENSTEIN (3)]. The contrast with the *Tractatus* is startling. It would probably be less startling if the transitional work which preceded them were published. That work is also interesting in another way. For it reveals that Wittgenstein came very close to the verificationism of the Vienna Circle before he abandoned the leading ideas of the *Tractatus*.

The Blue and Brown Books are related to *Philosophical Investigations* [WITTGENSTEIN (4)], which is the most important work of his later period, in much the same way that the *Notebooks* are related to the *Tractatus*. They are easier to read than any of his works that have been published so far. His thoughts develop unchecked with a fluency and continuity which could not survive the sort of revision that he thought necessary before publication. He never published them, but they were copied and circulated by others during his lifetime like books in the ancient world. He tried to revise the *Brown Book*, intending to publish it, but gave up the task in 1936, and began writing *Philosophical Investigations*, most of which he finished preparing for publication before he died in 1951. It came out two years after his death. He described it as 'the precipitate of sixteen years' philosophical investigations'. Selection, compression and rearrangement of his thoughts have given it a greater density and complexity than *The Blue and Brown Books*, and so it does not flow so naturally, but has to be read in a different way. He does not give all the connections between his thoughts but leaves us to discover many of them for ourselves.

Anyone who turns from his earlier to his later works is immediately struck by the fact that his way of doing philosophy has become more personal. The *Tractatus* is oracular in tone, like the voices of the dead in Japanese films; if we listen to the truth we shall hear it. But his later work is much more flexible, and evidently intended to start people thinking along certain lines for themselves rather than to give them definite conclusions. He had, in fact, discovered a method which was appropriate to the form in which he found it easiest to publish his thoughts. For in the *Tractatus*, too, his thoughts are arranged in a way that does not bring out all their connections. But such an arrangement is inappropriate to a classical philosophical treatise. It became appropriate only when he began to write philosophy in a way that required the reader to give up his passive role and participate.

His doctrines exhibit a similar shift from the impersonal to the personal. In the *Tractatus* language is detached from human life and behaviour and presented in a very abstract way, frozen and immobile. But in his later work this is completely changed. Language is put back in its place in human life, and the question that Wittgenstein always asks is not what its essential nature must be but how, in fact, it is used. The earlier theory was essentialist, and its cardinal concept was denotation: the later theory—in so far as he had one (and this is a very real qualification)—is empirical, and its cardinal concept is use.

The study of language in its proper setting naturally led to closer attention to detail. But though his later work became, to this extent, more like science, it became, at the same time, less like it in another way. For it is also characteristic of scientists to seek very general theories, which are similar in form to the theories of systematic philosophers—a similarity which is not accidental, since in the past systematic philosophy often grew out of scientific inquiry; but Wittgenstein avoided theorizing in his later work. So in this dimension it is very far removed from science. Indeed, the width of the gap is hard to understand. If he had merely refrained from producing a very general theory of language, that would have been easily explicable. For he no longer expected systematic results, because he had abandoned his belief in a single logical structure underlying the variety of language. But the avoidance of all theories whatsoever is more difficult to understand.

We might have expected to find modest theories, of limited scope, but what we find instead are techniques whose application is not precisely prescribed. At first sight it looks as if he is arguing for an instrumentalist theory of language. But, though he puts great weight on the connection between meaning and use, he never formulates a precise theory about it. He only employs it as a very general guide to strategy. The exact way in which it is to be applied to different kinds of case cannot be reduced to a formula, since it is an art. And the campaign gets its unity of purpose not from the theories that are defended—for there are none—but from those that are attacked.

If defending theories were the only positive thing that philosophers could do, Wittgenstein's later work would be completely negative. But perhaps there are other kinds of positive achievement in philosophy. After all, what do people who construct theories actually do? They classify phenomena, and trace necessary connections between them. But it is arguable that there is no special type of phenomena left for philosophers to classify. Even so, they might, of course, superimpose their own more general classifications on those of others. But, if they do this, what will be their purpose? In other disciplines an agreed nomenclature is needed for practical reasons, and its basis is seldom a matter for dispute. But philosophical nomenclature is superfluous from a practical point of view, and though, of course, it has another purpose—to produce understanding—there is no reason to believe that this will be completely achieved by a single classification with a single basis. So Wittgenstein's refusal to adopt rigid classifications may be right, and what he did instead, which was to insist on the enormous multiplicity of criss-cross similarities between linguistic phenomena, may be a better way of achieving the same purpose.

However, this does not explain his rejection of the other task that is undertaken by the constructors of theories, the tracing of necessary connections. The number and complexity of the necessary connections among linguistic phenomena should not deter philosophers from trying to trace them. For the general statements that report these necessary connections do not compete with one another in the way that classifications are apt to compete with one another, since no true general statement excludes any other true general statement. Admittedly, slippery nomenclature increases the risk of falsehood. But that is a danger that philosophers might face and overcome. It does not justify the abandonment of any attempt to construct theories.

The theory that comes under most continuous attack is the *Tractatus'* theory of language. However, logical atomism itself is only subjected to a brief direct assault, at the beginning of *Philosophical Investigations*. For Wittgenstein regards it as an outlying position, which will fall if the centre is destroyed. The centre is a formation of two concepts, denotation and analysis. Now the theory, that the meaning of a word is what it denotes, conceals more than it reveals. Of course, if the word is the name of a particular, there is not so much to be revealed. But if it is a general word, a lot is concealed. For the theory is, at best, an uninformative answer to the question what such a word means. But Wittgenstein thought that it was worse than uninformative, because it mistakenly assimilated the relation between a general word and its meaning to the relation between a proper name and its bearer. This criticism is directed against the part of the theory that was

34

left obscure in the *Tractatus*. Wittgenstein's idea is that the theory that some objects are universals is only a result of the mistaken assimilation. If we really want to understand the semantics of general words, it is no good invoking objective meanings.

Many arguments are adduced in support of this contention. Two of the most important are these: the theory wrongly treats all general words as if they functioned in the same way; and, even when it is applied to descriptive general words, for which it was designed, it looks in the wrong place for an explanation of their meaning. The second of these two arguments is, of course, connected with Wittgenstein's claim that the theory is based on a mistaken assimilation. For his point is that we ought to look at the way in which a descriptive general word is used, and after that we shall not feel the need to postulate an entity co-extensive with its application and analogous to the bearer of a proper name. And, incidentally, we shall probably find that the things to which it is applied are related to one another in a far more complex way than the postulation of a single common entity suggests. At this point the second argument leads straight back to the first one. For the assumption that all general words function in the same way is merely the result of neglecting this kind of complexity in a case where the things described happen to be linguistic.

These are pertinent criticisms not only of Wittgenstein's own earlier views but also of the views of other realists. Do they indicate support of conceptualism or of nominalism? Certainly Wittgenstein rejected anything like Locke's conceptualism; indeed, he shares some of his ideas on this subject with Berkeley. This came about in the following way. The study of language in its proper setting of human life and behaviour led Wittgenstein into the philosophy of mind. For when he ceased to rely on a simple linkage between word and object, it was natural for him to turn to the users of language and to ask what is contributed by them. A plausible answer is that something must go on in their minds. Now the *Tractatus* said little about the mind, but it did suggest that its contents are related to objects in the same simple way that words are. But Wittgenstein now argues that a word is not backed up by a single mental entity—for example, an image— which guides its application. The search for a unitary basis for the meaning of a word is no more successful in the mind than it was in the world outside the mind. Images need an interpretation

(Berkeley's point).[1] Even rules have to be interpreted. But perhaps it may be suggested that the intention of the person following a rule is the fixed point on which the explanation of meaning can rest. However, according to Wittgenstein, even his intention is not a thing that exists self-contained in the present moment leaving him no latitude in the future.

There is always latitude, since the pattern of human reactions is essentially flexible. This is one of the points where his attack on the idea of denotation can be seen to be equally directed against the idea of analysis. For an analysis uses a definition to bind us for the future, and this not only exaggerates the simplicity of the internal structure of most concepts but also fixes their boundaries in an excessively rigid way. Or perhaps we should say that it tries to fix them; for, according to Wittgenstein, it is impossible to eliminate the flexibility. Even when the previous application of a word seems to dictate our reaction to a new set of cases, we still have a choice. There are always alternative ways of developing a series. Is this nominalism? At least it is utterly opposed to realism. Universals must always wait and see what I shall do next. But often I must too. And this distinguishes Wittgenstein's position from most versions of nominalism, which imitate realism to this extent, that they choose one thing, such as similarity between particulars, which, they hope, will be a fixed point on which the explanation of meaning can rest.

The philosophical theory that is most likely to be attributed to Wittgenstein is behaviourism. But, though this is understandable, it is mistaken. One very simple cause of the attribution is his rejection of self-contained mental entities; e.g. according to him, a psychological verb, such as 'to intend', cannot be pinned on to a momentary event in the mind. Now those who support the kind of theory that he is attacking are apt to infer, without further thought, that his attack necessarily commits him to behaviourism. But, though he certainly shifts a lot of weight on to people's overt reactions, he was not a behaviourist. Psychological concepts are obviously no exception to his general doctrine of the complexity of conceptual structure, and the theory that gives them an exclusively external basis is no more likely to be correct than the opposite theory. What he did was to give them a basis that was

[1] See BERKELEY, Introduction; and for an account of Berkeley's views, WARNOCK. —Edd.

partly external and partly internal. But he connected the two in a way that has certainly contributed to the mistaken impression that he was a behaviourist. For, though he allowed that in a particular case a person can apply a psychological concept to himself immediately, without using external criteria, he thought that the general ability to do this depends ultimately on the fact that there are external criteria, since without them it would be impossible to establish a language for describing internal states.

The change in Wittgenstein's account of language produced a parallel change in his treatment of logical necessity. Here the result seems to be very paradoxical, and it is a pity that he did not work it out more fully. For the *Remarks on the Foundations of Mathematics* [WITTGENSTEIN (5)], in which it is to be found, is not a unified and finished book but only a selection made after his death from several notebooks. The view that Wittgenstein seems to have reached is that so-called logical necessity never dictates to us but only prompts us. For, however natural a particular logical inference may be, we are always free to reject it. This is, of course, extreme conventionalism, the theory that he avoided in the *Tractatus*. For there he had maintained that, though we exercise considerable freedom of choice about our symbolism, the structure of reality makes it inevitable that a choice made at one point in the system should bind us at other points in it. The view that our choices are connected in this way is a very plausible one, whatever the explanation of the connection may be. But, when Wittgenstein abandoned the ontology which he used to explain the connection in the *Tractatus*, he seems to have abandoned his belief in the connection itself. The result is a very paradoxical treatment of logical necessity, which is consistent with the account of following a rule that he gives in *Philosophical Investigations* but hardly sufficiently supported by it. It is really unbelievable that every time that we make an inference we are free to make the contrary choice and reject it.

Beneath the changes in Wittgenstein's views there was much that remained constant. The most obvious and perhaps the most important thing was his general conception of philosophy. For he still regarded it as a critique of language, concerned with the limit of what can be meaningfully said. However, this particular concern seems to have become less overriding in his later period, since the detailed description of what lies inside the limit had come

to interest him more for its own sake. And, of course, he completely abandoned the attempt to fix the limit in a systematic
way. Meaningless language, he thought, was language that had
somehow become disengaged from its use, and was running idle;
but he did not offer any general principle for discovering when
this had happened. He pointed out particular places where it had
happened, but he never tried to locate them on a single map.

It is this refusal to theorize that is really the most paradoxical
feature of his later philosophy. How could it be enough for a
philosopher to remind us of the uses of words by citing perfectly
familiar facts? How could this kind of writing avoid being chaotic
and superficial? How could it produce understanding without
organization and depth? But Wittgenstein rejected the analogy on
which these objections are based, the analogy between philosophical and scientific understanding. He believed that, since philosophy is an inquiry into the meaning of our thoughts and utterances, its data must be familiar to anyone who can think and
speak, so that it does not have to explore hidden depths in the
way that some sciences do. Its purpose is profound, to make us
understand the nature of our own thoughts; but its method is to
take perfectly ordinary kinds of things that we think and say, and
to describe them and their place in our lives with great sympathy
and care for detail. Understanding will come not through the
discovery of new facts but through seeing the significance of
familiar facts. This is the kind of work that has the profundity of
art rather than of science. Its results cannot be organized and
presented in a treatise, since they do not have the necessary order
and finality. It describes our thoughts and utterances from in-
numerable points of view, and there is no end to the relations in
which it places them to one another.

It is remarkable that, though this new view of philosophy contains a criticism of the view that he took in the *Tractatus*, they both
have the same idea behind them. For Wittgenstein's later refusal
to theorize is not completely explained by the complexity of the
phenomena of language, and it is partly the expression of an idea
that is also to be found in the *Tractatus*, the idea that philosophy
is a self-alienating subject, necessarily detached from life. It is true
that this idea found a very different expression in the *Tractatus*;
for there it did not prevent him from theorizing but only led him
to attribute an extraordinary status to philosophical theories. In

his later work, on the other hand, the statements that he made were, as far as their truth or falsity were concerned, exactly like ordinary statements, which could be used in the construction of ordinary theories; according to him, what kept them apart was their actual purpose, which was not to lead to theories but, rather, to remove the misunderstandings which, he thought, inevitably arise as soon as we begin to theorize about language instead of using it. For he had come to regard philosophy as a kind of psychotherapy. But it is still the same idea that is being expressed, the idea that philosophy is not one of the normal activities of the human spirit.

This idea, at least in the form in which Wittgenstein presented it, must be an exaggeration. Certainly philosophy is very different from anything else, and, if it shares its immediate subject-matter with semantics (or, as has sometimes been thought, with psychology), that makes it all the more difficult to say what the difference is. What seems to have happened is that, when Wittgenstein came to believe that philosophy is a critique of language, his conviction that it is totally unlike a scientific study of language led him to ascribe very peculiar characteristics to it both in his earlier and later periods. But perhaps the gap between philosophy and other subjects is not as great as he thought. His own doctrine that concepts are related to one another by a complex network of similarities and dissimilarities might be applied to philosophy. It could differ from other subjects without being so far removed from them. The transition need not be the beginning of exile.

2. ASSERTIONS AND ABERRATIONS

JOHN R. SEARLE

IN his paper 'A Plea for Excuses'[1] Professor J. L. Austin makes the following point. The expressions which we use to qualify descriptions of actions, expressions such as intentionally, voluntarily, on purpose, deliberately, etc., are not used to qualify an action unless the action is in some sense aberrant or untoward. It is linguistically improper, says Austin, to assert *or deny* of an action that it is intentional, deliberate, voluntary, done on purpose, etc., unless the action is aberrant. (A corollary of this point is that to state that an action is voluntary or involuntary, etc., is to imply that it is in some sense untoward or aberrant.) Austin says:

> The natural economy of language dictates that for the standard case covered by any normal verb no modifying expression is required or even permissible. Only if we do the action named in some special way or circumstances, different from those in which such an act is naturally done (and, of course, both the normal and the abnormal differ according to what verb in particular is in question) is a modifying expression called for or even in order.

He summarizes his thesis in the slogan 'no modification without aberration'.

In a paper defending Austin, called 'Must we mean what we say?' (2) Professor Stanley Cavell adds to Austin's thesis the qualification that the aberration can be 'real or imagined'.

This thesis has long puzzled me: On the face of it, it is a somewhat surprising thesis, for Austin is saying that, for example, it is neither true nor false that I came to write this article of my

---

[1] This paper is included in AUSTIN (2).

own free will, for unless there is some aberration, the concept of free will just does not apply to such cases. How does one state the thesis exactly? Austin's statement in the article seems to me to depart from his usual standards of exactness. And is the thesis true? If it is true, what kind of *impropriety* is involved in modifying without aberration? What is the force of Cavell's saying that the aberration can be real or imagined? Should it not arouse our suspicions to be told that a presupposition of an utterance need not be 'real' but can be merely imagined? If the thesis is true, what consequences does it have? How important is it?

I am puzzled by all this and more, and this paper is the result of my attempt to resolve this puzzlement. To answer the last question: the thesis certainly sounds very important, for note that it runs counter to a whole tradition of discussing these concepts in philosophy. For example, in discussions of free will from Aristotle to the present certain sorts of examples such as raising one's arm or walking across the room have been presented as paradigm cases of acting freely or voluntarily. What Austin is saying is that far from being paradigm cases, such actions are neither done freely nor not done freely, neither done voluntarily nor not done voluntarily, for unless certain conditions are satisfied these concepts simply do not apply to raising one's arm or walking across the room. It seems that if what Austin says is true these discussions cannot even get started.

Let us try to state the thesis again. There is a class of expressions (mostly adverbs) used to describe or qualify descriptions of actions. It is incorrect to use any of these expressions or their negations to describe or qualify a description of an action unless the action satisfies certain conditions, which conditions Austin denotes by the notion of an aberration. It is also suggested, though not by Austin, that these aberrations can be either real or imagined.

Now we have our thesis. Is it true? Well, if one considers the actual use of these words there seems to be a good deal in it. Consider the following sentence: 'He went to the Philosophical Society meeting of his own free will.' When would one naturally utter such a sentence? In describing a normal man under ordinary conditions attending such a society meeting? I think not. To imagine a case where we would actually utter the sentence would involve imagining rather special or aberrant conditions.

Or again consider the sentence: 'He tied his shoes on purpose.' It is not easy to imagine a situation where this would be in order. But try: 'He stepped on the dog on purpose.' Here it is easy to imagine a situation where this would be appropriate, and the reason seems to be that stepping on dogs is aberrant in some way that tying shoes is not.

So far, then, we have a thesis, and it seems to be true. What I now propose to do is to make five points about the thesis which will enable us to see it in an entirely different light from what I think Austin originally intended.

(1) It exemplifies a common pattern of analysis in contemporary philosophy. Similar points have been made by several philosophers. An obvious example which springs to mind is Ryle's discussion of the word 'voluntary' in the *Concept of Mind*. Ryle says that in their ordinary employment the adjectives 'voluntary' and 'involuntary' are used as adjectives applying only to actions which ought not to be done. He says: 'In this ordinary use, then, it is absurd to ask whether satisfactory, correct or admirable performances are voluntary or involuntary.'

Furthermore, this pattern of analysis is not confined to words we have been considering. Similar points have been made about certain other expressions.

In an article entitled 'Remembering' B. S. Benjamin says that if 'remember' is used in its usual sense there is 'an absurd inappropriateness' in speaking of Englishmen speaking English as remembering words in the English language, or to speak of oneself after signing a cheque as having remembered one's own name. One could, says Benjamin, 'generate' a sense of remember which would apply to such cases, but in the usual sense it is inappropriate to bring up the concept of remembering at all in such cases. The reason for this inappropriateness is that 'we reserve the use of these expressions for occasions when there is some possibility that one may not remember whatever happens to be in question'.

Some of the things Wittgenstein said about the verb 'know' suggest a similar view. Wittgenstein objects to saying 'I know I am in pain' or 'I know what I am thinking', and also in an unpublished work on scepticism he seems to object to some of Moore's uses of the verb 'know'. Moore imagines himself confronting a tree in broad daylight at point-blank range and

D

announcing, 'I know that that is a tree.' Wittgenstein finds this utterance in these conditions odd: 'I am sitting with a philosopher in a garden; he says again and again "I know that that is a tree" pointing to a tree near us. Someone else arrives and hears this, and I tell him: "This fellow isn't mad: we are just philosophizing." '

These views all seem to have a family resemblance. Ryle says it is neither true nor false that I bought my car voluntarily because the concept has no application to cases where there is nothing wrong with the action. Benjamin says that it is neither true nor false that I remember my own name, because the concept of remembering has no application to such cases. Wittgenstein says or seems to be saying it is neither true nor false that I know I am in pain or that Moore knows the object in front of him is a tree, and Austin says it is neither true nor false that I went to the society meeting of my own free will because unless there is some aberration, neither the concept of free will nor for that matter any other action-modifying concept at all is applicable to my coming here tonight.

In each case the author claims that a certain concept or range of concepts is inapplicable to certain states of affairs because the states of affairs fail to satisfy certain conditions which the author says are presuppositions of the applicability of the concepts. And in terms of the history of philosophy we see a pattern emerging. The traditional philosopher says such and such is a paradigm case of voluntary action, free will, knowledge, memory, etc. The linguistic philosopher replies: In the cases you are imagining it does not even make sense to use the expressions 'voluntary', 'free will', 'remember' or 'know' because each of these requires certain special conditions for its applicability, which conditions are lacking in your example. It might seem we could get a list of such words—let us call them for short A-words, and the conditions of their applicability A-conditions—a list which Ryle, Austin, Wittgenstein and Benjamin among others have begun. This leads me to my second point.

(2) The sorts of conditions exemplified by the slogan 'no modification without aberration' are not confined to the words which have interested philosophers but seem to pervade language in general and apply to all sorts of words. Consider the following examples:

(*a*) The President is *sober* today.

(*b*) The man at the next table is *not lighting his cigarette with a* $20 *bill*.

(*c*) Jones *is breathing*. (Or perhaps: Jones is still breathing.)

Now what I am suggesting is that these sentences are like the previous examples in that their utterance is only appropriate under certain aberrant or fishy conditions. Imagine circumstances in which they might be uttered.

(*a*) The first where it is a known fact that the President is an habitual drunkard.

(*b*) The second in a Texas oilmen's club, where it is a rule that cigarettes are lit with $20 bills, not $10 bills or $5 bills, much less matches, which are reserved for igniting cash.

(*c*) The third where Jones has just been pulled out of the water and is presumed drowned.

In such cases the utterance of such sentences would be in order. But they would not be appropriate in standard, non-aberrant situations, e.g.:

(*a*) when a normally sober company President is addressing the Board of Directors;

(*b*) when a man in an ordinary restaurant is lighting his cigarette with a match;

(*c*) when Jones is quietly listening to a public lecture.

And the inappropriateness or impropriety of uttering these sentences in non-aberrant, non-fishy conditions seems quite similar to the impropriety of uttering the philosophers' examples in non-aberrant, non-fishy conditions. As yet I am making no attempt to *characterize* this impropriety, but only calling attention to its *generality*. If we are to compile a list of A-words, it will not be confined to such philosophical favourites as 'intentional', 'voluntary', 'know', 'remember', etc.

(3) The third point I wish to make is that contrary to our initial supposition, the opposite or negation of an A-word is not an A-word. Thus, going through our examples:

I did not buy my car voluntarily, I was forced to.
I did not come of my own free will, I was dragged here.

I don't remember my own name.
He doesn't know whether the object in front of him is a tree.

and similarly:

The President is drunk today.
The man at the next table is lighting his cigarette with a $20 bill.
Jones has just stopped breathing.

An utterance of each of these in any of the situations, aberrant or non-aberrant, which we have considered, will be true or false. And indeed, as we shall see later on, in normal circumstances they would all be false, for their falsity is one of the things that makes the circumstances normal.

Thus, at this point there seems to be a serious assymetry between A-words and their opposites or negations. That is, to justify fully an utterance containing an A-word we need, first, evidence of an aberration or of one of the other special conditions, and, secondly, evidence for the truth of the utterance. But for the opposite or negative we need only evidence of the truth of the utterance. This, I should note, is my first flat disagreement with Austin's account. He says that both require an aberration. I will state later how the ambiguity in the notion of aberration led him to this view. But at this stage of the argument I want just to note that for every sentence which requires an A-condition, there is a negation or opposite sentence which does not require an A-condition. At any rate, we have found this to be true of the examples considered, and I suggest that it is true generally.

At this point we shall want to focus our attention on the vague and so far unexplained notion of an aberration. This notion is clearly the crux of the thesis 'no modification without aberration'. What is meant by the word 'aberration' as it occurs in the statement of the thesis?

(4) An aberration or A-condition for a sentence is in general a reason for supposing that the assertion made in uttering the opposite or negation of that sentence is or might have been true, or at least might have been supposed by someone to be true. An A-condition for a remark is just a reason for supposing the remark might have been false or might have been supposed by someone to be false.

46

Austin's account is misleading, for the slogan 'no modification without aberration' suggests that any aberration will justify modification. But, clearly, not just any old aberration will do. If, for example, I buy my car while strumming a guitar with my bare toes, though this is an aberrant way of buying a car, it gives no grip to the remark 'he bought his car voluntarily'. In order that this remark should be in order, there must be some reason for supposing, or for supposing someone might have supposed, that I might have bought it under compulsion or otherwise *not* have bought it voluntarily. And in all of the cases we have been considering, the aberrations which would render the remarks in order are reasons for supposing that the negations of the remarks might have been true. The 'aberrations' which would render our examples inappropriate are reasons for supposing I might have forgotten my own name; Moore might not have known that that was a tree; I might not have bought my car voluntarily; I might not have gone to the meeting of my own free will; the President might have been drunk; the man might have been lighting his cigarette with a $20 bill; and Jones might have stopped breathing.

We are now in a position to see that the thesis 'no modification without aberration' seems really to mean something like 'no modification without some reason for supposing the negation of the modification might have been true'.

(5) We cannot get a list of A-words, for whether or not a given word requires any aberration will depend on the rest of the sentence and on the surrounding context. Thus, e.g., 'he bought his car voluntarily' requires an A-condition; but 'he went into the Army voluntarily' just means he volunteered rather than was drafted. And an utterance of it requires no A-condition, it is just true or false (that is assuming that he did enter the Army). The reason for this, as we shall see, is that the standard way of buying a car is to do it voluntarily, but there is in that sense no standard way of going into the Army.

The point I am making now is: there is no such thing as a list of A-words. For any sentence in which a word requires an A-condition we can find another sentence in which the same word does not. The thesis 'no modification without aberration' at this stage, then, seems not to be a thesis about words but about sentences, and, as we shall see, it is only about sentences given a

47

background of assumptions about people's habits and expectations.

So far, then, my investigations of the thesis 'no modification without aberration' have yielded five tentative conclusions:

(1) It expresses a common pattern of argument in contemporary philosophy.

(2) It is a general thesis applying to all sorts of subject matter.

(3) For any sentence to which it applies it never applies to its negation.

(4) An A-condition for a sentence is in general a reason for supposing that the statement made in the utterance of the negation of that sentence might have been true (or might have been supposed by someone to be true).

(5) It is not a thesis about words but about sentences, and, indeed, only about sentences in certain contexts.

Now I wish to offer what seems to me to be the obvious explanation of all these five points.

There are standard or normal situations. (People normally, e.g., buy their cars voluntarily, go to meetings of the Philosophical Society of their own free will, know when they are confronting a tree, remember their own names, are sober, do not light their cigarettes with $20 bills and breathe.) It does not in general make sense simply to assert of a standard or normal situation that it is standard or normal unless there is some reason for supposing that it might have been non-standard or abnormal, or that our audience might have so supposed, or might have been supposed to so suppose. For to remark that it is standard is to imply or suggest that its being standard is (in some way) remarkable, and to imply or suggest that is often or in general to imply or suggest that there is some reason for supposing that it might not have been standard. If a speaker describing a situation knows of no reason why anyone might suppose the situation non-standard or aberrant, or of any other reason why its standard character is worth remarking on, then his assertion that it is standard is out of order.

Austin's point, then, is not, properly speaking, about words or even sentences. It is a point about what it is to make an assertion. To make an assertion is to commit oneself to something's being the case as opposed to that thing's not being the case. But if the possibility of its not being the case is not even under considera-

48

tion, or if its being the case is one of the assumptions of the discourse, then the remark that it is the case is just pointless.

Austin's slogan 'no modification without aberration' ought to be rewritten 'no remark without remarkableness' or, to steal and redefine a term from Dewey, 'no assertion without assertibility'.

As this explanation may not be clear I shall try to restate it. In general to remark that p, is to suggest that p is in some way remarkable or noteworthy. One of the characteristic ways in which p will be remarkable or noteworthy is for there to be at least the possibility of *not p* in the offing. All of the examples we were inclined to call A-sentences, were sentences which in standard situations could not be uttered to record something remarkable or noteworthy, because their not being remarkable is what makes those sentences standard. They could not, therefore, be appropriately uttered in such standard situations but could only be uttered in 'aberrant' situations, and the aberration was in general some reason for supposing that the negation of the proposed remark might have been true. This explanation accounts for all the five facts we noted.

(1) and (2) The point being about assertions in general is not confined to a certain class of words or a certain subject matter or to assertions about a certain subject matter.

(3) Since the opposite of a standard condition is non-standard, no A-condition is required for the utterance of the negation of an A-sentence. A-sentences mark standard situations; their negations do not.

(4) An A-condition is in general a reason for supposing the negation of the A-sentence to be true, because in general only where there is some reason for supposing a standard situation might have been non-standard is there any point to asserting that it is standard.

(5) Obviously, no set of *words* (except words like 'standard') can invariably mark standard conditions. For what is standard will depend on a variety of facts about people's culture and habits as well as about their language. It is possible to imagine a culture where it is non-standard to buy cars voluntarily. In such a culture our discussion of this example would have to be reversed.

We are also now in a position to see the point of Cavell's saying that the aberration can be real or imagined. An assertion will have a point both in cases where there is a good reason for supposing it might have been false and in cases where there is no good reason, but where people merely believe there is a good reason. Thus, to someone who thinks I was dragged to the meeting there is a point in saying, 'Searle came here of his own free will', whether his reasons for thinking I was dragged are good reasons or bad reasons.

I am suggesting that Austin and others have seen this matter in the wrong light. I now want to explain how that came about. Consider, e.g., the concept of intention.

Many verbs of human action have the notion of intention as it were built into them. To *do* X is just to do X intentionally. So as Austin saw, it is out of place to add the adverb 'intentionally' unless the situation is very odd. He also saw that to deny that X was done intentionally is to *assert* that the situation was very odd, odd just because it is odd to do something not intentionally. What he did not see is that the oddness necessary to assert 'X was done intentionally' is simply a reason for supposing it might have been true that 'X was not done intentionally'. Seeing the oddness in both cases and not seeing their relation, he concluded that only in odd cases *could one properly assert or deny that X was done intentionally.* But what I have been claiming is that the oddness or aberration which is a *condition of utterance*, for 'X was done intentionally' is *evidence*, etc., *for the truth* of 'X was not done intentionally'. And it is a condition of utterance for the one precisely because it is evidence for the truth of the other. Since, in general, unless there is some reason for supposing it was not done (or might not have been done, etc.) intentionally, there is no point in asserting that it was done intentionally.

What exactly is the nature of the dispute here? Both sides agree on the existence of certain data, data of the form: It would be odd or impermissible to say such and such except under certain conditions. But there is a disagreement about the explanation of the data. I say the data are to be explained in terms of what, in general, is involved in making an assertion. The view I am attacking says the data are to be explained in terms of the applicability of certain concepts. So far the claims I can make for my account are greater simplicity, generality and perhaps plausibility. But now it seems to me I am in a position to present actual counter examples to try to refute the view in a more knock-down fashion. It is argued that the conditions of applicability of certain concepts render certain statements in certain conditions neither true nor false. But now recall, as I mentioned earlier, that the negations of those statements are not neither true nor false but in standard conditions simply false. Recalling our examples:

I didn't go to the meeting of my own free will, I was dragged there.
I didn't buy my car voluntarily, I was forced to.
I don't remember my own name.
I don't know whether the thing in front of me is a tree.
He is not sober.
He is now lighting his cigarette with a $20 bill.
He has stopped breathing.

In the present standard or normal conditions there is nothing non-sensical about such utterances, they are all just false. Furthermore, if we get away from the very simple examples we have so far been considering, we shall see that these concepts are explicable without any of the conditions we have had in mind. Take the following examples:

The system of voluntary military recruitment is a total failure in California.
The knowledge of and ability to remember such simple things as one's name and phone number is one of the foundation stones of modern organized society.
It is more pleasant to do things of one's own free will than to be forced to do them.

These statements contain such words as 'knowledge', 'remember', 'free will' and 'voluntary', and their utterance is appropriate without any of the special conditions of the sort the philosophers I have considered said were necessary conditions of their applicability.

Now I wish to make some clarification of what I have been saying so far. First, I am not saying there are no conditions of applicability at all for such terms as 'voluntary', 'intentional', 'of one's own free will', etc., that any of these can be sensibly applied to any action; rather I am saying that the sorts of conditions expressed in Austin's slogan 'no modification without aberration' are not conditions of application of these concepts, but rather are conditions for making assertions in general.

The word 'voluntary' in particular seems to me to be an

excluder, like 'real' or 'normal'. A statement of the form: 'act A was done voluntarily' has a certain indeterminacy of sense until we know what is being excluded—compulsion, duress, force or what not; in the same way as the statement 'this chain is a real chain' has a certain indeterminacy of sense until we know what is being excluded: toy, papier maché or what not.

Nor, of course, am I attempting to rescue the traditional view that all voluntary and intentional acts are preceded by mental acts of volition and intention.

Furthermore, I am not saying that the possibility of something not being the case or not having been known or supposed to be the case is a necessary condition for making any assertion whatever. There are all sorts of conditions which will make a remark worth remarking and this is only one, though a rather important one, and one which has often been confused by philosophers with features of the analysis of particular concepts.

Now I wish to consider some possible objections which could be made to what I have been saying. The point of considering these objections will be both to forestall them and to clarify my argument.

First: Someone might object to my saying that there are true propositions which it is improper to assert except in certain conditions. Surely, someone might claim, this is paradoxical, for how can it ever be improper to tell the truth. I seem to be saying that it is true that Moore knew that the object in Trinity garden was a tree, that I remember my own name, that I went to the meeting of my own free will, etc., but that it is somehow logically improper to assert these true propositions except under certain special conditions which might call their truth in question. This seems paradoxical.

That this should seem paradoxical is a consequence of a failure to distinguish between propositions which form, as it were, the content of assertions (and other speech acts) and the speech acts themselves. I distinguish between the propositions that p and the act which I perform when I *assert* that p. That there is a distinction is shown by the fact that the same proposition can be a common content of such different speech acts as questioning whether p, commanding that p, warning that p, expressing doubt as to whether p, etc., as well as asserting that p.

And once we recognize the distinction between propositions

and speech acts it should no longer surprise us, or at least no longer surprise us *a priori*, that the conditions for the truth of the propositions are not the same as the conditions for the performance of the speech act of asserting that proposition. And just as I can only make a promise or issue a warning under certain conditions, so I can only make assertions under certain conditions. Just as I can only properly make a promise if there is some reason for supposing that the thing promised will benefit the promissee, and just as I can only issue a warning if there is some reason for supposing the thing warned about might harm the person warned, so I can only make an assertion if there is some reason for supposing the state of affairs asserted to obtain is worthy of note or in some respect remarkable. And in each case I am not saying that the proposition which forms the content of the speech act entails that the condition obtains—but that the speaker in performing the speech act implies that it obtains.

And if you still doubt that a speaker in making an assertion can imply more than is entailed by the proposition asserted, consider the following example from real life. When Dr Pusey was made President of Harvard, Senator McCarthy announced to the Press that in his opinion Dr Pusey was not a Communist. And I take it that Dr Pusey was not complimented by this assertion, because it suggests that what is, in fact, obvious is not obvious and is somehow noteworthy, that considering everything about Dr Pusey, and perhaps about Harvard as well, it is a notable fact that he is not a Communist.

I shall now consider a second objection, a modification of the first. Supposing everything I have said is true, still isn't it somehow only a psychological thesis about what people expect in conversation? Isn't it at best part of the pragmatics rather than the syntax or semantics of language? In response to this I should say first that I have never found this distinction, between pragmatics on the one hand and syntax and semantics on the other, very useful, as it seems to presuppose a particular theory in the philosophy of language, and thus beg several crucial questions at the outset. But in any case I should deny that I was making a contingent psychological point. The point I am making is about what it is to make an assertion, and therefore is a part of an analysis of the concept of asserting. But I am fully aware that this is only the beginning of an answer to these objections, and that a development of these points would require at least another paper, a paper about the concept of assertion.

There is also a methodological moral to be drawn from this discussion. It is characteristic of contemporary philosophers that they construe such traditional philosophical questions as what is a voluntary action, what is knowledge, what is truth, etc., as questions about the use of the words 'voluntary', 'true', 'know', etc. They make this identification in most cases because they hold a theory about meaning to the effect that the meaning of a word is its use. The trouble with this theory is that the notion of use is so vague as to engender confusion, and here is how, in the present case, I think that confusion has come about:—A philosopher wishes to analyse the notion of, e.g., voluntariness. He asks:

(1) What does 'voluntary' mean? And since he holds the view that meaning is use he takes this question as equivalent to—

(2) How is 'voluntary' used?

But then, by restricting his study of examples to rather simple categorical indicative sentences, that question is tacitly taken as equivalent to—

(3) How is 'voluntary' used in these simple categorical indicatives? Which question is then tacitly taken to mean—

(4) Under what conditions would we utter these sentences? Which is in effect equivalent to—

(5) Under what conditions would we call an act voluntary?

But this amounts to confusing the question 'What is it for an act to be voluntary?' with the question 'Under what conditions is it correct to call an act voluntary?' And this is only an instance of the general methodological error of supposing that the conditions in which it is correct to assert that p are identical with the conditions in which it is the case that p. But there is no reason at all to suppose that these are identical, since assertion is only one kind of speech act among many, with its own special conditions for its performance.

Without any coherent general theory of syntax and semantics on which to base particular linguistic analyses, the philosopher who looks to the so-called use of expressions has no way of distinguishing features of utterances which are due to particular words from features which are due to other factors, such as the syntactical character of the sentence or the type of speech act being performed.

3. THE FOUNDATIONS
OF KNOWLEDGE

ANTHONY QUINTON

I

THE idea that knowledge forms an ordered, hierarchical system is not a new one, but it has been particularly prominent in British philosophy in the last fifty years. It was anticipated by the theory of self-evidence put forward by Aristotle in the *Posterior Analytics* and assumed by Descartes in his pursuit of an indubitable starting-point for the reconstruction of his beliefs. But where Aristotle and Descartes took the ultimate truths on which the edifice of knowledge was reared to be *a priori* principles, the more recent adherents of this general position have understood them to be particular statements of empirical fact.

The inspiration behind the recurrences of this theory has in each case been mathematical and logical. Aristotle's version was in accord with his own discovery of deductive logic, and with the beginnings of Greek geometry in Pythagoras and perhaps Thales, eventually to be systematized by Euclid. Descartes was explicit about his debt to the pure mathematics of his own time, to which he extensively contributed, and was concerned also to found a systematic science of mechanics. In the case of Russell, the central figure of the contemporary revival of the doctrine, there is an equally close connection between theory of knowledge on the one hand, and mathematics and logic on the other. The essential aim of *Principia Mathematica* [RUSSELL–WHITEHEAD] was to demonstrate the identity of logic and mathematics by showing that the whole of mathematics could be derived from an improved deductive logic. The unitary discipline they composed was set out by him in a Euclidean manner as a vast body of theorems derived with the aid of three intuitively acceptable rules of inference from five equally self-evident logical axioms. By organizing a particular body of knowledge in a fully logically articulate way *Principia Mathematica* provided a model for the systematic presentation of knowledge in general. The idea of a comparable systematic presentation of our knowledge of empirical fact, in which the justification of every kind of thing we empirically know or have reason to believe is made clear by displaying its logical derivation from its ultimate empirical evidence, lies behind a long sequence of important and influential treatises: RUSSELL's *Our Knowledge of the External World, An Inquiry into Meaning and Truth,* and *Human Knowledge,* SCHLICK's *Allgemeine Erkenntnislehre,* WITTGENSTEIN's *Tractatus Logico-Philosophicus,* CARNAP's *Logische Aufbau der Welt,* C. I. LEWIS's *Mind and the World Order* and *Analysis of Knowledge and Valuation,* PRICE's *Perception,* REICHENBACH's *Experience and Prediction* and AYER's *The Foundations of Empirical Knowledge.*[1]

In each of these works it is said that knowledge has foundations and that the task of a philosophical theory of knowledge is to identify and describe these foundations and to reveal the logical dependence, whether deductive or inductive, of every other sort of justified belief upon them. As distinct from such earlier empiricists as Locke, Hume and Mill, the members of this tradition, which has been the standard or classical form of epistemology, in Britain at any rate, in this century, have been quite definite that their purpose is to give a logical analysis of knowledge as it actually exists and not a genetic or historical or psychological account of its growth. In Reichenbach's useful phrase, they are offering a rational reconstruction of our knowledge which sets out the reasons that logically justify our beliefs and not a narrative of the causes that in fact led us to adopt them.

This standard theory of the foundations of knowledge has been exposed to two kinds of criticism. In the first place it has had to contend with the objections of those who, while not denying that knowledge has foundations, disagree with the actual specification of them that Russell and his followers have given. Secondly, there have been more radical critics who reject the general presumption that knowledge has foundations at all. The traditional alternative to the doctrine of foundations is the coherence theory which argues that the elements of our knowledge do not stand in any

---

[1] For all these works, see the bibliography.—Edd.

sort of linear dependence on a set of self-evident basic truths about the given but hang together, rather, in systematic mutual corroboration. A version of the coherence theory was revived by some radical positivists in the 1930s, and another by Quine, under the influence of Duhem, more recently. In a series of publications stretching over the past thirty years Popper has argued for a fallibilism with interesting affinities to the critique of Cartesian intuitionism put forward by Peirce at the end of the nineteenth century. He does not deny that there are basic statements, but contends that their basicness is not absolute but relative. There are no statements for which further evidence cannot be acquired; but no further evidence need be sought for those which are not disputed by anyone. Goodman has also maintained that the basicness of a statement is relative, but in a very different sense. Bodies of assertions can be systematized in many alternative ways between which the analyst has a free choice. A statement is basic only in relation to a particular, freely chosen, way of systematizing the set to which it belongs. Finally, Austin has argued that the doctrine of foundations is altogether misconceived.

In what follows I shall first consider the arguments that have been advanced for the general thesis that knowledge has foundations. In particular I shall examine the infinite regress arguments that have been brought in support of the view that there must be some intuitive statements which have not been inferred from anything else and for the view that there must be some ostensive statements whose meaning is not introduced by correlating them with other statements whose meaning is already understood. Secondly, I shall consider the specification given by the standard theory of the detailed characteristics of these intuitive and ostensive statements as (*a*) certain or incorrigible, and (*b*) sensory or phenomenal. Thirdly, I shall look at the alternatives to these two specifications: the theories that basic statements may be probable or corrigible, on the one hand, and that they may report public, physical states of affairs, on the other. Finally, I shall turn to the more radical view that knowledge has no foundations of the kind the doctrine supposes, and thus that there are no absolutely or logically basic statements. A discussion of these topics will cover the main elements of epistemological controversy among analytic philosophers in the English-speaking world during the past fifty years.

II

The traditional form of the doctrine of foundations holds that there must be some intuitive beliefs if any beliefs are to be justified at all. By an intuitive belief is meant one which does not owe its truth or credibility to some other belief or beliefs from which it can be inferred. For a belief to be justified it is not enough for it to be accepted, let alone merely entertained. There must also be good reason for accepting it. Certainly some beliefs are justifiable by reference to others, but only if these other beliefs are themselves established or well confirmed. If every belief was dependent on others for its justification, no belief would be justified at all, for in this case to justify any belief would require the justification of an infinite series of beliefs. So if any belief is to be justified, there must be a class of basic, non-inferential beliefs to bring the regress of justification to a halt. These terminal, intuitive beliefs need not be strictly self-evident in the sense that the belief is its own justification. All that is required is that what justifies them should not be another belief.

The point can be made by reference to a widely accepted definition of knowledge. I know that p, it is often said, if I believe that p, if p is true and if I have sufficient reason for my belief in it. This sufficient reason cannot always be another belief since it will only be a sufficient reason if, besides being something from which the original belief can be validly inferred, deductively or inductively, it is also something which I know to be true. That today is the 30th is a logically sufficient reason for the conclusion that this month is not February. But only if the statement that today is the 30th is true, or some other statement is true which is a sufficient reason for the conclusion, will it be true that this month is not February; and only if I know that this or some comparable statement is true do I know that the conclusion is true. In other words not all beliefs can have other beliefs as their sufficient reasons but some must be justified by, for example, the occurrence of an experience or sense-impression. Valid inference only establishes the truth of a conclusion if the premises from which it is made are true. Inference cannot justify unless its ultimate premises are given. The argument for intuitive statements is simply a generalization of this argument in which the concept of justification has been widened to include making statements rationally credible or worthy of acceptance as well as their establishment as certainly true.

Empiricist philosophers are usually uncomfortable at the mention of intuition, which they identify with some perhaps mystical, and at any rate uncheckable, alternative to observation. But it is being used here in an approximately Kantian sense which would count our ultimate observational beliefs as themselves intuitive. To say that a belief is intuitive is to say that it does not owe its justification to other justified beliefs from which it can be validly derived. It is desirable at this stage to distinguish three possible senses of the word 'intuition'. There is, first, the common-or-garden, vernacular sense of the word in which it refers to the capacity to form correct beliefs in the absence of the sort of evidence ordinarily required to justify them. Unless the beliefs formed are, at least predominantly, correct, this is just guessing. They can be shown to be correct only if there is an authoritative, laborious and inferential way of justifying the beliefs in question. Secondly, there is a psychological sense of the word in which the formation of a particular belief by a particular person may be said to be intuitive if he has not got or cannot provide any reason for accepting it. Thirdly, there are what may be called logically intuitive beliefs where the belief is of such a kind that no reason in the form of another supporting belief is required for it to be worthy of acceptance. Beliefs that are logically intuitive will ordinarily be psychologically intuitive as well. But they do not have to be. From the fact that statable reasons are not *required* it does not follow that they are not *available*. Equally psychologically intuitive beliefs need not be logically intuitive. First we find ourselves inclined to accept a belief, then we look round for reasons in support of it. Finally, no common-or-garden intuition can be logically intuitive though all will be psychologically intuitive.

There do not have to be common-or-garden intuitions but there are, and it is a good thing that there are for otherwise the accumulation of knowledge would be a very plodding, laborious and uneconomical business. There must be psychologically intuitive beliefs if there are logically intuitive beliefs, and also, it would seem, if the number of beliefs held by a person at any given moment is finite. At any rate, if there was a time before which he had no beliefs at all, this must be so since he could have had no reason for his first belief or beliefs. These first beliefs may cease to be intuitive in this sense if he acquires reasons for them, but then some of these reasons will have to be intuitive since they cannot be based on the beliefs that they are used to support.

The traditional form of the doctrine of foundations is clearly concerned with logically intuitive beliefs. What it maintains is that there must be a set of statements which do not require for their justification the establishment of any other beliefs.

III

This familiar line of argument has been supplemented and fortified in recent times by an analogous train of reasoning which derives the necessity of foundations for knowledge not from the conditions which must be satisfied if any belief is to be justified but from the conditions which must be satisfied if any statement is to be understood. It seeks to show that there must be ostensive statements, in other words, statements whose meaning is not explained in terms of other statements already understood. Its starting-point is the fact that we often explain the meaning of a form of words by asserting it to be the same as that of some other statement or statements, and it argues that to avoid an infinite regress of explanation there must be a class of statements whose meaning is explained in some other way, not by correlation with other statements but by correlation with the world outside language. The parallels between this theory of ostensive statements and the theory of intuitive statements are obvious. Both rest on infinite regress arguments; in one case applied to the idea that all statements are explained by definition in terms of others, in the other applied to the idea that all statements are justified by inference from others.

The classic presentation of what might be called the pure theory of ostensive statements is to be found in the account of elementary propositions in Wittgenstein's *Tractatus* [WITTGENSTEIN (2)][2]. He contends that if any statement is to have a definite sense it must be, or be equivalent and so reducible to, a statement or set of statements which correspond directly to the facts of which the world is composed. The underlying principle of this theory is less original than the way in which it is expressed. For what it really does is to present in a new way a generalized version of the

[2] On this, see also D. F. Pears' article in this book, particularly pp. 25–31 *seq.*—Edd.

principle of traditional empiricism that all ideas or concepts must be, or be definable in terms of, ideas or concepts that are directly derived from and correlated with experience. But in Wittgenstein there is no commitment to the empirical nature of terms of the analysis. The novelty of Wittgenstein's version of the theory is that it takes the ultimate units or elements of meaning to be not words but sentences. Underlying this assumption is a theory of the logical priority of sentences to words, first propounded by Frege in his precept of philosophical method: 'Never to ask for the meaning of a word in isolation, but only in the context of a proposition.' In closely similar words Wittgenstein remarks: 'Only propositions have sense; only in the nexus of a proposition does a name have meaning.' This fact is concealed by the occurrence of intelligible one-word utterances, such as 'fire' or 'stop'. But to make anything of such one-word utterances we have to take them as sentences by supplying the missing elements, for example, 'there is a fire here', 'this place is on fire', 'fire that gun', 'light the fire', etc. To understand the meaning of a word is necessarily to understand the kinds of sentence in which it can occur. As our mastery of language increases we realize that many groups of words play similar syntactical parts, and this makes the definition of single words in terms of other words possible. When told that 'spinster' means the same as 'unmarried woman' I understand that the defined word can occur in all the sentences in which I already understand the defining phrase to be capable of occurring significantly.

IV

The arguments for intuitive and ostensive statements are connected as well as similar in form. The ostensive statement is given its meaning by correlation with some kind of observable situation. It has a meaning to the extent that observable situations are divided into those of which it is true and those of which it is not. To know what it means or to understand it is to be able to pick out the situations in which it is true, or at least to have been trained to respond to such situations with an inclination to utter it. Now the occurrence of a situation of the appropriate, verifying kind will be the sufficient reason for the assertion of an intuitive statement, the non-inferential kind of justification required to bring an end to the infinite regress. Intuitive statements must be ostensively learnt, for if they were explained in terms of other statements these latter could serve as premises for an inference to them; and ostensive statements must be intuitive, for the occurrence of a situation of the kind by correlation with which they were explained would be a sufficient reason of a non-inferential kind for their acceptance. As will emerge more fully later, it would be going too far to say that all ostensive statements are intuitive in the sense that the sufficient reason for their acceptance must always be non-inferential. For if we have found that when and only when an ostensive statement o is true, another statement p is true, we can reasonably infer from a new case of the truth of p that o is true even though we are unaware of the non-inferential sufficient reason for asserting it in this case.

From now on I shall refer to statements that are both ostensive and intuitive as basic. Basic statements are the axioms of the system of factual or empirical knowledge. Non-basic or derived statements are explained in terms of them and are established or confirmed by inference from them. Derived statements can be divided into two classes at this stage. First, there are those which are equivalent to some closed or finite set of basic statements, the conjunctions, disjunctions and conditionals called molecular propositions by Russell and Wittgenstein. Secondly, there are general propositions, equivalent to an open set of basic statements. The former can be established conclusively by deductive inference from the closed set of basic statements that makes up the ultimate evidence for them. But the latter can be confirmed only inductively by establishing some finite subset of the open set of basic statements that follow from them. It is worth noticing that this way of classifying the main elements of discourse does something to support the traditional view of induction, to be found in the writings of Mill, as primarily a matter of confirming general statements by establishing their singular, basic, consequences and thus as the inverse of deduction. A less restricted idea of induction is now widely accepted which defines any inference as inductive in which the conclusion is supported but not entailed by the premises (cf., for example, STRAWSON (4)). But unless the relevance of the premises of a non-deductive inference to its conclusion is established by the fact that they follow from it, and thus are part of its logical content, this relevance can be established only by reference to a general statement which has been confirmed in the primary, traditional way.

Basic statements, defined as intuitive and ostensive, have been given a variety of names in recent works on the theory of knowledge. They are the atomic propositions of Russell's logical atomism, the elementary propositions of Wittgenstein's *Tractatus*, the protocol propositions of the Vienna Circle. Schlick called them constatations, Lewis expressive judgements. But however they have been described they have been taken to be the ultimate statable evidence of all the factual assertions we have any good reason to assert, and to constitute the ultimate analysis of everything we can significantly assert. They are held to be the indispensable support of whatever we know or have reason to believe and to be entailed by everything significant that we say.

So far I have treated them in a purely formal and generalized way. But most theorists of basic statements, with the exception of Wittgenstein, have gone farther. In the first place they have maintained that all basic statements are certain, usually stating or implying the corollary that no derived statement can be more than probable. Secondly, they have identified them with phenomenal reports of immediate experience, expressed in the first person singular and in the present tense. But both of these consequential theories have been firmly rejected by some of those who accept the general principle that there must be some basic statements if any statement is to be understood or rationally accepted. Russell has always been doubtful of the certainty or incorrigibility of any contingent statement whatever, and has been content to claim that phenomenal basic statements are less uncertain and corrigible than anything else, a position endorsed by Ayer in his first book [AYER (1)], but later abandoned by him. Price, in his lecture *Truth and Corrigibility* [PRICE (2)], and Ayer, in his essay 'Basic Propositions' [AYER (4)], have both considered the possibility of basic statements that are no more than probable; but their consideration has been only in a conjectural, exploratory spirit. As to the phenomenal or experiential interpretation of the concrete character of basic statements, this was ruled out by the theory of physicalism which occurred as a kind of left-wing deviation within logical positivism; and, with a certain licence, a theory similar to physicalism can be attributed to Ryle, whose *Concept of Mind* [RYLE (2)] does seem to imply a general theory of knowledge of the kind that sees knowledge as a structure with foundations.

V

It has been widely assumed that basic statements must be certain and incorrigible. The most general argument for this assertion is not often stated, but it is similar in character to the arguments used to establish that intuitive and ostensive statements are indispensable if any beliefs are to be justified or understood. It is clearly presented by Lewis in his *Analysis of Knowledge and Valuation* [C. I. LEWIS (2)], where he writes: 'If anything is to be probable, then something must be certain. The data which support a genuine probability must themselves be certainties.' One merely probable statement may be supported by another, but 'such confirmation is only provisional and hypothetical, and it must have reference eventually to confirmation by direct experience, which alone is capable of being decisive and providing any sure foundation' [C. I. LEWIS (2), Ch. 11]. What lies behind this conviction is the view that probability is essentially relative in character, that no statement is probable by itself but only in relation to its evidence, the presumed truth of some other statement. Clearly, if this were correct it would follow that not all statements could be no more than probable. The chain of probabilifying evidence could never be completed. Price, in his *Truth and Corrigibility* [PRICE (2)], has drawn a useful distinction between hypothetical and categorical probability. A statement of hypothetical probability is non-committal with regard to the acceptability of its evidence. 'If he has caught the train he will probably be there by six', leaves the question of his having caught the train open and says only that he will probably arrive by six *if* he has caught it. A statement of categorical probability, set out in full, is of the form 'since he has caught the train he will probably be there by six', and any such statement as 'he will probably be there by six' presupposes the acceptance of some such since-clause.

What makes Lewis's argument suspect is that certainty would appear to be just as much relative to evidence as probability. For just the same reasons exist for denying that certainty is an intrinsic property of statements as for denying that probability is. Both properties of statements vary with time. What was not, in the light of the evidence available a month ago, either probable or certain may be probable or certain now. So the more or less Cartesian identification of the certain with the necessarily true is a mistake. A statement is necessarily true, if it is, whether anybody has any good reason for thinking so or not. It has always been necessarily true that there is no largest prime number, but before Euclid discovered his proof of the fact it was not certain that this was so.

We are faced here by another version of the difficulty we discovered in accepting as a general account of the conditions under which it was correct to say 'A knows that p' the requirements that X believes that p, p is true and X has sufficient reason for believing p. And the difficulty can be circumvented by the same manoeuvre of distinguishing between the type of evidence or sufficient reason that can be expressed as a statement and the type that cannot. We can allow that both certainty and probability are relative to evidence provided that we admit that the evidence may be propositional, in other words, a belief, certain or probable, from which the initial statement can be inferred with certainty or probability, or experiential, the occurrence of an experience or awareness of the existence of some observable situation. The infinite regress argument rules out the idea that there must be propositional evidence for every certain or probable statement but, if evidence is allowed to be experiential as well, the argument cannot be brought to bear against the view that all statements that we have any reason to believe must rest on evidence.

In PRICE (2) Price opposes to the view that probability presupposes certainty a conception of the intrinsic probability of statements. He suggests that it is possessed by statements of perception, introspection and memory. Such statements, he continues, will be as corrigible as any other empirical assertions, but they will differ from these others in being also, as he puts it, 'corrigent', that is to say, 'capable of correcting other judgements, as well as receiving correction from them'. But he confesses to some doubts about the concept of intrinsic probability, wondering if it is not as nonsensical an idea as that of being intrinsically longer. Recognition that if probability is relative so is certainty, together with the distinction between propositional and experiential evidence, should go some way towards removing these doubts. Instead of 'intrinsic' we can speak of 'experiential' probability, contrasting it with the propositional probability of a statement relative to the statable evidence for it. But these doubts cannot be wholly set at rest until a positive account is forthcoming of the manner in which experience confers intrinsic probability on statements.

Another general argument for the view that probability presupposes certainty, outlined in an essay of Hampshire's on 'Self-Knowledge and Will' [HAMPSHIRE (1)], will help to show what sort of thing this positive account of experiential probability must be. Hampshire says that to understand a statement is to be aware of the conditions in which it can be known to be true. There is, he says, 'a necessary connection between learning the meaning of an expression and learning what are the standard conditions of its use'. So for every statement whose meaning is understood there must be some conditions in which it can be known for certain to be true, namely, conditions of the sort that are standard for introducing someone to the meaning of the statement in question. Hampshire's point is a seemingly inevitable development of the idea that the meaning of a statement is given by its truth-conditions. One weakness of the argument as Hampshire puts it is that it can only apply to ostensive statements. The statement that this stone is infinitely divisible has an intelligible meaning (perhaps several), but, except on an interpretation that renders it analytic, it is hard to see that we can envisage circumstances in which we should conclude that it was certainly true. But is it even correct to say that ostensive statements must be incorrigible?

In his first discussion of the subject in AYER (1) Ayer held that there were no incorrigible empirical statements on the ground that a sentence could refer to nothing outside the current experience of the speaker only if it consisted entirely of demonstrative expressions. But if so, it would not be a genuine statement which must contain, as well as a demonstrative to indicate what it referred to, a general predicative term, whose application to the object of reference involves a comparison of that object with other objects satisfying the same predicate and serving as the standard for its application. In his later essay, AYER (4), however, he says that, in applying purely sensory predicates to our current immediate experience, we describe it, not by relating it to anything else, 'but by indicating that a certain word applies to it in virtue of a meaning rule of the language'. Meaning rules of this ostensive kind are necessary for any language that can be used for purposes of empirical description.

> Unless one knows how to employ (these rules), one does not understand the language. Thus, I understand the use of a word if I know in what situations to apply it. For this it is essential that I should be able to recognize the situations when I come upon them; but in order to effect this recognition it is not necessary that I should consciously compare these situations with memories of their predecessors.

But, he continues, although a language must have ostensive meaning rules, these do not have to be of the kind which conclusively establish the truth or falsehood of the statements they are used to introduce. Meaning rules can be of this certifying kind, and Ayer believes that the rules governing the use of such statements as 'this looks green' and 'I am in pain' actually are. But they do not have to be, they could be merely probabilifying, so to speak. 'It might be that the rules were such that every correct description of an empirical situation involved some reference beyond it; and in that case, while the use of the sentence which was dictated by the given meaning rule would be justified in the given situation, its truth would not be conclusively established.' In other words ostensive rules determine the conditions in which it is correct to make a statement or in which one is justified in doing so, but to do this is not necessarily to lay down the conditions in which the statement is conclusively established and thus known for certain to be true. Ayer's distinction between the correct use as that in which the making of a statement is justified and as that in which it is conclusively established as certainly true, and so, as it were, absolutely justified, removes the obstacle to Price's hypothesis of intrinsically probable statements presented by Hampshire's argument. To understand the meaning of an ostensive statement is to know in what circumstances it is correct to make it and these need not, *a priori*, be those in which it is certainly true.

VI

While it has been widely, though not universally, assumed that basic statements are incorrigible, it has not usually been deduced in Lewis's way that this is so from the concept of a basic statement.

A common procedure has been to say that the basic statements of our language are, in fact, phenomenal or sensory statements about our immediate, current experience, whether perceptual or introspective, and that these phenomenal statements are, as it happens, incorrigible. On the other hand, however, the identification of phenomenal statements as basic is not ordinarily presented simply as a matter of straightforwardly discoverable fact about our use of language. It is supported by the principle that the ultimate source of our knowledge about matters of fact is experience, observation or perception. At the level of common sense it might seem that a statement reporting what we experience, observe or perceive would refer to medium-sized material things currently in our fairly close environment. But the usual view of observation statements is that they report the current sense-impressions of the speaker. And the main reason for this is that statements about material things are susceptible to doubt and correction, that, by carrying implications about what may be observed at other times, or with other senses, or by other people, they go beyond what we directly apprehend or are aware of and so embody an element of inference. Thus Price, in his *Perception*, says 'When I see a tomato there is much that I can doubt . . . One thing, however, I cannot doubt: that there exists a red patch of a round and somewhat bulgy shape (which) is directly present to my consciousness' [PRICE (1), Ch. 1]. This patch of colour, private to my consciousness, is what is given in perception, it is the type of empirical datum from which all the rest of my factual beliefs are inferred. And Ayer, in *Foundations of Empirical Knowledge*, takes basic statements to be those which we discover by direct awareness and he defines 'direct awareness' as entailing that 'if someone is directly aware of an object *x*, it follows that *x* exists and that it really has whatever properties it is appearing to have' and again 'that whenever we are directly aware of a sense-datum, it follows that we know some proposition which describes the sense-datum to be true' [AYER (2), Ch. 2]. The upshot of these accounts of the matter is that in every perceptual situation, in every situation in which we perceive or think we perceive something, it is at least certain that we seem to perceive something and this is held to be equivalent to the statement that we know for certain that a seeming object, or sense-impression, in other words, exists.

The standard view, then, is that the basic statements which are the foundations of our knowledge of matters of fact are phenomenal reports of our immediate experience. These are incorrigible in the sense that since they do not go beyond what we are directly aware of and have nothing predictive about them, they cannot be falsified by any subsequent experience. Statements about material things, on the other hand, are subsequently corrigible. The implications they carry may turn out to be false. But the only ways in which statements about impressions can be false are by the deliberate intent of the person who has the impression being reported (for since they are contingent there is no contradiction in denying them), and by merely verbal error. Statements about material things are or seem intuitive in the psychological sense. We do not ordinarily, if ever, infer them consciously from statements about impressions. But, it is argued, since they are corrigible conjectures about what is going on outside the field of our direct awareness they cannot be logically intuitive, but must be implicitly inferred from statements about impressions if their assertion is to be justified.

Initially, two main lines of objection were developed to this theory of the phenomenal character of basic statements. The first of these started from the difficulty of giving an acceptable account of the way in which beliefs about material things were supported and justified by reports of immediate experience. Statements about objects could only be confirmed by statements about impressions that followed logically from them, and they could only have a definite meaning if they were capable in principle of translation into ostensive impression statements. But the only acceptable-looking translations failed to eliminate the reference to material things from the translation. 'There is a table in the next room' did not entail 'if I were having the impression of being in the next room, I should be having the impression of a table', but only 'if I actually were in the next room, I should be having the impression of a table'. Another difficulty arose from widely felt insufficiency of any set of hypothetical statements, however extensive, to add up to a categorical statement about material things.

More important than this negative objection, which led to no clear alternative account of the problem and no serious scrutiny of its underlying assumptions, was the criticism of Carnap and Neurath which was directed against the private and uncommunicable character of the facts reported by phenomenal statements.

They argued that science, and therefore ordinary common knowledge, was a public, intersubjective affair and could not be based on private experiences that individuals had no way of communicating to one another. Neurath further objected to the momentary and unfalsifiable nature of phenomenal basic statements like Schlick's constatations. As momentary they could only be used to confirm or refute other beliefs at the instant of utterance and as unfalsifiable expressions of subjective conviction they were foreign to science. Schlick defended the phenomenal theory, in his essay 'On the Foundation of Knowledge' [SCHLICK (3)], partly by admitting the momentary character of constatations but declaring it to be harmless, arguing that they were used antecedently to suggest and consequently, at any time the question arose, to confirm derived, theoretical statements, and partly by criticizing the conventionalism of the alternative theory proposed by Neurath, which, by regarding the acceptance of basic statements as a matter of social convention, was open to the objections traditionally raised against the coherence theory. But there are other difficulties connected with the privacy of phenomenal basic statements which undermine them more effectively: first, that our private languages seem to be based on public language rather than the other way round and, secondly, that a strictly private language is, according to Wittgenstein, an impossibility.

VII

If it is phenomenal statements that are basic, not merely must we say that all public statements, to the extent that they are justified at all, are inferred from or supported by them, we must also admit something much harder to accommodate: that all public statements acquire their meaning from correlation with statements in an *antecedently understood* private language. It is plain that the private language we actually have, that in which we report our own sensations and emotions, is taught to us by other people on the basis of our publicly observable behaviour. Furthermore, we draw on the public language in developing it. We describe our sensations in terms of the material things that cause them and our emotions in terms of the behaviour to which they incline us. The theory that phenomenal statements are logically intuitive could be saved only by claiming that the inference from them to other statements was implicit. Similarly, the theory that phenomenal statements are ostensive can be saved only by the claim that basic statements are originally private in a double sense, being expressed in some internal symbolism or imagery as well as referring to private entities, and that we must have acquired the capacity to use this inner language not from teaching by others but by having made it up for ourselves. The teaching of language as a social activity clearly begins with statements about material things. If phenomenal statements alone are basic, we must come to understand the statements about material things that we are taught by correlating them with the already understood phenomenal statements of our inner language which are present to our minds in the circumstances in which the teaching is taking place.

In his *Philosophical Investigations* Wittgenstein argued that this exceedingly unplausible conjecture was in fact a senseless one. A language is a practice of utterance governed by rules which distinguish correct utterances from incorrect ones. It might seem that a man could construct a private, inner language by naming a particular experience, and adopting the rule that every subsequent experience of the same kind should have the same name. But how, he asks, are we to tell whether any subsequent experience is of the same kind? It will not do to say that I call this experience 'x' because I remember the experience used to introduce the term 'x' and see that they are the same. For it is always possible that my memory is mistaken in any particular case and this is a doubt that I can never set at rest since memory is my sole mode of access to the standard experiences by means of which the terms in my private language were introduced. In these circumstances the private introduction of names for experiences is an 'empty ceremony'.

VIII

The phenomenal basic statements that report sense-impressions are expressed in ordinary language by means of the verbs 'looks', 'appears' and 'seems'. To say that one is having a sense-impression of a brown box is to say that there looks or appears or seems to be a brown box where one is, or that it seems or appears that one can see a brown box. It is clear that in every perceptual situation, which has been defined as one in which we perceive something or think that we do, there appears to be something present to us.

The supporters of the theory of a phenomenal basis for knowledge go on from this to conclude that in every perceptual situation there is a private object, an appearance or sense-datum, which is directly present to my mind in the sense that I know for certain that this private object exists. These appearances are never identical with material things or with any parts of them for they are private to a single observer, depend for their existence, like the ideas of Berkeley's philosophy, on the fact that they are being perceived and have all and only the properties that they appear to have.

For some time doubts have been felt as to the validity of this transition from the unquestionable statement that in a perceptual situation I appear to be aware of a material thing to the conclusion that in a perceptual situation I am aware of a non-material appearance. It has been held that this 'reification of appearances' is mistaken and that it commits the 'sense-datum fallacy'. As it stands the move is not obviously legitimate; but it is not obviously illegitimate either. In general, this kind of grammatical transformation of verb into noun is not puzzling or disputable. There is no objection to saying 'he gave the door a kick' instead of 'he kicked the door' or 'she took up a position at the end of the line' instead of 'she placed herself at the end of the line'. But this absence of trouble might be ascribed to the fact that we do not exploit these permitted transformations to ask questions about the nature of kicks and positions and do not assume that they are some sort of objects in the way that doors and lines are. Again there are transformations of this general variety which we should be less willing to endorse. We should not be pleased with the replacement of 'it is probably dark down there' by 'there is a darkness-probability down there'.

In an article on 'The Problem of Perception' [QUINTON] I have tried to show that statements about what appears to be the case are used in two broadly distinguishable ways, in the primary and more usual of which the reification of appearances is unacceptable. In this primary, epistemic sense of 'appears' to say that there appears to be, or that it appears that there is, such-and-such a thing here is not to describe the current state of one's visual field but rather to express an inclination to believe that there actually is such-and-such a thing here, in other words, to make a tentative, qualified statement about the material world. 'It appears that p',

I suggested, is the way in which we make a qualified claim about observable facts when the evidence is experiential, 'it is probable that p' being more appropriate to the case when the evidence is propositional. An epistemic statement about what appears is not, then, a description of appearances, it is a hesitant statement about public, material objects.

There is, however, a secondary, derivative, use of the verb 'appears' in which it is employed for some rather specialized purposes to describe the current character of our sensory fields. At the instance of oculists and art teachers we can, by an effort of attention, suppose that, for example, what we see is all situated on a flat surface a few feet in front of us in conditions of normal illumination. We then describe our visual field by saying what we should be inclined to believe was in front of us if we in fact knew that these special and peculiar conditions of observation prevailed. The result is a genuinely phenomenological statement about patches of colour of various shapes and sizes arranged in a certain way. The conditions mentioned are chosen for the purpose of phenomenological description because they are visually ideal, are those in which, when they actually do obtain, the danger of visual error is minimized. The phenomenological use of the verb 'appears', it should be noticed, is not merely a rather sophisticated one, it is also a development of the more usual, epistemic, one. We say 'there appears to be an x here' when we are not sure that the conditions of observation are ideal or that they are unideal in a way that we can allow for. We could say instead, 'I should say that there definitely is an x here if I were sure that the conditions of observation are what I am taking them to be; but I am not sure of it.' More important is the effort of attention that we have to make in order to give a phenomenological description. We have to see things as we know, or have very good reason to believe, they are not. Now the ability to adopt this phenomenological frame of mind is one that has to be learnt after that for the perception of the material world has already been mastered. The language in which its findings are expressed is derived from that with which we describe material things and the rules defining the attitude involved are stated in public, material terms. So unless we first make up a private phenomenological language for ourselves ordinary statements about material things cannot acquire their sense from correlation with basic phenomenal statements. Furthermore, the phenomenological attitude or frame of mind, in which by an effort of attention all our background knowledge of where we are and what is around us is suppressed and replaced by a feigned assumption of ideal conditions, is inevitably exclusive of the ordinary frame of mind in which we confront the observable world. We cannot look at the world ordinarily and phenomenologically at the same moment. It follows from this, and is fairly obvious on its own account, that we are very rarely in a phenomenological frame of mind. It cannot, therefore, be the case that our beliefs about material objects are generally inferred from phenomenological statements about appearances or sense-data. For the very much greater part of our conscious life the phenomenological evidence is simply not there for statements about material things to be inferred from. Unless we can be subconsciously in a phenomenological attitude at the same time as we are consciously looking at things in the ordinary way, and unless we subconsciously register the deliverances of this attitude, the only alternative to the view that statements about material things do not have a phenomenological foundation is that the very great majority of our beliefs about the material world never have any justification at all.

Some empirical confirmation for the view that we are only very exceptionally aware of the phenomenologically describable state of our sense-fields is provided by the fact that if asked for a phenomenological report of a past experience, we normally have to reconstruct it from our recollection of the material scene we actually perceived, together with our background knowledge of where we were situated within the scene. What we can reasonably do is to infer that in every perceptual situation our sense-fields are in some appropriate condition, and we can work out what this was in any particular case by working out what phenomenological report we should have given at the time if we had been in the appropriate frame of mind. These conjectured states of our sense-fields may be interpreted as the phenomenological causes of our perceptual beliefs. We can refer to them, for instance, when we want to explain errors of perception. But this is not to admit them as reasons for our perceptual beliefs. Though they can be used as reasons for such beliefs in exceptional cases, and then only in the light of antecedently established correlations between the phenomenological condition and the observable state of affairs in question, they cannot serve as reasons in all cases in which we have some reason for the perceptual beliefs we form.

In its ordinary use an epistemic appearance statement of the form 'there appears to be an *x* here' does not, then, describe a substantive appearance. Its function is to make the assertion that there is an *x* here in a guarded, qualified way. It makes clear that the speaker regards the statement as no more than probable. We can raise these statements to higher probabilities and even certainty, in Moore's sense of absence of reasonable doubt rather than incorrigibility,[3] by assembling other consilient statements of the same sort. 'There appears to be an orange here, but perhaps not, since wax fruit is to be found in places like this. But it also appears to be cold and hard and this room does not appear to be refrigerated.' This artificially circumspect soliloquy shows how epistemic appearance statements mutually corroborate each other. More usually the requisite corroborative material is already to hand embedded in our background knowledge, (in the example given, perhaps, that this room is a prison larder).

What I suggest is that these epistemic appearance statements are ways of affirming, in an explicitly qualified fashion, the experientially probable basic statements whose possibility was argued for earlier. To say 'there is an orange here' may be no more than probably true. In saying 'there appears to be an orange here' the fact that it is no more than probable is made explicit. By putting in the explicit qualification the statement is protected from the kind of falsification wrought by the discovery that the object involved is in fact made of wax. These appearance statements have, then, a kind of certainty. But it is rather the unqualified statements which we have an inclination to believe, and not the qualified appearance statements associated with them, that are basic on the theory that I am advancing. Ordinary statements about material things, I claim, are, as they appear to be, both the ostensive basis in terms of which all other statements are introduced and the intuitive basis by reference to which they are confirmed. In themselves, they are never more than probable. But associated, as they commonly are, with a large background of other statements, probable and certain, they can attain certainty, at least in the straightforward, Moorean sense.

It remains to be shown how, in the process of ostensive teaching

---

[3] Cf., e.g., the article 'Certainty' in MOORE (4).

of ordinary statements about material things, they are endowed with the experiential probability that the theory ascribes to them. This can be shown by a consideration of the way in which their meaning is learnt. I learn when to say 'this is an orange', or its infantile equivalent 'orange', by being exposed to oranges in carefully selected situations, that is, where my teachers have assured themselves that the object involved really is an orange, and not a piece of wax fruit or a piece of soap or a rubber ball, and where the conditions of observation are favourable. Equipped by this training I start to make use on my own of the statement I have learnt and, still unaware, in my ostensive innocence, of the existence of orange-like non-oranges, and again of the effect of fog on the look of traffic lights or of distance on the look of large orange globes, I make mistakes. These mistakes are corrected and my understanding of the statement 'this is an orange' undergoes a change. It becomes loaded with theory, as it were, for I find out about the insides of oranges, their characteristic taste and their causal dependence on orange trees. I learn that vision is not enough to certify the belief that there is an orange here. But unless my utterances of 'this is an orange' are more often mistaken than not, this saddening achievement of conceptual maturity will not deprive the statement of its intrinsic probability.

An important consequence of this discussion is the undermining of an assumption which has not been questioned hitherto. It has been assumed that a statement is either ostensive or verbally introduced, that it must be wholly the one or wholly the other. According to this theory of basic statements ordinary assertions about material things are first taught ostensively, but this correlation with observable states of affairs does not complete the teaching process. It has to be supplemented by knowledge of the circumstances in which our inclination to believe something about our material surroundings must be controlled by collateral information about those surroundings. On this theory there are no purely ostensive statements. Partly ostensive basic statements acquire an intrinsic probability from experiential evidence alone, but this is never complete, never sufficient to render them certain. It may well be that Hampshire is correct in saying that the ostensive conditions under which the use of a statement is taught constitute the criteria of its certainty in so far as *purely ostensive* statements are concerned. But in the language we actually have the basic statements in which our observations are reported are not purely ostensive. So the conjecture of Price and Ayer that there could be a language whose basic statements were no more than probable is confirmed in the best possible way, by the fact that what they envisage as a possibility is true of the language we actually have. The initial infinite regress arguments proved that some statements must be ostensively learnt, and that some statements must derive their justification from experience rather than other statements. But these two requirements are satisfied by an account of basic statements which represents them as initially, but not wholly, taught by ostension and as justified to some extent, but not beyond reasonable doubt, by experience.

IX

A complete rejection of the doctrine that knowledge has foundations implies the acceptance of a coherence theory of truth and knowledge. This theory had a central place in the absolute idealism of Bradley, who worked out its consequences with great elaboration. Bradley's idealism was the dominant academic philosophy against which Russell and Moore rebelled, and Russell's earliest strictly philosophical writings, in the first decade of the century, were directly concerned to refute the coherence theory. Some of his criticisms do not apply to it if, as in this discussion, it is restricted to the domain of empirical fact. Certainly we must accept the truth of the laws of logic if the concept of coherence is to be applied; but there is no circularity in this if it is only the truth of non-logical statements that coherence is used to define. Again there is nothing self-refuting, or rather self-enfeebling, about the consequential thesis that no statement is wholly true if the reference of this thesis is not supposed to include itself. Indeed, if Russell's theory of types, by which all self-reference is ruled out, is accepted, the thesis cannot be formulated in this self-destructive way. There remains the crucial difficulty that coherence, while it may be the necessary condition of the truth of a body of statements, cannot be the sufficient condition, since more than one system of statements, all of which are coherent with the other members of the system, can be constructed where there will be members of one system that are incompatible with members of another. The same point is less formally made by the argument

77

that the business of justification can never begin unless some of the statements up for consideration have some ground for acceptance other than their relation to the others.

In the light of these criticisms recent philosophers have seldom openly endorsed a full-blooded coherence theory. Nevertheless, several have taken up positions which commit them to it by implication. The left-wing positivists of the 1930s, abandoning Schlick's view that basic statements were the direct and incorrigible reports of experience, concluded that their nature and their acceptance was a matter of convention. Unwilling to admit that any sense could be attached to the idea that some statements rested on experiential evidence, because of its purportedly metaphysical assertion of a relation between language and fact, they seemed to have no other recourse than conventionalism. Their attempt to show that the actual convention they proposed was not an arbitrary one by pointing to its coincidence with that adopted by scientists, was unsuccessful. In the first place the expedient was viciously regressive in presuming the antecedent truth of some statement about the basic statements actually adopted by scientists. Secondly, it inverted the logical relation between the concepts of a scientist and a basic statement. It is not that a basic statement is one that a scientist accepts without question or further inquiry, but rather that a scientist is one who systematically exposes his beliefs to the judgement of basic statements.

X

Two negative views of the doctrine of foundations of more recent origin, which avoid difficulties by the simple expedient of failing to present an alternative to it, deserve some consideration. In his *Structure of Appearance* [GOODMAN] Goodman rejects the concept of an asymmetrical relation of epistemological priority between basic and derived statements. In his view logical priority is always relative to a particular system and it is well known that the same body of assertions can be equally well derived from different, alternative sets of axioms or primitive propositions. Applying this to systems setting out the definitional relations of empirical concepts, he argues that it is a matter of free choice for the builder of the system as to which concepts he selects as primitive and undefined. He should be guided in his choice by such strictly

78

formal considerations as that of the simplicity and elegance of one choice as compared with another. Certainly there is a formal sense of priority or basicness which is relative to a given way of setting up a system of statements. But philosophical analysts are not concerned simply with the construction of formally consistent systems: their aim, in the first instance, is to set out, as systematically as possible, the order of logical dependence of the apparatus of concepts and statements that we actually possess. But more than this, a formally consistent system may be epistemologically inconsistent. If Wittgenstein's argument against the possibility of private languages is valid, a system in which physical concepts are defined in terms of strictly phenomenal ones, though it might be perfectly consistent as a formal system, would nevertheless be epistemologically impossible and incapable of being used as a language.

In his *Sense and Sensibilia* [AUSTIN (3)] Austin delivers a lively but somewhat superficial onslaught on the doctrine of foundations, which he mistakenly identifies with the theory that our knowledge of matters of fact must rest on an incorrigible basis. He agrees that such philosophers as Ayer are right to hold that the truth of some statements must be determined by non-verbal reality, and he asserts that most words are learnt ostensively. To accept these points is to concede the truth of the greater part of the doctrine of foundations, and so a more precise account of the actual object of Austin's criticism must be sought. At one stage of the argument he singles out for criticism the view that it is the particular business of some sub-class of sentences to be evidence for or to verify the rest. Against it he says that no kind of *sentence*, understood as a form of words in a given meaning, could do this job. A given sentence will sometimes be used to express a conclusion from evidence, at others to make a direct report of observation. A given sentence can be used to make many different statements, depending on who is making them and on where and when they are made. This is true but doubly irrelevant. The doctrine of foundations can perfectly well be formulated in terms of statements and to the extent that it has not been it is because of the peculiarities of the German word 'Satz'. But, in fact, this is not to go far enough, since two people can make the same statement but only one of them be making a basic statement. Suppose *A*, looking down a well, says, 'There is water at the bottom.' *B*, who is standing beside him and not looking down, may affirm that there is water at the bottom at very much the same time and in exactly the same words because he has heard what A said and believes A to be a reliable person. In strictness we should perhaps say that a given statement can be made as basic or as derived. But provided we realize that to say that A's statement is basic is not to say that the same statement made by B is also basic and is *a fortiori* not to say that every statement made by the use of the sentences A utters is basic, no confusion need be caused by the less pedantic way of speaking.

Austin argues penetratingly against the view that there are any strictly incorrigible statements. Every statement can, he maintains, be retracted, and any that are so understood that their seeming to their speaker to be true is a guarantee of their truth, are not really descriptive at all. This, as we have seen, does not invalidate the doctrine of foundations. He goes on to say that in general we do not have to produce or even have evidence for our assertions about material objects. As far as this refers to propositional evidence I have argued that it is correct. But it is not a criticism of the theory of basic statements, only of the identification of them with phenomenal reports. If it refers to experiential evidence as well, it is false, for it suggests that we can assert any material object statement with justification by mere whim. What he perhaps intended to say was that we do not ordinarily call the experience that justifies a statement about material things evidence for it. This would not be very interesting even if it were true. But if a man who, looking into a room, says, 'There's a fire in here', is asked if he has any evidence for saying so, when he has in fact seen the fire, it would be ridiculous for him to answer, 'No.' The proper answer would be, 'Yes, I can see it.'

The real point of Austin's criticism is his claim that 'in general ... *any* kind of statement could state evidence for *any* other kind'. 'It is not true, in general,' he goes on, 'that general statements are "based on" singular statements and not vice versa; my belief that *this* animal will eat turnips may be based on the belief that most pigs eat turnips; though certainly, in different circumstances, I might have supported the claim that most pigs eat turnips by saying that this pig eats them at any rate.' It is true that the belief of any particular man that a given pig, not before him, eats turnips may be based on and owe what justification it has to his antecedent conviction that most pigs eat turnips. But there is an obvious asymmetry in the logical relation between the two beliefs. For the general belief, although formally evidence for the singular one by itself and independently of whether there is any reason to accept it, will actually confirm or justify it only if it is itself already supported. This support will normally be provided by the establishment of a number of statements of the form 'this pig eats turnips', and of not more than a very few of the form 'this pig does not eat turnips'. This recourse to the empirical basis may be postponed. That most pigs eat turnips may be inferred from the further generalizations that most curly-tailed animals eat turnips and that all pigs are curly-tailed. And these, if they are really to support it, must themselves rest either on singular statements about particular curly-tailed animals eating turnips and particular pigs being curly-tailed, or else on further generalizations which possess, at some finite remove, singular evidence of the same kind. In other words, general statements can only be contingently or derivatively evidence for singular ones, whereas singular statements are the primary and indispensable evidence for generalizations. We can have sufficient reason for thinking that this pig eats turnips without having any justified belief about what pigs in general do; but we cannot have reason for thinking that most pigs eat turnips unless we have some justified beliefs about the eating habits of particular pigs. That most pigs eat turnips, then, while it does not presuppose for its justification the establishment of any particular statement to the effect that this pig does so, does presuppose that some statements of this kind have been confirmed or established. But the statement that this pig does so, while it may owe its justification to the antecedent establishment of some general statement about pigs in a particular case, does not in general require the establishment or confirmation of any such generalization.

Most specific issues in the theory of knowledge can be conceived as problems about the epistemological priority of one class of statements to another. It has been questioned whether statements about impressions, present memories, behaviour, observables, natural events and feelings of pleasure and pain are epistemologically prior, respectively, to statements about objects, past happenings, mental states, theoretical entities, supernatural beings and values or whether, on the other hand, the types of statement coupled in this list are logically independent of one another. One does not have to accept the reducibility of any of the items in the second part of the list to their partners in the first part to attach sense to the concept of epistemological priority which is involved in the theories that they are so reducible. And whatever may be said about these contentious cases the priority of singular statements to general ones is really too obvious to need labouring.

XI

The most substantial criticism of the doctrine of foundations that has been put forward in recent times is that made by Popper, in his *Logic of Scientific Discovery* [POPPER (1)], particularly in the fifth chapter, and in his *Conjectures and Refutations* [POPPER (4)], particularly in the introductory chapter. Popper's theory of knowledge is a sustained attack on a traditional body of ideas which he divides into empiricism, the theory that the foundation of knowledge is observation, and inductivism, the theory that knowledge is developed by the generalization of theories from this observational basis. He rejects these theories both as psychological or genetic accounts of the way in which knowledge actually grows, and as logical reconstructions of the order of dependence in which the elements of knowledge stand as regards their justification. On the matter of growth he maintains that theories precede observation and are not, and cannot be, mechanically excogitated from it. There is no such thing as pure observation; we must always observe under the guidance of some hypothesis which directs our attention by telling us what to look for. Theories or hypotheses are not derived from observable facts by applying the rules of a non-existent inductive logic to those facts. They may be suggested by facts to some extent, but an indispensable part is played in the business of theoretical conjecture by the background of knowledge already achieved, as well as an understanding of the unsolved problems that it presents, and by the constructive or imaginative power of the individual theorist. This seems truer of the more strictly theoretical parts of science than of the instantial laws of, say, natural history, and, again, truer of scientific theorizing than of the broad and continuous tide of subconscious, or at any rate not consciously directed, generalization that augments our ordinary knowledge of the world. On the matter of justification he points to the logical asymmetry between general theories and singular descriptions because of which theories can be falsified by observations but not established or verified by them. Science, then, as the most developed method of acquiring knowledge, is defined by him as a method of resolutely seeking for observations that will falsify our theoretical conjectures. It requires us to formulate our theories in as falsifiable a way as possible and to expose them as vigorously as possible to the test of observation and experiment and to the criticism of others. Our theories can never be certain, but to the extent that they have escaped falsification, without being so formulated as to avoid it, they are corroborated and worthy of provisional acceptance.

Bringing his accounts of the historical order of discovery and of the logical order of justification together, the following picture of the growth of knowledge results: first of all, theories, in the form of general statements, are put forward as conjectures; from them singular statements about observables are derived by deductive logic; these observations are empirically tested; if they pass the tests, the theory is so far corroborated, if they fail, it is refuted and must be replaced by another. The nature of the empirical test to which the observation statements are subjected is plainly crucial in this progression. Popper is prepared to describe these vital singular statements about observable states of affairs as basic, but he does not admit that they can be regarded as certain or as descriptions of experiences. It would appear, he argues, that three possible views can be taken about the status of basic observation statements. First, a dogmatism which accepts them as true without question; secondly, a psychologism which somehow reduces them to or identifies them with perceptual experiences; finally, the acceptance of an infinite regress. His own view of the matter is presented as a combination of elements from all three theories which he believes is free from the defects of all of them.

His theory is that in genuinely rational and scientific thinking we adopt as basic, statements about observable material things and events situated at a definite time and place. The acceptance of basic statements is a matter of convention and thus far dogmatic, but not viciously so since the convention can be abandoned if the convention of some other investigator comes into conflict with it. There is nothing permanent about the convention, and so the dogmatism involved is of a harmless because temporary and provisional kind. If a basic statement is challenged, it can itself be exposed to test by deriving further basic statements from it, together with already accepted theories. This possibility introduces an infinite regress, but it, too, is not vicious. We do not have to go on deducing basic statements from one another *ad infinitum*, but only from any given basic statement if anybody challenges it. And in fact most statements of the form he takes as basic are not challenged. Finally, a measure of dependence on perceptual experience is introduced to explain why we make the conventions that we do, why we choose to accept so very few of the basic statements from among all those that, being significant, are formally suitable for adoption. Experience does not, he says, verify basic statements but it does motivate us to adopt some rather than others.

This is an original and important attempt to solve the problem of the basis of knowledge, and I believe it to be very nearly successful but I do not think it can be accepted as it stands. The first difficulty concerns the idea that experiences do not justify but simply motivate the acceptance of certain singular statements about observables. We may assume that this motivation is not inexorable and can be resisted, in particular, by those who have reflected on the principles of rational thinking. If it could not be resisted, speculations about how one ought, if rational, to manage one's beliefs would be devoid of point. The vital difficulty is this: either the fact that an observational belief is motivated by experience is a reason for accepting it, in which case experience is not just a motivation, or else no belief whatever is justified at all. Unless experience actually supports the beliefs that it prompts us to hold, why should we choose to adopt them in preference to those which are prompted by wishful thinking or the desire to save ourselves trouble or any other emotional factor? In practice, to the extent that we are rational, we resist the promptings of hope and laziness because of their well-established tendency to conflict with the beliefs we are induced to form by experience. But why should we show this partiality as between the different emotional determinants of belief unless there is some necessary connection between experience and the acceptability of the beliefs that it inspires in us?

No conjecture, whether theory or observation statement, derives any support from the mere fact that someone entertains or conjectures it. Before it deserves acceptance a theory must be corroborated by the discovery that the basic statements which could falsify it are in fact false. But, on Popper's theory, should this not apply to basic statements as well? Either a basic statement derives some support from the experience that underlies its conventional adoption, in which case it is qualified to refute or corroborate antecedently conjectured theories, or the convention is a completely arbitrary one. If basic statements have no intrinsic probability, then the derivation of further basic statements from them cannot, for however long it is continued, add anything to their justification.

Why, furthermore, should conventional adoption be restricted to basic statements and not extended to theories themselves? For, as Popper has argued, theories are just as psychologically intuitive, just as much matters of subjective conviction, as basic statements are. It will not do to say that it is because they can at least be subjected to the negative test of exposure to falsification, for this is true of basic statements also. Popper might argue that we confine conventional adoption to basic statements motivated by experience because we find that there is very little disagreement about them, whereas there is a great deal of disagreement about theories and about basic statements motivated by wishful thinking or laziness. But, waiving the somewhat rhetorical objection that asks how this comforting fact is discovered, we must inquire whether it is simply a happy accident. Even if it is correct it only shows that the most economical or socially harmonious way to go about controlling our beliefs will be by subjecting them to the test of what experience has motivated. But is this relevant? The corroboration of theories will be accelerated by this convention and it will be a more sociable affair, but will it be any better calculated to approximate to truth than the convention of accepting basic statements on grounds of their euphony? Why should the fact that it satisfies our desires for economy and social harmony be regarded as justifying the second-order convention of adopting only those basic statements that are motivated by experience? Popper, in fact, has not really escaped his trilemma. If no statement is worthy of acceptance until it has been corroborated by way of the consequences deducible from it, then a vicious infinite regress ensues and no statement can be justified at all. If some or all statements are justified to some extent by the mere fact of being entertained

85

or conjectured, then his position is arbitrarily dogmatic. The only alternative is to allow himself to be impaled, at least a little, on the remaining horn of psychologism by allowing that basic statements can derive some support from the experiences that motivate them and are not entirely dependent for justification on the consequences that can be derived from them.

This modification of Popper's theory of basic statements, which holds that they acquire some, perhaps small, initial probability from the perceptual experiences that prompt them, is in effect the corrigibilist theory considered by Price. It is wholly consistent with Popper's fallibilist conviction that no statement of fact is ever finally and unalterably established, and that every statement, basic or theoretical, can be corroborated by its consequences. It maintains that the structure of our knowledge has foundations, but does not hold that these are absolutely solid and incorrigible, and while it asserts that it is through their connection with experience that basic statements derive that initial support without which no statement whatever would have any justification, it does not require them to be mere descriptions of experience. If the truth of the matter does lie in some such close interweaving of the correspondence and coherence theories, it would at once explain why the conflict between them has continued for so long and bring it to a conclusion which would not require the unconditional surrender of either contestant.

4. SENTENCES, STATEMENTS AND PROPOSITIONS

E. J. LEMMON

IN July 1950 there appeared an important article by P. F. Strawson entitled 'On Referring' [STRAWSON (2)]. One of the aims of this paper was to show that Russell's theory of descriptions, inasmuch as it was designed to give an account of the use of definite descriptions (expressions of the form 'the so-and-so') in ordinary language, embodied certain fundamental mistakes. In order to understand the mistakes that Strawson believed he had detected in Russell's theory, it will be as well to begin with a brief account of the theory itself.[1]

Consider the sentence:

(1) The present king of France is bald,

which contains as its grammatical subject the definite description 'the present king of France'. It would seem that this sentence is meaningful, and yet what exactly does it say about what? A natural answer is to reply that it says of some object, referred to by the phrase 'the present king of France', that it has the property of being bald. For, if we were asked the same question about the similar sentence:

(2) Khruschev is bald,

we should naturally reply that it says of some object, referred to by the name 'Khruschev', that it has the property of being bald. And yet this answer cannot be right in the case of (1), just because, in 1962 at least, there *is* no object referred to by the phrase

[1] The theory is most simply expounded in RUSSELL (1).

'the present king of France', so that there does not, at the present time, seem to be *anything* for (1) to be about.

The difficulty here can be seen more clearly, perhaps, if we turn to another sentence containing the same definite description:

(3) The present king of France does not exist.

We are inclined to say not only that this sentence is meaningful, but also that it is *true*, even if, no doubt, oddly put; indeed, it seems to be precisely a way of putting the truth that there is no present unique king of France. But if we ask the question 'What exactly does (3) say about what?', we again find it awkward to answer. For the natural reply—that it is about an object referred to by the phrase 'the present king of France' to the effect that there is no such object—so far from making the sentence appear true, makes it appear not only false but actually self-contradictory: the sentence refers to an object and then claims that there is no such object to be referred to, on this analysis.

Russell's escape from the difficulty is to claim that, while (1) and (3) are *grammatically* very much like (2), all three being of the same grammatical subject-predicate form, this structure is *misleading* as to the actual content of (1) and (3). When submitted to a proper logical analysis, (1) and (3) turn out to be respectively a complex existential claim and the denial of an existential claim; the subject-predicate façade disappears. For (1) Russell proffers a logical analysis into:

(4) There is something which (*a*) is a present king of France, (*b*) is unique in being a present king of France and (*c*) is bald;

and for (3) an analysis into:

(5) It is not the case that there is something which (*a*) is a present king of France, and (*b*) is unique in being a present king of France.

In these analyses, the definite description 'the present king of France', which appeared to refer to some unique object, has disappeared, and the special force of the definite article 'the' has been rendered by clause (*b*) in each case. It also follows from Russell's analysis that (3) is after all true, since (5) is evidently true; and that (1) is in fact *false*, since there is nothing which satisfies condition (*a*) of (4), and hence *a fortiori* nothing which satisfies all of conditions (*a*)–(*c*). It should be fairly easy to see from these examples how a Russell-type analysis can be applied to sentences of other kinds containing definite descriptions, in such a way that the definite descriptions are eliminated in favour of other less misleading locutions.

Strawson begins his attack on this theory by drawing attention to a class of expressions, which we shall call *uniquely referring expressions*, whose normal use in discourse is 'to mention or refer to some individual person or single object or particular event or place or process' [STRAWSON (2), p. 320]. This class includes ordinary proper names ('Venice', 'Napoleon'), demonstrative pronouns ('this', 'that'), personal and impersonal pronouns ('I', 'he', 'it'), and definite descriptions. He then makes a distinction between (*a*) these expressions themselves, (*b*) a *use* of one of them and (*c*) an *utterance* of one of them; and correspondingly, between (*a*) a sentence (say, beginning with a uniquely referring expression, such as (1) and (2) above), (*b*) a use of a sentence and (*c*) an utterance of a sentence. For suppose a man to utter the sentence (1) during the reign of Louis XIV and again during the reign of Louis XV: then the same *sentence* will have been uttered, but it will have been put to different *uses* on the two occasions. For example, the statement made by using it on the first occasion may well have been true, while the statement made by using it on the second occasion may well have been false. This illustrates the contrast between (*a*) and (*b*), both for uniquely referring expressions and for sentences. Again, suppose that during the same reign simultaneously two men utter sentence (1). Both men, since they refer to the same king and say the same thing about him, will now have put the same sentence to the *same* use, and made the same statement, either true or false; but there will be two distinct *utterances* of sentence (1) and of the phrase 'the present king of France'. This illustrates the contrast between (*b*) and (*c*) in each case, as well as between (*a*) and (*c*).

The contrasts between (*a*), (*b*) and (*c*) do not always hinge on the time of utterance of expressions and sentences, as in the examples given. They may hinge on the place of utterance, or even on the person uttering. For example, two people *A* and *B* may both utter the same sentence:

(6) I am hot,

but, if they do, will be putting it to different *uses*, since, such is the meaning of 'I', *A* will be referring to *A* and *B* to *B*, so that *A*'s statement may well be true and B's false. On the other hand, if B utters, not (6), but (addressing A):

(7) You are hot,

at the same time that A utters (6), then it is reasonable to say that A and B have now put different sentences to the same use, and made the same statement, either true or false. For both have referred to A and said the same thing about him.

It will be convenient to summarize Strawson's conclusions up to this point in the following two *dicta*: (α) the same sentence may be used in different contexts of utterance to make different statements, some true and some false; and (β) the same statement, either true or false, may be made by using different sentences in different contexts of utterance. (Similarly, the same uniquely referring expression may be used in different contexts of utterance to mention or refer to different things; and the same thing may be mentioned or referred to by using different uniquely referring expressions in different contexts.)

I am inclined to accept as true the *dicta* (α) and (β), though there remains some unclearness in the notion of 'same statement' to which we shall return. But the conclusions which Strawson bases on these claims, and with which he hopes to refute Russell's theory of descriptions, may, I think, be doubted. He concludes that we cannot say *the same things* about sentences and their uses, or about uniquely referring expressions and their uses. In particular, *meaning* is a function of the sentence or expression, while truth and falsity and mentioning and referring are functions of the *use* of a sentence or expression. 'To give the meaning of a sentence is to give *general directions* for its use in making true or false assertions' [Strawson (2), p. 327]. Hence we cannot, according to Strawson, ask the question 'What is the sentence about?': this question can only be asked about some *use* of a sentence to make a statement. Similarly, we cannot ask the question 'Is the sentence true or false?': it is the statements that we use the sentences to make that are true or false, and, indeed, a sentence such as (1) will be used to make a true or false statement only if the uniquely referring expression 'the present king of France' is successfully used, in the context of utterance, to refer to some object, i.e. if there is, at the time of utterance, a unique king of France.

Strawson elsewhere [Strawson (4), p. 4] reinforces the point that truth and falsity are functions of statements not of sentences as follows: 'We cannot identify that which is true or false (the statement) with the sentence used in making it; for the same sentence may be used to make quite different statements, some of them true and some of them false.' Now this is, in fact, an unsatisfactory argument. It is as though one were to say that we cannot speak of a gate as having a definite colour, because the same gate may have different colours at different times. The proper consequence of *dictum* (α) is that, if we wish to speak of *sentences* as true or false, then this talk must be *relative to context of utterance*, just as talk of the colour of a gate is relative to date. Thus, we might say that sentence (1) is true at one date but false at another (as the gate is red at one date and green at another); and that sentence (6) is true, perhaps, on my lips but false on yours. Strawson's examples do not show that we cannot speak of the truth or falsity of sentences: only that many sentences cannot be viewed as *absolutely* true or false.

And this is an important conclusion; for many logicians do seem, at least tacitly, to have supposed that sentences were all absolutely true or false. This is perhaps not surprising when we recall that modern logic is characteristically concerned with arguments in mathematics and the natural sciences, where there is good reason to suppose that sentences do not wait upon the context of utterance for their truth-value.[2] In fact, this contextual dependence is a much more deep-seated feature of sentences than one might at first sight suppose. Consider:

(8) Brutus killed Caesar.

We naturally say that this sentence is true if uttered today (though, of course, false if uttered in, say, 55 B.C.). But this is only because most contemporary contexts of utterance would disclose that the reference of the proper names 'Brutus' and 'Caesar' were the well-known Romans of that name. It is easy to imagine a contemporary context, in which the reference was to two dogs with the same names, such that (8) was in fact false. Our linguistic conventions are such that *no* ordinary proper names are uniquely assigned to a single object, so that there is always an element of contextual

---

[2] 'By the *truth value* of a sentence I understand the circumstance that it is true or false . . . For brevity I call the one the True, the other the False.' FREGE (1); GEACH-BLACK, p. 63.

dependence in their reference and, consequently, in the truth-value of sentences containing them.

Let us now return to Strawson's attack on Russell. Strawson agrees with Russell that (1) is meaningful, and that anyone now uttering it would be saying something true only if there was at present a unique king of France; but he denies that anyone now uttering (1) would be saying anything true or false, and that part of what he would be saying would be that there was a unique present king of France. (Russell is committed to both these positions by the analysis into (4), as we have seen.) For Strawson, anyone uttering (1) today *fails* to refer successfully, his use of the sentence is a *spurious* use, and the question whether his statement is true or false fails to arise for just this reason [STRAWSON (2), pp. 329–31]. And he believes that Russell failed to see this just because he failed to make the distinction between sentences and their uses to make statements, and so assumed that the only alternative to a sentence's being true or false was for it to be meaningless.

If we bear in mind, however, that, while we accept Strawson's distinction between sentences and statements, we see no good reason to withhold the labels 'true' and 'false' from sentences because of it, we can recast Strawson's view of (1) as follows: the sentence (1), if uttered today, is *neither true nor false*, because the uniquely referring expression in it 'the present king of France' has today no reference; and it is a prerequisite of sentence (1)'s being true or false that there be a unique king of France at its date of utterance, though this is no part of what is claimed by (1).[3] But it is important to notice that this rephrasing of Strawson's position hinges not at all on the contrast between sentences and statements; this was pointed out by Quine [QUINE (2)], who accepts Strawson's strictures on Russell's theory of descriptions regarded as an analysis of the ordinary use of such expressions, but is worried by the postulation of statements as opposed to sentences: 'In appealing thus to "statements" . . . Mr Strawson . . . runs a certain risk. The risk is that of hypostatizing obscure entities, akin perhaps to "propositions" or "meanings" . . . , and reading into them an explanatory value which is not there.'

Now this raises several questions. Does the notion of a state-

---

[3] If we do say that this is part of what (1) claims, as opposed to what it *presupposes*, then we are back, of course, to something like (4), and are forced to conclude that, since there is no present king of France, (1) today is actually false.

ment have any explanatory value? If it does (as seems at first sight so from Strawson's own examples), how do statements relate to propositions or meanings? Again, if Strawson's views about the 'truth-valuelessness' of certain sentences in ordinary speech are correct, how is it that logicians (including Quine) can continue successfully to use Russell's theory of descriptions, as is certainly the case? These questions are interconnected, and we shall gain some insight into their solution by considering the position of Frege [FREGE (1)], who puts forward a view in many respects similar to that of Strawson.

Frege begins his article 'On Sense and Reference' with a puzzle about identity. Consider the two sentences:

(9) The morning star is the morning star.
(10) The morning star is the evening star.

We naturally say that (9) is a trivial truth of logic, an example indeed of the law of identity that $a = a$, while (10) is a far from trivial astronomical fact, dependent for its truth not on logic but on the way the world happens to be. Yet it is hard to see how they can be so different: for they are both *about* the same object, Venus, and say of it the same thing, that it is the morning star, i.e. that it is the evening star (which *is* the same thing since the morning star *is* the evening star). This puzzle is deeper than it looks, and Frege's way out is to distinguish between the *reference* of uniquely referring expressions and their sense.[4] Their reference is simply the object, if there is one, to which they uniquely refer. It is clear that the expressions 'the morning star' and 'the evening star' have the same reference, namely, the celestial object Venus.

---

[4] Frege's distinction between *sense* and *reference* is closely related to Mill's between *connotation* and *denotation* [MILL (1, 2), para. 5]. But, while Frege applies his distinction only to uniquely referring expressions, Mill applies his to all terms or 'names': roughly, the denotation of a term for Mill is the class of things of which the term is truly predicable (we all, for example, belong to the denotation of the term 'human being'), and its connotation is the class of attributes which anything *has* to have in order to belong to its denotation (to be a human being one has to be rational, so that the attribute of rationality belongs to the connotation of 'human being'). Thus 'white' denotes any white thing, but connotes the attribute whiteness. Mill's distinction is in turn related to an older one, that between a term's *extension* and its *intension*: again roughly, by a term's intension is understood its meaning, whilst its extension is the class of *subspecies* of its denotation (in Mill's sense). Thus the *class* of whales belongs to the extension of the term 'mammal'; any individual whale belongs to its denotation. See JOSEPH, Ch. VI. I should add that these terms are used in varying ways by different authors.

What the sense of an expression is is less clear, but examples may help. No one would say that 'the morning star' *meant* the same as 'the evening star', and so we may say that the two expressions have different senses. On the other hand, 'the morning star' *does* have the same sense as its correct French translation 'l'étoile du matin'. Again, 'the man whom Brutus killed' and 'the man who invaded Britain in 55 B.C.', though they have the same reference, Caesar, have different senses, while 'the man whom Brutus killed' and 'the man who was killed by Brutus' have not only the same reference but also (presumably) the same sense. Frege nowhere *defines* sense, but he explains it as the *mode of presentation* of the object which is the reference.

It is similarly natural to speak of sentences as a whole as having a sense:[5] this will be, for example, what the sentence has in common with its correct translation into other languages. This sense will be a function of the sense of any expressions occurring in the sentence; Frege called it a *Gedanke*, but it is convenient to translate this 'proposition' rather than 'thought' in order to avoid misleading psychological implications [CHURCH, p. 26]. Following Frege's terminology that uniquely referring expressions and sentences *express* their sense, we may say that a sentence expresses a proposition which is its sense.

Clearly, (γ) two different sentences may express the same proposition (have the same sense); clearly, also (δ) the same sentence, if it contains some ambiguous word or phrase, may have two different senses and so express two different propositions. These results are akin to Strawson's *dicta* (α) and (β) above, and we shall pursue this affinity later.

As to (9) and (10), we can say that, since all uniquely referring expressions in both have the same reference, they both have the same truth-value, namely, are both true, but that, nevertheless, since the *sense* of 'the morning star' is different from that of 'the evening star', (9) and (10) have different senses and express different propositions. Thus the puzzle about identity ceases to be puzzling.

Frege also draws attention to the fact that many uniquely referring expressions (one of his examples is 'the least rapidly converging series', but 'the present king of France' will do as well)

---

[5] Frege also allows that sentences have a reference, and this turns out to be their truth-value; but this piece of doctrine need not concern us here.

have a perfectly clear sense but no reference. What of a sentence, such as (1) at least if uttered today, which contains such an expression? Then the sentence as a whole may have a perfectly clear sense (express unambiguously a proposition), but it will *lack a truth-value*, be neither true nor false.[6] This is exactly Strawson's position, as rephrased by us earlier.

However, there is a difference between Frege's position and Strawson's. Frege never makes clear, at least in 'On Sense and Reference', that the reference of a uniquely referring expression may vary from context to context, even though the sense does not change:[7] witness Strawson's example of 'the present king of France' uttered in different reigns. Indeed, he suggests rather the reverse, that to a given sense there will correspond a unique reference, when he writes [FREGE (1), p. 58]: 'The regular connection between a sign, its sense, and its reference is of such a kind that to the sign there corresponds a definite sense and to that in turn a definite reference.' If Frege did believe that sense determined a unique reference in this manner, then he seems clearly to have been wrong: it is its sense *taken in conjunction with the context of utterance* that in general determines the reference of a uniquely referring expression.

We are now in a position to compare Frege's notion of a proposition (the sense of a sentence) with Strawson's notion of a statement (what sentences are used to make): both, of course, are to be viewed as distinct from sentences, which are merely taken to be sequences of words belonging to a given language; but how do they relate to one another? A little reflection shows, I think, that they are distinct notions. For consider again our original imaginary situation in which (1) was uttered in different reigns: there, we agreed, different *statements* were made because different kings were referred to; but, inasmuch as the *sense* of (1) remains unchanged at the different dates of utterance, the *proposition* expressed (in Frege's sense) is the same. And now suppose a different situation: let (1) be uttered during the reign of Louis XIV and let:

(11) The previous king of France was bald

---

[6] See Frege's discussion of 'Odysseus was set ashore at Ithaca while sound asleep' [FREGE (1), pp. 62–3]. Frege also says [p. 61], with Strawson, that the use of a uniquely referring expression *presupposes* a reference for it (cf. footnote 3).

[7] Contrast FREGE (2).

be uttered during the reign of Louis XV. Here two distinct sentences have been used to make the *same* statement (Louis XIV has been referred to on both occasions, and the same thing said about him); but inasmuch as the two sentences are evidently not synonymous, two distinct propositions have been expressed.

Similar remarks apply to (6) and (7). No one would claim that these two sentences had the same meaning; hence they express different propositions; but they may be used in the right context to make the same statement. Conversely, if you and I both say (6), then, though we make different statements, we express the same proposition, since we use the same words in the same sense.

Despite the similarity, therefore, between (α) and (β) on the one hand, and (γ) and (δ) on the other, statements that sentences may be used to make are quite distinct from the propositions that they may express. (α) and (β) hinge on the fact that reference is partly determined by contextual factors; (γ) and (δ) are explained by the fact that languages contain synonymous and ambiguous terms. It should be fairly clear by now that, given two utterances, the questions whether these are of the same sentence, or of the same statement, or of the same proposition, are quite independent of one another. Admittedly, in the examples given so far where the same proposition has been expressed on two different occasions, the same sentence has in fact been used; but by changing one of the utterances to an utterance of the correct French translation of the same sentence, we vary the sentence without changing the proposition.[8]

We have then, intuitively at least, three distinct notions: that of a sentence, that of a statement and that of a proposition. All three —sentences, statements and propositions—may be said to be true or false, though no doubt in different senses. A sentence may be said to be true (false), relative to a particular context of utterance, if, in that context, it is used to make a true (false) statement. A proposition may be said to be true (false) relative to a context of utterance, if there is a sentence, true (false) relative to that context, which expresses it.

Of course, in the last paragraph I have taken it for granted that

---

[8] The hardest situation to envisage is that of two distinct utterances of the same sentence to make the same statement, even though two distinct propositions are expressed. But it can be done. The interested reader should consult (δ) before trying to work out an example for himself.

one understands what it is for a statement to be true or false, and defined a sense of 'true' and 'false' for sentences and propositions in terms of this understanding. It is arguable, however, that the ascription of truth and falsity to sentences is in fact more basic than their ascription to statements, if only because it seems difficult to identify uses of distinct sentences as making the *same* statement without already knowing that the sentences, in their respective contexts, have the same truth-value, though, in fact, a way of doing so will be suggested later on. Perhaps, therefore, we should suppose it known what it is for a sentence to be true (false), and define a statement as true (false) if there is a true (false) sentence which in some context can be used to make it. This puts both propositions and statements on the same footing with respect to sentences, but involves also the assumption that all propositions and statements are expressible by or can be made by the use of some sentence in some language. How reasonable is this assumption? What, for example, of the proposition (statement) that neutrinos have no mass? This was presumably as true in 500 B.C. as it is today, though no doubt not expressible in any language in use at that date. This objection seems to me specious: a suitable account of languages and the sentences belonging to them can ensure that the English sentence 'Neutrinos have no mass' existed to express the proposition in question as surely in 500 B.C. as it does now, though the speakers at that time were, for historical reasons, unable to make use of it to this end.[9] Yet may there not be propositions or statements which no language will ever find the means to express? I think here we can say what we please: whether we postulate such entities or not, in any case they can have, for obvious reasons, little interest for us.

Sentences, then, will vary in their truth-value, as we have seen, from context to context; so for that matter will propositions, as the senses of sentences. By contrast, statements are true or false once and for all. The statement that Brutus killed Caesar is true

---

[9] Or, if this seems paradoxical, we may take the 'is' of 'there is a sentence' in the above definitions to be timeless, i.e. equivalent to 'was, is or will be'. The view adopted here, that languages and the sentences belonging to them are timelessly given, is a common one among logicians (see, for example, CHURCH, p. 27, footnote 72). The contrasting picture, that languages change in time, is no doubt needed by linguists and historians of ideas. That these two stand-points are not necessarily exclusive of one another, i.e. that different concepts of meaning may be useful in different fields of study, is argued in COHEN.

for all time,[10] even though the sentence (8), which in normal contexts today would be used to make it, may in other contexts be false.

If a sentence containing a uniquely referring expression is used in a context such that this expression lacks a reference, then, according to both Frege and Strawson (at least as rephrased), the sentence lacks a truth-value. But it still has a sense, so that in addition to true and false propositions we have to admit truth-valueless ones. Are we also to admit truth-valueless statements? This seems to be merely a matter of terminology: we may either say that in these special contexts no statement at all has been made, or that in them the statement made is neither true nor false. Strawson himself seems committed to the latter alternative [STRAWSON (4), p. 175], but the former seems just as viable as a form of expression; if we follow it, then all statements are either true or false, which may be viewed as a satisfactory consequence.

One merit of employing all three notions of sentence, statement and proposition is that it reveals a deep-seated ambiguity in the notion of *saying the same thing*. If I say 'I am hot', and you say, to me, 'You are hot', then in one sense we have said the same thing (made the same statement). If I say 'I am hot', and you say 'I am hot', then in a different sense we have said the same thing (uttered the same sentence). If I say 'I am hot', and you, being French, say 'J'ai chaud', then we have neither uttered the same sentence nor made the same statement; but there is still a sense in which we have said the same thing, namely, expressed the same proposition.

Another merit of employing the notion of proposition in addition to those of sentence and statement is that it enables us to give an account of such fairly common idioms as 'it used to be true that . . .' and 'it is no longer true that . . .'. Suppose we say:

(12) It used to be true that the population of London was under 4 million, but this is no longer true today.

Then what is it that used to be true and is no longer true? This cannot be a statement because, as we have seen, statements are

---

[10] It was true, presumably, even before 44 B.C., when it might have been made by using the sentence 'Brutus will kill Caesar'. Here we brush by the problem of future contingents. There is space only for me to say that 'Che sera sera' is a truth of logic, not a version of determinism.

timelessly true or false, and cannot change their truth-value. Nor can we say that (12) is about a certain *sentence*, say:

(13) The population of London is under 4 million,

to the effect that it was true at a certain date and is not true today. For sentences, as sequences of words, belong to some language, and if we wish to talk about them, we need to employ some special device for doing so, such as quotation marks. Thus (12) has to be contrasted with:

(14) 'The population of London is under 4 million' used to be true, but is no longer true today,

in that (14) is a sentence, in English, about an English sentence, in a way that (12) is not. This point emerges clearly if we translate (12) and (14) into another language, say French; for a correct translation of (14) will leave the words inside the quotation marks *unchanged*, yielding a French sentence about an English sentence. It should be obvious that the 'that'-clause in (12), as opposed to the quotation marks in (14), make reference to a *proposition*, namely, the proposition expressed by the English sentence (13), and the whole sentence says of this proposition that it used to be true, but is no longer so.

Incidentally, we here observe an ambiguity in the 'that'-construction. While sentences are perhaps best referred to by the device of quotation marks, both statements and propositions can equally well be referred to by 'that'-clauses,[11] and only a careful inspection of surrounding circumstances will reveal in general which is being spoken of. It is perhaps worth adding that the distinction between statements and propositions is only worth upholding in any case in connection with those sentences whose truth-value is contextually dependent. In the case of general sentences belonging to the natural sciences ('All ravens are black') or to mathematics ('$7 + 5 = 12$'), truth-value is timelessly given, and there seems little point and little sense in making a distinction here between the propositions expressed and the statements such sentences are used to make.

But this matter may be clearer when we have seen whether the notions of proposition and statement, so far discussed merely

[11] So, for that matter, can *facts*. But perhaps facts are best construed as a kind of proposition or statement: see D. MITCHELL, pp. 109–15.

intuitively, can be defined with any rigour. For so far all we have really seen is that propositions in Frege's intuitive sense are distinct from statements in Strawson's, and that to uphold the distinction may help to clarify some puzzles. To these other questions we should now turn.

It must be admitted, in the first instance, that the ontological status of statements and propositions is peculiar. For they are certainly not linguistic entities, as sentences are—do not belong to a language—nor are they spatio-temporal particulars, locatable at a position in space-time, like physical objects or even events and processes. Thus, there is a *prima facie* case against postulating them, if only in accordance with Ockham's razor, unless we have to. On the other hand, as abstract objects, they are perhaps no worse then qualities (e.g. colours) or even works of art such as symphonies (as opposed to their performances, which no doubt are spatio-temporal events).

Whether the notion of proposition can ultimately be justified depends really on whether the notion of meaning or sense and the closely related notion of synonymy can be adequately defined. A vigorous attack on all these notions has been launched in recent years by Quine.[12] It would be beyond the scope of this paper even to attempt to meet Quine's criticisms, but a few rather scattered remarks may be in order.

In the first place, there is little doubt that we shall have a clear criterion for the identity of propositions if the notion of synonymy can be made clear. For we can say that two sentences S_1 and S_2 express the same proposition just in case they are synonymous. However, Quine argues [QUINE (4), Ch. II, esp. paras. 14–16] that no firm empirical basis can be given to the general notion of synonymy, mainly on the grounds of a fundamental indeterminacy in the idea of translation from one language to another: different and incompatible translational schemes (which Quine calls analytical hypotheses) can be adopted which all fit the empirical linguistic data. Still, the situation here seems no worse than in science generally, where it is commonly the case that discrepant theories will fit all the facts—a choice is made rather on grounds of simplicity, elegance and the like. Quine himself admits [QUINE (4), p. 75]:

---

[12] See QUINE (4), for the most recent onslaught: the related literature is cited in his bibliography.

The indefinability of synonymy by reference to the methodology of analytical hypotheses is formally the same as the indefinability of truth by reference to scientific method. Also the consequences are parallel. Just as we may meaningfully speak of the truth of a sentence only within the terms of some theory, so on the whole we may meaningfully speak of interlinguistic synonymy only within the terms of some particular system of analytical hypotheses.

It seems to be a consequence of this view that, once a translational scheme is more or less agreed on (as is certainly the case between the familiar European languages, but may be less true in the case of, say, English and Hawaiian), we *may* speak profitably of synonymy. Of course, there is no doubt that the notion of synonymy is in need of proper clarification. But Quine has not shown that such clarification is unobtainable; rather he has revealed some of the difficulties that might stand in the way of it. It may, indeed, be some comfort that the notion of truth, with which few logicians or philosophers would wish to dispense, is only different in degree of clarity perhaps but not in kind from the notion of synonymy. I conclude that synonymy, as a basis for propositional identity, if unsatisfactory, is certainly not doomed by Quine's arguments. There is certainly, however, no room here to attempt to clarify the notion.

Later in the same book [QUINE (4), Ch. VI, esp. paras. 40, 42, 43], Quine launches a new and separate attack on propositions, on the grounds that they are in any case theoretically dispensable. He claims first that any sentence (such as (1), (6) or (7)) which is dependent on context for its truth-value can be expanded, in a given context of utterance, into an *eternal sentence* which is not so dependent and will be absolutely true or false; examples of sentences which are already eternal sentences in this sense are, of course, theoretical sentences in mathematics and the sciences. The expansion consists in the first instance of replacing tensed verbs by tenseless ones, together with time-indicators; secondly, of replacing 'indicator words' such as 'I', 'now' and 'this', by exact and objective spatio-temporal references; and thirdly, of filling out incomplete descriptions and proper names so as to secure a unique for-all-time reference [QUINE (4), p. 194]. It may, however, be doubted whether this expansion is in principle always possible; certainly Quine nowhere illustrates it. We have already seen that

(8) is not in fact eternal, if only because there may be dogs called Brutus and Caesar. But even if we expanded (8) into:

(15) Brutus, the Roman Senator who lived from 85 to 42 B.C., killed Caesar, the Roman general who lived from 102 to 44 B.C.,

we are in theory no better off. For it is in principle still possible that there were two such senators or two such generals, or even two Romes. No such definite description or proper name, however 'complete', carries a *logical* assurance of contextfree unique reference, which is what Quine's expansion seems to demand.[13]

However, we may leave this difficulty on one side for the moment. Supposing that the expansion into eternal sentences is possible, Quine contends that talk about propositions can in most contexts be replaced by talk about eternal sentences, so that there is no need to postulate the existence of the former. Several remarks are pertinent here. First, it is *statements* rather than *propositions* that eternal sentences might replace.[14] For eternal sentences, like statements but unlike propositions, are supposed to be timelessly true or false. Hence there is no reason to suppose that eternal sentences can hope to explain idioms such as those exemplified in (12). Propositions are in fact called in, as distinct from statements, precisely as the constant senses, from context to context, of *non*-eternal sentences. Secondly, it is not clear that eternal sentences will do in place of *statements*, just because eternal sentences belong to a language in a way that statements do not, so that distinctions such as that between (12) and (14) are obscured. A sentence to the effect that an eternal sentence is true is a sentence about a language, in a way that a sentence to the effect that the corresponding statement is true is not.[15] Thirdly, it is arguable that it is theoretically simpler to postulate the existence of statements as entities than to rely on a putative and complex translation into eternal sentences—provided, at least, that clear criteria for the identity of statements can be given.

---

[13] This argument is chiefly prompted by a similar line of thought in STRAWSON (3), Ch. 1, part 1.

[14] Quine concedes this at the beginning of para. 43 of QUINE (4).

[15] Quine [QUINE (4), 213–14] rejects this sort of argument, but only because it turns on the notion of synonymy.

It is to this problem, therefore, leaving propositions behind, that we shall now turn. What are sufficient and necessary conditions for two sentences uttered in different contexts to be used to make the same statement in Strawson's sense? Up to now, we have merely relied on examples, such as (6) and (7), and the intuitive notion that the sentences should both, in their separate ways, say the same thing about the same thing.

Let us consider, first of all, an example slightly different from (6) and (7). Suppose A says:

(16) The driver of the van had no hair,

and B says:

(17) Tom Jones was bald,

and the contexts of their utterances are such that they are both, the one by using a definite description and other by using a proper name, referring to the same person at the same date. Then, since to be bald is just to have no hair, we incline to say that they are both making the same statement by using different sentences in different contexts. Now to say that to be bald is to have no hair is to say that anyone is bald if, and only if, he has no hair. Let the context in which A utters (16) be c_1, and the context in which B utters (17) be c_2. Then sufficient and necessary conditions for (16) in c_1 to be used to make the same statement as (17) in c_2 are (a) that the reference in c_1 of 'the driver of the van' be the same as the reference in c_2 of 'Tom Jones', and (b) that anyone is bald if, and only if, he has no hair.

To generalize slightly: let $S(a)$ be a sentence containing the uniquely referring expression a, and $T(b)$ be a sentence containing the uniquely referring expression b. For any uniquely referring expression e let $rc(e)$ stand for the reference of e in context c. Then $S(a)$ in c_1 is used to make the same statement as $T(b)$ is used to make in c_2 if, and only if, $rc_1(a) = rc_2(b)$,[16] and for any x, $S(x)$ if, and only if, $T(x)$.

This definition is not completely correct as it stands, partly because of complexities concerning quotation-marks into which it would be tedious here to enter. A more serious defect is that it only takes account of sentences containing one uniquely referring

---

[16] We use '=' here, as is logical practice, simply to mean 'is the same as'.

expression each; but generalization to the case of many such is fairly straightforward.[17]

A consequence of the definition, as we should hope, is that $S(a)$ in c_1 is true if, and only if, $T(b)$ in c_2 is true, if they are used to make the same statement. For suppose $S(a)$ is true in c_1. Then, since, for any x, $S(x)$ if, and only if, $T(x)$, in particular $S(a)$ if, and only if, $T(a)$. Hence $T(a)$ is also true in c_1. But, since $rc_1(a) = rc_2(b)$, $T(b)$ will be true in c_2. The converse argument is similarly seen to hold. Thus, our criterion for the same statement is such that statements are absolutely true or false, a *desideratum* for the notion of statement.

A word should be added concerning the matter of time-reference. For it to be the case that (16) and (17), in their respective contexts, are used to make the same statement it is clearly necessary that both A and B be referring to the same date. Hence, strictly, the sentences should be expanded by the insertion of words such as 'yesterday' or 'on 1st January 1962 A.D.', in order to include such a reference. But such words as 'yesterday', 'today', 'then', 'now' raise new problems for us. For suppose A to say at 10.15:

(18) Tom Jones is now bald,

and to utter the same sentence again at 10.30 on the same day. Has he made the same statement or not? We are inclined to say yes; but, given that by a near-miracle Tom Jones might have gone bald precisely between 10.15 and 10.30, this answer will apparently commit us to saying that the same statement may be false when first made by A, and true on the second occasion—a conclusion at conflict with our view that statements are timelessly true or false.

One solution is to say that 'now', taken strictly, refers only to an instant of time, so that A's two utterances of (18) do indeed make different statements, since the reference of 'now' changes with the time of utterance. But let us suppose that 'now' may more loosely refer to a fairly indeterminate *period* of time surrounding the moment of utterance but sufficiently broad to in-

[17] To be explicit and formal, for a moment, $S(a_1, \ldots, a_n)$ in c_1 makes the same statement as $T(b_1, \ldots, b_n)$ in c_2 if, and only if, $rc_1 (a_i) = rc_2 (b_i)$ for $1 \leqslant i \leqslant n$ and, for any $x_1, \ldots, x_n$, $S(x_1, \ldots, x_n)$ if, and only if, $T(x_1, \ldots, x_n)$. The order in which uniquely referring expressions occur in the two sentences can be rearranged to suit this definition.

clude, let us say, 16 minutes each way; hence A's two utterances make the *same* statement by our present criteria, since his two 'now's refer to the same vague period. ('Today', 'this afternoon', etc., do refer to periods in this way.) Then, in *that* sense of 'now', it is not at all clear what the truth-value of (18) in *either* context is, in case Tom Jones loses his hair during the period in question: it is neither clearly false at 10.15, in view of what is about to happen, nor clearly true at 10.30, in view of what has just happened. And this unclearness is brought about by the inexactness of the predicate 'bald' rather than by the vague reference of 'now'. If this inexactness is removed, then the truth-value of the sentence (18) in its two contexts of utterance will be settled in the same way, and we have again no exception to our conclusion that statements are timelessly true or false.

A rather tighter criterion for two sentences $S(a)$ and $T(b)$ to be used to make the same statement is to stipulate not merely that, for any x, $S(x)$ if, and only if, $T(x)$, but rather that it be *analytic* that, for any x, $S(x)$ if, and only if, $T(x)$. I shall not pursue this suggestion further here, but it is worth remarking that, while the notion of analyticity is as suspect from Quine's point of view as the notion of synonymy (with which it is indeed interdefinable), the actual criterion put forward above for the identity of statements contains, so far as I can see, no features with which Quine would quarrel. It is, in textbook jargon, a purely extensional rather than an intensional notion.

So far, I have argued that propositions are acceptable as entities if synonymy can be clarified sufficiently, and that this undertaking has not been shown by Quine to be hopeless; and that reasonable criteria for the identification of statements can also be put forward, so that they too, if we wish it, can be admitted into our ontology. There is a final question, raised earlier, which I should like to discuss, concerning the admissibility of truth-valueless sentences, statements and propositions.

Let us admit, with Strawson, that for some sentences used in some contexts the question of the truth-value of the statements there made by using them can fail to arise, and that this will often if not always be the case where the sentence in question contains a uniquely referring expression which in that context fails to refer. We may say, with Quine, that such situations give rise to *truth-value gaps* [QUINE (2), p. 439]. Then it is a standing tendency of modern formal logic, as exemplified in Russell's theory of descriptions, to close these gaps: to assign, that is to say, a definite truth-value, true or false, to sentences in this situation. Can this tendency be justified? Certainly not, of course, if it is one of the functions of formal logic faithfully to reflect every idiosyncracy of ordinary speech.

But formal logic is not called upon to do this. One of the aims of formal logic is to regularize and standardize the conditions under which sound argumentation takes place, and in situations where ordinary speech is unclear or undecided this very standardization may involve departures from familiar practice. So long as these are recognized as departures, so long, that is to say, as we admit that a formal analysis of an ordinary sentence is not necessarily equivalent to it in every respect, it is hard to see that harm is done.

In the particular case of uniquely referring expressions, it is a presumption of ordinary discourse that a speaker using one in a given context knows enough about the context to ensure that unique reference is in fact secured by his use of it. Thus, sentence (1) will only ordinarily be used by speakers in contexts in which there is in fact a unique king of France. And in such contexts Russell's analysis into (4) is entirely satisfactory: for it will render (1) true in case that unique king is bald, and false in case that unique king is not bald. If this presumption is not satisfied, then in ordinary speech we may say that the sentence is neither true nor false, while, as logicians following Russell, we shall say that it is false. It is almost possible to say that it is the speaker's own fault if what he says turns out to be false on logical analysis; for he should have made sure that there was a unique present king of France before uttering (1). One can say, in fact, that a certain logical fallacy is committed by someone who employs in a reasoning situation a uniquely referring expression which lacks a unique reference.[18]

It may be conceded that the logician has the right, in standardizing the conditions for sound argument, to depart to some extent from ordinary language, and yet be argued that any such departure should at least be justified. In the case in question, why is it more

[18] This fallacy is committed by Euclid, *Elements*, I, 1, who speaks of 'the point at which the circles intersect' before he has shown that the circles in question intersect at all (in fact, they intersect at *two* points). The fallacy vitiates his proof, in fact.

satisfactory to treat (1) as false when there is no unique king of France, rather than neither true nor false? The answer, I think, is very simple: the gain to the logician in closing truth-value gaps is that he is then able to treat *all sentences as true or false*—an assumption which leads to an extremely simple logical structure. The familiar method of truth-table testing becomes available to him as a means of recognizing certain sentences as embodying logical laws, and so on. On the other hand, if the logician is to acknowledge truth-value gaps in his formal work, a considerable price in complexity has to be paid. And the desire to stay close to ordinary usage does not seem a sufficient motive for paying this price.[19]

If this *pragmatic* justification for the closing of truth-value gaps is felt to be worthy, we may accept Russell's theory of descriptions for purposes of logical analysis, and conclude that in logic we have no need for truth-valueless sentences, and consequently no need for truth-valueless propositions or statements either.[20] And we are finally able to see that the original dispute between Strawson and Russell rests on a misunderstanding: if Russell thought he was expounding the ordinary usage of definite descriptions, then probably he was wrong in much the way that Strawson describes; but this is in no way to impugn the utility of Russell's theory as a logical tool for the analysis of sentences used in serious argumentation. This utility has been demonstrated over and over again by the employment of the theory in the logical analysis of mathematical and scientific arguments.

[19] Similar observations are made in COHEN, pp. 250–1.

[20] This conclusion is exaggerated, of course; for we have not considered how to treat proper names (e.g. 'Odysseus') which may ordinarily fail of reference; for a treatment of the problems raised by them, see QUINE (4), para. 37.

5. PARTICULAR AND GENERAL

R. HARRÉ

ANY attempt to devise a systematic logic of science must cope with the fact that the results of observation and experiment must be expressed in particular statements, while the laws of nature, for which they are in some sense the basis, are stated as generalizations. Different methods of attacking the problem of devising a logic for that part of scientific reasoning concerned with the relation between particular and general statements stem, in part, from different views as to the way in which particular statements are the basis for generalizations. For instance, particular statements could be regarded as the premises from which generalizations are inferred; or particulars could be regarded as providing tests for generalizations arrived at in some way other than by inference from particular premises. Those who have held that there is an inferential relation between particular and general statements have tried to construct formal schemata for this relation, that is, have attempted to construct *inductive* logics:[1] while those who have held that particulars express test cases of generalizations have employed deductive logic to give an account of scientific reasoning which has come to be called the *hypothetico-deductive* theory.[2] Neither account is free from difficulties of a very fundamental kind, but their respective difficulties, as we shall see, are two aspects of the same deep-seated problem.

Nothing is easier than to generalize. Our language is very well equipped with expressions for expressing generality. Indeed, just by dropping the particularity of reference of a descriptive statement we arrive at one which is general, without using any special

[1] For example VON WRIGHT, Chs. 2–5.   [2] Cf. BARKER.

linguistic device. For instance, Newton discovered in a series of experiments that colours separated by the prism are not further separable. The result of each experiment could have been stated in the form of a particular—'This instance of homogeneal light has a colour corresponding to its degree of refrangibility which cannot be changed by reflection or refraction'; and the results of the finite series of experiments in a finite set of particular statements like the instance above. Instead, Newton states his discovery quite generally just by dropping any particularity of reference—'Homogeneal light has a colour corresponding to its degree of refrangibility and that colour cannot be changed by reflections and refractions' (Opticks: Prop. II, Theor. II). The problem is not 'How can we *make* general statements?' but 'How can we be persuaded that those we have made are worthy of belief?'

If we construe the relation between particular and general statements as an inferential one, that is, if we choose to say that general statements are inferred from particular statements, then we can argue from the analogy of deductive logic, where correct inference from true premises gives a true conclusion, that 'correct inference' from true particular statements gives us a general statement worthy of belief. The problem then becomes a double one: of finding the rules for 'correct inference' in this situation, that is, rules which will lead to statements of the required general form, and incidentally of showing in what sense general statements arrived at by employing such rules are worthy of belief. We might be persuaded to attempt this somewhat as follows:

Some instances of P are Q
therefore
All instances of P are Q

Rule: Given a set of true particular statements asserting some matter of fact, and given that there are no true particular statements which deny that matter of fact, the generalization asserting that matter of fact generally can be inferred.

But is the generalization *true*? The temptation is to say that the more instances favourable to the generalization which we can discover, the more highly the generalization is confirmed, and hence the more worthy is it of belief. Those who have succumbed to this temptation have come to be called 'inductivists'.[3] There is an in-

[3] MILL, Bk. III, Ch. XXI, Sect. 2–3.

ductivist form of the hypothetico-deductive account of scientific reasoning too. Though those who espouse the hypothetico-deductive theory do not see generalizations as the result of inferences from particular matters of fact, there are, nevertheless, those who see the confirmation of generalizations as the result of the piling up of more and more favourable instances, in the absence of any instances unfavourable to the hypothesis.[4]

It has been recognized for a long time that the acceptance of an inductivist account of the role of particular statements in relation to the truth of a generalization, commits one to a kind of circularity of reasoning. The difficulty arises in this way: the inductivists' grounds for holding a certain generalization are found in some growing set of favourable instances. But to use this set for this purpose presupposes that it will continue to grow in the same manner, that repetition of tests will continue to yield favourable instances. But this presupposition involves reference to future times and other places, in which it is quite conceivable that the generalization under test does not hold. This difficulty would be quite easily overcome if it could be demonstrated that nature was such that regularities once discovered would continue to be exhibited under the appropriate circumstances. But to demonstrate this general empirical truth would require, for an inductivist, the building up of a growing set of favourable instances of the hypothesis; and he would then have no means left to justify his faith that *this* set would continue to grow in the same favourable way.

It should now be clear that there is some sort of problem here— how are we to devise a set of rules for that part of scientific reasoning where particular and general statements are brought into relation with one another, which escapes the difficulties to which inductivist accounts seem to commit their followers? Perhaps no set of rules can be devised for the move from particular to general, for what one might call the *enlargement* of statements.

Attacks upon the problem of how we are to use particular statements of ascertained truth to justify generalizations have lately been supplemented by two novel methods.

(1) *The Linguistic Critique.* In accordance with the principles of analytical philosophy, the existence of an intractable problem is a sign that something is wrong in the way the problem has been set up, and the insoluble questions posed. Language has gone astray,

4 See, e.g., HEMPEL (2).

so that distinguishable concepts are hidden under one word. This leads either to a conflation of many questions into one; or to the situation in which a question is formulated using a certain key word in one way, while the problem is of such a kind that answers to the question necessarily require the key word to be used in some different way. It has been suggested by P. F. Strawson[5] and P. Edwards [EDWARDS] that the problem of induction is just such an intractable problem, and depends for its appearance of intractability upon ambiguities in the uses of the word 'justify' and its synonyms. When we set up the question 'What justifies our belief in an empirical generalization?' we are tempted to want answers in terms of strict logical or *deductive* justification; while the context of the question determines a sense of 'justify' which is not that of 'deduce from true premises'. Hence any answer modelled upon deductive justification can be faulted from the context of the question. All that is needed to dissolve the problem and to start to answer the question is to see this. Then we look for the senses of 'justify' used in the description of empirical investigations, and so find answers adjusted to whatever sense the question may have.

Finding answers to the question and identifying the appropriate sense of 'justify' are closely connected, for each sense of 'justify' is tied to some paradigm case of its use, that is, a case which we could use to explain that sense of 'justify'. That is, we look for cases in which people agree that a generalization is justified by certain evidence and we can make the following moves:

Question: 'What justifies our belief in *this* sort of empirical generalization?'
Answer: '*This* sort of evidence.'

Then to the general question:

'What justifies our belief in empirical generalizations?'

we answer:

'Empirical evidence.'

And if anyone asks for *more* justification in a particular case than the production of evidence which is generally held to be satisfactory, he can be satisfied if what he means by 'more evidence' is 'more evidence of the same kind'. But if he is demanding that he should be shown a deductive link between evidence and generalization in virtue of which the generalization can be known to be true, he has not realized that this demand is inappropriate in the context, since it is an empirical investigation that is going on.

It is tempting to suppose that this argument settles the matter finally, and that further progress would consist only in identifying those kinds of evidence which are regarded as justifying various kinds of generalizations, and thus identifying the acceptable forms of non-deductive reasoning by reference to them. But one might well accept the linguistic critique without accepting the conclusion just drawn from it. To suppose that the study of non-deductive reasoning is now shown to be no more than a matter of *identifying* forms which are accepted, is to confuse the descriptive with the normative function of logic. There still remains the question whether the forms of reasoning which *are* identifiable by their *being* accepted, *ought* to be accepted. That is, we can still raise questions of the standards of non-deductive reasoning, which are not to be answered by the formula that each accepted method defines a standard. For instance, we might set about devising some standards by investigating the requirements that have to be met by a theory in order for it to be judged satisfactory, and then choosing only those accepted methods of accrediting generalizations which lead to the selection of those which fit into acceptable forms of theory. If there are such standards, then *a fortiori* there are general principles for assessing the worth of generalizations, and we find ourselves once more looking for a logic. But, thanks to the linguistic critique, we need no longer feel obliged to take deductive logic as our model or valid deducibility as our standard of justification. We are free to look elsewhere; to the courts,[6] to the arts,[7] to certain mathematical procedures,[8] for our models of reasoning among particular and general statements.

The linguistic critique, in effect, advises one to preserve the realities of reasoning and reform logic to fit them.

(2) *Searching for the Falsifier.* The account of the logic of the relations of particular statements of fact and generalizations due to K. Popper,[9] and expounded also by J. W. N. Watkins [WATKINS] and J. Agassi [AGASSI], depends upon turning this advice round

---

[6] TOULMIN (2), Chs. III, V.   [7] HARRÉ, Ch. VII.

[8] JEFFREYS, Ch. III.   [9] POPPER (1), Chs. I–VI.

about. One is advised instead to preserve logic and reinterpret scientific reasoning to fit the logic. However, the problem of this chapter was not the main source of Popper's characteristic ideas, and his method of dealing with our problem arose out of his answer to another question; the problem of the demarcation of those statements which ought properly to be called scientific or empirical. Though the problem is not at present much discussed it played a central role in the formation of much that is characteristic of modern English philosophy, since the profoundly influential doctrines of logical positivism could be said to have developed out of attempts to solve it.

Briefly, the origin of the problem is this: how can we find a way of detecting and thence eliminating metaphysical statements from the sciences? The answer given to this question by the philosophers of the Vienna Circle was simple in outline. An empirical statement is one for which a method of verification is possible in principle, and hence those statements for which a method of verification cannot be described are non-empirical, metaphysical and should be eliminated from the sciences. Unfortunately, as the subsequent history of this doctrine has shown,[10] it is extremely difficult to justify in detail. (A further development, important to philosophy generally, was made by the Vienna Circle and by Professor Ayer in England [AYER (1)]: it was claimed that statements for which no method of verification is possible were not only non-empirical, but meaningless.) Popper, dissatisfied with the shortcomings of the verification criterion, proposed his own. A statement is empirical, or scientific, if it is possible for evidence to falsify it. This criterion must be carefully distinguished from one of a more traditional cast, that an empirical statement is one whose contradictory is not self-contradictory. It might be argued that if a statement is to be identified as a falsifier of a general empirical statement, it must be the contradictory of that statement, and it must be possible for it to be true; that is, it must not be the case that it is self-contradictory. Thus it might be made to seem as if the criteria of Popper and traditional philosophy were identical. But this is not so, since it is a key part of Popper's doctrine that there are statements whose contradictory is not self-contradictory and yet which are not scientific, in so far as all the relevant evidence which turns up concerning them is treated as

---

[10] See AYER (1), Preface to 2nd edition.

confirmatory, so that in the context they cannot be falsified.[11] So the test for whether a statement is empirical (scientific) or not is to ask whether it is such that the truth of some particular statement could be formally contradictory of it, and hence show it to be false (not, of course, that there *is* some true particular statement which *does* show it to be false).

However, even though the origin of Popper's philosophy of science is in this problem of demarcation, the particular form that his doctrine takes has another source. We have already seen the insuperable logical difficulties that arise when we regard the role of particular statements as either premises for the inference of general statements, or as providing confirmatory instances of general statements. But in Aristotelian formal logic particular statements can falsify general statements—and this is the role to which Popper assigns them. Particulars which agree with a general statement are not, it is implied, worth seeking, since they add nothing to its probability; but particulars which would *dis*agree with a given general statement are worth seeking, since if we could find one, it would show the generalization to be false. There is an ambiguity in the presentation of this doctrine which many commentators of Popper's views have noticed. It is not clear whether we are to regard him as claiming that this is what scientists actually do experiments for, seeking falsifiers, whatever they may think to the contrary; or whether we are to regard the doctrine as a logician's advice to scientists as to what it is profitable for them to do.

Put simply Popper's contention about the logical form of science seems to be this. The 'traditional' account of the relation between particular and general could be expressed as follows:

(I)   *Hypothesis*   All S is P
       Discovered matter of fact therefore Some S is P
                                             All S is P

is in some degree confirmed.

Furthermore, the more instances of S which are instances of P, the more highly is the hypothesis confirmed. But this is bad logic, since it rests upon the invalid inference

Some S is P

therefore

All S is P

[11] For instance, general existential statements in contrast to particular assertions of existence.

Even if we suppose the 'premise' only to add probability to the general statement, we still gain nothing from the support of particular cases, since they cover only a finite section of a potentially infinite class of cases and hence leave the probability of the generalization untouched.

On the other hand, the discovery of a contrary instance does get us somewhere, since if

(II)   All S is P

is our hypothesis, to discover that

Some S is not P

is true, enables us to infer without reservation, according to Popper, that

All S is P

is false.

This leads us back to the demarcation problem, for it is claimed that hypotheses for which such a form as (II) cannot, in principle, be constructed, are not scientific hypotheses. So we can reach the criterion of demarcation from a consideration of the proper role of particular statements. Since we find that the only role which Aristotelian logic will permit them to play is that of falsifiers, potential falsifiability must be the criterion of an empirical statement, for all empirical information must be expressed in particular statements.

On the source of our general statements Popper argues, in effect, that there can be no logic of scientific discovery, that is no rational account of better or best ways of generalizing particular pieces of information that is not a description of the psychology and cultural background of scientists. I think he is to be understood in flat contradiction to Newton, who says 'the theory, which I propounded, was evinced by me, not by inferring 'tis thus because not otherwise, that is, not by deducing it from a confutation of contrary suppositions, but by deriving it from experiments concluding positively and directly' [*Phil. Trans.* (vii, 1672, 5004–5)]. And 'In experimental philosophy we are to look upon propositions inferred by general induction from phenomena as accurately or very nearly true, . . . till such time as other phenomena occur, by which they may be either made more accurate or liable to exceptions.' Newton, whose views may have some weight in the matter, evidently regarded phenomena which were counter-instances to his laws as stimulating the investigator to make his laws more accurate (to correct them), or to find in this way the limitations to the application of his laws in nature. But Popper's analysis cannot be refuted so long as the laws of nature and the results of experiment are expressed in the forms of Aristotelian logic. I hope to show, by analysing the formal structure of a class of laws of nature, that the observation that a particular negative instance renders a general affirmative statement *false*, the corner-stone of Popper's doctrine, is insufficiently precise for explaining the relation between many laws and their counter-instances. Fol-lowing the hints from Newton I shall argue that in many scientific contexts, the judgement 'L is false', where L stands for some general statement expressing a law of nature, conceals distinctions of the greatest importance. My argument leads to the proposal that we substitute for the simple appraisal 'L is false' the more refined judgements 'L is incorrect' and 'L is limited in application', and to the conclusion that within the simple Aristotelian scheme offered by Popper subtler formal inference schemes can be found.

To find such logical schemata we need to begin with an adequate analysis of the forms of scientific reasoning. According to the recommendations of the linguistic critique a formal analysis will depend upon an adequate understanding of the forms of general statements which are actually made by scientists. In one important respect the logician's understanding of this form has been in-adequate. What I have to say about the logic of particular and general statements in the sciences depends upon what I believe to be an important distinction between kinds of general statements made in the sciences. The distinction I have in mind I shall call that between taxonomic generalizations and functional generaliza-tions. It depends upon the way the instances of which the generali-zations are supposed to be true are treated. The extension of a general term can either be treated as an ordered set of objects, events, properties, etc., or any order which could be given to the objects, etc., forming the extension, can be disregarded.

Since a set of objects, states or events can be ordered in a variety of ways, and since my argument to a more refined logic of par-ticular and general statements depends heavily upon the identifi-cation of order in the sets of objects, states or events which are the extensions of general terms, it is important to investigate such orderings more closely.

Consider some general term A. Suppose the intension of that term is some set of predicates F, and suppose the extension of A to be some set of objects $a, b, c, \ldots$. Some object n is a member of the extension of A, that is of the set $(a, b, c, \ldots)$, if and only if Fn is true. The propositional function Fx can then be treated as a criterion for membership of the extension set. The set of objects, states or events $(a, b, c, \ldots)$ is ordered, if there is some relation R such that if x and y are both members of the set, then

$$\text{If } x\text{R}y \text{ then } not\text{-}y\text{R}x \tag{1}$$
$$\text{If } x\text{R}y \text{ and } y\text{R}z \text{ then } x\text{R}z \tag{2}$$
$$not\text{-}x\text{R}x \tag{3}$$

It follows from this that any object n for which Fn is true has a unique place in the set of objects; that is, to assert both that it is between say p and q, and between q and r, where p, q, r and n are related in such a way as to satisfy (1), (2) and (3) above, leads to a contradiction.

There are a great many relations which, given the appropriate kind of entities in the set, could be interpretations for R in (1), (2) and (3) above. For instance, if $a, b, c, \ldots$ are any length measures, then by interpreting R as 'greater than', we can order the set $(a, b, c, \ldots)$. In general if $a, b, c, \ldots$ are numerical, we can find an R (though not necessarily one and only one R) such that with respect to that relation $(a, b, c, \ldots)$ is ordered. Other relations yielding unique orderings are, for instance, 'parent of' where the members of the set are organisms, 'to the left of' where the members of the set are objects linearly disposed. Whether we choose to order the extension of a general term is a matter for decision, and we are not compelled to order any extension set in any particular way, though for any given interpretation for $a, b, c, \ldots$ there are some relations which cannot be used to order the set, since the $a, b, c, \ldots$ may not be such that they can properly be treated as terms of the proposed relation.

Once we have chosen to treat a set of objects as having an order it is easy to see that the logical relations between particular propositions about members and general propositions about the set are not quite the same as when the set of objects is treated as unordered. Since it is upon this difference that my whole argument turns, it must be examined in some detail. Suppose we assert the hypothesis that for some set of objects, states or events, all the members of the set have some property G. We can represent this by the unlimited conjunction

a has G, and b has G, and c has G, . . ., and n has G, . . .
or Ga and Gb and Gc . . . and Gn . . .

We suppose that some experimental investigation shows that Gk is false. What are we to conclude about the truth of the hypothesis that all members of the set have G?

1. *Macrologic*

From received formal logic we draw the conclusion that the hypothesis is false, and this logic makes no provision for further steps in reasoning.

2. *Micrologic*

There are now two further possibilities open, depending upon whether the objects, states or events a, b, c, . . . are treated as an ordered set or are not so treated.

(i) *Unordered Set.* If $(a, b, c, . . .)$ is unordered then k might be anywhere in the set. This is the force of the disjunctive interpretation of particular propositions. That is, that if we know that some member does not have the property G, all we are entitled to assert is that

Either a does not have G, or b does not, . . .

so, if k cannot be placed uniquely in the set $(a, b, c, . . .)$, all the particular propositions Ga, Gb, Gc, . . . are equally cast into doubt.

(ii) *Ordered Set.* If $(a, b, c, . . .)$ is an ordered set, then k can be given a unique location in that set. Clearly it is not at all certain that the same degree of dubeity can be cast upon particular propositions about members of the set remote from k, as can be cast upon propositions about members adjacent to k.

To put this in another way; if the extension of general terms can be treated as ordered sets, then particular propositions about members of that extension cannot be treated as disjunctions covering the entire set, each of which might have the same contradictory force against the general assertion. This is particularly so when we know beforehand that some of those particular propositions are true.

Generalizations which refer to sets of objects that we do not treat as ordered and which therefore exhibit the micrologic of unordered sets are those I shall call taxonomic, and those which refer to sets of objects which we do treat as ordered and which exhibit the micrologic of ordered sets are those which I shall call functional.

Taxonomic generalizations are more characteristic of those parts of science where we classify things and substances, while functional generalizations are more characteristic of those parts of science where we describe processes in, and interactions among, things and substances. In classifying animals the order in which one collects specimens does not have to be considered in the logical analysis of the relations between statements describing particular organisms and statements defining or describing biological species. In physics, on the other hand, experiments are done over ranges of conditions, and the position of the conditions in which a particular experiment has been carried out, within the range of conditions, is of crucial importance in deciding what effect favourable and unfavourable instances have upon the acceptability of a functional generalization.

When philosophers of science have noticed that the varying of experimental conditions is an essential feature in the assessment of putative laws of nature, they have not taken sufficient account of the fact that in varying the conditions to produce additional particular facts, the conditions are not only different from those in which a relation was originally discovered, but they can also be ordered with respect to those conditions. Further, by reference to the ordered set of conditions under which particular phenomena occur, those phenomena can be ordered. To put this another way, hypotheses about the world are tested under as wide a range of conditions as possible. The experimental conditions in which hypotheses hold can be ordered because the particular conditions which make up a range of conditions can be ordered. A simple example of this is the experimental testing of the laws governing the rate of chemical reactions. Roughly speaking, the rate of a reaction depends upon the concentration of the reactants and the temperature at which the reaction takes place. Both 'temperature' and 'concentration' are concepts with a built-in possibility of order, since they are specified numerically. So the hypotheses of mass-action can be said to hold in a range of experimental conditions which are ordered, and ordered by the order of the temperatures and concentrations in terms of which they are specified. It does not matter that this case shows a two-dimensional ordering, for test cases for any one or any set of the experimentally variable conditions can be placed uniquely in the ordered set of experimental conditions. It is the place of particular specifications of general laws in the ordered sets which are the extensions of their terms that fails to find a place in the logics of Frege and Aristotle. There is no way of specifying which S's are P when we express our knowledge of a particular fact in the form 'Some S is P', nor is there any way of specifying which x has the property F when we symbolize a particular statement in the sentence-form $(\exists x)Fx$. Aristotle's and Frege's logics of the relations between particular and general statements are the logics of taxonomic generalizations and unordered sets of particulars. In attempting to construct a set of rules for scientific reasoning it is essential that we take account of the fact that for a great many laws of nature the effect of a favourable or an unfavourable instance will depend upon the location of the instance in the ordered set of conditions under which the generalization is tested. It looks as if some modification of accepted logic will be necessary in order to find the rules for this part of scientific reasoning.

The logic of taxonomic generalizations and their instances would seem to be that of Aristotle; for the instances of taxonomic generalizations are not treated as having a location in an ordered set of instances. We could regard the unspecific character of Aristotelian particular sentence-forms as sufficiently reflecting this feature of taxonomic reasoning to be an adequate representation of favourable and unfavourable or counter-instances. If this is so, then it may be the case that Popper's account of the asymmetry between the alleged confirmation and the actual falsification of general statements by relevant particular statements applies not too badly to taxonomy.

Functional relationships may take various forms and be variously defined, but for the purposes of my argument it is sufficient that a functional relationship between observables is expressed by an algebraic function of variables and constants, where the algebraic variables stand for variable and numerically measurable observables. For instance, $s = vt$ is a functional generalization standing for the functional relationship between distance, velocity and time of travel of a body moving uniformly.

Let us suppose that we have arrived at a functional generalization by 'enlargement', that is, simply by stating a particular discovery generally. How should we express such a functional generalization? To begin with we should notice that when we hold a functional relationship to be generally applicable, this generality is, as it were, in two dimensions: we suppose it to hold for all times and places, and we suppose it to hold for all conditions determined by the possible values of its variables. Let us set aside spatio-temporal generality for the moment. What we have left is a functional relationship between variables together with the implicit assertion that this functional relationship will be exhibited by all measurable values of the observables. The numerical values of the variables are ordered sets, for instance, 'temperature' or 'pressure' are such that the relations between temperatures or pressures are transitive and asymmetrical; that is, if t_1 is higher temperature than t_2, and t_2 than t_3, then t_1 is higher than t_3: and if t_1 is higher than t_2 then t_2 is not higher than t_1. Combining the ordered sets of values of relevant variables we get an ordered set of experimental conditions. When a functional relationship between observables is stated generally, then one dimension of this generality is that of experimental conditions, that is, the functional relationship is asserted to hold at all experimental conditions.

One further feature of ordered sets of conditions needs to be noticed. When we specify the experimental conditions by some set of parameters, not only can we order particular experimental conditions but we can assign a zero to this order, a lower bound. Ranges of experimental conditions are orderable as sets of values of the parameters bounded at one end and open at the other. This feature of the logic of functional generalizations arises from the fact that all the parameters which we use to represent physical properties are defined only for positive values. For instance, it is easy to see that no sense can be attached to a pressure of less than o gm/cm^2 or to a volume of less than o cm^3. We do, on occasion, use negative integers for the values of some parameters, but it can be shown that in each case the range of values is not open. There are three obvious cases. We may be using negative values for a parameter because we are operating our scale from a 'false' zero.

For instance, there are temperatures below $0°$ C. But we also know that temperature has a 'true' zero defined by $0°$ K $= -273°$ C; and this sets a lower bound to the range of possible temperatures. Again, we may use negative values of a parameter to define a new parameter. This case occurs with the parameter 'charge', where we treat negative and positive charges as different sorts of charge; as, for instance, in the way we use charges of different sign to distinguish different classes of fundamental particles. Finally, there are those uses of negative values for parameters that we find with vectors. Here the negative value is not to be taken as an indication of the negative value of the quantity, but as a sign of direction.

This feature of sets of conditions we shall see reflected in the logic of particular and general statements; for slightly different rules apply to instances between the zero and a particular favourable instance, from the rules for instances in the unbounded upper regions of a set of experimental conditions.

If for the sake of simplicity of exposition we take the experimental conditions to be a one-dimensional ordered set, then we could represent the general assertion of a functional relationship as follows:

Let $F(x, y, \ldots)$ be the functional relationship, and let $Rc_0 \ldots$ $c_n \ldots$ be the ordered set of experimental conditions, then the general assertion of the functional relationship could be represented by

$$F(x, y, \ldots) \, Rc_0 \ldots c_n \ldots$$

But this does not yet represent the state of knowledge at any one time. It is necessary to distinguish in the ordered set of conditions between those which are definite, that is in which experiments have been done, and those which are, at any time, hypothetical, that is in which experiments have not yet been done. To represent the situation we can divide the ordered set of experimental conditions $Rc_0 \ldots c_n \ldots$ into hypothetical and definite cases. That is, what one might call the 'candid' form of this kind of law of nature is

$$F(x, y, \ldots) \, Rc_0 \ldots c_m \, \text{(Hyp)} \, \& \, Rc_{m+1} \ldots c_n \, \text{(Def)} \, \& \, Rc_{n+1} \ldots$$
$$\text{(Hyp)}$$

I locate the definite cases within the hypothetical, as this represents the most common situation. For instance, 'room temperature' is that in which experiments usually begin, since lower and higher temperatures are more difficult to achieve.

This formulation of a law of nature of a certain kind represents an advance upon both the Aristotelian formulation 'All S is P' and the Russellian formulation '$(\forall x)(Fx \supset Gx)$', in two ways.

(i) The 'all' and the universal quantifier '$(\forall x)$' ('for all x') conceal the methodologically, and as I hope to show, logically vital difference between hypothetical and definite cases.

(ii) Counter-instances and favourable instances when expressed in the Aristotelian system as 'Some S are not P', 'Some S are P'; and in the Russellian system as '$(\exists x)(Fx \ \& \sim Gx)$', '$(\exists x)(Fx \ \& \ Gx)$' do not carry any indication of where, in the ordered set of experimental conditions, they were discovered. But the forms

$$not\text{-}F(x, y, \ldots) \ c_k$$
$$F(x, y, \ldots) \ c_j$$

which can be derived from the experimental tests of particular substitutions of the variables in $F(x, y, \ldots)$—e.g. '$(F(a_k, b_k, \ldots)$ is false' and '$F(a_j, b_j, \ldots)$ is true'—do carry an indication of just where, in the ordered range of cases they occurred.

It is demonstrable in science that what judgements we make of a general assertion of the functional relationship kind, and what we do in case of a counter-instance, depend upon where, in the ordered range of cases, that instance comes. To find the acceptable schemata we must notice two features of scientific reasoning.

(1) Provided that apparatus and standards of measurement remain unchanged we do not admit counter-instances within the range of already established definite cases. If we do find apparent counter-instances, we reject them as mistakes, due to some fault in the apparatus or clumsiness of the experimenter; for instance, the way scientists take no notice of the stream of counter-instances to all the well-known laws which are continually being discovered by student scientists. The whole procedure of a teaching laboratory, with its central concept of 'right result', depends upon this feature of scientific reasoning and is unintelligible without it.

(2) (i) A favourable instance in the hypothetical part of the range of cases serves to extend the definite part of the range of

cases, but leaves the remaining cases hypothetical. A counter-instance in the hypothetical range of cases, *in the first instance*, does not count against the law, in the sense of showing it to be false, with the suggestion of 'wrong in all instances'. Rather it is used to limit the application of the law to a certain restricted range of cases. It counts against the openness of the range of hypothetical cases. In ordinary language this is represented by the distinction between a counter-instance leading to the judgement of a generalization as 'false', i.e. 'untrue', and leading to the judgement of a generalization as 'false', i.e. 'only partly true'. The bald judgement 'false' conceals this vital difference.

(ii) Under the circumstances that the limiting conditions can be explained theoretically, a second move is possible. The old law can be combined with the limiting conditions, interpreted in the concepts of the theory, to yield a new law, which accommodates the limiting conditions of the old law as definite cases of the new law's application.

Following Newton I distinguish these functions of the particular counter-instance as 'limitation' and 'correction'. Let us now look at a classical example of limitation followed by correction to see if the doctrine which has just been outlined needs any limitation or correction.

The general gas law was first enunciated in the form

$$PV = RT \quad \text{(under all conditions)} \tag{1}$$

Experiment disclosed that

$$PV = RT \quad \text{(except under high pressure and low temperature)} \tag{2}$$

That is, the discoveries that the law does not hold at high pressures and low temperatures are used to limit the range of experimental conditions in which it is claimed to hold. Using the kinetic theory of gases the limiting of experimental conditions can be expressed in terms of the concepts of that theory.

$$PV = RT \quad \text{(except when the volume of the gas molecules is not small with respect to the total volume occupied by the gas, and intramolecular forces are significant)} \tag{3}$$

Let b be the volume of the molecules of the gas and a/V^2 a measure of the intramolecular forces. The condition just enunciated can be expressed in these symbols.

$$PV = RT \quad \text{(except where } b \text{ is not small with respect to } V \text{ and } a/V^2 \text{ is not small with respect to } P) \tag{4}$$

The corrective move which follows these limiting moves is to accommodate the theoretically interpreted restrictions in the functional relationship; that is, to modify $PV = RT$ as some function of b and a/V^2. This gives us the well-known formula

$$(P + a/V^2)(V - b) = RT \tag{5}$$

The generality of (5), the new functional relationship, is now open to test, since we have stated it unrestrictedly. The whole series of moves (1) to (5) can be repeated yielding functional relationships both of greater particular precision, and of wider definite application.

The argument of this section can be summed up by contrasting the logical principles of the Aristotelian treatment of the relation between particular and general statements, where cases are not ordered; and the principles which, I have suggested, are to be extracted from actual instances of reasoning, where the general statements refer to ordered ranges of cases and the particulars are always stated with respect to cases whose position in the ordering is known.

1. *Aristotelian Principles*

(*a*)   Some S is not P
                        contradicts
(*b*)   All S are P.

That is, if (*a*) is true, then (*b*) is simply false.

(*c*)   Some S is P
                        contradicts
(*d*)   No S are P.

That is, if (*c*) is true, then (*d*) is simply false.

2. Principles of Limitation and Correction

Let L stand for some functional relationship. Let $c_1 \ldots c_n \ldots$ be the ordered set of experimental situations or cases in which L could be tested. Then there are at least the following laws:

A1. Law of Minimum Extension

If L under $c_1 \ldots c_m$ (def.) & $c_{m+1} \ldots$ (hyp.) and L under $c_n \ldots c_p$ (def.) & $c_{p+1} \ldots$ (hyp.), then L under $c_1 \ldots c_p$ (def.) & $c_{p+1} \ldots$

A2. The Law of Minimum Contraction

If L under $c_1 \ldots c_k$ (def.) & $c_{k+1} \ldots$ (hyp.) and not-L under c_m $(m > k)$ (def.), then L under $c_1 \ldots c_k$ (def.) & $c_{k+1} \ldots c_{m-1}$ (hyp.)

A3. The Law of Hypothesis

If L under c_m (def.), then L under $c_1 \ldots c_{m-1}$ (hyp.) & L under $c_{m+1} \ldots$ (hyp.)

A4. The Law of Initial Limitation

If L under some c (hyp.) and not-L under $c_1 \ldots c_m$ (def.), then L under $c_{m+1} \ldots$ (hyp.)

A5. The Law of Final Limitation

If L under some c (hyp.) and not-L under $c_m \ldots c_p$ (def.), then L under $c_1 \ldots c_{m-1}$ (hyp.)

A6. The Law of Correction.

If L under $c_n \ldots c_p$ (def.) & L under $c_{p+1} \ldots$ (hyp.) and not-L under $c_j \ldots c_k$ $(j < k < m < n)$, then L' under $c_1 \ldots c_p$ (def.) and L' under $c_{p+1} \ldots$ (hyp.); where L' is some function of L and $c_j \ldots c_k$ such that $L' \longrightarrow L$ when $c_k \longrightarrow c_n$.

If the laws of limitation are correct representations of scientific reasoning, then they exclude outright falsification of an hypothesis by the production of one contrary instance. From the Law of Initial Limitation it follows that it is always logically possible to continue to maintain an hypothesis for remote cases provided that the contrary instances discovered fall in the initial part of the set of possible cases. From the Law of Final Limitation it follows that final and outright rejection of an hypothesis is only logically forced upon one when the class of cases of which it is the true description is 'squeezed up' to zero.

No inductive problem arises in this dimension of generality, since the assertion that the functional relationship holds generally is not the *assertion* that it holds unrestrictedly, for the differential role of favourable and counter-instances shows that the range of experimental conditions in which the functional relationship holds must be treated as consisting of definite and hypothetical cases, since only if this is the case can we give a rational account of limitation and correction.

Such a solution cannot be adopted in the dimension of temporal generality; for what happened in the past is not open to experimental test, at least before the sixteenth century when most of our systematic records begin. What will happen in the future cannot be discovered now, whatever experimental ingenuity we exercise. However, one might be tempted to say that the dimension of spatial generality is theoretically, though not practically, open to test. Using Einstein's definition of simultaneity we could, theoretically, arrange for a simultaneous test of some functional relationship in remotely different regions of space. But in order to correlate the results at any one point they must be signalled to that point; and we know that all signal velocities are finite. It follows that to have any faith in the accuracy of the results which reach us in this way, we should have to suppose signal invariance, and that depends upon faith in the invariance of certain processes with time. We cannot therefore escape the necessity of the assumption of temporal generality. We are left then with a residual problem—how to justify the assumption of temporal generality.

To see just what the problem is, we need to distinguish between the premises which are required to complete the cogency of any piece of reasoning, and the conditions which must hold for there to be any reasoning at all. Philosophers have, not uncommonly, treated the assumption of temporal generality as a premise which must be added to the inference of a prediction to make the predictive reasoning cogent.[12] If the assumption is treated as a premise, then *a fortiori* it is being treated as a statement which might be true or might be false. It is then deemed proper to ask what is the evidence for this statement, and the use of the evidence, say, of

---

[12] MILL, Bk. III, Ch. III, Sect. I.

past successes in prediction, is then seen to depend itself upon the assumption of temporal generality. This circularity, so easily generated, is surely an indication that something is wrong with the way the problem has been interpreted. If, instead of treating the assumption of temporal generality as a premise in every prediction, we treat it as a condition for making predictions, then we cannot so immediately be driven to asking ourselves whether it is true, and so be forced to argue in a circle.

A moment's reflection shows that the assumption of temporal generality is the condition, not only for making predictions, or at least for placing any reliance on them, but for every intellectual and practical act whatever. In particular, the assumption of the relative stability of the senses of words, which is a condition for any use of language, is a special case of the assumption of temporal generality. To give up any particular generalization may be painful, but leaves the possibility of science unimpaired. But to give up the assumption of temporal generality is to give up, not only the scientific enterprise but even the possibility of having a language in which doubts about that very assumption of temporal generality can be expressed. It does not make sense to give up the assumption of temporal generality, since upon that assumption the possibility of sense depends.

6. GOD AND NECESSITY

ANTHONY KENNY

IN most times and places there have been philosophers interested in the implications of philosophical trends for religious beliefs. Contemporary England is no exception. About five years ago several groups of writers attempted to present an account of religious belief acceptable to the currently influential school of British philosophy. *New Essays in Philosophical Theology* [FLEW–MACINTYRE],[1] a collection of papers published in 1955, was followed in 1957 by two further symposia, *Faith and Logic* [B. MITCHELL] and *Metaphysical Beliefs* [HEPBURN–TOULMIN–MACINTYRE], and by Professor Ramsey's *Religious Language* [I. T. RAMSEY] and Professor Braithwaite's *An Empiricist's View of the Nature of Religious Belief* [BRAITHWAITE]. Few readers, whether philosophers or believers, found the analyses of religious language presented in these books wholly satisfactory. I do not propose to give a summary of the views presented in these books or others which followed them. Instead, I propose to follow the fortunes of a single argument concerning natural theology which has been pursued in philosophical publications in this country during the last twenty years.

God, it is often said, is a necessary being; all else is contingent. One of Leibniz's proofs of the existence of God concludes that there exists 'a necessary Being, in whom essence involves existence, or in whom it suffices to be possible in order to be actual. Thus God alone (or the necessary Being) has this prerogative, that he must necessarily exist if he be possible.' Many of the philosophers whom we are considering appear to have derived their impression of natural theology either directly or indirectly from the writings of Leibniz. The attempt to understand the concept of *God* has

[1] Throughout this article, this collection will be referred to as 'F–M'.—Edd.

131

therefore frequently taken the form of an attempt to make sense of the notion of *necessary being*. Several philosophers, finding this notion incoherent, have concluded that the concept of *God* is unintelligible.

'The only necessity that exists,' wrote Wittgenstein in the *Tractatus Logico-Philosophicus*, 'is *logical* necessity. There is no compulsion making one thing happen because another has happened' [WITTGENSTEIN (2), 6.37]. Moreover, Wittgenstein maintained that the propositions of logic, which alone were necessary, were all tautologies; and that tautologies gave no information about the world. 'The propositions of logic are tautologies. Therefore the propositions of logic say nothing. (They are the analytic propositions)' (6.1, 6.11). Since Wittgenstein at this time accepted the thesis of *Principia Mathematica* [RUSSELL–WHITEHEAD] that the whole of mathematics could be exhibited as a continuation of logic, the word 'logic' in these quotations refers also to mathematics. 'It is . . . remarkable that the infinite number of propositions of logic (mathematics) follow from half a dozen "primitive propositions". But in fact all the propositions of logic say the same thing, to wit nothing' (Ib., 5.43).

The doctrine that the only sense of 'necessity' is 'logical necessity', and that the necessary truths of logic and mathematics were necessary only because they were tautologous, was one of the most influential theses of the *Tractatus*. The doctrine was particularly attractive to empiricists, and in particular to the logical Positivists. It enabled them to maintain, with Hume, that all our information about the world was derived from experience and contingent, without having to deny, with Mill, the *a priori* and necessary nature of mathematical truths. Tautologies say nothing about the world: logic and mathematics, if they are tautologous, are necessary only at the price of not being factual.

Thus Professor Ayer wrote in 1936 as follows:

The principles of logic and mathematics are true universally simply because we never allow them to be anything else. And the reason for this is that we cannot abandon them without contradicting ourselves, without sinning against the rules which govern the use of language, and so making our utterances self-stultifying. In other words, the truths of logic and mathematics are analytic propositions or tautologies . . . They none of them provide any information about any matter of fact. In other words they are entirely devoid of factual content. And it is for this reason that no experience can confute them. [AYER (1), 77–9]

To philosophers who think along these lines the notion of *necessary being* has naturally been a scandal. In 1942 Professor A. N. Prior published a dialogue entitled 'Can Religion be discussed?' [PRIOR (1)]. In this dialogue one of the characters, named 'Catholic' attempts to state the difference between God and all other beings in the following manner:

> What the medieval schoolmen said—and I have yet to learn that their work in this field has been improved upon—was that the Being of God is necessary, while that of all other beings is contingent. All the objects we commonly encounter can be imagined not to exist—they exist, so to speak, by chance,—but for God there is no such possibility of non-existence. He occupies the field of Being securely; his dislodgment from it is unthinkable; indeed the supposition of his dislodgment is nonsense—it cannot even be talked about; we are not really speaking of God when we say such things. God *is* his own Being. Similarly, all other beings are *what* they are 'by chance'; at least their 'properties' are contingent; one could imagine them being otherwise; all other good things, for example, even some supremely vast and good being whose vastness and goodness tempt us to worship him, are good 'by chance'; they might have been otherwise. But God couldn't have been other than good, and there is no chance of his losing his goodness; the supposition of his losing it is nonsense, because God *is* his own goodness, and all goodness. [F-M, p. 4]

Another character in the dialogue, called 'Logician' criticizes this exposition as containing, in the sentence 'God is his own goodness' a confusion between abstract and common nouns. The same thing may be said, Logician concedes, either by abstract nouns or by common nouns, and either way does equally well. We may say either 'The people were very happy' or 'The people's happiness was great'. But we must opt for one method or the other.

> We cannot have it both ways, and use a word as an abstract noun and a common noun at once, as you try to do in your sentence 'God is his own goodness'—that's just bad grammar, a combining of words which fails to make them *mean*—like 'Cat no six'. [F-M, p. 4]

'Catholic' is given no reply to this argument, and we are left to conclude that there is nothing to do except to call in 'Psychoanalyst' (a further character in the dialogue) to explain why people utter such meaningless jumbles of words.

Six years later, the concept of *necessary being* was criticized at greater length by Professor J. N. Findlay in a paper entitled 'Can God's Existence be disproved?' [FINDLAY (1)]. Analysis of the meaning of the word 'God', Findlay argued, could show that His existence was impossible. If God is to be an adequate object for religious attitudes, then He must be infinitely superior to His worshippers. He cannot therefore be a being which just happens to exist: His existence must be identified with His essence. His existence must be 'something inescapable and necessary, whether for thought or reality'. Moreover, He must possess in a more than accidental manner the excellences in which His creatures participate. Only if God is in some way indistinguishable from His own goodness is He worthy of *latria*. But an adequate object of worship, as described in these terms, is inconceivable.

The Divine Existence is either senseless or impossible. The modern mind feels not the faintest axiomatic force in principles which trace contingent things back to some necessarily existent source, nor does it find it hard to conceive that things should display various excellent qualities without deriving them from a source which manifests them supremely. Those who believe in necessary truths which aren't merely tautological, think that such truths merely connect the *possible* instances of various characteristics with each other; they don't expect such truths to tell us whether there *will* be instances of any characteristics. This is the outcome of the whole medieval and Kantian criticism of the Ontological Proof. And, on a yet more modern view of the matter, necessity in propositions merely reflects our use of words, the arbitrary conventions of our language. On such a view the Divine Existence could only be a necessary matter if we had made up our minds to speak theistically *whatever the empirical circumstances might turn out to be* . . . The religious frame of mind seems, in fact, to be in a quandary; it seems invincibly determined both to eat its cake and have it. It desires the Divine Existence both to have that inescapable character which can, on modern views, only be found where truth reflects an arbitrary convention, and also the character of 'making a real difference' which is only possible where truth doesn't have this merely linguistic basis. If God is to satisfy religious claims and needs, He must be a being in every way inescapable, One whose existence and whose possession of certain excellencies we cannot possibly conceive away. And modern views make it self-evidently absurd (if they don't make it ungrammatical) to speak of such a Being and attribute existence to Him. [F-M, p. 55]

In January 1949 two articles appeared in answer to Findlay [HUGHES, RAINER]. Professor G. E. Hughes, in the first of these, suggested that phrases like 'necessary being' and 'contingent being' were unfortunate, and thought it better to conform to modern usage by reserving the terms 'necessary' and 'contingent' to describe propositions. Restated in accordance with this restriction, Findlay's contention would be that it was self-evidently absurd to hold that 'God exists' is a necessary proposition. Findlay's proof of this conclusion was, Hughes suggested, a conflation of two arguments, neither of them convincing.

First, Findlay had argued that modern philosophical research had established that all existential propositions are necessarily contingent, and that all necessary propositions are necessarily non-existential, since they merely reflect the conventions of language. Hughes replied that the conventionalist theory was a theory merely about the propositions of logic and mathematics. and the theory that all existential propositions are contingent applied only to empirical propositions. But no theist suggested that 'God exists' was either an empirical proposition or a proposition of logic or mathematics. Even if we accept the conventionalist theory, therefore, we are not committed to saying that 'God exists' cannot be a necessary proposition. Findlay, Hughes suggested, was begging the central question, namely, whether there can be any necessary non-tautological propositions.

Secondly, Findlay appeared to argue that if God exists, then His existence must be inescapable for thought; but God's existence is not inescapable for thought, since some modern philosophers find it possible to conceive that there is no God; therefore God does not exist. Hughes retorted that this argument rested on a confusion between a proposition's being necessary and its being *seen* or *known* to be necessary. No theist had ever maintained that God's existence was inescapable in the sense that anyone who ever thought about the proposition 'God exists' found himself forced to accept it. If a proposition is necessary, then anyone who thinks clearly and who clearly understands the subject-matter involved, will find himself forced to accept it; and if 'God exists' is a necessary proposition, then it is in this sense inescapable. But it still does not follow that 'God exists' is self-evident even to human reason at its best: for it might be the case that the subject-matter here in question was one which no human being could understand clearly enough. In fact, theists have been divided on this point. Anselm held that the proposition was self-evident to human reason at its best; Aquinas held that it was not, but was inescapable only in the sense that it was entailed by other propositions which we had sound evidence for believing to be true. Professor Findlay's 'Ontological Disproof', Hughes concluded, failed of its object. [F–M, pp. 56–64]

A more plausible argument on the same lines, Hughes suggested, would run thus. If 'God' is defined as 'necessary being', then 'God exists' becomes a tautology, since it predicates of God something already contained in the definition of God. But no tautology can be existential. Therefore 'God exists' cannot assert that God exists. Which is absurd.

This argument does not involve the contentious premise that only tautologies are necessary. None the less, Hughes maintained, it is invalid. It is true, that if 'blue', for example, were part of the definition of 'x', then 'x is blue' would be a tautology; but 'exists' is not a predicate like 'blue', and so the matter is different here. Professor Ryle, among others, has pointed out that if, in 'God exists', 'exists' is not a predicate, save in grammar, then, for the same reasons, in the same statement 'God' cannot be, save in grammar, the subject of predication. Hence, in Ryle's words, ' "God exists" must mean what is meant by "something and one thing only is omniscient, omnipotent, and infinitely good" (or whatever else are the characters summed up on the compound character of being a god and the only god)' [RYLE, 1 : FLEW (1), 15–16]. So analysed, Hughes observed, the statement 'God exists' is not a tautology. The theist must maintain that, despite this, it is a necessary proposition. Findlay's argument had in no way shown this position to be untenable. Hughes concluded:

> The most that 'modern' views about such propositions can tell us about the contention that 'God exists' is a necessary proposition is that if it is we cannot here be using the term 'necessary' in quite the same sense as that in which we say that logico-mathematical

propositions are necessary, and that we cannot be using the term 'exists' in quite the same way as when we say that tables and chairs exist. But these are statements with which the theist need have no quarrel. [F-M, p. 67]

Another theist critic of Findlay, Mr A. C. A. Rainer, was prepared, unlike Hughes, to deny that 'God exists' was a necessary proposition. He wrote as follows:

> The necessity of God's existence is not the same as the necessity of a logical implication. It means, for those who believe in it, God's complete actuality, indestructibility, *aseitas* or independence of limiting conditions. It is a property ascribed to God, not a property of our assertions about God ... For us, both the assertion of God's necessary existence and the assertion of his necessary possession of the properties of a Perfect Being are contingent. [F-M, p. 69][2]

To say that God cannot exist necessarily because we cannot necessarily assert his existence, Rainer concluded, was to commit the converse fallacy of Anselm's ontological argument.

Findlay's reply to his critics [FINDLAY (2)] was surprisingly irenic. His argument, he said, was not so modern after all: it was merely a development of Kant's criticism of the Ontological Argument.

> Kant said that it couldn't be necessary that there should ever *be* anything of any description whatsoever, and that *if* we included 'existence' in the definition of something—Kant of course didn't think we *should* so include it, as existence 'wasn't a predicate'—we could only say, *hypothetically*, that *if* something of a certain sort existed, then it *would* exist necessarily, but not, categorically, that it actually existed. And he also said that if one were willing to deny the existence of God one couldn't be compelled to assert any property of him, no matter how intimately such a property formed part of his 'nature'. Now, Kant, of course, didn't make existence (or necessary existence) part of God's nature, but I have argued that one *ought* to do so, if God is to be the adequate object of our religious attitudes. So that for all those who are willing to accept *my* account of an adequate religious object, and also Kant's

[2] I. M. Crombie agreed with Rainer that 'God exists' is a contingent proposition [CROMBIE: F–M, pp. 113–4]. On the other hand, Professor H. D. Lewis supported Hughes [H. D. LEWIS]. So did S. A. Grave, who wrote: 'If there is a God there is at least one analytic existential proposition—a proposition which is analytic for God, but merely necessary for us' [GRAVE, p. 30].

doctrine of the hypothetical character of necessary predications, it must follow inevitably that there cannot be an adequate object for our religious attitudes [F-M, pp. 72–3].

He considered, however, that there was perhaps little difference between the position of a theist who thought that God existed in a sense of the word different from the ordinary sense, and his own attitude of unquestioning reverence to an imaginary ideal. 'When theists say,' he concluded, 'that their God exists in some sense quite different from created objects, there seems but a hairs-breadth between them and such atheists as place their ideal, with Plato and Plotinus, ἐπέκεινα τῆς οὐσίας' [F-M, p. 74].

In 1951 views similar to Findlay's were expressed in a public lecture at the University of Adelaide by Professor J. J. C. Smart [SMART (1)]. Smart in this lecture presented and criticized various arguments for God's existence. He presented the cosmological argument as follows:

> Everything in the world around is *contingent*. That is, with regard to any particular thing, it is quite conceivable that it might not have existed. For example, if you were asked why you existed, you could say that it was because of your parents, and if asked why they existed you could go still further back, but however far you go back you have not, so it is argued, made the fact of your existence really intelligible. For however far back you go in such a series you only get back to something which itself might not have existed. For a really satisfying explanation of why anything contingent (such as you or me or this table) exists you must eventually begin with something which is not itself contingent, that is, with something of which we cannot say that it might not have existed, that is we must begin with a necessary being. [F-M, pp. 35–6]

'Necessary being' in this context, according to Smart, means the same as 'Logically necessary being'. A logically necessary being is a being whose non-existence is inconceivable in the sort of way that a triangle's having four sides is inconceivable. But the concept of such a being is a self-contradictory concept. For since 'necessary' is a predicate of propositions and not of things, 'God is a necessary being' must mean the same as 'The proposition "God exists" is logically necessary'. But necessary propositions—such as '$3 + 2 = 5$', 'a thing cannot be red and green all over', 'either it is raining or it is not raining'—are guaranteed solely by the rules for the use of the symbols they contain. It follows that no existential proposition can be logically necessary.

> The truth of a logically necessary proposition depends only on our symbolism, or to put the same thing in another way, on the relationship of concepts . . . [But] an existential proposition does not say that one concept is involved in another, but that a concept applies to something. An existential proposition must be very different from any logically necessary one, such as a mathematical one, for example, for the conventions of our symbolism clearly leave it open for us either to affirm or deny an existential proposition; it is not our symbolism but reality which decides whether or not we must affirm it or deny it. The claim that the existence of God should be *logically* necessary is thus a self-contradictory one. [F-M, pp. 38–9]

The necessity of God, therefore, is not a logical necessity. Instead, Smart prefers to say that God's existence is a 'religious necessity' by which he means that 'it would clearly upset the structure of our religious attitudes in the most violent way if we denied it or even entertained the possibility of its falsehood' [3] [F-M, p. 40].

The essays of Findlay and Smart were republished in 1955 in the symposium *New Essays in Philosophical Theology* [F-M]. In a review of this book Professor Raphael Demos [DEMOS] used against the critics of necessary being an argument of a pattern familiar in anti-positivist polemic. What was the status, he asked, of the proposition 'Only analytic propositions are necessary'? If it is analytic, then it merely records Smart and Findlay's determination to use certain terms in a particular way. If it is meant to be an inductive generalization, then the statement 'God exists' which is claimed as an exception, must be examined on its own merits and not rejected *a priori*. There is no third alternative for Findlay and Smart, since they are committed to excluding the possibility of necessary synthetic propositions.

Demos commented that it was ironical that Findlay and Smart should attack the notion of necessary being in the name of contemporary philosophy: for the distinction between analytic and synthetic propositions, on which their attack was based, had recently been called in question by influential philosophers of the school to which they appealed.[4]

---

[3] Smart repeated his argument several years later: see SMART (2).
[4] See, for example, QUINE (1).

The basis of the criticism of the notion of necessary being was indeed increasingly called in question. Prior, with whose criticisms this discussion began, published in 1953 a paper with the title 'Is Necessary Existence Possible?' in which he attacked the thesis that the only necessity is logical necessity. [PRIOR (2)]

The line of argument to prove that 'necessary being' is a senseless phrase, Prior observed, starts from the position that existence is not a predicate. What is not rightly thought of as attaching to a subject at all is not rightly thought of as attaching to a subject necessarily. But the belief that existence is not a predicate, Prior now wished to contend, is perfectly compatible with the belief that 'necessary existence' makes sense.

Prior accepted the customary analysis of existential propositions which derived from Moore. According to this analysis, 'Lions exist' asserts that the concept of *lionhood* is exemplified, and 'unicorns do not exist' that the concept of *unicornhood* is not exemplified. Now one can distinguish between the necessary and contingent non-exemplification of concepts: it is contingent that *unicornhood* is not exemplified, it is necessary that *non-cubical cubicity* is unexemplified.

Why should there not be a similar distinction, Prior asked, between *exemplified* concepts? Since there are properties of concepts which preclude their exemplification, why should there not also be properties of concepts which necessitate their exemplification? Prior admitted that he did not know of any such necessarily exemplified concept: he rejected the suggestion that self-complementariness (the property of *being x or not being x*) might be such a concept. Someone might propose the property of *exemplification* for the role. To this proposal Prior replied as follows:

> We must reply that that is not the sort of necessitation intended; and to indicate what *is* intended, we may simply say that we are using 'necessitates' in such a sense that to say that '*B* is necessitated by *A*' is in some way to account for *B*. Logical necessitation will not do here—you do not account for *X*'s being *Y* by saying that *X*'s being *Y* necessitates *X*'s being *Y*, though this in a sense is true. And logical necessity, I should further contend, is itself to be defined in terms of this other sort. To say that *A* is a logically necessary proposition is to say that *A*'s truth is (pre-logically) necessitated by its logical form. [PRIOR (2), p. 547]

The recognition of another sort of necessity alongside, and prior to logical necessity, marks a departure from the *Tractatus* doctrine that the only necessity is logical necessity. Recently, Professor Kneale has pointed out that the *Tractatus* itself contains elements which contradict this doctrine. In one place Wittgenstein explained negation in the following manner:

> The negating statement determines a logical place *other* than that determined by the negated statement. The negating statement determines a logical place with the help of the logical place of the negated statement, by describing it as lying outside this latter. [WITTGENSTEIN (1), 4.0641]

This implies, Kneale observes, that the possibility of using a negative particle significantly depends on the objective incompatibility of various thinkable states of affairs. For the otherness here spoken of is presupposed by the construction of negative statements and must therefore be a relation independent of our use of a negative sign. In fact, inconsistency of general terms presupposes incompatibility of characters; and from this it follows that necessity cannot be merely a product of linguistic rules and customs. [KNEALE, pp. 633–9]

Ayer himself, in the introduction to the second edition of *Language, Truth and Logic,* had recanted his former account of *a priori* truth.

> I now think that it is a mistake to say that they [*a priori* propositions] are themselves linguistic rules. For apart from the fact that they can properly be said to be true, which linguistic rules cannot, they are distinguished also by being necessary, whereas linguistic rules are arbitrary. At the same time, if they are necessary it is only because the relevant linguistic rules are presupposed ... In Russell's and Whitehead's system of logic, it is a contingent, empirical fact that the sign '⊃' should have been given the meaning that it has, and the rules which govern the use of this sign are conventions, which themselves are neither true nor false; but given these rules the *a priori* proposition '$p . \supset . q \supset p$' is necessarily true. Being *a priori*, this proposition gives no information in the ordinary sense in which an empirical proposition may be said to give information, nor does it itself prescribe how the logical constant '⊃' is to be used. [AYER (1), p. 17]

The necessity of logical truths is thus put forward as being the consequence of, and not identical with, the adoption of a set of rules. But this consequence is itself necessary: it is not a contingent fact that, given the relevant rules, '$q. \supset . p \supset q$' is necessarily true. And this consequence is itself necessary only in virtue of what Prior called 'pre-logical necessity'. It is, as Ayer says, an empirical fact that the symbol '$\supset$' has been given the meaning that it has; and the rules for its use are based on a convention. But it is not because of any further convention that, given '$\supset$' has the use it has, '$q. \supset . p \supset q$' is true; nor is it an empirical fact that the convention for the use of '$\supset$' is one which it is possible to make.

The doctrine that necessary propositions are merely uninformative by-products of our linguistic conventions thus proves impossible to uphold. Kneale has suggested that the popularity of the doctrine is due to its being a distorted version of an important truth about *a priori* knowledge:

> Anything we come to know *a priori* is a second-order truth about the relations of propositions or a truism derivative from such a truth, and in either case it is learnt by reflection on the meaning of words or other symbols. An animal such as a dog may perhaps be said to know a contingent fact such as that there are two sheep in a field, but it seems absurd to say that a dog can know even a very simple truth of arithmetic such as the proposition that $2 + 2 = 4$; and the reason can scarcely be that all non-human animals lack the special kind of intuition which according to Kant enables us to learn arithmetical truths. Many misleading accounts of *a priori* knowledge have been inspired by Plato's notion of contemplation ($\theta\epsilon\omega\rho\iota\alpha$) as a kind of intellectual gazing in which the soul may read off facts about super-sensible objects; and if we are to free ourselves from the influence of these it is no doubt important that we should realize the connection of *a priori* knowledge with the use of symbols. [KNEALE, p. 636]

It is possible to agree with Kneale that all *a priori* truths are learnt by what Mill called 'the artful manipulation of language', without following him in his belief that all *a priori* truths are truths *about* the symbols of a language. In arithmetic, for example, it seems *prima facie* that by manipulating numerals and other symbols we come to know truths about numbers which are not themselves symbols. And Kneale himself elsewhere writes as if this were the case.[5]

So far, in this paper, I have not made any division between necessary propositions of different kinds. I have written as if the

[5] See the passage referred to on page 144 below: KNEALE, p. 707.

terms 'analytic', '*a priori*', 'necessary' and 'tautological' were, if not synonymous, at least co-extensive in application. In this I have followed some of the authors whose discussion of *necessary being* it has been my purpose to record. It is time now to draw some necessary distinctions.

The term 'analytic' was given currency by Kant. The judgement that A is B is analytic, according to Kant, if the predicate B belongs to the subject A as something which is contained in the concept A; otherwise it is synthetic. Kant's dichotomy as it stands applies to judgments, and not to propositions, and among judgements applies only to those of subject-predicate form. If we wish to give it application to propositions of various forms, we do better to take a different definition of 'analytic'—one which is nowhere put forward by Kant, but which is implicit in the use which he makes of the term. We may say that a true proposition is analytic if, and only if, its negation is self-contradictory.

Some analytic propositions are tautologies in the strict sense in which Wittgenstein introduced this term into logic. In this sense, a tautology is a compound proposition which is true no matter what may be the truth-values of the propositions which enter into its composition. All tautologies are analytically true by the definition given. But not all propositions which are analytically true are tautologies. 'Either some Greeks are philosophers or none are', 'All actresses are female', 'Three o'clock comes one hour after two o'clock' are all analytically true propositions. But none of them is a tautology.

The notion of *tautology* and the distinction between analytic and synthetic truths is a distinction belonging to the field of logic. The distinction between *a priori* truths and *a posteriori* truths, on the other hand, is drawn from theory of knowledge or epistemology. *A priori* truths are truths which are known on logical grounds alone; *a posteriori* truths are truths which are known only by experience. It is being increasingly recognized that not all *a priori* truths are analytic. Kneale lists several examples of such truths which are not analytic.[6]

An example which has often been discussed is the proposition that nothing can be both red and green all over at the same time.

[6] Kneale's definition of 'analytic' is broader than the one I have given; but any proposition which is not analytic in Kneale's sense is *a fortiori* not analytic in my sense. On the same topic, from a different viewpoint, see PEARS.

Another is the proposition that the relation of temporal precedence is transitive but irreflexive. Furthermore, if we can ever be sure that certain perceptible characters and relations provide a model satisfying the postulates of an abstract geometry, this too must be a piece of knowledge *a priori* but not analytic. [KNEALE, p. 637]

No analytic proposition is existential. A denial of existence can never be self-contradictory. But since the class of logically true propositions is wider than that of analytic propositions, it does not follow that no existential proposition can be established *a priori*. The thesis that there are no logically true existential propositions has, indeed, long been popular. As Kneale has observed, it can be quite easily refuted by the production of counter-examples from mathematics. It is not a fact of experience that there is a prime number greater than a million [KNEALE, p. 707]. Someone might object, as Kneale himself, in another mood, appears to do, that such a truth is really a second-order truth about the relations between propositions, and does not deal with 'real existence' as empirical existential propositions do. If so, then the objector must give some account of the difference between real and non-real existence. The presence or absence of an existential quantifier can no longer be regarded as the criterion of whether a proposition is really existential.

The distinctions which I have just drawn were sometimes denied, and sometimes ignored, by the authors whom we have been considering. Only when they have been drawn can one fruitfully consider the meaning of the terms 'necessary' and 'contingent' as applied to propositions. We must first ask whether the dichotomy between necessary and contingent corresponds to the dichotomy between analytic and synthetic, or to the dichotomy between *a priori* and *a posteriori*, or to neither of those dichotomies. In this field, the ground was usefully cleared in 1958 by Mr Richard Robinson in an essay entitled 'Necessary Propositions' [ROBINSON].

Robinson distinguished four senses in which propositions have been called 'necessary'. By 'a necessary proposition' one may mean:

(1) A proposition which one cannot not believe.
(2) An apodeictic modal proposition.
(3) An analytic proposition.
(4) An unrestrictedly general universal proposition.

Each of these senses is independent of each of the others: a proposition may be necessary in one of these senses without being necessary in any of the other senses.

Used in any of these senses, Robinson suggests, the word 'necessary' has a perfectly clear meaning. Leibniz, for instance, used it in the third sense. He wrote: 'A truth is necessary when the opposite implies contradiction, and when it is not necessary it is called contingent.' A necessary truth he seems to mean, is a truth whose contradictory is self-contradictory. This is the definition which, we have seen, best fits Kant's use of the word 'analytic' when the concept of *necessary proposition* has become thoroughly muddled. Robinson illustrates the confusion from Kant's writings, and concludes:

> Kant thought he had found a necessary proposition whenever he felt compelled to believe (sense 1) a proposition which either asserted that something *must* be so (sense 2) or had a self-contradictory (sense 3), or asserted something with unrestricted universality (sense 4). [ROBINSON, p. 293]

One confusion which is still prevalent concerns the relationship between necessity and truth. Is a necessary proposition by definition a true one? If we take 'necessary' in the first, second or fourth sense, we must admit that some necessary propositions are false. Some of the propositions which some people cannot help believing are false; some propositions which say that something *must* be so are false; some propositions which say that something universally *is* so are false. But if we say that an analytic proposition is one whose contradictory is self-contradictory, then all propositions which are necessary in the third of the senses listed above are true.

To avoid confusion, Robinson suggests that we define analytic propositions as those of which either the assertion or the denial is self-contradictory. Thus, the pairs of terms 'analytic/synthetic' and 'necessary/contingent' in all their senses, will divide *all* propositions, and not only *true* propositions.

It is only in its third sense that Robinson takes 'necessary' seriously as a useful term in philosophy. He introduces his other three senses only for purposes of illustrating and pruning the confusions which he detects in Kant. Accordingly, he is left with two pairs of terms, 'analytic/synthetic' and 'necessary/contingent' to refer to a single distinction. He ends with a plea, on aesthetic grounds, that the distinction be marked by the terms 'necessary' and 'contingent' rather than their alternatives.

I shall follow Robinson in dismissing, for our present purposes, the first, second, and fourth of the listed senses of 'necessary'. I shall not, however, follow his proposal that we should use 'necessary' only as an elegant synonym for 'analytic'. For the rest of this essay I shall continue to use 'analytic' in the sense defined, since I believe that there are senses of 'necessary' other than those listed by Robinson which are of philosophical importance.

In the first place, most people would agree that all logical truths are necessary truths, and that whatever is *a priori* false is necessarily false. But if, as we have seen reason to believe, there are *a priori* propositions which are not analytic, then there are some necessary propositions which are not analytic.

If this were all, however, the distinction between necessary and contingent propositions would still be superfluous. 'Necessary', though no longer a synonym for 'analytic', would become simply an elegant variant of '*a priori*'. But given the current view of the nature of propositions, I think we can go no farther. Kneale suggests that there may be necessary truths which are not truths which can be known *a priori*; not because they can be known *a posteriori* but because they cannot be known at all. He writes:

> It does not seem absurd to suggest that there may be necessary truths about unperceived qualities or relations which no one can ever know because (as Locke might say) no one has the requisite ideas. [KNEALE, p. 637]

In this context he defines necessary truths as 'truths without alternatives'. It is difficult to make sense of this unless 'necessary truth' means the same as 'necessarily true proposition'. But if it does, then it is hard to see how what is here said can be reconciled with Kneale's view that the word 'proposition' refers to the common feature of actual or possible utterances that resemble each other completely as vehicles of communication [KNEALE, p. 593]. A possible utterance is an utterance which somebody can make. Nobody can make an utterance if he has not the ideas requisite for its making. If there are ideas which nobody *can* have, then no utterances are possible which presuppose such ideas: there are, therefore, no corresponding propositions. If, on the other hand, the ideas which Kneale postulates are ideas which *can* be acquired, but which nobody in fact possesses, then the truth of the propositions in question *can* be known also, provided only that the ideas have first been acquired. On the view of propositions which Kneale accepts, therefore, no difference has been made out between *a priori* propositions and necessary propositions.

If, however, we reject the current doctrine that no proposition can change its truth-value, then it becomes possible to use the words 'necessary' and 'contingent' to mark a distinction which is not marked by any other pair of terms. For we may say that a contingent proposition is a proposition which *can* change its truth-value, and a necessary proposition is one which *cannot* change its truth-value. On this view, all analytic and *a priori* propositions are necessary, for analytic truths and logical truths are always true, while self-contradictory statements and *a priori* falsehoods are always false. But the converse does not hold: not all propositions which are necessary in this sense are either analytic or *a priori*.

On the current theory of the nature of the proposition, no proposition can be at one time true and at another false. A sentence such as 'Theaetetus is sitting', which is true when Theaetetus is sitting, and false at other times, would now commonly be said to express a different proposition at different times, so that at one time it expresses a true proposition, and at another time a false one. And a sentence asserting that 'Theaetetus is sitting' *was true* at time *t* is now commonly treated as asserting that the proposition which ascribes *sitting at time t* to Theaetetus is true timelessly. No proposition is significantly tensed, but any proposition expressed by a tensed sentence contains a reference to time and is itself timelessly true or false.

There is another way of looking at a proposition, which was classically expressed in Aristotle's *De Interpretatione*. On this account, a sentence such as 'Theaetetus is sitting' *is* a proposition, in the sense in which a particular piece of shaped metal is a shilling. This proposition is significantly tensed, and is at some times true and at others false. It becomes true whenever Theaetetus sits down, and becomes false whenever Theaetetus ceases to sit.

Arguments have been put forward recently to show that this second account of the nature of the proposition is to be preferred to the one now common.[7] I shall not now discuss whether these arguments are convincing. What here concerns us is that the *De Interpretatione* view was the one accepted by those Aristotelian philosophers who traditionally described God as a necessary being. It is impossible to make sense of this notion without taking seriously the possibility of propositions changing their truth value.

If we accept the view that mathematics does not concern itself with real existence, then we must admit that the modern criticisms we have been considering establish that it is absurd to say that 'God exists' is an analytic or *a priori* proposition. The Leibnizian notion of *necessary being* must therefore be abandoned. It remains to be seen whether 'God exists' can be said to be necessary in the Aristotelian sense, and whether the Aristotelian notion of *necessary being* may be preserved.[8]

God is, by definition, eternal: those who believe in God believe that He is and always was and always will be. A being, however magnificent, which came into existence or which passed away would not be God. It follows that 'God exists' is a necessary proposition by our new definition of 'necessary'. For if 'God exists' is true, then it always has been true and always will be true. And if 'God exists' is false, then it always has been false and always will be false. The proposition 'God exists', whether true or false, cannot change its truth-value. By our definition, therefore, it is a necessary proposition. Furthermore, since God possesses His attributes unchangingly, 'God is good', 'God knows whatever is to be known' and 'God the Father loves God the Son' are all necessary propositions. But not only propositions about God are necessary by our criterion. Apart from *a priori* propositions, any propositions, true or false, ascribing everlasting existence are necessary. When Aristotelians stated that the heavenly bodies were eternal, and when Lucretius claimed everlasting existence for his atoms, they asserted propositions which, by our criterion were necessary.

It was pointed out by Rainer that when scholastics said that God

---

[7] Notably by Prior in PRIOR (3 and 4).

[8] In calling this notion 'Aristotelian' I mean no more than that it is a notion implicit in discussions of necessity by Aristotelian philosophers. For a fuller and documented account of the topics treated in this last part, see my article 'Necessary Being' [KENNY]. Aristotle's own doctrine of necessity is complicated by the fact that, believing that what can happen sometimes does happen, he was committed to the belief that what is always true is necessarily true. Cf. ANSCOMBE–GEACH, p. 35

was a necessary being they meant that He was eternal and imperishable. It is because God is necessary in this sense, that the proposition 'God exists' is necessary in the sense we have defined. The necessity *de dicto*, the medievals would have said, follows from the necessity *de re*: the property of the proposition about God derives from the property of the concept of *being God*. With Leibnizian necessary being, the converse was the case: a suppositious property was ascribed to God on the basis of an alleged property (e.g. self-evidence) of the proposition 'God exists'.

Again, when it is said that God possesses His attributes necessarily, no more need be meant than that God is wholly unchangeable. How then are we to take those expressions—such as 'God in His wisdom'—which Prior found so puzzling in the essay with which we began?

The most satisfactory modern treatment of them is that given by Mr Geach in his account of Aquinas' theory of *form*.[9] Geach insists that when Aquinas speaks of 'form' he is not referring to any entity such as 'that of which "wisdom" is a proper name'; for Aquinas was no Platonist, and without Platonism one cannot admit that 'wisdom' is a proper name at all. Nor, strictly speaking, would 'the wisdom of Socrates' stand for a form: for Aquinas says that forms are as such multipliable. 'The wisdom of Socrates' does not mean: wisdom, which Socrates possesses. 'Of' does not denote a special relation of possessing. Geach suggests that the phrase should be divided into two members thus: 'The wisdom of . . .' and 'Socrates.' It is a phrase such as 'The wisdom of . . .' which best expresses what Aquinas had in mind when he talked of forms: this is what he meant when he said that a form was *entis* and not *ens*—it must be followed by a genitive. [AQUINAS, Ia, 45, 4]

Geach here draws an analogy from mathematics. 'The square root of 4' does not refer to an entity called 'the square root' which stands in the relation *belonging to* to the number 4. Logically, the phrase must be divided 'The square root of/4': the first part of the phrase, which is to be followed by some number-expression or other, is the sign of a *function*; and the numeral '4' completes this function-sign with the sign of an *argument*. 'The wisdom of Socrates' is not a form *simpliciter*, but a form *of Socrates*, just as 2 is not the square-root function, but is that function *of 4*.

9 GEACH (3); ANSCOMBE–GEACH, pp. 77 *seq.*, 121 *seq.*

Applying this to the doctrine of God's 'simplicity', Geach writes:

> When Aquinas says things like *Deus est ipsa sapientia* he is not meaning that God is that of which the name 'wisdom' is a proper name, for the Platonists are wrong in thinking that there is such an object, and Aquinas says they are wrong. But we can take it to mean that 'God' and 'the wisdom of God' are two names of the same thing . . . for we can significantly say that 'God' and 'the wisdom of God' and 'the power of God' are three names with the same reference; but 'the wisdom of . . .' and 'the power of . . .' have not the same reference, any more than the predicates 'wise' and 'powerful' have. [GEACH (1)]

Here again, the mathematical analogy is helpful. 'The square of . . .' and 'the double of . . .' signify two quite different functions, but for the argument 2 these two functions both take the number 4 as their value. Similarly 'the wisdom of . . .' and 'the power of . . .' signify different forms, but the individualizations of these forms in God's case are not distinct from one another; nor is either distinct from God, just as the number 1 is in no way distinct from its own square.

It does not seem to have been shown, therefore, that the notion of *necessary being* employed by the medieval scholastics is an incoherent one. In spite of Kant, if our argument has been correct, it is possible to accept a proof of God's existence from the things He has made without being committed to an acceptance of the manifest fallacy of the Ontological Argument.

The following argument is sometimes used against the possibility of any proof that there is a God. Such a proof must either contain only *a priori* premises, or must contain in addition to *a priori* premises some *a posteriori* ones. If the former, it can prove nothing about real existence. If the latter, then the existence of God will be at best a revisable empirical hypothesis.

In fact, the traditional causal demonstrations of the existence of God claimed to start from indubitable premises (e.g. 'some things change') and proceed according to the normal rules of logic to the conclusion that there is a God. Such a proof, if valid, would lead to an indubitable conclusion: 'there is a God', if proved by such means, would be no more a revisable hypothesis than 'some things change' is. On the other hand, 'some things change' is not *a priori true*; so there is no difficulty in principle

about this premise leading to a conclusion concerning real existence.

The Five Ways of St Thomas Aquinas were supposed to be
proofs of just this sort. Whether any of them is valid, I do not
know. No serious work on them has been done by philosophers
of the school we are considering. Philosophers have frequently
been led to believe that work on them would be a waste of time
by the erroneous opinion that the type of being whose existence
they professed to establish was a self-contradictory *Unding*. I
hope that this essay has done something to show that the impression is mistaken.[10]

[10] Some prolegomena to a consideration of the Five Ways are put forward by
Geach. [GEACH (3)]

7. IMAGINATION

HIDÉ ISHIGURO

FOR too many years Imagination was the ugly duckling of the philosophical world. Although Hume, and above all Kant, had noticed and stressed the importance of imagination in their theories of knowledge, their arguments have never been properly discussed or developed by their successors. One reason for this lies in the fact that 'Imagination' is an ambiguous term which has meant different things for different people. It is also due to the fact that people often confused the psychological or empirical investigation into how imagination works and the philosophical analysis of what it is to imagine. Anxious to preserve the purity of philosophical inquiry, many brilliant thinkers have kept away from this subject. Imagination was treated as a non-rational faculty the understanding of which had little to do with our knowledge of other mental activities. It was linked with our feelings and our senses but not with our intelligence.[1] Especially in Britain the study of the imagination was considered as the examination of our mental images or as belonging to theories of art, appropriate to psychologists, art and literary critics, or muddle-headed philosophers who were victims of associationism or some such psychological dogma.[2]

Fortunately, the situation has changed greatly in the last two decades. In both Britain and Europe eminent philosophers have tried to show that the philosophical study of imagination is a respectable and important part of the philosophy of mind. In fact, the study of imagination is one of the subjects where the problems

---

[1] Some idealistic philosophers, e.g. Croce, who did think that the intellect was influenced by the imagination, nevertheless maintained that the imagination was altogether independent of the intellect.

[2] The most substantial writer on the subject of Imagination in Britain was the romantic poet Coleridge, and more recently Collingwood, an admirer of Croce.

raised by philosophers of the two isolated worlds of Europe and Britain most resemble each other. The difference between Sartre's *L'Imaginaire* (1940) [SARTRE] and the notes concerning imagination in Wittgenstein's *The Blue and Brown Books* [WITTGENSTEIN (3)] or the chapter on imagination in Professor Ryle's *The Concept of Mind* [RYLE (2)] is much smaller than the difference between *L'Imaginaire* and the works of Sartre's French predecessors or that between Ryle's inquiry and those of the British empiricists of the Humean tradition.

The object of this paper is not to characterize what it is to be imaginative but to elucidate the concept of forming a mental picture, running through a tune in one's head, doing sums in one's head and the like, mainly through the investigation of the ideas of Ryle and Sartre. Although I have not arrived at a satisfactory solution, I hope to indicate where the difficulties of the problem lie and point out in what direction the answers might be found.

It is amusing to observe philosophers who claim to use completely different methods and profess the greatest mistrust of each other's methods yet managing to arrive at similar conclusions and even coming to similar deadlocks. For at first glance nothing seems more different than the treatment of the problem of imagination by Professor Ryle and by the continental phenomenologists, notably Sartre. Sartre asserts that since Descartes 'We know that a reflexive consciousness gives us absolutely certain data' and thus all we must accept is 'what reflection will tell us'. His 'simple method' consists of 'producing images in ourselves and then reflecting upon these images in order to describe them, in other words to determine and classify the characteristics distinguishing them' [SARTRE, p. 14]. On the other hand, Ryle, the most behaviourist of British analytical philosophers, denies the value of introspection as a method of finding out facts about our mind, and tries to show throughout his controversial book how people since Descartes have been misled into believing that by introspection we can have indubitable knowledge of what happens in our mind. Ryle not only denies the value of introspection, but seems to deny the existence of those inner mental processes which people have believed to be discernible by introspection.

> The radical objection to the theory that minds must know what they are about, because mental happenings are by definition conscious, is that there are no such happenings, there are no

occurrences taking place in a second-status world, since there is no such status and no such world and consequently no need for special modes of acquainting ourselves with the denizens of such a world. [RYLE (2), p. 161]

One can sympathize with Ryle's scepticism about introspection. People who believe in the value of introspection have often described psychological facts which are of very little interest to philosophers. For example, Bertrand Russell wrote that the word 'or' corresponds to a state of hesitation and that hesitation arises when we feel two incompatible impulses neither of which is strong enough to overcome the other [RUSSELL (5), p. 84]. Titchener reports in even greater detail about his image of 'but'.

> It was my pleasant duty, a little while ago, to sit on a platform behind a somewhat emphatic lecturer who made a great use of the monosyllable 'but'. My feeling of 'but' has contained ever since a flashing picture of a bald crown with a fringe of hair below and a massive black shoulder, the whole passing swiftly down the visual field from north-west to south-east. [TITCHENER, Lecture V]

If this is the kind of thing that one discovers by introspection then one can justly deny that introspection has any special place in philosophy. The facts discovered are as contingent as any particular fact observed in the world.

In spite of their radically opposed principles the methods of Ryle and of the phenomenologists are not very dissimilar. The introspection or the 'reflection' of the phenomenologists does not aim at discovering psychological facts like the ones above. Indeed, one of Husserl's enterprises was to denounce the infection of philosophy by empirical psychology. And in *L'Imaginaire* what Sartre discovers by 'reflecting on his mind' is not the content of the particular images he has, nor the various patterns of association of ideas. His work shows that what he means by reflecting is the asking of questions like 'Can I go on discovering new facts about the things I imagine as I do when I perceive things?', 'Does it make sense to say that one has found a new feature of an object one is imagining which one hadn't realized before?', 'Do I see or observe the objects which I imagine in the same way in which I see or observe things in the world?', 'When I picture something do I think that it belongs to the spatio-temporal world in which I find myself?' This method of inquiry is not very far from that of Ryle, which we will now examine. After all it is not very surprising to find a similarity between the ideas of the French phenomenologist and of Ryle. In his early years Ryle lectured on Husserl and Brentano at Oxford, and was the first to introduce *Sein und Zeit* [HEIDEGGER] to England.

It is easy to see why the study of Imagination is important for Ryle in his programme of demolishing the Cartesian dualism of mind and body. In order to combat the view that there are mental events and physical events taking place side by side when human beings act, one has to give a satisfactory explanation of the activities of our mind when it is preoccupied with imaginary objects. For, as Ryle says, 'imaginary' is usually taken to be synonymous with 'mental'. An imaginary object is considered as the mental entity *par excellence* which exists in a universe independent of the physical world.

The chapter on Imagination is consequently a section of the *Concept of Mind* about which the greatest amount of dissatisfaction has been expressed by various British philosophers, even those belonging to the analytical school. The world of our imagination people usually consider as being private and internal, and accessible only to introspection. Even if one agrees with Ryle that mental terms do not always simply refer to introspectible mental entities or events (for example, Ryle seems to be right to point out that a 'belief' refers not to any mental occurrence or process but to a disposition to do certain things, etc.), one finds it difficult not to think that one has a privileged access to one's own world of imagination. Now Ryle thinks that when we do sums on a piece of paper or when we read a book, we are not doing two things, one of them private and the other public, at the same time. We do not first do sums mentally and then put them down on paper, nor do we arouse in ourselves a purely inner process called reading by moving our eyes across the page and perceiving certain letters. The publicly observable behaviour of putting the sums down on paper *is* the mental act of doing sums, and perceiving groups of letters in a certain way *is* reading. He says, '. . . when we describe people as exercising qualities of mind we are not referring to occult episodes of which their overt acts and utterances are effects: we are referring to those overt acts and utterances themselves' [RYLE (2), p. 25]. How would Ryle's argument work in the case of imagination? When we imagine things we do not usually perform any publicly observable acts at the same time. Would anything remain of imagination after being operated on by Ryle's razor?

People might say that all mental activities are in essence private and internal and, therefore, that there is nothing specially occult and inaccessible about the workings of our imagination. Why should our having a pain, for example, be less public than our picturing things? In the case of pain, however, there usually occur certain symptoms or natural behaviour which the person exhibits. And although there is no logically necessary connection between the statement that someone is in pain and the statement that someone is exhibiting certain symptoms or behaviour (since one can be true and the other false), yet there is a connection between the meaning of the word pain and certain patterns of human behaviour. Imagination betrays no such symptoms and is accompanied by no natural gestures. As Ryle himself writes: 'If you do not divulge the contents of your silent soliloquies and other imaginings, I have no other sure way of finding out what you have been saying or picturing to yourself' [RYLE (2), p. 61]. Can he sensibly admit this and deny that the process of imagining is introspectible at the same time? The workings of the imagination seem to resist explanation in terms of publicly observable behaviour.

Before going any farther into the discussion, I will try first to indicate the main points of Ryle's arguments.

The *Leitmotiv* of Ryle's chapter is that imagination is not a purely sensuous faculty which occupies itself solely with imaging, and that imagining is not the seeing of mental objects, but a way in which we make use of our knowledge without performing overt acts. Ryle begins by claiming that the question 'Where do the things and happenings exist which people imagine existing?' is a spurious one. Because we use the same kind of words to describe the things which we perceive in the world and the things which we imagine, we take it for granted that the above question is as meaningful as, for example, the question 'Where do the things we perceive exist?' We are being misled by language. Readers might recall that Sartre made precisely the same point when he attacked Hume in his book *L'Imaginaire*. Sartre claimed that our habit of thinking about objects in space in spatial terms had led people mistakenly to suppose that images are in the mind, and the objects of imagination are in the imagination. When I picture Julius

Caesar to myself, the proud-looking Emperor that I am imagining is not in my mind in the same way in which the historical Julius Caesar was in Rome. The object of my imagination, both Sartre and Ryle are eager to tell us, is not a mental entity, an image which has the characteristic of being like the real Caesar but no other qualities, like a painting without a canvas. I imagine the historical Caesar and not the image of him. In Ryle's words: 'Much as stage murders do not have victims and are not murders, so seeing things in one's mind's eye does not involve either the existence of things seen or the occurrence of seeing them' [RYLE (2), p. 245].

Ryle is quite right to think that when I picture an object, the image of the object is not located in my mind in the same way as this painting I see or this piece of sculpture which I touch is located in time and space. If one were to say that mental images existed in the mind simply because the person alone can be aware of the objects he imagines, then by the same kind of reasoning one would be able to say that the objects of perception exist in the mind (as many have indeed said). My visual field can only be *my* visual field, and the things I see are all in this field. One can properly talk of temporal and spatial location only after identifying and establishing a public time and space. Even if one were to talk of the location of objects in private time and space, as in the case when I say that an event preceded another in my dream or that I saw an apparition in the centre of my visual field, the objects of my imagination could still not be described as being located 'in my mind'. It does not, however, follow from this fact that one cannot, as Ryle assumes, meaningfully ask where the things and events are which people imagine existing. This derives from the ambiguity of the reference of the words 'things' and 'events'. The point can be illustrated by considering the fact that in answer to the question 'What are you painting?' one can answer, for example, either 'A mural' or 'The last supper'. We will come back to this point later on and, in the meantime, proceed with Ryle's arguments.

In order to explain why imagining things does not involve the existence of mental images, Ryle tries to show the difference between 'seeing' in one's mind and seeing. His argument against Hume's mistake of assimilating seeing and having mental images is again very much that of the phenomenologist tradition. As Ryle points out, Hume was never able to make a clear distinction between 'impressions' (sensations) and 'ideas' (images in our terminology). Hume thought that one could distinguish the two kinds by their vividness, i.e. 'ideas' or 'images' are according to Hume less lively. But, of course, we do not have perceptions of a neutral kind, scrutinize them and then decide by their vividness whether we are perceiving things by our senses or imaging.[3] We do not see mental images as we see things. As a matter of fact, according to Ryle, we do not see mental images at all, except in a metaphorical sense. He points out that this can be brought out more clearly by thinking of 'smelling'. When one smells the smithy one visited as a child one is not smelling a special smell. One is not smelling a faint smell nor a copy of a smell. One fancies one smells: it is a game of make-believe. Thus, Ryle claims that just as mock-murder is not the committing of a mild or faint murder, picturing is not seeing a faint object: 'imaging occurs but images are not seen,' 'I have tunes running in my head but no tunes are being heard.'

Some people may feel that this statement is preposterous. When I picture my mother's face what I see need not be a faint replica as Hume suggests, nor need there be any danger of confusing my act of picturing with my really seeing her. Nevertheless, it seems true that I am seeing an image since I have an experience such that I can describe what I am picturing to myself.

In order to understand the point of Ryle's thesis, one should perhaps reflect on some of the disputes about the 'logic' of 'see-ing' which have occurred among the analytical philosophers in the last twenty years. Many of them have tried to cast doubt on the sense-datum theory prevalent in Britain previously, which asserted that we never see or directly perceive material objects but only see sense-data, i.e. our sense-perceptions. Analytical philosophers have endeavoured to show that this sense-datum theory is based on a conceptual muddle. When we see something we are, of course, aware of the fact, i.e. we have a certain kind of inner experience. Having this experience is, however, not the only criterion by which we judge that a person sees.[4] For example, if a person with his

---

[3] Even many contemporary philosophers are victims of this confusion. For example, Professor Price writes: 'An image of a yellow patch, it might be said, is actually itself yellow, as a buttercup seen in full daylight is, and an image of a squeak is itself squeaky. This claim, I think, is not altogether justified. The image does not seem to me to have the characteristic of intensiveness or sensible forcefulness which the actual percept has' (1) [PRICE (3), p. 155].

[4] I refer to the fact that one of the criteria by which other people judge that I see is the report I give of my experience.

eyes firmly shut were to say that he sees a table, we would not be willing to grant him that he really sees it, even if there happened to be a table before him. Similarly, if someone were to say, 'I see a table, but there is none', our first reaction would be to say that he was mistaken. And it has been claimed that the person must either *think* that he sees a table when he doesn't, or he sees something which looks like a table. One cannot claim, it has been argued, to see something which does not exist simply because we would not call this 'seeing'. It is not a question of idioms or ordinary language. The point is that the concept of seeing which we use is tied to many assumptions about public objects, visual organs, human behaviour, etc., and is not uniquely related to our having certain experiences. In order to discover these assumptions, and thus to understand the concept, it is never sufficient just to 'reflect on our consciousness'. It is necessary to examine the occasions when we would be prepared to say that we see and in what circumstances we do say so. Ryle's point is that when I picture something, what I am doing does not satisfy the ordinary accepted concept of seeing, which is intimately linked with our ideas about visual sensations and about the existence of things seen. If I can picture something with my eyes closed, the act of picturing is compatible with having no sensations and nothing akin to them. It cannot be confused with my seeing a picture.[5]

I will now indicate an unnecessary confusion in Ryle's arguments. When he attempts to distinguish seeing in one's mind or 'seeing' from ordinary seeing, he lumps together many other mental activities which are quite dissimilar and follow a different 'logic'. (Ryle writes that even people who treat picturing as a kind of seeing realize that there is a difference and often use the word seeing with inverted commas.) He discusses not only picturing but also seeing in dreams, in a delirium, under hypnosis and in conjuring shows, as examples of 'seeing' and claims that all are distinct from seeing just as a forged signature is distinct from an authentic signature. I am not even certain whether they are all (logically) distinct from ordinary seeing as Ryle says, but even if they were the difference between them is so great that I believe it will only obscure the problem at issue to consider them as a

---

[5] Sartre asserts precisely the same thing when he writes that images and perceptions far from being psychic factors of similar quality, exclude each other. [SARTRE, p. 156]

group.[6] (For example, I can scrutinize and discover new facts about the objects I see in a state of delirium tremens, and this brings it closer to ordinary seeing than 'seeing'.) I think that even people who falsely thought that to have imaginative powers was to see a host of mental images, would not have considered a man suffering from delirium tremens or a man taken in by a conjuring show to be exercising his imagination. I will thus only consider what Ryle calls seeing or hearing or smelling, etc., in one's mind, and discuss Ryle's arguments in so far as they concern this problem. I will not consider any of the cases where a person mistakenly thinks that he perceives when he does not.

If Ryle does not think that picturing consists in seeing mental images, what does he think it is? He believes that 'seeing' is a kind of pretending, i.e. one of the many kinds of games of make-believe that we can play. When we picture x we are pretending to see x. When we run through a tune in our heads, we are pretending to hear it. We should not think, however, that Imagination is solely occupied in fancied viewings and hearings. The exercise of Imagination is a sophisticated function of intelligence which can be shown in many ways, such as in writing a novel, reading a novel, inventing a machine, acting or in pretending; and it is an intellectual exercise similar to that of entertaining an hypothesis. (This shows even more definitely that Ryle cannot group dreaming and seeing things in hallucinations together with picturing. It would be absurd to say that when we have dreams, we are pretending to see. One can say that Macbeth did not see the dagger, since he was mistaken and merely thought that he saw it when he did not, but one cannot say that he pretended.) We have no special faculty of imagination of a purely sensuous kind as some have believed. Thus, according to Ryle, 'imaging', i.e. picturing, having a tune running through one's head, etc., is one of the many kinds of acts of pretending, and pretending is one of the many ways in which we exercise our imagination, which in turn is a way in which we make use of our knowledge and intelligence.

Pretending to do x, Ryle says, has a logic which is more complex than doing x, since the description of pretending to do x involves the knowledge of what it is to do x. The person who pretends to do x, models his actions intentionally upon those of a man who does x. He cannot pretend to be jealous unless he knows

---

[6] J. M. Shorter makes a good analysis of this confusion. [SHORTER, p. 528]

what it is to be jealous. Neither would we be able to understand the man who pretends to be jealous unless we knew what it was to be jealous. Yet it is important to understand that the person who pretends to be jealous, is not doing two things at the same time—contemplating jealousy and acting in a jealous way. In Ryle's words pretending to do x does not involve two actions, one of meditating x and the other of doing the acting. One evidence of this is that even if a person cannot give a verbal description of x, as long as he can mimic x we say he can pretend to be x. And we can, he claims, paraphrase 'picturing x' into 'pretending to see x' because it has the same complex logical structure.

Is it true that we cannot have a mental image of x unless we know x? Of course I can picture Julius Caesar without having seen him or can even visualize an inhabitant of Mars who may not exist, but this is because I have formed a notion of Caesar through the statues I have seen and the impressions I have got through my reading of Roman history, and the illustrations which adorned my school copy of *De Bello Gallico*, and I expect a Martian to be light-weight, intellectually advanced and so on, because of the influence of science fiction. Ryle is quite right when he says that it would be absurd for someone to say, 'I see something vividly in my mind's eye, but I cannot make out what sort of thing it is' [RYLE (2), p. 265]. As one cannot say, 'I am pretending to be something but I don't know what', one cannot picture something of which one cannot give any description. Thus, according to Ryle, though I could see a face in my mind's eye without being able to give it a name or run through a tune in my head without being able to attach a name to it, I must know how the tune goes or what sort of face I am picturing.[7]

Consider an example given by Wittgenstein. Someone claims that he imagines King's College on fire. We ask him, 'How do you know that it's King's College you imagine on fire? Couldn't it be a different building very much like it?' The absurdity of such questions seems to show how imaging is connected with our intentions and that the qualities of objects which we image are not discovered as are the qualities of perceived objects.

However, the fact that the logic of 'pretending to perceive x'

---

[7] Sartre makes the same point when he says that when one pictures a printed page, one does not read it or strictly speaking even look at it, since one knows already what is written. [SARTRE, p. 21]

and 'imaging *x*' are similar and that they are both more complex than that of ordinary perceiving does not prove that they are equivalent. Also, since it is very difficult (as we shall see later) to understand what is involved in pretence, reducing imaging to a kind of pretending does not necessarily make things clearer. Ryle explains that when one pretends to do *x*, one intentionally models one's action upon those of a man who does *x*. Thus the actor who acts the murder scene on the stage deliberately moves about, changes his expressions or handles his weapon as he thinks a real assassin would do. There is, however, no set of overt actions for seeing or hearing or smelling. If I were blind but also had reasons for concealing this fact, I might act like a person with normal eyesight. I might, for example, pretend to see the doorway when I did not and walk straight on as I fancy other men would without stretching out my arms and feeling about. It is easy to see that when we picture something, say Mont Blanc, we do not 'pretend to see' it in the same way in which the blind man pretends to see the doorway. Certainly, visualizing Mont Blanc with its icy ridges on the one hand, and acting like a man who would actually be gazing at the peaks from the Chamonix valley on the other, are quite different things. Ryle could not mean that to picture is the same as to pretend to see in this latter sense, for Ryle himself writes that picturing is not sham-seeing in the way that sparring is sham-fighting.

Here we are faced with a difficulty. If to see something in the mind's eye or to run through a tune in one's head is a kind of pretending, and if this pretence involves no overt actions, would this not lead us back to inner mental processes again? Isn't the pretence a pretence of having certain inner experience which we actually do not have?

In order to circumvent this Ryle uses two arguments. First, Ryle says that there cannot be such a thing as an *overt* act of pretending to see or hear simply because there can be *no* act of pretending to see or hear either overt or secret. Seeing, hearing or any sort of perceiving is not bringing anything about. It is getting something or keeping it, but it is not a doing at all.[8] It is not an

---

[8] This corresponds to the distinction of 'achievement verbs' and 'performance verbs', which Ryle makes elsewhere. Ryle illustrates this by pointing to the difference between running a race and winning. Winning is not a performance as running is. It is an achievement you accomplish by running. A performance has a duration which an achievement has not. One can be ordered to perform but not to achieve.

act which can be witnessed. One cannot pretend to perceive in the same way as one can pretend to box or murder. But if perceiving is not a doing at all, could one pretend to perceive? What does one pretend when one pretends to perceive?

Here Ryle introduces yet another concept: that of 'refraining' or 'inhibition'. People often suppose that we sing tunes to ourselves in our heads before ever singing them out loud, or that we first acquire the capacity to do mental sums before we learn how to write them down on paper or say them out loud. Ryle thinks that it is the other way round. After knowing how to sing aloud, one then, by refraining from doing it overtly, can run through a tune in one's head. Similarly, after learning to manipulate numerals and knowing how to do it on paper, or after being able to say the multiplication tables and sums out loud, one then learns to inhibit the overt expression and acquires the sophisticated skill of doing sums in one's head. This capacity of pretending to do something or to be something without engaging in any publicly observable act is imagining or fancying. Picturing and 'hearing' a tune in one's head are two of the many kinds of imagining. Ryle writes 'imagining oneself talking or humming is a series of abstentions from producing the noises which would be the due words or notes to produce if one were talking or humming aloud' [RYLE (2), p. 269].

Thus by an analysis of concepts such as 'seeing in one's mind' and 'running through a tune in one's head', Ryle has arrived at the following conclusions:

(1) The exercise of the imagination does not consist solely in imaging and is closely connected with mental activities like supposing and pretending.

(2) Imaging ('seeing', 'hearing', etc.) is not seeing mental pictures or objects of a special personal or shadowy kind.

(3) Imaging is only one kind of imagining, i.e. imagining that one perceives. It is a sophisticated use of our knowledge of perceiving and is logically dependent on it.

(4) Unlike ordinary acts of pretending, imagining does not consist of deliberately going through certain acts with an intent to imitate. It is a more sophisticated exercise of the imagination where one refrains from overtly performing certain acts and yet pretends.

We will now examine whether Ryle's arguments are convincing and conclusive.

First, let us examine Ryle's view that to imagine is not to see mental images and that seeing in one's mind does not involve the existence of any mental objects.[9] I will picture the birth of Venus to myself. I see a female creature with long golden hair. She is looking at the waves round her with a slightly disdainful look, her lips are pouting, her arms are plump. Now what does Ryle deny that I am doing? If he is saying that he refuses to call it 'seeing mental images of Venus' merely because what I am doing differs, as we have seen, from standard cases of seeing, then it will be a quarrel over language. Anyone, including Hume, with all his confused terminology, would have realized that there was some difference between picturing and seeing. If, in spite of that, many philosophers called picturing 'seeing mental images', it was because they thought the similarity between the two processes more important than the difference. The boundaries of a concept or a meaning of a word are usually vague and elastic. It is for us to decide whether we should change the boundaries or not. One cannot stretch a concept at the expense of making it self-contradictory or too vague to be of any use, but at times one has to be willing to extend or narrow the boundaries fixed by ordinary usage, if one finds it more appropriate to do so. After all it is human beings who decide whether a concept is used metaphorically in a certain case or whether it is used literally. With this in mind I will show why I still agree with Ryle that it is misleading to describe my act of picturing Venus as seeing a mental picture of her.

Ryle's main argument seems to be that a person can see things only when he has his eyes open and when his surroundings are illuminated and that since I can visualize an object without having any visual sensations, I cannot be seeing. This is a weak argument. Naturally, when I picture something, I am not seeing anything in the world. But the believers in mental images, whom I will call Imagists for short, have never claimed that when I picture Venus, I see Venus. They merely said that it was *as if I were seeing a picture of Venus*. Imagists were quite aware of the fact that my optical

[9] Again Sartre makes the same point by using his metaphysically sounding term 'Nothingness'. He says that the objects of imagination are grasped as a 'nothing' or 'non-existent'.

organs were not receiving any external stimuli, but thought that in spite of this difference I was having a similar experience to that of seeing, i.e. to that of seeing a picture of Venus.

One can here put a stronger argument against the Imagists. It is simply wrong to think that I have an experience very similar to that of seeing a picture when I visualize. When I look at a real picture, for example, when I look at Botticelli's 'Birth of Venus', I can see it and describe it without knowing what it is a painting of. I can describe its colours, I will see that it is a nude woman rising from the sea. I can scrutinize and discover more and more details about the painting. When I picture something in my mind, it is entirely different. I cannot have a mental image without knowing what it is an image of. A mental image does not have qualities by itself as a painting does. There is no mental image as such. I have an image of a red object, but I do not have a red image. I do not behold an image which I then discover looks like a Venus, since my mental image consists solely of the description I am willing to give to Venus. As Ryle says, when I fancy I hear a very loud noise, I am not really hearing either a faint or loud noise. It would be absurd to ask, 'Do you have a soft replica of a loud noise in your mind?' Thus, having mental images is quite different from perceiving.

This argument is not an original discovery of Ryle. Wittgenstein had pointed this out, and it is a familar argument of the phenomenologists, which we find explicitly stated in Sartre's L'Imaginaire. Sartre wrote that the expression 'mental image' is misleading because it suggests an object of some kind. When I picture Pierre I do not, he claims, have an awareness of an image of Pierre, but rather a special kind of awareness of Pierre himself; an awareness which could be better described as an 'awareness of Pierre-in-image' or 'imaging awareness of Pierre'. And Sartre describes this by saying that an image is not a mental object, but a relation. Sartre also points out how wrong it is to describe imaging as a kind of perceiving, although in doing so he often lapses into confused terminology. When we perceive an object, we are perceiving it from one of its infinite aspects. We can go on learning new things about the object. In Russellian terminology, 'The object always goes beyond my awareness of it.' When we picture things, it is quite different. We cannot learn new things about what we picture. 'An Image,' Sartre writes, 'is defined by its intention.' We can never learn new things about it because it only has the qualities that we have put into it. Sartre expresses this somewhat misleadingly and says, 'The object of imaging is never anything more than the awareness one has of it.'[10] This expression, with its ambiguous use of the word 'object', would seem to contradict his view that an image is not an object, but a relation. For when I picture Pierre, the man Pierre is the object of my awareness, and not, as Sartre himself says, the image of Pierre. And Pierre is certainly much 'more' than the awareness I have of him! We should perhaps rephrase this expression of Sartre and interpret it as meaning that in imaging there is nothing more in the person's awareness of the object than what the person puts in.

Although both Ryle and Sartre correctly point out the fundamental difference between picturing and seeing a picture, it seems that neither gives a satisfactory analysis of imaging. Sartre says that an image is not a mental object, but a relation. What then is it a relation to? According to Sartre, whether I perceive him or imagine him, it is the man Pierre who is the object of my awareness.[11] It is easy to establish at least that there is a relation (in a Humean sense) between Pierre and my awareness when I perceive him in front of me,[12] but how is my awareness related to him when I picture Pierre who is absent? And when I picture the birth of Venus, what is the object of my awareness? In this case, to say that the object of imagination and perception is the same is to give no explanation at all, since there is no Venus either present or past to be perceived. There is another difficulty. When I picture Venus to myself and when I picture Brigitte Bardot, I seem to be doing the same kind of thing, although the objects of my awareness are

[10] [SARTRE, pp. 20–1]. Some people might object and say no, we do learn new things about our images. When we want to prove a geometrical theorem we often learn from our mental images. We sometimes put down our images as diagrams and discover facts from them. This is, however, wrong. We never discover new facts from the diagrams as we would about ordinary objects of perception. We discover or see what is entailed by the ideas we already had or postulated by the aid of diagrams. Even when we draw a triangle badly, we read in that the three angles form 2π and are not bothered by the actual difference.

[11] Thus the question 'Where do things exist which people imagine' is not a spurious question for Sartre as it is for Ryle. In many cases, e.g. when I imagine my friend Pierre or picture Mont Blanc, the answer is 'In the world' or 'In Paris', 'On the Swiss-French border', etc. 'Things imagined' does not have to mean any mental entities, and I am sure that if the question is taken in Sartre's sense, Ryle will also consider it as being meaningful.

[12] A relation between Pierre in front of me and my awareness can be established by others (in a Humean sense) by correlating their observations of Pierre and the reports I give of my awareness.

radically different; one being a mythological fiction and the other a woman in the flesh. Could this be explained without positing mental objects?

We might say that when I picture *x* the object of my awareness is not *x*, but the description of *x*. In other words, I am thinking of the description of *x*. As the description of Venus and the description of Brigitte Bardot are not so qualitatively different (?), it is not surprising that I do very similar things when I picture them. This, however, makes my picturing (or hearing in my mind, etc.) a purely conceptual or verbal act, which clearly is not the case. Even Ryle, who thinks that there is a close connection between imagining and supposing or entertaining an hypothesis, does not consider that picturing is a verbal process. Although picturing something is connected with having a knowledge of the thing, knowledge is not, for Ryle, necessarily verbal. He claims that seeing a face in my mind's eye is one of the things which my knowledge of the face enables me to do; and describing it in words is another and a rarer ability. But as Ryle never makes it quite clear what the difference consists of, and as he so confidently declares that when a person pictures 'there *is* nothing akin to sensations', one is unable to grasp what Ryle thinks imaging is like.

Another philosopher [SHORTER, p. 528] has tried to correct Ryle by suggesting that if picturing is sham-anything at all, it is sham-depicting and not sham-seeing. Ryle was correct to point out that visualizing is not seeing a mental picture, but he was wrong to think that it is a mock-seeing. The logic of 'visualizing' is parallel to that of 'depicting', and this, it is claimed, is a *doing*. For example, one can be ordered to depict or visualize something, although one cannot be ordered to see it.

It is probably true that the logic of 'visualizing' is somewhat similar to that of 'depicting'. As Wittgenstein says 'seeing an aspect and imagining is subject to the will' [WITTGENSTEIN (4), p. 213]. Ordered to picture Venus, I would try to draw up a picture of her in my mind similar to what I would do on paper. It does not, however, at all follow from this that visualizing is a pure *doing* or that it has nothing akin to seeing. We can make this clearer by considering the so-called paradigm case of *doing* or performance and of *getting* or achievement: 'running' or 'observing' expressing performances and 'winning' or 'seeing' expressing achievements. I can run or observe successfully or unsuccessfully, but cannot win or see successfully or unsuccessfully. I merely win or lose, see or not see. People can order me to run or observe, but not to win or see. The most they can order me to do is to try to see or win. To which of these groups do the concepts 'depicting' or 'picturing' belong?[13]

If I am ordered to depict Brigitte Bardot, I will try to do so in words or by drawing. The result may not be successful. You may say that I depict her incorrectly or poorly, although I am forming sentences or drawing lines with the intention of capturing her looks. You are then thinking of 'depicting' in a performance sense. However, if my attempt is too unsuccessful, you may no longer want to describe me as depicting Brigitte Bardot, but may say that I have not depicted Brigitte Bardot. In this case 'depict' is taken in its achievement sense. My drawing or writing did not count as depicting. Thus we see that 'depicting' is a complex or ambiguous concept in between concepts expressing performance and concepts expressing achievements. This ambiguity derives from the complex nature of the fact itself, which involves elements that depend on my intention and elements which do not.

Let us consider 'picturing'. I am ordered to visualize Venus, but am unable to do so. I try; I think of various Greek myths concerning Venus, but I see nothing in my mind's eye. In this case I will surely not say that I am picturing Venus unsuccessfully or poorly. I will confess that I do not picture her. Just as one cannot win every time one wishes to win, one cannot picture every time one wants to.[14] Picturing is not a pure *doing*; it is a *happening* or an achievement as well. The word 'picturing' is taken even less than 'depicting' in a pure performance sense, which makes it more like 'seeing'. And I believe, against Ryle and Shorter, that there is a quality of *picturing* which can best be described as analogous to seeing, and in general a quality of imaging which can be best described as analogous to perceiving (in spite of differences which should be remembered) and which perhaps can only be described in this way.

A person who pictures is not simply a fanciful man who can

[13] I will not consider here the other criterion which Ryle uses to determine whether a verb expresses a performance or an achievement: that of duration. This is because the criterion is dubious and because it simplifies a complex problem.

[14] I know a person who is incapable of picturing the face of his mother to whom he is very close.

entertain complicated hypotheses or build up sophisticated suppositions. Picturing seems to be a distinctly visual capacity as well, just as hearing tunes in one's head is an auditory capacity. Ryle correctly says that imaging is not a function of pure sentience. It is wrong to ignore, however, that there is an element of 'given' in it, which is beyond control. If other people can postulate certain axioms, I can postulate the same ones. I can entertain any hypothesis that you can so long as it is meaningful to me. I am unable, however, to picture some things that other people can, regardless of the knowledge I have of them. This can be brought out clearly by considering images which are not visual. If someone orders me now to follow the tune of the 'Goldberg Variations', I am unable to do so, although I know the piece in the sense that I will recognize it if it is played, and even though I can give a description which will uniquely identify it, e.g. that it consists of thirty variations, that it was published in 1742, etc. Try as I may, I cannot succeed in running through the tune in my head. The best way to describe my failure seems to me to say that I do not hear it. Similarly, if I have to wait for several minutes before I can picture Brigitte Bardot's face, I would say that I could not see her face for a while. (Even Sartre, who denies that images are mental objects, writes that when one pictures something, the thing comes to the mind 'en bloc', like a particular object of perception, and that this distinguishes it from a concept. He also admits that often an image of a thing appears with greater clarity than any perception one ever had of it.) [SARTRE, pp. 21, 55]

To admit that there is an element in our experience of imaging which is similar to that of perceiving should not damage Ryle's general thesis. We still agree with Ryle against the sense datum theorists that there is an essential difference between perceptions and images. We agree that the object of our imaging is the thing itself, and not the mental picture of the thing. It seems, therefore, unnecessary and wrong for Ryle to ignore any kinship between them, since, as I will point out later, a better understanding of the exercise of the imagination will be obtained by examining its intimate connection with perception. We are, of course, agreed with Ryle that imagination is not a faculty of pure sentience, for although we have tried to show that imaging is connected with sensory experience, we by no means think that imaging is the only way in which we exercise our imagination. There are many ways in which we can engage in imaginative work without having any images or having anything resembling sense experience. I can describe a country which I have never visited, as well as one which I have, quite vividly with the verbal knowledge I possess, and this is also an exercise of my imagination. I am supposing a situation which is not there, and in Ryle's words I am operating with suspended judgements: I am engaged in a game of pretence. It seems to me that if one has vivid images of certain kinds, one will be aided to be imaginative in certain ways. If I 'hear' various tunes, it would be easier for me to compose.[15] If I visualize things easily, I can more likely set up hypothetical situations which can be described. The converse, however, does not hold.

Thus, mental images are, at most, necessary tools for a *limited number* of people in *certain kinds* of exercise of the imagination and are, for many people, merely psychological accompaniments which occur when they are engaged in imaginative work and not the essence of it. As Ryle says, imaging is not the nuclear operation common to all exercises of the imagination. I will thus now leave the problem of imaging and examine Ryle's general explanation of what it is to do things in the mind, or to imagine.

Here Ryle expresses himself in rather negative terms. He is eager to point out, as we have seen, that there is no one operation which all exercises of the imagination have in common. He considers 'imagining' as a special brand of pretending or make-believe where no overt behaviour is exhibited, and thus holds that the concept of imagining is intimately connected with that of supposing or entertaining hypotheses. What then does pretending consist in? What remains of pretence when, as Ryle says, the overt behaviour is restraint? How can we, to take Ryle's example, listen for certain notes in a hypothetical manner, if there is nothing akin to sounds that can be heard? When we do mental arithmetic or run through a tune in our heads, we are not continually restraining an urge to make sounds in the way in which someone with a severe pain has to force himself not to groan.[16] This seems to follow from the difference in the relationship which holds between a pain and an expression of a pain, on the one hand, and doing sums and writing down sums on the other. The former are two happenings

---

[15] For example, it is a known fact that Mozart constantly 'heard' the tunes he composed.

[16] This was pointed out to me by Mr M. Dummett.

which can be said to have a causal relationship with each other, whereas in the latter case we do not merely not observe any causal relationship, but we do not even know whether there are two separate happenings. Although it is easy to understand what it would be like to restrain the groaning when the pain is there, it is difficult to see what is left when one restrains oneself from writing down sums. Obviously, reading silently is quite different from suffering pain in silence. The sounds were not suppressed in the same sense in the former case as in the latter, for, as Ryle himself says, when we do sums on paper it is not at all necessary that there are two happenings going on side by side.

Ryle seems to be hindered from digging deeper into the problem by unnecessarily holding an assumption based on the confusion of two distinct theses. The two theses are: (*a*) the meanings of words expressing mental activities are connected with certain patterns of behaviour as well as a whole set of notions which we have about our bodies and the world. Thus the criterion for the correct use of such words cannot consist solely in our having certain inner experiences. To take the example Wittgenstein gives in the *Philosophical Investigations* [WITTGENSTEIN (4)], if 'reading' only meant a certain mental process which a person usually has when he sees words written in a language he understands, what should we say of a person who claims that this mental process is going on in his head when he is uttering words which have no connection to the things written in the page before him, or of a person who goes on reading correctly but asserts that he has no such feeling of reading? Thus 'reading' cannot refer solely to such a mental process or awareness. And (*b*) there cannot be any inner processes or mental acts denoted by words expressing mental activities, if the criterion for the use of such words does not consist in being aware of these processes or acts. Although Ryle seems to assume both, I believe that (*a*) is an important truth brought to light by analytical philosophers, whereas (*b*), at least expressed in this way, is highly doubtful if not wrong. To deny the 'occurrence of acts of seeing' imaginary objects, and to deny the occurrence of any introspectible mental happenings when we exercise our imagination are two quite different things. The second thesis is not entailed by the first which Ryle has brilliantly put forward.

Ryle is probably right in saying that we learn to talk to ourselves by refraining from speaking out loud, and that we learn to follow

tunes in our heads by repressing our humming. But if it is true
to say that in general, when we do things in our mind or in
imagination we are making use of our knowledge of how to do
certain things while refraining from performing public acts, we
must make clear what such knowledge is a knowledge of. It cannot be merely a knowledge of how to perform certain overt acts,
for if that is the case one cannot be said to be making use of that
knowledge when one is not performing these acts. For example,
when we learn to follow tunes in our heads, we are not making
use of our knowledge to utter certain sounds, but our knowledge
of a melody which we learned through humming. When I talk
to myself in my head, I am not making use of the knowledge how
to utter words out loud, but my knowledge of how to form propositions, to reason and so on. Of course, as Ryle says, we can
only learn to do these things by learning to do certain overt acts.
It is in his words a 'knowing how' rather than a 'knowing that'.
But the question remains: when I make use of my 'knowing how'
without performing any overt act, am I not undertaking a mental
act, and isn't this a process which takes place in time? I am not
saying that there is an inner process or an act which goes on side
by side with my humming out loud or speaking, and that when I
do things in my imagination, the inner process takes place without
the outer one. I quite agree with Ryle that when I hum, I am not
necessarily doing two things at the same time. But if my humming,
which is a manifestation of my 'knowing how', is a definite act
which takes place in time, why shouldn't my following a tune in
my head, which is a similar kind of use of my knowledge, be considered as an act which takes place in time as well? If one says, as
Ryle does, that they are 'inhibitions', it is strange that they should
not be events or acts.

I will illustrate my point by comparing 'imaging' or 'doing
things in one's mind' with 'knowing' or 'believing' which, as
Ryle has correctly pointed out, do not necessarily express hidden
processes or acts. One sees what a person has done in his mind by
attending to the results he obtains and expresses. For example, we
see that a person has done mental arithmetic by hearing the
answer he produces, just as we see that a person can tie a reef-knot
or that he knows French by seeing him tie a knot or by hearing
him speak French. The fact that he does tie a reef-knot when the
occasion arises or that he makes himself understood in French

is what we mean by claiming that he knows how to tie a reef-knot or speak French. There is no continuous inner process or mental state of 'knowing', which must exist in addition to the occasional manifestations of the knowledge. (Even if there were some brain traces corresponding to every kind of skill and knowledge we acquire, this is a matter for physiologists to investigate. We do not call brain traces 'knowledge'.) Thus, there need not be any mental state of 'knowing how to tie a reef-knot' or 'knowing French' prior to the manifestation of the knowledge. In contrast to this, if a man writes down correct answers after being given certain arithmetical problems, it is not his having given the answer alone which makes us say that he knows how to do sums. His answer plus the mental act we think he has carried out make us speak of his knowledge, just as in a calculation that has been written out step by step, not only the final answer but each step counts as evidence of his knowledge. That is why producing an answer after calculating in one's mind is a manifestation of knowledge in a way in which a conjuring trick is not and a miracle is not.[17] When a person produces an answer after doing mental arithmetic, we presume that he has done a mental act prior to his answer giving. It seems to me that Ryle has not made out the case for his denial of the 'occurrence of the acts of seeing' things in one's mind.

One must not think that Ryle's failure to give a satisfactory account of 'doing things in the mind' or 'imagining' is necessarily a proof that his so-called 'analytic method' is at fault. Ryle would not have obtained any better results by merely relying on introspection. Sartre confesses this at the end of the first section of *L'Imaginaire* when he describes the deadlock which confronts him in the 'terrain sûr' (!) of phenomenological description. 'We know,' he writes, '. . . that in mental images there is a psychic datum which functions as representational material (analogon), but the moment we want to determine the nature and components of this we are reduced to making conjectures' (which is empirical

---

[17] In a different chapter of *The Concept of Mind* Ryle does write that in judging that a performance is or is not intelligent we have to look beyond the performance itself: 'For there is no particular overt or inner performance which could not have been accidentally or mechanically executed by an idiot, a sleep-walker, a man in panic, absence of mind or delirium, or even sometimes by a parrot.' However, he immediately adds that 'in looking beyond the performance itself, we are not trying to pry into some hidden counterpart performance enacted on the supposed secret stage of the agent's inner life' [RYLE (2), p. 45].

science and not phenomenology). 'We can describe what the image is an image of and discover by reflection the qualities of the imagined object', but 'we cannot hope to grasp the content of our picturing mind through introspection'.

It is indeed difficult to give a clear philosophical analysis of the exercise of the imagination. Ryle and Sartre realize that as the exercise of the imagination can be done without an overt behaviour or expression, people try to introspect in order to catch it at its work, and only get empirical psychological data which are in most cases personal and contingent. Thus, they try to grasp the difference between the concepts of imagining and perceiving; Ryle by examining the logical behaviour of the expressions describing such mental activities, Sartre by describing the difference of the relation of the objects and awareness in each case. We have seen that what they actually do is not very dissimilar. What comes out most clearly from such analyses are the characteristics of the working of the imagination which resemble those of other kinds of thinking. For both of these philosophers, in spite of their beliefs to the contrary, mental images are very close to descriptions. Sartre explicitly says that images are neither things which accompany thoughts nor interfere with thoughts, but constitute a subclass of thoughts [SARTRE, p. 158]. Yet, when it comes to the positive characterizations of the exercise of the imagination, neither Ryle nor Sartre is successful. We have seen, for example, that in his attempt to characterize imaging, Sartre often lapses into talking about mental images as if they were objects: a view which he explicitly denies. As for the explanation of what we usually call 'the capacity to do things in the mind', i.e. our capacity to show our 'knowing how' without any overt behaviour, the one offered by Ryle is far from adequate.[18] Sartre tries to give one by finding in our mind a 'nihilating (anéantissant) power' which can detach itself from what it perceives, and posit imaginary objects, that is to say, form objects which are basically characterized by 'Nothingness'. However, as this 'Nothingness', which is the converse of the 'real' or the 'being', is an irreducible primitive concept for Sartre, this does not take us much farther.

[18] Ryle points out that knowing how to do things does not entail the knowledge of propositions or the citing of appropriate rules to oneself before the act; but his explanation of what it then is, is inadequate in spite of the fact that he even has a section in another chapter of the book entitled 'The Positive Account of Knowing How' [RYLE (2), p. 40].

According to Sartre, when people exercise their imagination the objects of their thoughts are imbued with the features of unreality: they are aware that these objects are not perceived, that they are not there and that they escape the laws of the perceived 'real' world. Perceiving and imaging are, he claims, two irreducible and mutually exclusive attitudes of the mind. But is this dichotomy of the real and unreal or of the perceived and imagined as evident as Sartre suggests? Sartre says, for example, that when I look at an actor mimicking a person X, so long as I am aware of the actor and his movements, I am perceiving him, and thus the object of my awareness is 'real'. When I no longer see him as the actor himself, but as the person X whom he is mimicking, and when his gestures become for me the gestures of X, the object of my awareness is no longer the actor, but X who is not there. I cannot be said to be perceiving X, but, according to Sartre, I have an image of X: an awareness of X, who is not there to be perceived as a real object. We can in a way make sense of Sartre's assertion that the object of perception is real whereas that of the image is not. If I perceive the actor, then given the same conditions, other people should be able to perceive him as well. Everyone who comes into the theatre will see this man on the stage. Whereas if I see the actor as X, it does not follow that all people do or would have to see him as X. X is not a public object which is there in the way in which the actor is there. Thus, it does follow that if I see something as X, I could not be perceiving the real X at the same time.

Sartre's claim is, however, a stronger one than this. He thinks that when I see the actor as the person he is mimicking, I cannot be really perceiving the actor. Similarly, if I see a painting as a portrait of X, according to Sartre I am no longer perceiving the painting [SARTRE, p. 156]. And this seems to me to be evidently wrong. If I see Laurence Olivier as Hamlet, I must on the contrary also be perceiving Laurence Olivier. One cannot see X as Y without seeing X. It is probably this fact which led philosophers to assume that when I picture Y in my mind, there must be a mental object which I see as Y; or that I must be perceiving a mental image of Y. Although this latter view is mistaken and, as we have seen, the fact that I picture something does not entail that I see a mental picture of the thing, it serves no purpose to twist facts as Sartre does and assert that whenever we have an 'imaging awareness' of something we could not at the same time be perceiving anything at all. On the contrary, it seems that we will arrive at a better understanding of what it is to image and to do things in our mind, if we examine more closely the intricate relationship that holds between imaging and perceiving or between *seeing as* and seeing.

I have suggested that Ryle's interesting inquiries into the problem of imagination were unnecessarily checked from going farther by an implicitly assumed dogma that there are no occurrences of mental acts of an entirely private kind, i.e. acts which are not in some *de facto* way connected with publicly observable phenomena. Sartre, on the contrary, seems to be hindered from pursuing a more exact investigation by too easily establishing a dichotomy of 'real' and 'unreal' or of 'perceived' and 'imagined'; of too readily accepting certain features of our mental activities as being in no way dependent on the world of perception.

In order to understand such an elusive and private exercise of the mind as that of the imagination we must avoid the temptation to deceive ourselves with a magic word, which gives the appearance of solving everything without making anything clear, and with explanations which impress us more by the neatness and beauty of their structure than by their correctness or thoroughness. The somewhat prosaic method of conceptual analysis, if applied with care and without being mixed with unproved dogmas, can, I believe, lead people to solid and hence exciting facts about our Imagination precisely because the method was born to combat such a temptation. And although those works on Imagination by analytical philosophers which have appeared up to now have been far from satisfactory, the problems raised and the direction of inquiry suggested by some of them are, as we have seen, valuable. Although I myself find it hard to get a better grasp of the problems involved in imagination, I can think of nothing so exciting on this subject as the various questions raised by Wittgenstein in his *The Blue and Brown Books* and in his *Philosophical Investigations*.

It is in these sharp penetrating observations about small precise problems that the most unexpected and exciting resemblances between the philosophers divided by the English Channel can be observed. We have already seen an example of this in the analysis that has been made of the distinction between perceiving and

imaging. Another remarkable example can be found in Wittgenstein's remark that 'to see as . . .' is similar to 'having an image
of . . .' [WITTGENSTEIN (4), Part II, Sect. 11; especially p. 213],
and the almost exactly similar view running through Sartre's book
as he examines portraits, caricatures, mimics, symbols and other
specific phenomena in detail. This is one of the key problems of
imagination which might be fruitfully discussed together by philosophers on both sides of the Channel, and it will establish, I
believe, a common ground between the almost comically separated worlds of the pedestrian articles of *Mind* and the verbose
works of the late Merleau-Ponty (whose theories on perception,
comportement and the world are closely connected with the problem
of 'to see as . . .'). For even people who deny having any mental
images and people who think that the problem of imagination has
no important place in the philosophy of mind, could scarcely deny
that they are constantly 'seeing things as' something; at the same
time, even the most ardent metaphysician would be reluctant,
I am sure, to consider this as something 'irreal' or 'nihilating'.

8. FACT, VALUE AND IDEOLOGY

ALAN MONTEFIORE

THERE can hardly be anyone—anyone, that is, who is prepared to accept these as terms of debate at all—who would not agree that the relations between judgements of value and statements of fact constitute one of the great central issues of moral and political philosophy. Could a study of the facts of our social situation, of the purposes of our Creator, of the likely outcome of our actions or of our own or other people's desires ever even in principle provide us with logically compelling reasons for holding any one course to be better or worse, more or less obligatory than another? It all depends on whether facts as facts can ever determine our values. And it has been a characteristic, if not always translucent dogma of much recent British philosophy that they cannot, that value judgements stand in proud logical independence of all and any assertions that are not themselves in some way evaluative.

It would be quite mistaken, of course, to suggest that this view has been in any way exclusive to this country. Nevertheless, the form or mode of its acceptance by British philosophers has on the whole been somewhat different from that which it has taken elsewhere. Where some Continental writers have spoken, for example, of the inescapable human predicament of having, like it or not, to create one's own values in the face of a world which blankly refuses to supply them, British philosophers, operating within their framework of more or less linguistic analysis, have treated the independence of values as a simple consequence of (and hence guaranteed by) the laws of logic alone.[1] For some time, indeed, this logical independence of values was a matter of largely

[1] See, for example, POPPER (2).

unquestioned assumption among all those who saw philosophy in this dominant light. In the last few years, however, it has come back into vigorous and widespread dispute. The attack has a variety of sources and takes a variety of forms. But the main object of this paper is not so much to join in attack or defence as to give one particular account of how the problem re-emerges to face analytic philosophers; and of how in so doing it forces those who come from this movement to grapple with issues that belong more recognizably to the same family as those faced by their Continental contemporaries than may have been the case in the past.

This means to say, then, that the argument must take on semi-historical form. To see why the issues are now posed in the way that they are is to see how they grow out of the discomfort of previous positions. But, since many 'analysts' might well disagree with this version of the situation, the 'history' is also an argument, the argument that this *is* a network of problems that has now to be faced. Hence it is also to some extent a form of semi-autobiography; history only as the explanatory confession of a laborious shift of mind.

For many of us who came to the subject in the Oxford of the years just after the war, modern moral philosophy seemed to begin with the critical rejection of what was broadly known as 'objectivism'.[2] There was, I think, reasonable awareness of the persistent elusiveness of terms such as 'objective', 'subjective', 'absolute', 'intrinsic', 'intuition' and so on, and of the fact that they could severally and together be made to take on a whole range of varying meanings. But the problems here involved seemed to be essentially problems of formulation; 'objectivism' was the family name of all those doctrines which took values to have some independent existence of their own, as being what they were independently of the wishes, purposes or attitudes of any subject or body of subjects. And while it was easy enough to understand that one might *wish* to treat one's fundamental values as part of the very fabric of the universe, it seemed difficult to see how anyone of impartial and unmuddled intelligence could actually *believe* them to be so. (Except, perhaps, within the context of some explicitly religious outlook; though, quite apart from

[2] The objectivists in chief included such philosophers as G. E. MOORE, Sir David ROSS, and H. A. PRICHARD. For Moore see also SCHILLP.

the peculiar philosophical problems raised by religion, to make values dependent on God was not in any case to assign them their own independent objectivity.)

All the same, the rejection of 'objectivism' was in no way tied to any commitment to 'naturalism'. On the contrary, while we were far from denying the possibility of 'natural' explanations of why different people or communities should have created or adopted the standards of value that they have, virtually all of us fully accepted the apparently self-evident doctrine that values were strictly non-definable in natural or indeed in any other kind of purely factual terms.[3]

All this, however, was largely negative. We did not believe values to be objective, nor did we believe value judgements to be reducible to statements of fact. But what more positively did we believe them to be?

The suggestion with which most of us were probably most familiar was that put forward by A. J. Ayer in his version of the theses of the Vienna Circle in *Language, Truth and Logic* (first published in 1936) [AYER (1)]. This was a book of ruthless and striking simplicity. There were, it appeared, only two classes of meaningful propositions; analytic propositions, whose truth depended solely on the meanings of the words therein employed, and empirical propositions, the truth or falsity of which depended in principle on the outcome of some verifying observation. Value judgements, including moral judgements, fell into neither of these categories and were, therefore, literally meaningless. The strictly moral or evaluative elements in these pseudo-propositions functioned to express the feelings of the speaker or to direct the actions of others.

The theory of *Language, Truth and Logic* may have been crude as well as simple. But the same fundamental position had subsequently been given a more subtle and elaborate treatment by C. L. Stevenson, most notably in his substantial *Ethics and Language*, published in 1944 [STEVENSON (4)];[4] and in 1949 Ayer himself had just published a restatement along similarly developed lines [AYER (3)]. Thus, we learnt to talk of moral judgements as

---

[3] The rejection of naturalism in this sense had, in fact, been given a famous, if pretty thoroughly confused, formulation by Moore in his doctrine of the Naturalistic Fallacy [see MOORE (1)].

[4] See also his articles, STEVENSON (1-3).

elements in a highly complex pattern of behavioural attitudes, though still within the framework of a theory which, while making a now generous allowance for associated descriptive meanings, nevertheless still saw evaluation primarily in terms of self-expression on the one hand and persuasion on the other. It need hardly be said that when value judgements are so treated, no question arises of the logical derivation from ordinary statements of fact.

In its more sophisticated versions this was and still is a powerful as well as a striking theory. It did, however, invite attack as one according to which the processes of moral argument are fundamentally irrational. Everyone knows that it is not always the most truthful, valid or relevant remarks or arguments that are the most effectively persuasive. As for the feelings or attitudes to which people may give expression, these are but facts to be recorded, phenomena to be stimulated or repressed, and as such neither rational nor irrational. (There are, of course, senses in which feelings or attitudes may be said to be rational or irrational; an irrational feeling of fear, for example, would be one whose object would not be regarded as an appropriate cause for such reaction.[5] But a feeling is not something which can figure as premise or conclusion in any piece of rational argumentation, and any causal connection between feelings and such argumentation can only be contingent—and, in fact, of a pretty unreliable contingency at that.) Yet surely, many people felt, at least some moral arguments are genuine in their use of rational procedures, and not all of them are concerned with moulding the feelings or actions of others.

Ayer and Stevenson had, of course, answers to offer to this complaint. For, as they were able to point out, there are many cases in which effective persuasion will depend on the outcome of some genuinely factual dispute, or on getting one's opponent to see that there is some formal inconsistency in his position as stated. But while this answer may serve to explain why one so often gets the impression of listening to or of being oneself involved in some rational moral argument, it still appears to provide no rational account of the connection between the facts adduced and the judgement 'You ought to do X'. 'You ought to do X, because . . .'—but the 'because' seems on this view a bogus one, since what follow are not *reasons*, but what the speaker hopes may

[5] For a fuller discussion of this and related topics see EWING and H. M. WARNOCK.

be causal factors making for a favourable attitude on the part of his audience. Any such factors might do, provided only that they were associated with a favourable attitude on his own part and/or were reasonably reliable for success.

One attempt to remedy this position appeared in 1950 with S. E. Toulmin's *The Place of Reason in Ethics*.[6] Broadly speaking, his thesis was that factual considerations could provide perfectly good reasons for evaluative conclusions, and that any fuss to the contrary came simply from the mistaken belief that all valid inference must be either deductive or inductive. In fact, said Toulmin, there are within any community certain widely accepted rules by which to determine what kinds of behaviour are morally admirable or obligatory. Moral reasoning consists first in the application of these rules to particular cases, and secondly, in the testing of the rules themselves against the general criteria of social harmony and happiness. So, for instance, the generally accepted rule that one ought not to lie, licenses the inference from the statement that a story is false to the judgement that one ought not to repeat it. This is not, to be sure, a strictly deductive inference; no formal contradiction would be involved in the conjunction of the premise with the contradictory of the conclusion. But one must remember that circumstances alter cases and that it is only natural that moral reasoning should leave a logical gap for exceptions. The peculiarly evaluative inference is none the worse for that, and the gap for exceptions is not one to leave any disturbing logical hiatus between fact and value.

The central thesis of this book struck me at the time as impressive in execution but depressing in implication. There was for one thing its apparently built-in conservative bias. With all allowances made for the flexibility of Toulmin's own approach, good ethical reasons, it still appeared, were quite simply those which were generally considered to be so; this, indeed was what was meant by calling them 'good'. But more important was the way in which it seemed to blur crucial distinctions. It was all very well to talk of the rule that one ought not to lie as licensing certain sorts of inference. But this was a very different sort of licence from that provided by more strictly formal rules or procedures. That one ought not to lie was after all a substantial rule of conduct, and the problem was still one of whether one remained in principle free to

---

[6] TOULMIN. For a more recent work of the same general temper see BAIER.

adopt or to reject it as a general rule in the face of any and every situation of fact. To talk of rules of conduct or of value as if they were also rules of inference was to muddle rather than to solve this problem.

These second sorts of objections were very much those that R. M. Hare had to bring against Toulmin's and similar theories, in particular in his book *The Language of Morals* which appeared in 1952.[7] This book, together with Hare's subsequent explications and defence of its theses, has remained a centre of controversy ever since and, whether its stimulus has been to agreement or to disagreement, one of the most influential books of the decade.

Hare never actually arrives in *The Language of Morals* at a formal definition of the term 'value judgement' or of its closely related cousins. There is, it is true, an entry in the index—'value judgements; defined'—as well as a reference on page 172 to 'my definition of the word "evaluation"', which suggest that he thought that he had in fact given such a definition; but the index reference is to page 168, where what is provided is only a defining criterion of the use of the particular judgement 'I ought to do X' in an evaluative sense. All the same, his main view is in general clear enough. Value judgements, according to him, have universal import and entail imperatives; that is to say that they are derivable from universal principles, of which they are but the applications to particular cases, and that these may be characterized as prescriptive, principles for the advisory guidance, as opposed to the persuasive moulding, of one's own and other people's actions. Within this framework Hare, too, is able to elucidate a sense in which evaluative choice is essentially rational; the principle on which a value judgement is based, provides a reason for holding its object, and by implication any other which may exhibit the same relevant features, to be right or wrong, good, bad or indifferent as the case may happen to be. But at the same time his doctrine of the action-guiding nature of evaluation provides him with the basis for an emphatic reaffirmation of the so-called (and perhaps miscalled) Autonomy of Morals, i.e. the non-derivability of value judgements from non-evaluative premises. For, he maintains, while it is impossible to derive imperatives from non-imperative premises, whether from analytic propositions or from

---

[7] HARE. The important sequel, HARE (3), which he has just published appeared too late for account to be taken of it in this paper.

the indicatives of statements of fact, the essentially prescriptive nature of value judgements is shown precisely in their entailment of imperatives. And here he insists—contra Toulmin—on the preservation of clear-cut criteria of inference; though whether Hare himself fully succeeded in working out such criteria is another and possibly controversial question.

This is, of course, a highly condensed account of a fairly complex theory. But one at any rate of its most notable features is the way in which it makes the relation between evaluation and a certain readiness for action into a defining condition of the former. 'I ought to do X', Hare maintains, is to be counted as a value judgement only when it can be understood as entailing the command 'Let me do X'. There are a number of problems in the way of working out just what is involved in this entailment, and this is not the place to go into such detail. But given the way in which Hare develops his account of entailment, it certainly seems to follow that no one who said, 'I ought, I believe, to do X, but have no intention even of trying to do it' could be taken sincerely to mean 'I ought to do X' as a truly evaluative judgement. As someone under the impression of having quite often deliberately avoided doing what I thought I ought to do—and not always out of mere weakness of will—I should perhaps have found some comfort in the adoption of Socrates' paradox; but in fact it left me, for one, puzzled and ill at ease.

A second source of discomfort was the extreme form in which Hare states his doctrine that all value judgements must be derivable from fully universal premises. This has to do, no doubt, with the logical spirit of his enterprise. 'Ethics as I conceive it,' he declares in his preface, 'is the logical study of the language of morals.' Hence his treatment of value judgements as a class of sentences and of the principles on which they are based as characterized by the logical features of the terms in which they are cast. A fully universal principle must on Hare's view be one in which there occurs no singular term, and in which no reference is made to any particular individual. But it seemed difficult for one thing to see in logic alone any clearly infallible measure by which to determine what for these purposes was to be counted as a particular. Of course, part at least of Hare's purpose was clear enough. He wished to rule out of evaluative court all such judgements as 'You ought to do X—even though I, who may be in effectively the same position, have no such obligation.' Here it is obvious what sort of particular is being vetoed. But at this point one may become uneasy about the substance of the doctrine; in particular, if one wants to retain the reverse logical possibility of recognizing obligations for oneself without having therefore to impose them as obligations on anybody else, even somebody who may appear to be in the same sort of situation as oneself; but in general because it becomes a little hard to distinguish between universalizability as a logical thesis and the thesis of universality as a moral standard.[8]

In general, then, I was uneasily impressed by the way in which this *prima facie* purely analytic study of a particular area of language appeared somehow to embody a characteristic 'evaluative' or 'ideological' position. For Hare, it seemed, a man's readiness to act and to prescribe the same courses of action for others are, in the last resort, the necessary criteria both of the values in which he believes and even perhaps in a sense of what he himself is. But one may call this position 'evaluative' only as long as one is careful to put the word between inverted commas; for whatever sense may be intended, it could scarcely be one that Hare himself would have recognized. There was no principle of choice here involved between what he might have seen as possible alternatives; he was simply engaged in the conceptual analysis of what it is to make judgements of value. It could well be argued, moreover, that empiricist theories of meaning can only permit the preservation of the obviously to be preserved contrast between what one says and what one really believes, by referring the latter to the test of action in principle observable and distinct from the statements comprised in the former. So what one has here is perhaps not so much a chosen standpoint of evaluation as a framework of understanding of human character and belief; but which, so it seemed to me, could not fairly be called neutral as against other frameworks in which human beings would be differently understood.

In spite of these doubts, however, I myself continued to take the central question to be one of the exact nature and import of the distinction between value and fact rather than whether there was necessarily any such general distinction to be drawn; for this I continued to take confidently for granted. But this problem was not simply one of how best to characterize evaluative as opposed

[8] On this and related topics see, also, SINGER.

to non-evaluative judgements—room though there was for debate over Hare's concept of evaluation. It was also, as we have seen, one of the precise nature of the logical relations that might or might not hold between them. And here the notions of 'contextual implication' and 'logical oddness', as put forward by P. H. Nowell-Smith in 1954 [Nowell-Smith (1)], offered a noteworthy alternative to those both of 'entailment' and of 'evaluative inference'.

To recapitulate briefly: When Hare maintained that value judgements are logically underivable from non-evaluative premises, he meant that there can be no relations of entailment between them; and of entailment he said that 'for my present purposes it may be defined accurately enough as follows: A sentence P entails a sentence Q if, and only if, the fact that a person assents to P but dissents from Q is a sufficient criterion for saying that he has misunderstood one or other of the sentences.' This, as Hare himself puts it, makes of 'entailed' a strong word; the contrast with Toulmin's 'evaluative inference' is clear enough. Entailments spring from the meanings of words, evaluative inferences from the existence of generally accepted codes of social harmony and happiness. But if the contrast seems sharp at first sight, the introduction of 'contextual implication' may serve to soften it once more.

Nowell-Smith's own original version of this concept is as a matter of fact unsatisfactory in various respects.[9] But whatever the details it did embody the recognition that words and phrases are often linked with each other by rules of usage or of meaning to which there may, nevertheless, be permitted certain types of exceptions. It may be odd of someone to say that he enjoys smearing treacle on his books; even so, his meaning is clear, the oddness lies simply in his taste and in his readiness to give it public expression. But if he claims that he is glad to do things that he dislikes doing, he says something that needs further interpretation if it is to be fully intelligible. The oddness is no longer a mere eccentricity of taste or behaviour; there is a *prima facie* clash of meaning between 'being glad' and 'disliking'. Not that the clash amounts to an actual contradiction, for there may well be contexts in which the apparent paradox has a perfectly

[9] For a much more recent and considerably revised discussion of the same topic, see Nowell-Smith (2).

meaningful point; e.g. 'When they are for your sake, I am glad to do things that I dislike doing.' But one can say that the oddness of the original, as yet unexplained remark is 'logical' in that it arises from the meanings of the crucial terms therein juxtaposed. Conversely, one cannot say that 'I am glad to do X' entails 'I don't dislike doing X', as one could if there were an outright contradiction between 'I am glad to do X' and 'I dislike doing X'. So one says less stringently that the one contextually implies the other, which is to say that anyone is entitled by the rules of customary meaning to assume the second from the first unless he has been given some specific indication to the contrary.

But now, when the point was put, there seemed little doubt that while entailment may be the appropriate relation for systems whose terms are governed by rules of strict or formal definition, contextual implication is for most purposes more suitable to the informalities of the languages in which we all normally talk and think. (To talk in terms of contextual implication, moreover, still allows recognition of such invariant commitments as may be found among the terms of ordinary, non-formal language; for contextual implications that turn out to hold for all contexts come to the same thing as entailments.) This conclusion seemed likely, however, to raise some difficulty for the would-be strict autonomist. The trouble as I saw it was that 'in the informal logic of everyday speech . . . there is no difficulty at all in moving from (conjunctions of) statements of facts such as "He is a kind man, honest, generous and hard-working, etc." to judgements of value such as "He is a good man".' For how does one decide whether a contextual implication holds or not? Only, presumably, by finding out how people react to conjunctions of assertions and judgements such as the above. If they find them hard to *understand* (as opposed to hard to *believe*) without further special explanation, then one must say that they are related by a contextual implication. But 'the ordinary man would surely be just as baffled by . . . a sentence such as "X is unkind, unhelpful, dishonest, etc., but is a good man" as he would be by "Y cannot bowl, does not know how to bat or wicket-keep, and is a clumsy fielder, but is a good cricketer." '[10]

These difficulties were enough to convince me, not indeed of the untenability of any clear-cut distinction between value judge-

---

[10] I take these extracts from an article published in 1958 by R. F. Atkinson and myself. (See ATKINSON and MONTEFIORE.)

ments and statements of fact, but certainly that it could be neither discovered nor preserved by any mere inspection and report of the state of natural languages. On the contrary, I was now inclined to suggest 'that there was in the end no substitute for the simple recognition that to record on the one hand and to approve or disapprove on the other were two irreducibly different ways of approaching the facts' [MONTEFIORE (1), Ch. 13]. Once given this recognition it should, I thought, be possible to show that not only was the only sort of description or record from which value judgements could strictly be derived one in which some element of approval or disapproval was already implicit; but also that it would always be possible in principle to eliminate such evaluative elements by the simple expedient of an explicit disavowal of the approval or disapproval which might otherwise be contextually implied. (For example: To say of someone that he had cheated might normally convey disapproval; but to say 'He cheated, but I neither approve nor disapprove of him for that' would be to limit oneself to an explicitly neutral report.) Not that I supposed that everyone did regularly and systematically recognize this distinction, nor that it was already embodied as an explicitly necessary principle in every possible language. But I did try to argue that it was one whose general application virtually everyone could be *brought* to recognize, in virtue of the fact that everyone, or virtually everyone, must already know by his own experience what it was to be favourably or unfavourably inclined towards some state of affairs or other.

This was all very well. But there was no denying that there remained many difficulties in this position. It is never wholly satisfactory to find oneself with no resource but to appeal to people to examine their personal experience to see if they do not there recognize what one claims to recognize in one's own; and it is easy to understand the philosopher who prefers to draw their attention to the plain, public facts of the ways in which they speak. In this case one further obvious objection was that the notions of approval and disapproval were far too indefinite and vague to take the full weight of the distinction between value and fact. They called indeed for a good deal of further analysis.

Neither approval nor evaluation had in my view anything very much to do with the entailment of imperatives; nor was I tempted by Hare's full-scale thesis of universalizability. But I did rely very

189

heavily on a thesis of partial universalizability, claiming (or stipulating) that it was at least one defining characteristic of approvals when interpreted as evaluative that they should be based on reasons. I pointed out, too, that 'value judgements are, or claim to be, detached from personal interests and feelings in a way in which likes and dislikes very obviously are not' [MONTEFIORE (1), Ch. 10]; and hoped in this way to mark off 'genuine' value judgements from mere assertions or expressions of liking. All the same I had to admit that this was no sharp dichotomy, but a matter of more or less.

> Many likes and dislikes are in fact supported by reasons, and some people's principles of evaluation have no application to any but their own actions and efforts. Moreover, the fact that likings and approvals are both generally to be understood not as single experiences of some pure and uniquely identifiable type, but rather as dispositions to feel and behave in a variety of more or less loosely related ways, makes it even more impossible to draw one sharp boundary line between them. [Ib., Ch. 10]

There were, of course, other difficulties, of only some of which I was then aware. But of these perhaps the most notable was the fact that, as I then put it, 'in some contexts alternative ways of recording what is believed to be the case, may be inextricably linked with different general attitudes or world-views' [Ib., Ch. 13]. Here once again was the problem that had seemed to emerge from *The Language of Morals*, the problem of an 'evaluative' or 'ideological' position so embedded within the framework of a language that it may perhaps resist even the most emphatic and explicit of disavowals.

At the time I still thought that I could deal with this difficulty adequately enough—though I was working only with one or two highly sketchy examples. There was, for one instance, the problem of how one might wish to describe the circumstances of a strike in a capitalist economy. If a Marxist formulates his description in terms of class struggle and so on, the 'liberal' will protest at the intrusion of unnecessary and tendentious theorizing; for the Marxist, the liberal's own more 'straightforwardly factual' account could be equally tendentious in what it left out. But why not just stick to the fact that certain workers were on strike, leaving the theory of class struggle, if one wants it, to the further context of explanation? The trouble is that there is no convenient dividing line between description and explanation, the latter depending on an appropriate formulation of the former within the same family theoretical framework. Of course, the Marxist and the liberal can agree on whether and for how long there was a strike, their languages overlap, they live after all in the same world. But this the Marxist cannot count even as a full description of the circumstances. Not that the existence of alternative theoretical descriptions itself necessarily involves parallel alternative attitudes of approval or disapproval; but in this instance, where one description assumes the absence and the other the existence of some fundamental conflict of interests, the choice of terms may willy-nilly commit one to an at least indirect support of or opposition to one side or the other.

To meet this difficulty I tried to argue that the notion of a neutral statement—one that would be equally compatible with any explicit expression of being either for or against the facts which the statement claimed to report—only made sense from within any given system of concepts and not as between one system and another. Thus anyone, Marxists included, might be brought to acknowledge the difference between approving and reporting and hence to an admission of the autonomy of value judgements. Even though his statements of fact might be framed within the language of Marxism and, therefore, in a sense unneutral with respect to the language and outlook of liberals, he could obviously appreciate—would indeed wish to stress—that their evaluation of social situations might be very different from his. Nor need this kind of non-neutrality of descriptive language mean that there will be some specifiable statement of fact from which a value judgement might be derived as a matter of entailment. For if the value judgement is formed from within the same set of concepts as that to which the factual statement belongs, then the value/fact dichotomy applies with all its force; while if the judgement is formed from without, there can be equally little case for any entailment between it and any statement of fact within the system which it may be about.

All this was, of course, not so much an argument as a suggestion for one. It was one thing, however, to sketch suggestions and another to see just how they might be further worked out, and here I was admittedly more hopeful than certain as to how to proceed. Meanwhile there was another aspect of the problem that called for attention; namely, the possibility that might seem to exist of bridging the gap between reporting and approving via the so-called functional words.

Functional words so-called are, in fact, perhaps miscalled. They come in many and quite widely differing types; and it might be better to speak of criteria-setting words, of which functional words proper could form a mere sub-class. However, this question of entitlement is of no great importance in itself, and functional words may very roughly be characterized as those whose meaning ing includes a reference to what the objects or persons in question are for or to what they are supposed to do. I have inherited an old paper-knife inscribed with the motto 'Every tool, if it does that for which it has been made, is well'. Most people might agree that this assertion can be taken as analytic. It would follow that any other assertion obtained by substituting the name of a particular tool for the general term would also be analytic. The following argument could thereupon be set up:

(i) Augers are for boring holes.	(Analytic)
(ii) If an auger does that for which it has been made, it is well.	(Analytic)
(iii) This object is an auger.	(Factual)
(iv) This object bores holes.	(Factual)

Therefore

(v) This object, being an auger, is well.	(Apparent value judgement)

In other words, we appear to be committed by our recognition and understanding of the facts that the object is an auger and that it bores holes to (some degree of) approval of it as the sort of object that it is. Which commitment could, needless to say, be highly embarrassing for anyone determined to refuse any fully committing passage from (statement of) fact to (judgement of) value.

Hare had, in fact, already had a look at this problem both in *The Language of Morals* (from which comes the example of an auger) and in a subsequent paper, HARE (2), written in answer to P. T. Geach's earlier 'Good and Evil' [GEACH (2)], in which Geach tried to show that to say that something was good, was less to commend it than to describe it as being of a certain kind. (Geach is among those philosophers whose attack on the doctrine of Autonomy owes much to Aristotelian and in some cases to more specifically Thomist influences.) Hare himself was unworried by the apparent commitment, taking the line that a word such as 'auger' already includes as part of its meaning a reference to an end which the object is intended to serve, and hence to a standard or viewpoint from which it is to be judged. On this view the premise 'This is an auger' would thus be partly evaluative, presenting a criterion according to which augers are to be graded. The evaluative conclusion to the argument would, therefore, be in order after all.

All the same, there remained many unclarities. Of these the most immediately puzzling seemed to be the question of the exact nature of the end to which reference was made in 'This is an auger', and, if *this* statement was partly evaluative, how one might then state all the facts without such evaluative reference as might commit one to approval or disapproval.

A first temptation might be to try and eliminate the idiomatic complexities of functional words by replacing 'This is an auger' by a conjunction of the pattern 'This is an object of a certain characteristic physical description and has been made for boring holes'. Here the reference to end and associated standard has been clearly separated out. It still appears, it is true, as a matter of fact, the fact that the object had been made for boring holes. But now it seems possible to argue that any value judgement that may be implied, could be so only contextually. For suppose that someone says, 'I made this object for the purpose of boring holes and, as it turns out, it will (or won't) do what I meant it to do; it is therefore all right (or no good).' There is a standpoint, certainly, from which his argument is conclusive enough, the standpoint of the speaker's creative intentions; and no doubt that this standpoint would normally be implied through the context. But no one can be finally committed through his recognition of an object's functional origin to making his own evaluation from this particular standpoint. The value judgement is in other words in the nature of a hypothetical, dependent on the adoption of a standpoint which anyone is free to adopt or to reject. It is not one into which he can be forced by the facts of what the object's creator happened to have in mind at the time of its creation; not even, when one comes to think of it, if the creator was himself at some time in the past.

But this argument, whatever its force, has after all no direct application to the case of functional words; for one cannot, in fact, accept 'This is an object of a certain characteristic physical description and has been made for boring holes' as an equivalence for 'This is an auger.' It is not impossible, for instance, that a craftsman should make an auger intending it in this particular case for ornamental purposes or as an effective and yet unsuspicious instrument for stabbing his wife. It may be that the statement that it is an auger contextually implies that the man who made it, intended it for boring holes; but there is no entailment. It is not even impossible that no one actually concerned in the physical shaping of augers should have any idea or concern about what they might be for; while those responsible for the production setup might care only about their real hole-boring capacity in so far as this was a necessary condition of their effective sale—which in the short run and under conditions of high pressure advertising might not be very far. It may be true by definition that augers are for boring holes, but there is no *a priori* way of pinning the intention so to design or to use them on to any specific set of persons. We may say rather that their's is a socially determined function. And this being so, we seem forced to ask again whether the individual has the same logical freedom to reject the evaluative standpoint built into the common meaning of the term 'auger' as he apparently had to reject that of the individual creator of some individually determined object.

Among philosophers with an especial interest in functional or criteria-setting terms, Mrs Philippa Foot is a leading example of those whose way of dealing with them differs wholly from that of Hare—against whom, indeed, a great deal of her argumentation is directed [FOOT (1–4)]. She is not, in fact, prepared to argue her case in terms of 'value judgements' at all, claiming not to understand a term which she regards as essentially a technical invention. Her argument is couched rather in terms of what is good or bad, right or wrong, just or unjust and so on. Thus, she makes use of various criteria-setting terms to show that it would in general be absurd to pretend to individual freedom to choose what a person or object was to be like if he or it was to be good or bad. No one, for example, could say 'that a good knife was one which rusted quickly, defending his use of the word "good" by showing that he picked out such knives for his own use' [FOOT (4)]. But although she makes great use of criteria-setting terms by way of illustration her thesis has in fact a much wider scope. No one presumably would say that coal was to be defined in terms of its functions; yet, Mrs Foot argues in another example, the uses of coal in our society being what they are, it is a matter of common fact rather than of individual choice whether any given load of it is good or not. And in general she is prepared to argue that individual choice is virtually never either a necessary or a sufficient condition of the goodness of objects, persons or of states of affairs.

One of the most interesting things here is to see how much manoeuvring may be needed before Mrs Foot and an autonomist like Hare can be got to line up squarely in face of each other. For no one is called upon to deny that what may count as a good X is largely or even wholly determined by common understanding for a very wide range of X's. The question for such an autonomist is rather how far such assessments are evaluative. Hence it is to him of crucial importance to distinguish the properly evaluative from the merely descriptive uses of words such as 'good', a distinction for which Mrs Foot can find no intelligible ground. She, however, concedes that 'sometimes a particular man's interests determine what is good or bad' in the sense that they determine what is 'good for his purposes'; and though she at once adds that 'given his purposes, and in general his interests, it is a plain matter of fact that particular As will be good *for his purposes*, or *from his point of view*' [FOOT (4)], this particular restriction need cause no serious worry to an autonomist, except perhaps as to the minor matter of its formulation. But this being so, one may begin to wonder why they fight so sternly with each other. For could one not settle the dispute on purely terminological lines—with the autonomist marking out as evaluative uses of 'good' some such sub-class as might be interpreted 'good from the speaker's viewpoint' (or, if this might be misleading, 'good in the speaker's view'), and Mrs Foot sticking to her preference for not introducing this particular distinction or label?

It is indeed possible that some such compromise might be worked out. At the same time we need to be clear as to the issues at stake. No one need excite himself over coal or augers for their own sake. We could all comfortably agree that while private interests may differ, meaning and facts together place pretty tight limits on what would commonly be recognized as the goodness or badness of such commodities or tools; and if philosophers like to argue over the interpretation of this situation in terms of evaluation, what matter? But shall we say that the question of whether the value of our conduct as parents or children, employers or employees, lovers, artists or citizens is similarly determinate, is in the same way a mere matter of technical terminology? Yet this is what would be implied unless some relevantly sharp line could be drawn between examples such as those of augers and coal and those of the sort apparently more relevant to morals.

Can such a line be drawn? It hardly needs saying that this is in itself a highly controversial question. There are those who claim, for instance, that one crucial difference between men and augers lies in the fact that while augers, if bad enough, tend to drop out of the class altogether, men, however deplorable, remain obstinately men. There is some truth in this. If an object, whatever its shape, were so soft or so brittle as to render it fundamentally useless for boring any sort of hole in any sort of material at all, then we should presumably be as unwilling to call it an auger as we should be to call coal something that was not, say, 40 per cent but 98 per cent stone. But men of ultimate badness do not seem to be peculiar in remaining themselves. When sight gets so bad as to disappear altogether, then no doubt it is no longer sight; but can a bad eye so degenerate out of its class? Or a book? Or the weather? Or apples? It all seems to depend on whether there is any connection between the characteristics that make for bad quality and those that make for bad instance. But whether the presence or absence of this connection can be correlated with any other major distinction is by no means so clear. Nor, indeed, is it so clear what the force of such a correlation would be, if it could be established. Friends who are sufficiently bad can hardly be counted as friends; yet many people might feel that to judge the quality of a man's friendship is to make some moral judgement of the man himself. The worst of apples are apples; but this is not to say that there are no commonly determined criteria for their goodness or badness. In short, while none of this shows (or could show) that there are not many fundamental differences between augers and men, it may be very hard to discover any crucial differences of structure between arguments as to the value of citizens or even men and arguments as to the value of augers or coal.

(It must not be supposed, however, that the question—still an open one—of the structure of argument in cases of moral and non-moral evaluation, is the same as that of the relations between moral judgements and value judgements. It has to be admitted that there has been a persistent tendency in much recent discussion to slip backwards and forwards from talk about moral judgements to talk about value judgements as if the two came to the same thing—while yet relying in other and sometimes adjoining contexts on a distinction between the two. Hare at times provides an example of such indecision.)

This brings us back to the question of what, if anything, hangs on the particular terminology of evaluation other than the use of the terminology itself. It seems to me now that something very important is at stake. If the autonomist is ready to concede that what counts as a good X may be largely or even wholly determined for a very wide range of X's, this is only because he can regard himself as uncommitted by the use for conventional description of generally accepted standards to any genuinely evaluative commendation of his own. The anti-autonomist, on the other hand, does not insist on the irrelevance of personal choice to the goodness or badness of X's merely in order to establish a point about the idiom of neutral description. For him, to say that something is good is typically to say that it is worthy of approval (from whatever the standpoint from which it is being considered); and to say this is in effect for the speaker to approve of it himself.[11]

So what this seems to come to is that the doctrine of the logical incommensurability of value and fact is associated with a certain thorough-going individualism and anti-authoritarianism. This, for most autonomists, is something that goes very much beyond the defence of the (admittedly logically impregnable) autonomy of personal taste. For to approve of X is, as we have seen, not necessarily the same thing as to like it. If it were, there would be no problem; for no one pretends that statements or expressions of liking might actually be entailed by any other set of statements (even functionally) descriptive of the X concerned. (It may be that

[11] For an interesting discussion of related points see SEARLE.

the old style reduction of approval to liking is in the last resort the only consistent way of preserving individual autonomy in matters of value. The only trouble is that it is not very plausible.) In contexts where the distinction is admitted, however, there seems clearly a sense in which an assertion of approval would normally make more important claims that a mere assertion of liking. Its connections with the idea of a reference to a standard, to principles or reasons, to independence of purely personal or momentary feelings, combine to lay claim to common acceptance or at the least to a deeper respect than would an expression of simple personal preference. And here the terminology of evaluation can be used to underline the distinction. The notion of approval, after all, though often standing in contrast, yet at other times comes idiomatically very close to that of liking. But though values have, certainly, been interpreted in a very wide diversity of ways—as conditioned by the long-term or consistent preferences or purposes as opposed to those of the changing moment, by those which are most general in scope, by those which are consecrated by religion, by those which pertain to society, to the nation, to the race, to the individual and much else besides, yet whatever the terms of the contrast, those purposes and standards are marked out as constitutive of values which are seen to have the greatest significance or importance.

If this is the line of distinction between values and simple personal preference, this can, of course, only reinforce the insistence of the extreme individualist that such commitments can never be determined by mere concomitance of fact. Preference may vary with the particularities of subjective feelings and attitudes, but value judgements must be based on principles of universal import. Likes and dislikes, moreover, may be treated as the outcome of causal conditioning, but value judgements spring from the decisions of free individuals. For if principles are to count as truly evaluative, the individual must make them his own by his own act of will. This freedom of evaluation—a freedom that has obvious affinities with that proclaimed by the logical autonomists' Continental existentialist cousins—raises, no doubt, a whole thicket of theoretical and perhaps practical difficulties; but it is at any rate invulnerable to external authority. Genuine evaluation can never be forced on the individual by the mere recognition of the facts of somebody else's views. Conversely, if a recognition of facts *were* ever to carry an entailed commitment to any sort of approval or evaluation, the individual would have lost his unconditioned freedom to determine his values on the basis of personal decision alone. The issues here at stake are *not* simply terminological.

They may not be simply; but terminological, nevertheless, they are also. Someone for whom values are essentially matters of free individual commitment, but for whom at the same time they are to be marked off from the idiosyncrasies of personal preference, will naturally frame for himself a language in which the whole network of evaluative concepts embodies and obeys these demands. (Though he could not, of course, start on or even envisage any such task did not the materials lie to hand in the familiar concepts of the language which he already speaks.) Possessed of such a language he will find some way of dealing with any and every situation; and since all that he understands of evaluation will be determined by the concepts with and within which he works, he can scarcely conceive how non-autonomists might be clear-headed and honest at one and the same time. But the non-autonomist will for his part enjoy similarly restrictive advantages. If Hare and Mrs Foot are really to take themselves and each other systematically and seriously, each will be *ipso facto* disabled from seeing how the other can actually mean the apparently preposterous things that he or she says.

How is one to characterize a situation in which outlook and language are so spun together in one conceptual thread. I am tempted to the notorious risk of the term 'ideological', if only because I cannot think of a better. As long ago as 1949 W. B. Gallie was arguing that 'the question "One morality or many?" is the most important question facing moral philosophy to-day' [GALLIE]. But there is clearly a sense in which one might acknowledge the existence of two or more fundamentally different moralities from within one and the same conceptual framework. Autonomists, in fact, maintain that different men may base their lives on radically different principles; the possibility is an integral part of their thesis. No confusion of language, no misunderstanding of perspective need be here involved. One man may opt for reward in proportion to contribution as the basis of justice, another may ignore contribution in distributing rewards according to need; their practical disagreement may be fundamental and systematic, while conceptually all is clear between them. If we have to settle on labels, we might here speak of a straightforward clash of moralities, where opponents use the same language to set forth their opposed standards and programmes. It is at any rate to be distinguished from the case, which I am trying to articulate, where the divergence is doubly obscure. Not only does it enter into the recesses of language; but since the alternative languages are each systematically applicable to every possible particular situation, there can be no specific course of action in which autonomists and non-autonomists are as such bound to collide. It is in their conceptions of the world that they differ, not necessarily in what they do in it. (Though it could doubtless be misleading to suggest that what they do is to be identified independently of the ways in which their actions might be conceived by themselves or others.)

So we may perhaps take the term 'ideological' to refer to the way in which certain perspectives on the world may be locked within systematically intermeshed nets of concepts; partly to distinguish this case from that of disagreements, however basic, from within the same conceptual family, and partly because the ramifications of such alignments may extend far beyond what may normally be thought of as morality. But Gallie was surely right to point out that ideological divisions of this sort may occur not only between social groups, but even within one and the same individual. This could happen in a fairly obvious way to people who happened to belong to more than one group and were thereby bilingual or biconceptual in the relevant way. But it could happen, too, to whole communities of people in any period of ideological transition; for different areas of thought will show differing degrees of resistance to such conceptual refocusing, while the boundaries between the areas may themselves be indefinite and shifting. Thus, a Hare and a Mrs Foot may both find support within the language of our internally unstable society. From an ideological starting-point firmly within one part of this chequered cultural field, either may extend their own systematical account of evaluation to all other adjoining areas. The less firmly anchored thinker, with his inherited muddle of conflicting presuppositions, is open to conviction by whichever gains his attention, precisely because in either case their presuppositions are already his.

For myself, I can now see that I have been dimly preoccupied with the sorts of problem here involved for longer than I realized at the time. There was already the discomforting impression that the apparently formal analysis of *The Language of Morals* yet contrived somehow to express a certain way of looking at life. But though this did lead me to the view that behind or within such concepts as 'sincerity', 'belief', 'evaluation' and, for those who are interested, 'sin', may lie sets of divergent presuppositions so systematically entwined with the concepts in which they find expression as to constitute what I now tend to see as another and overlapping case of 'ideological' divergence; still the 'ideological' aspect of the autonomy of values was much slower to emerge from beneath the edge of my horizon. In the article from which I quoted earlier I referred to the matter in a mere couple of lines; in the subsequent book there was no more than a speculative footnote. Indeed, I was there, in effect, working out my own version of the thesis of logical individualism. Small wonder, an opponent might say, that I was forced to such elaborate and perhaps only dubiously successful pains to distinguish 'liking' from 'approval'. For if approval as the basis of evaluation is to be accounted a purely individual affair, the two are indeed entangled with each other as variations on the same essential theme. It was only in the closer consideration of functional words that the problem became openly inescapable.

All the same, for me at least it remains depressingly obscure. There are, it now seems clear, many possible alternatives to the extreme individualist scheme. In a certain kind of religious framework, for example, God's purposes, wishes and commands might be marked out as having supreme evaluative status in virtue of his position as the Creator of all things. Or, again, such status might be given to the interests and purposes of the social group as a whole. But the hardest puzzles seem to arise when one asks how one might choose between one framework and another. How, in fact, can choice come into the matter at all? For it seems that to envisage a choice between frameworks of evaluation is in effect already to opt for the autonomist or individualist position—or rather perhaps to give expression to the fact that this is the position from which one looks out on the world. How can one claim to be equally aware of such alternative possibilities? And what would this awareness imply for one's own evaluative position? What becomes of my attempt at a definition of a 'neutral statement' and of the suggestion that neutrality must be sought within languages rather than between them, if in a radically functional language 'is' may entail 'ought' after all?

To those familiar with the sociology of knowledge, it may seem extraordinary that even a British moral philosopher should be so slow in working round to such questions. Perhaps it is. The fact, at any rate, is that writers such as Karl Mannheim (or, for that matter, such as Collingwood) have had but the slightest of impacts on contemporary British philosophy in general and on its moral philosophy in particular. In my own case a certain amateur interest in sociology and in Continental writing must have had its contributory influence.[12] But in the working of actual argument I have, rightly or wrongly, struggled out from my starting-points in my home context. It is worth noting, incidentally, in face of Gallie's view that 'the "logic of ethics" is . . . powerless to decide whether or not different languages, or for that matter any one language, can be used to express a number of different moralities', that I personally have been led to the problem precisely through an attempted study of this sort of 'logic'. In any case, it can hardly be said that sociologists have as yet provided the precise and detailed underpinning for the notion of an 'ideology' that is certainly needed. It does seem that the possibility of an individualist logic and ethic must depend on the availability somewhere in the language of non-functional categories of sufficient and appropriate generality, as well as on a general understanding that it at least makes sense to regard the individual as a supreme arbiter of values. But here too, as far as I know, the convincing details of such dependence remain to be worked out.

If this is the present position,[13] it would be pleasant to think of it as one of fruitful confusion; of the confusion, at any rate, one can be tolerably sure. My own immediate hunch is to pursue the

[12] It is always hard to identify particular influences. But I know that I have received much stimulus from the writings of Lucien Goldmann in France.

[13] Compare WOLLHEIM (1). Wollheim rightly points to S. Hampshire's *Thought and Action* [HAMPSHIRE (2)] as an outstanding example of a book which, while in the analytic tradition, nevertheless brings the celebrated gap between fact and value into fundamental question and the substance of discussion closer to some of that of the Continent. For a much more obviously Continentally and Hegelian flavoured work see FINDLAY (3); in being so flavoured, however, this work is inevitably less representative of movements in contemporary British philosophy.

elusive notion of 'neutrality'. Not, of course, that of some 'absolute' neutrality, a neutrality with respect to all possible viewpoints at once, for to this notion it no longer seems possible to attach any plausible sense; but rather a sense or senses of 'neutrality' which will depend in some way on the nature of the terms between which neutrality is sought. The trouble with hunches, unfortunately, is that they do not always come off.

9. THE ANTECEDENTS
OF ACTION

ALASDAIR MACINTYRE

I

WE are haunted by the ghosts of dead concepts. The trouble with ghosts is that they do not replace the living satisfactorily and yet do not leave us with an entirely vacant hearth either. One such dead concept is the concept of the will; its ghost is the philosophical theory that the line which can be drawn between what is a human action and what is a mere happening is such that actions cannot have causes in the way that happenings can. When I speak of the concept of the will I do not, of course, refer to pellucid colloquialisms as in 'Where there's a will there's a way' or 'a strong will'; I refer to the concept built up in post-mediaeval philosophical psychology—in Hobbes, in Hume and in Kant, for example.

The exercise of the will in Hobbes distinguishes human action from animal behaviour because it presupposes a capacity for deliberation. 'In deliberation, the last Appetite, or Aversion, immediately adhering to the action, or to the omission thereof, is what we call the WILL; the Act, (not the faculty), of *Willing*' [Hobbes, I, 6]. The exercise of the will in Hume distinguishes human action from muscular or nervous responses because it involves consciousness. 'I desire it may be observed, that, by the *will*, I mean nothing but the internal impression we feel, and are conscious of, when we knowingly give rise to any new motion of our body, or new perception of our mind' [Hume (1), II, iii, 1]. The exercise of the will in Kant marks out the human action from mere physical movement by making action movement in accordance with and in obedience to precepts or rules. 'Everything in nature works according to laws. Rational beings alone have the faculty of acting . . . according to principles, i.e. have a *will*' [KANT, Ch. II].

The concept of acts of will which emerges from these quotations is one according to which the will is a special kind of efficient cause, the necessary cause of any human action. To make an act of will is to make a conscious and rational decision. It is to embody a precept for action in an instruction to oneself. Saying to oneself 'So I will do such-and-such' sets one's limbs in motion. On occasion one may fail to set one's limbs in motion, just as any other cause may fail to operate if prior causes intervene. One's limbs are paralysed or shot away. The first step in explaining an action therefore is to assign a proximate cause to the action by pointing to a prior act of will. In Hobbes and Hume appetite or aversion inspire and inform such acts; in Kant the causal chains which terminate in inclination may always fail to operate because of the prior intervention of that uncaused cause, the autonomous rational will obeying its self-imposed categorical imperative.

This ancestry makes it less surprising that the concept of acts of will was later called upon to play opposite parts by different philosophers. In the mechanistic psychology which the utilitarians took over from Hartley all human actions are the determinate effects of prior causes, and in the causal chain the act of will is the immediate cause of the action. In some anti-determinist writers the will is the intervening cause which prevents human action being the mere outcome of events in the brain or the nervous system. So participants of both determinism and free-will invoke 'the will'. For both parties acts of will possess two characteristics which are used by later writers to attack their existence: they are events distinguishable from actions, always as a matter of contingent fact preceding them; and they are events necessarily connected with actions in that without them what followed would not be an action. It was in this way that H. A. Prichard, for example, wrote of acts of will (see various papers in PRICHARD). And it is in this way that his critics have written of them in order to cast doubt on their existence. But the point at which genuinely sharp criticism of the concept of the will began was not here; it was the dualism which the concept implied that first attracted hostile critical attention.

II

The doctrine of acts of will from Hume to Prichard was formulated by philosophers who accepted a dualist view of body and mind, and to this extent were true children of Descartes. This dualism may have been refuted by Hegel, but in England, until recently, Hegel and mystification were almost synonymous. The refutation of Cartesian dualism was therefore in England the work not of Hegel but of Professor Gilbert Ryle, a chapter of whose *The Concept of Mind* [RYLE (2)] is explicitly devoted to the will, but whose argument throughout the book is extremely relevant.

The central argument of *The Concept of Mind* is that the criteria for the application of those expressions which we use to describe mental activity are all criteria of success or failure in performance in the realm of overt behaviour, and that therefore we neither need nor have reason to postulate a realm of specifically mental acts above and behind such behaviour. Foremost among the reasons which have misled philosophers into supposing that there are such mental acts is a false view that those bodily movements which are to count as human actions must have a special sort of mental cause. The application of this doctrine to what I shall now call the traditional view of acts of will is obvious.

Ryle in *The Concept of Mind* does not (at least not usually) want to deny the occurrence of any of the familiar 'inner' events such as twinges or pains at one end of the scale or musings and interior monologues at the other. What he does want to deny is that these could have the characteristics which mental acts are alleged to have in the traditional doctrine. In the case of acts of will, Ryle argues that we cannot identify such acts (which he calls volitions) with 'such other familiar processes as that of resolving or making up our minds to do something' or setting ourselves to do something. For we know that there are many human actions which do not, in fact, follow on such familiar processes, without thereby ceasing to be human actions. But in the traditional doctrine any action springs from an act of will. Hence these familiar processes and events cannot be what the traditional doctrine wished to identify as such acts.

Moreover, and here we return to Ryle's central argument, when we describe actions by using such characteristic predicates as 'voluntary' or 'responsible' or 'done on purpose' or when we insist that such-and-such a movement was not an action ('He was pushed', 'He slipped'), we seek to establish the truth of our description by reference to properties of the overt performance. We never deem it logically appropriate to inquire as to the presence or absence of acts of will. But if the traditional doctrine were correct, this would be the appropriate and the only appropriate question.

Ryle himself seems to place great weight on another line of argument with which it is less easy to be happy.

> No one ever says such things as that at 10 a.m. he was occupied in willing this or that, or that he performed five quick and easy volitions and two slow and difficult volitions between midday and lunch-time ... Novelists describe the actions, remarks, gestures and grimaces, the daydreams, deliberations, qualms and embarrassments of their characters; but they never mention their volitions. They would not know what to say about them. [RYLE (2), Ch. 3]

This appeal to what 'no one ever says' or to what everybody does say is in itself ambiguous. It may simply be a way of underlining the point that actions can be adequately characterized in all possible ways without bringing in the notion of acts of will and that the occurrence of such acts is therefore an unnecessary hypothesis. But it suggests something else, in the form in which Ryle advances it, namely, treating ordinary non-philosophical modes of speech as canonical for philosophical analysis.

If this is the thesis, it may once again be construed in two ways. A weak and unobjectionable version of the thesis is simply that any distinctions marked in ordinary language are likely to point to differences which philosophers ignore at their peril. But there is a stronger version of the thesis which must appear much more disputable. This is the thesis that 'ordinary language is in order, just as it is' and that in the elucidation of what human action is, common speech is not merely a source of suggested distinctions, but provides us with hard criteria.

A quite different type of argument, which Ryle has used against what he takes to be mythological mental acts has been advanced by A. I. Melden, specifically against the occurrence of volitions [MELDEN (1), and (2), Ch. 5]. Melden argues that the concept of a volition involves an infinite and vicious regress. For, on the traditional view, to move my limbs I must first perform an act of will. But an act of will is itself an action which I perform. And every action has to be preceded by an act of will. So the performance of an act of will must itself be preceded by an act of will, and so proceed *ad infinitum*. So an infinite number of acts must precede any action and no action could ever be performed. This argument is clearly valid and effective, and, like Ryle, Melden supposes that whatever the traditional theorists were talking about when they spoke of acts of will, they were not speaking of our familiarly experienced making of resolutions, coming to decisions and so on. About this one might be faintly dubious, if one remembered what Hobbes and Hume and Kant actually said. But for the moment let us put these doubts on one side.

III

The act of will was presented as the cause of the human action. But if there are no acts of will, as Ryle and Melden argue, do actions lack causes? Or have they quite other causes than acts of will? The discussion which has followed on from attempts to answer these questions can only be fruitful if we distinguish carefully between three senses of 'cause', or at least between three ways in which causal questions can arise. There is first of all what is usually spoken of as Humean causality. This is the view of causality which springs from one of Hume's several and incompatible accounts and which was further developed by J. S. Mill. On this view one event is the cause of another, if and only if events of the former type have uniformly been observed to precede events of the latter type, and events of the latter type have uniformly been observed to follow events of the former type. The occurrence of the earlier event is both a necessary and a sufficient condition of the occurrence of the later event.

It is this concept of causality whose application has aroused controversy over determinism. If actions are the determined outcome of prior events, and presumably of prior physiological events, it has seemed difficult to draw a distinct line between an action and a mere reflex, and certainly difficult to draw the kind of distinction which would lead us to impute responsibility in one case and not in the other. It is, perhaps, because overtones of the determinist controversy lie in the background that discussions of the causality of actions have been directed so overwhelmingly towards Humean causality. But, in fact, no discussion could be carried to a successful conclusion unless it attended to at least two other senses or analyses.

One of these is the sense of 'cause' which is equivalent to 'necessary, but not necessarily sufficient, condition', a sense which is apparently rather than really simple. For very often when we speak of 'the' cause of an event, for instance at a coroner's court in assigning responsibility for an accident, we point to a condition, by itself necessary but not sufficient for the occurrence of the accident. We do so when events were in train such that without the condition in question being satisfied the event would not have occurred. Taken by itself the condition was necessary but not sufficient. Taken in conjunction with all the other prior events its satisfaction was sufficient to bring about the accident. So it is with the ice-patch on the otherwise safe road. The point to note here is that what is by itself only a necessary condition for the occurrence of an event can be used to bring about the event, or can be referred to in giving a causal explanation of the event provided only that we know when its addition to other conditions is sufficient to produce the event. But by referring to such an occurrence as a cause we do not commit ourselves either to a generalization of the form 'Whenever ice-patches occur there is an accident' or to one of the form 'There is never an accident unless there is an ice-patch', but only to one of the form 'Whenever such-and-such other conditions occur, then, if there is an ice-patch, there will be an accident.' The importance of generalizations of this type needs much more attention, but for the moment we should only note that the task of detecting necessary conditions as it leads up to this type of generalization is inseparable from the task of detecting sufficient conditions and thus of formulating generalizations of the Humean type.

The third sense of 'cause' or the third point about the sense of 'cause' is one that is not incompatible with, but required by the other two. This is the sense which was underlined by Professor H. L. A. Hart and Mr A. M. Honoré in *Causation and the Law* [HART–HONORÉ]. Here a cause is a lever, a means of producing some other event. There could be no well-established Humean generalizations unless we were able to interfere with the course of nature and so discover whether apparently uniform sequences were genuine ones or not. But the Hart–Honoré analysis brings out the importance for causality of the concept of what would have happened if the cause had not operated. All causal explanation presupposes a background of generalizations about what occurs in the absence of the cause. This is true both of cause understood in Hume's sense and of cause understood as necessary condition.

IV

This very inadequate sketch of causality is a necessary prelude to examining the two main attempts to show that actions cannot have causes, at least in the Humean sense. The first of these derives from an attempt to correct the assumption that the necessary and sufficient conditions of human action are to be found in prior physical events, an assumption which depends upon a companion assumption that human actions are in fact only extremely complex physical movements.

Against whom is this insistence directed? The answer is that a great deal of physiology and psychology has taken it for granted that this is correct. All attempts to explain human action by building cybernetic models assume that human actions are of the same kind as the movements of such models. The greatest of the behaviour theorists of modern psychology, Tolman and Hull, set themselves the explicit goal of explaining human actions as very complex exemplifications of fundamentally simple patterns of physical movement. Those philosophers who have tried to show the falsity of this have clearly wanted a concept or set of concepts which will perform the function that the traditional concept of the will performed. But they have moved in a quite different direction.

In an article which tries to show that Hobbes and Hull were both essentially pursuing the same goal of mechanical explanations of human action R. S. Peters and H. Tajfel [PETERS–TAJFEL] have pointed out that bodily movements cannot be the genus of which human actions are a species, because the same bodily movements can be used in performing quite different actions and the same action can be performed by means of quite different bodily movements. So these bodily movements which are employed in writing a man's name may be used in signing a cheque, or giving an autograph, or authorizing a representative. Equally, the same action of paying a debt may be performed by those

bodily movements involved in signing a cheque or by those involved in handing over coin. In other words, the criteria which
we imply in judging that two bodily movements are the same or
different are quite other than the criteria which we use in judging
that two actions are the same or different.

Actions then cannot be identified with bodily movements. But
while on the traditional view actions were bodily movements plus
something else, namely, an act of will, for the more recent view
this is equally incorrect and misleading. For to speak of human
actions is to speak at a different logical level from that at which we
speak of bodily movements. To call something an action is to
invite the application of a quite different set of predicates from
that which we invite if we call something a bodily movement. If I
say 'I moved my arm', I do not say either the same or more than I
say if I say 'My arm moved.' I bring what occurred under a different form of description. We can bring out this difference in a
number of ways. First, if we ask 'Why did your arm move?', we
invite a causal answer including perhaps a story about conditioned
reflexes and a story about muscles and nerves. If we ask 'Why did
you move your arm?', we invite a story about intentions and
purposes. Equally, if on being asked to explain a piece of behaviour I start to give an account in terms of muscular and nervous mechanisms, I thereby treat the behaviour as a piece of
physical movement and not as an action. If, on the other hand, I
talk about purposes, goals, desires, intentions or the like, I thereby
treat the behaviour as an action. Secondly, if I say 'I moved my
arm', then the question 'What reason did you have for doing
that?' is always in place, even if the answer is, 'I do not know why
I did it.' To say 'I do not know' here is not to say 'There is a
reason, but I am ignorant of it' (except in psychoanalytic contexts,
which demand special treatment). It is to say in effect 'I had no
reason, though I might have done.' And nobody can know my
reasons or lack of them, unless I tell or otherwise betray them.
Here I have special and unique authority. But when it is a case
where it is appropriate to say 'My arm just moved', I have no such
special authority in giving explanations. What is needed is not the
authority of the agent as to his own intentions and purposes but
the authority of the physiologist on matters concerning conditioned reflexes, nerves and muscles.

Thirdly, in the standard cases at least where I say 'I moved my arm', there is no room for the question 'How do you know?' The reason for this can be brought out as follows. The point of asking 'How do you know?' is to ask for the credentials of a claimant to knowledge in cases where the claimant to knowledge may be in either a better or worse position to back up his claim. 'Pegasus won the 3.30.' 'How do you know?' 'I was on the course', 'I saw it on television', 'My bookmaker told me', 'I saw it in a dream' are all possible answers—of quite different value. But where self-knowledge of my own present actions is concerned, there is no question of being in a better or worse position to know. And so there is no room for the question, 'How do you know what you are doing?' But there is room for the question 'How do you know?' where not actions but bodily movements are the subject of the inquiry. Usually, of course, the answer is very simple: 'How do you know your arm moved?' 'I felt it move.' But from a partially anaesthetized man, lying so that he could not see his arm, the answer 'I saw it in the mirror' would make sense. And so would any other answer which appealed to observation or inference. Whereas this type of answer would make no sense as a reply to the question: 'How do you know that you moved your arm?' (Indeed, this question, as I have already pointed out, lacks a sense except perhaps in some very special contexts. It does not follow that a man may not say 'I moved my arm' outside those contexts and be mistaken. Where the question 'How do you know?' lacks application there is still room for error.)

Fourthly, in cases where it is appropriate to say 'I moved my arm' rather than 'My arm moved' the future tense used before the event would express an intention, not a prediction, if used in the first person. Moreover, if it is appropriate to say of the event afterwards 'I moved my arm', then neither I nor anyone else could predict that I would move my arm except on the basis of a knowledge of my intentions. It does not however follow, as has sometimes been argued, that where an event is the object of my intention it cannot be the object of my prediction. What does follow is that the expression of my intention is never the expression of my prediction. But the expression of an intention and the expression of a prediction can be closely related; for if I express an intention, I license others to predict. Of course, whether they are wise to predict or not depends upon the evidence they possess as to how far I am usually faithful to my declared intentions. Now their beliefs (or their knowledge) on this point will be expressible upon occasion in the form of Humean generalizations. Moreover, I can acquire such knowledge about myself. A man may come to recognize his own reliability or unreliability. Consequently, even if it is psychologically out of the way, it is not conceptually odd for a man to say 'I fully intend to do it tomorrow, but I know how unreliable I am, and so perhaps you are right and I will fail to do it again tomorrow.' What is more, in the very framing of his intentions a man's self-knowledge and predictions about his own reliability inevitably come into play. Hence, in cases where it is appropriate to say 'I shall move my arm', prediction is dependent upon knowledge of intention, but intention need not be entirely divorced from prediction; nevertheless, prediction depends not at all on knowledge of intention where it is in place to say 'My arm will move'.

Fifthly, the point of distinguishing between 'My arm moved' and 'I moved my arm' is brought out very clearly in just those border-line cases where we are uncertain which to say. We are all familiar—from novels if not from experience—with cases where as we say the body seems to have taken control. In Sartre's novel *L'Age de Raison* the hero—no, the protagonist—Mathieu, intends to say to his mistress 'I love you' and finds himself saying 'I don't love you.' Do we describe this as something he said or as words (or perhaps sounds) that come out of his mouth? Is it action or bodily movement? How we answer the question in this particular context does not matter for our present purposes. What does matter is that we cannot evade asking it, that we cannot escape the distinction between action and bodily movement.

Yet what follows about causality? Only that if we are to look for the causes of human actions, then we shall be in conceptual error if we look in the direction of the causes of the physical movements involved in the performance of the actions. It does not follow that there is no direction in which it would be fruitful to search for antecedent events which might function as causes. What has suggested this further conclusion is the way in which the investigation of concepts very close to the concept of action, such as that of intention, has been carried through. Wittgenstein wrote: ' "I am not ashamed of what I did then, but of the intention which I had." And didn't the intention reside *also* in what I did . . .' [WITTGENSTEIN (4), Part I, para. 644]. Just because the intention resides *in* the action, it comes too close to it to play a causal role; nor could we say what the action was, apart from specifying the intention to at least some degree. An intention, unlike a cause, does not stand in an external, contingent relation to an action. When Miss G. E. M. Anscombe investigates the concept systematically in *Intention* [ANSCOMBE], the whole discussion moves away from any kind of explanation in terms of causality, a topic to which Miss Anscombe alludes only in rare passages. One, but only one, reason why this is so can be brought out by considering how either in the kind of case which Miss Anscombe would classify as one of 'mental causality' (I am startled by a noise and jump) or in the hard case where I make a decision and later act on it (with which Miss Anscombe does not deal) we should be missing the point if we looked for a Humean generalization to connect the noise and the jump or the decision and the action. I can know that I jumped because of the noise or that I acted because of the decision and know perfectly well that the generalizations 'Whenever there is a noise of that sort, I jump in this way' and 'Whenever I decide to do something, I do it', are false. Hence this kind of explanation of these actions at least must be in terms other than those of causality. Beginning from this point, the argument is sometimes generalized in the following way.

It is bodily movements which are to be causally explained and not human actions. Human actions are made intelligible by reference to intentions, purposes, decisions and desires. These do not function as causes. They do not function as causes for at least two distinct reasons. The first is that to say 'He did it because he intended so-and-so', or 'He did it because he decided to', or 'He did it because he wanted to' is in each case not necessarily to refer to two separately identifiable events, the doing on the one hand and the intending or desiring or deciding on the other. There may be cases where we first frame an intention, come to a decision or experience a desire and then act; but the concepts of intention, decision and desire are equally applicable where the action is itself the expression of intention, decision or desire and to refer to our intention, decision or desire in either explanation or justification of our action is not to refer to an antecedent event. But a cause must, so it is argued, always be a separate event from that which is its effect. So intentions, decisions and desires cannot be causes. Secondly, intentions, decisions and desires cannot be causes, for they are not causally but logically related to the relevant actions. How do I know that this intention relates to this action? Not by any observed correlation such as would be relevant in the case of causality. But because both intention and action are mine and the intention contained a description of the as yet unrealized action. The action is related to the intention as being what is described in the forming of the intention. 'I'll have another cigarette in ten minutes' time.' When I light up in ten minutes, I am faithful to my intention, but my intention has not made me light up.

Considerations such as these are invoked to support one of two theses. Either the weaker assertion is made which I have already described, that actions are to be explained in terms of intentions and kindred concepts and therefore, in so far as this is the case, they are not to be explained causally; or else the stronger assertion that causal explanations are out of court altogether so far as actions are concerned. Unfortunately, the most extended statement of this case [MELDEN (2)], is ambiguous to a certain extent. Melden says:

> What I shall be concerned to deny . . . is that the term 'cause' *when employed in these sciences* [sc. physics and physiology] is applicable to those matters which, familiarly and on a common-sense level, we cite in or derto explain action: the motives, desires, choices, decisions, etc., of human beings. I do not, of course, deny that there are appropriate senses of 'cause' which can be intelligibly employed in these cases. . . . [MELDEN (2), pp. 16–17]

And again he writes:

> Indeed, it must appear problematic at best that the physiological psychologist who purports to be attempting to explain human action is addressing himself to his ostensible subject matter. [MELDEN (2), p. 72]

While still later he says:

> Here [sc. in cases where I am predicting what someone whom I know will do] nothing is hidden; it is because I understand him, not because I am aware of events transpiring in some alleged mechanism of his mind or body, that I am able to say what he will do. [MELDEN (2), p. 208]

These quotations can lend themselves to an interpretation in which all that Melden claims is that to explain actions citing purposes, intentions, desires and the like is not to assign causes (in the Humean sense) or to another interpretation in which Melden is claiming that causal interpretations of human actions are ruled out of court altogether on conceptual grounds. The second quotation—apart from the fence-sitting use of 'it must appear problematic at best'—seems to ensure that the latter is meant, but what I will presently try to do is to show that while the latter thesis is certainly untenable, even on the former interpretation Melden's thesis needs amendment. Before that, however, an even more radical version of this view must be considered. It is more radical because it is more systematic. It arrives at the same conclusions as Melden's but it derives them from independent foundations. The best-known exposition of this point of view is Dr Friedrich Waismann's in 'Language Strata' [WAISMANN (2)]. Waismann wished to campaign against the view that language is unitary, all of a piece, that truth, rationality and meaningfulness are one and the same for every sort of statement. Against this he urged the notion of language as composed of different strata, each with its own criteria of truth and meaning. An expression may be ambiguous in that it can figure in different contexts in different strata, and so take on different meanings. With this thesis so far my present argument does not require me to raise any questions. But Waismann then, although he allows that there are relationships between strata, characterizes the ambiguity of the word 'action' in such a way as to exclude relationship between the stratum in which it is proper to speak of causes and that in which it is proper to speak of motives. It follows that anything which can be explained by reference to motives cannot be explained by reference to causes and *vice versa*.

In like manner we may say that each stratum has a logic of its own and that this logic determines the meaning of certain basic terms. In some respects this is obvious. Whether a melody is a sequence of air-vibrations, of a succession of musical notes, or a message of the composer, depends entirely on the way you describe it. Similarly, you may look at a game of chess, or on the pattern of a carpet from very different aspects and you will then see in them very different things. Notice how all these words—'melody', 'game of chess', etc.—take on a systematic ambiguity according to the language stratum in which you talk. The same applies to 'doing a sum', 'writing a letter' or to any action indeed. An action may be viewed as a series of movements caused by some physiological stimulus in the 'Only rats, no men' sense; or as something that has a purpose or meaning irrespective of the way its single links are produced. An action in the first sense is determined by causes, an action in the second sense by *motives* or *reasons*. It is generally believed that an action is determined both by causes and by motives. But if the causes determine the action, no room is left for motives, and if the motives determine the action, no room is left for causes. Either the system of causes is complete, then it is not possible to squeeze in a motive; or the system of motives is complete, then it is not possible to squeeze in a cause. 'Well now, do you believe that if you are writing a letter you are engaged in two different activities?' No; I mean that there are two different ways of looking at the thing; just as there are two different ways of looking at a sentence: as a series of noises produced by a human agent; or as a vehicle for thought. For a series of noises there may be causes but no reasons; for a series of words expressing thought there may be reasons, but no causes. What is understood is that the word 'action' has a systematic ambiguity. [WAISMANN (2), pp. 30–31]

V

What is at stake in these arguments? Not only philosophical clarity, but also the question of the nature of the human sciences. For if philosophical argument can show that actions cannot have causes, then a good deal of science is fatally confused, since scientists do in fact attempt to offer causal explanations of action. Some physiologists have, indeed, done us a disservice by offering explanations of reflexes and calling these explanations of action, but in more than one field there appear to be genuine, if tentative, causal explanations of action. I refer to criminology and also to the study of the effects of drugs. (The study of hypnosis is interesting, but raises special issues.)

Some changes in the chemistry of the body which are brought about by taking drugs correlate with highly specific alterations in behaviour. More than this, we can alter the way in which people behave by inducing such changes in body chemistry. These changes range from the medical use of insulin in highly artificial laboratory experiments to buying a man a drink. What is correlated with the chemical change is a type of action and not just a type of bodily movement. That is to say, the framing of intentions, deliberations, reflection on wishes and desires and the like all play their normal roles. It may be that in many cases the type of action which is produced by the chemical changes cannot be narrowly specified. That is, we can say that to give this type of man this type of drug will make him act more irritably or unscrupulously or excitably rather than specify in more detail what he will do. But in these cases we are none the less involved in explaining behaviour.

Again, in criminology the work that has shown that there is an hereditary element in criminality is much to the point. The key studies on inherited characteristics in human beings are those which compare the degree to which such characteristics are shared by two siblings in the case of monozygotic and dizygotic twins respectively, for it would seem an unassailable conclusion that a clearly higher concordance in cases of monozygotic twins would indicate an hereditary factor. This is how the existence of an hereditary factor in tuberculosis was established for a study in New York in 1943, for example, which showed a 62 per cent concordance in monozygotic twins and only an 18 per cent concordance in dizygotic, while one in London in 1957 showed a 30 per cent concordance in monozygotic and only a 13 per cent concordance in dizygotic. Now, in exactly the same way, an hereditary factor in adult criminality can be established. For on the basis of five studies we have a concordance with monozygotic twins of 68 per cent and one with dizygotic of only 35 per cent. I need to insist that what were studied here were criminal actions, and that the fact that nobody supposes that heredity is more than a partial (and perhaps not enormously important) explanation of criminality does not make this any the less a causal explanation. Nor, if it makes sense to use such figures to provide an explanation, could it make nonsense if the figures turned out to be different, to be, for example, 100 per cent in the case of monozygotic twins and 0 per cent in the case of dizygotic. This would make our explanation somewhat less partial.

What then are we to make of this situation in which some philosophers appear to assert that causal explanations of human action cannot be given, while some scientists assert that they have produced them? Can we safely treat the scientists as we would treat men who claimed to have invented a perpetual motion machine?

Or are the philosophers like the old lady at the zoo who looked at the giraffe and said 'It's impossible'?

VI

Let us begin with the most general form of the argument that actions cannot have causes, Waismann's. It is beyond the scope of this paper to question in general terms the widely influential, but profoundly misleading view of language contained in Waismann's paper. What one must note is that unless there were expressions and criteria which transcended the divisions between his language strata, he could not distinguish them in the way he does. He can, for instance, recognize, and has to recognize in order to specify the ambiguity of 'action' in the way he does, that certain movements caused by physiological stimuli use the movements which are the 'single links' of this particular action and of no other. So that we are able to say 'These movements' (one stratum of language) 'belong to this action' (a quite different stratum). It follows that statements are not necessarily confined to one particular logical order or type or stratum (however these are specified). And now we have to note that an expression that cannot be so confined is the word 'cause', and its logical kith and kin. For Waismann speaks of the bodily movement by which an action is 'produced'. And 'produce' is certainly a causal verb. Moreover, he speaks of a melody as though to speak of a sequence of air vibrations is to remain within one language stratum, but to speak of a succession of musical notes is to move to another. But clearly one cause, in a perfectly acceptable and unambiguous sense of 'cause', of a set of notes succeeding one another in a piece of music to which we are listening is precisely the sequence of air vibrations which the orchestra have produced. Without having read Waismann, we might well want to say that the notion of colour is of a different logical order from that of a wavelength of light. But we unhesitatingly explain alterations in colour as caused by changes in the wavelength of light. So that, although the notion of bodily movements may be of a different logical order from that of an action, it certainly cannot follow that the word 'cause' is restricted to the stratum to which 'bodily movement' belongs and denied to the stratum to which 'action' belongs.

If we then disallow Waismann's contentions, the arguments that actions cannot have causes are best dealt with not by denying the importance of the type of example to which such arguments appeal, but by considering counter-examples. The suggestion will be that all the ordinary senses of causality apply *in some cases* to human actions and that therefore the 'ordinary language' use of 'cause' in this connection is by no means as remote from Humean causality as some suggest. (For an 'ordinary language' use, consider 'The Minister, receiving the Woman at her father's or friend's hands, shall cause the Man with his right hand to take the Woman by her right hand . . .' (Book of Common Prayer, Form of Solemnization of Matrimony).)

The first example is of *giving a reason* or *affording a motive* as causes. I may discover that when you are in a certain frame of mind I can get you to act by giving you information which affords a motive or a reason. Your action bears testimony to the fact that it was this motive or reason on which you were acting (as returning a ring with a reproachful letter is testimony that the girl's motive arises from her information about the man's behaviour). Thus the connection between affording the motive and the action is not one of a Humean kind; we do not depend on a universal generalization, of whose truth we need to be assured in order to make the connection. Even if on another occasion affording the same kind of motive does not produce the same action, we should not have grounds for doubting what caused the girl to act in the way she did on the first occasion. And the word 'caused' is in place precisely because of our third sense of causality. Affording a motive or a reason is performing a separately identifiable and desirable act, the performance of which is a lever that produces as its effect an action. And it is quite compatible with the thesis that motives, reasons, decisions and intentions cannot be causes that affording motives, giving reasons, giving grounds for decisions and for framing intentions can be. Nor is this merely something that others can do to me; I can in deliberation do this to myself. (This is not to be committed to the view that deliberation is always conversation with oneself, but only to the view that it can on occasion be.)

Secondly, 'the' cause of an action may, like 'the' cause of an accident, be a necessary condition the satisfaction of which is with other circumstances sufficient to produce the action. An insult may not make me violent when I am sober; and when I am even mildly drunk I may be extremely pleasant except when and until I am insulted. So the insult plays in relation to the action the part that the icy patch on the road plays in relation to the accident.

Thirdly, we are already well on the way to formulating explanations of actions in terms of Humean causality. I am puzzled by why I become angry when playing cards. Both others and myself presently observe that it occurs five minutes after I have started to lose. This connection is uniformly observed to hold until I become aware of it. People who wish to make me angry have learned that I become angry and perform angry actions if they bring about my defeat at cards. This is a perfect case of Humean causality and nothing is affected if I change my behaviour on discovering its cause. For the generalization which needed to be discovered by observation was that 'Whenever I am losing at cards, and so long as I do not know what is going to happen to my behaviour as a result, I shortly after become angry.' Or it may be that I cannot alter my behaviour. Obviously, it does not follow that I am inevitably going to be angry; but if I wish to avoid angry behaviour then I must not lose at cards, and probably I must not play cards.

These examples only skim the topic of the causality of action. What they do show is the danger of any generalization of the form 'Actions cannot have causes' or even 'Actions cannot have Humean causes'. Such generalizations are necessarily as erroneous as were the generalizations of the eighteenth-century mechanists who thought of every action as caused. What we need is a much fuller characterization of the concept of the human person in which the role of both causes on the one hand and of motives, reasons and intentions on the other, will become clear. But about two distorting features of the discussion hitherto we can now perhaps become clear.

The first is that the dichotomy 'logical connection' or 'causal connection' is much too easy, here as elsewhere. Consider the kind of case where an insult always leads to taking offence. 'Every Celt when insulted uses whatever weapons lie to hand' can be the expression of a good Humean generalization (even if false). Now the description of the first action as 'an insult' and of the second as 'taking offence' brings them under descriptions which are conceptually and internally related. But the two events are separately identified and we can correlate them. We know what it would be for the causal generalization to be falsified by an insult not causing offence or offence being taken without insult. The root error here is to think of actions as standing in relationship to the agents' motives and reasons or to other agents' behaviour independently of the alternative forms of description under which behaviour can fall.

The second distorting factor is the fear of determinism. This perhaps springs from accepting a determinist view of the Hume–Mill concept of causality. But to show that an action is caused is not necessarily to show that it must have happened, that the agent could not alter what he did. For to assign a cause to a happening is to go some way to informing us both how to produce and how to inhibit the happening in question. It follows from this that to assign causal explanations to actions is not to show that the actions in question are inevitable and unalterable. Nor does it even follow that if the explanations in question are explanations of *my* actions, *I* cannot alter them. But it certainly does follow that the more I know about possible and actual causal explanations of my behaviour the more likely I am to be able to intervene successfully and control what I do. Free, responsible, controlled behaviour is then behaviour where I have at least the possibility of successful intervention (though this is to state only a necessary, and not a sufficient, condition for being entitled to characterize a piece of behaviour in this way).

This argument needs one addition. My freedom as an agent depends upon my ability to frame intentions which are capable of being implemented. This capability is dependent on the reliability of my beliefs about the world and about myself: it is not just that given motives, desires and intentions of a certain sort, I act. A presupposition of successful action is a knowledge of what I will do unless I intervene in various ways. So the concept of intention cannot be understood in isolation from the role of belief and knowledge in our behaviour. The way in which this is so is brought out most clearly by the argument of HAMPSHIRE (2), especially Ch. 3. Hampshire uses the distinction between intention and prediction in a much more illuminating way than it is used by those who are trying to separate action and causation. For, as I argued earlier, there is a positive connection between intention and prediction. Unless I am able to predict what will happen if I do and again what will happen if I do not frame a given intention,

I am in no position to frame intentions at all. Thus, what I can intend depends upon what I can predict, and the dependence of the concept of human action upon the concept of intention does not exclude the possibility of prediction based on causal explanation from the realm of human action, but actually depends upon that possibility. That others can predict my actions does not matter unless they are able to predict what these are, no matter what my intentions are. My freedom consists, as Hampshire has argued, not in my unpredictability but in my ability to form clear intentions *and* to implement them. And this freedom depends on my ability to intervene in causal sequences, including those which have resulted in parts of my own behaviour to date.

The mistake that we might make in conclusion would be to suppose that because my main argument has been an attack on the generalizations of others, nothing definitive follows from it. I followed through the attack on the doctrine of acts of will and showed that the corollary to its destruction was the need to elaborate a much more complex view of the person. But some very simple conceptual truths still need emphasis, and one of them at least belonged to the view of the will which Ryle and Melden attempted to destroy.

The exponents of the traditional doctrine of acts of will were clearly wrong to hold that every act of a rational agent is preceded by an act of will which is its cause. They took what they thought to be the paradigm case of rational action, deliberation leading to conscious decision which issues in action, and supposed that the characteristics of the paradigm case must hold in every case. But were they wrong in their characterization of the paradigm? Where I act without deliberation or on impulse, where I provide one of the cases which appear to Ryle and Melden to destroy the traditional doctrine, what makes me responsible for what I do? Or where causal explanations of my anger are in place, what, if anything, makes me responsible? Presumably, that I could, had I reason so to frame an intention, decide not to do what I in fact do, not to let my impulses have their way or not to be angry; that I could deliberate (the 'could' means here that it makes sense to speak of my deliberating; in many actual occasions I might have no time or opportunity to deliberate) and decide on some other course of action. In other words, that I could perform an act of will in the traditional sense. If we read Hobbes, Hume and Kant as characterizing not the necessary prerequisites for something to be classed as an action but as characterizing the type of action which one must be able to perform on occasion, the type of intervention, inhibiting one course of action or unleashing another, which one must be able to make on occasion if one is to be classed as a responsible and rational agent at all, then the arguments of Ryle and Melden become irrelevant. For acts of will are, as the traditional authors clearly state, the familiar and unassailable processes of resolving, deciding and intending, and not the mysterious and occult 'volitions' with which Ryle and Melden make so much play. There is nothing here with which novelists and ordinary agents are not familiar in their everyday transactions; and there is no requirement that every action shall be preceded by a volition, which may result in an infinite regress. There is only the requirement that we shall recognize that it is in virtue of what they can be and not of what they always are that men are called rational animals.

10. MARXISM AND EMPIRICISM

CHARLES TAYLOR

THE question to which I shall address myself in this paper is that of why Marxism and the Marxist tradition has had so little impact on Britain and British philosophy. Indeed, in any discussion of Marxism in Britain, this is the first question which comes to mind. Not only has Marxism been a minority phenomenon in working class movements, and even in working class socialist movements, but Marxism as an intellectual tradition has had very little importance on the British scene. This is all the more true if one restricts one's purview to the academic scene.

True, one period stands out as an exception to this, and that is the 1930s. In that decade, under the impact of the deep economic crisis, Fascism, and the threat of war, the Labour movement seemed to be evolving closer to Marxism in its ideological outlook; and, what is more immediately relevant to the subject of this article, there was an intellectual flowering of Marxism such as Britain had never seen. Intellectuals not only of the Communist Party but also of the Labour Party (such as Harold Laski) turned to it as to the key that would unlock the secret of their society's critical condition. These works went beyond analyses of the immediate political situation, such as for instance, the Labour thinker John Strachey's *The Coming Struggle for Power*. With such Communist intellectuals, as, e.g., Ralph Fox, and the brilliant Christopher Caudwell, we find the elaboration of a critique of bourgeois civilization as a whole in Marxist terms, as seen through its art, literature and ruling ideas. Caudwell's work particularly represented a real development of the basic ideas of Marxism, a reflection on man and his history which was more than a transcription into English of what was said elsewhere, but which constitutes a real addition to the international corpus of Marxist thought.

As is well known, Fox and Caudwell met a tragic and untimely death on the battlefields of Spain. But what is surprising, and in another way hardly less tragic, their thought went into eclipse only a few years later. In fact, the extraordinarily fruitful period of the 1930s proved to be not a beginning but an interlude in British intellectual history. The post-war period has seen a decline in the importance of Marxism, both intellectually and politically, to the *status quo* of the 1920s. As though, once the crisis was over, the British wanted to revert to their traditional paths.

This decline of Marxist thought in general in the country has precluded its effecting any serious penetration of the academic community. Of course, even at its apogee in the 1930s Marxism was not important in the academic world. This is, of course, not surprising. Many of the more important innovations in thought have had to be effected outside the conservative atmosphere of the university, in order to break their way in after they are too well established to be denied access any longer. The vivacity of Marxist thought in the thirties did lead to some beginnings of academic recognition, but then this narrow sphere of influence atrophied and declined as did its counterpart outside. To some considerable extent the identification of Marxist thought with academics who were members of the Communist Party constituted both a symptom and cause of this decline; it symbolized the isolation of Marxism in British university life and certainly contributed to the widespread discredit from which it suffered. Such thinkers as Maurice Cornforth in philosophy and Arnold Kettle in literature are largely ignored by their academic colleagues, and their Marxist analyses have always been suspect, the suspicion being that they were vitiated by an element of special pleading in favour of the strategy of a political party. The fact that these thinkers have often been required by their allegiance to the Party to engage in such special pleading, albeit outside the academic context, has not made their task easier within it. Of course, the rare non-Communist Marxist thinker, such as, e.g., the philosopher Alasdair MacIntyre, does not suffer from this disability. But it is interesting that the work which recommends him to his colleagues is not specifically Marxist, not that it is not connected to his basic

Marxist orientation but that it is of the kind that can be and is accepted by others from a quite different standpoint.

The one exception to this general isolation of the Marxist academic in the post-war period lies in the field of history. Marxist historical work was sufficiently important after the war to justify the founding of a review *Past and Present*. And the work done by Christopher Hill and others could not be ignored. The reason for this is perhaps to be found in the fact that history is a discipline into which Marxist ideas and a Marxist approach have already penetrated very deeply, so that there is not such a gap between a Marxist historian and his non-Marxist colleague as there would be, for instance, among philosophers. For this very reason, however, the influence of a specifically Marxist school of historiography is harder to assess, and with the break-up of the original group of Communist intellectuals around *Past and Present*, assessment becomes even more difficult.

This sketchy and very incomplete review of the position of Marxism in the British university should not, however, lead the reader to believe that the average British student of philosophy, history or social science never comes in contact with the thought of Karl Marx. On the contrary. In a sense interest in Marxism is very alive in British universities. How could it be otherwise when one-third of the world lives under régimes which proclaim themselves Marxist? Many students of political thought have written on this subject; to mention only a few, Berlin, Carew-Hunt, Plamenatz and Popper. But the characteristic of this writing is that it represents a study of Marxism from the outside. At its worst, it so to speak takes the measure of an ideological enemy, and can even degenerate into Cold War polemics; but at its best, it can only approach the sympathetic and detached study normally accorded to Oriental religions. Marxism may be of burning interest for all sorts of reasons, but never because it might be *true*.

How to explain the relative absence of such an important stream of contemporary thought from the British scene? To explain in a full sense of the word would, of course, involve an historical and political study. This is beyond the scope of the present article as it is beyond the scope of the present writer. But one can still cast some light in the question if one takes it at a purely intellectual level, if one tries to examine why Marxism never found a congenial home in the British intellectual climate, if one tries to delineate the obstacles to its naturalization into the British republic of letters.

One could, of course, answer this question on a superficial level by repeating phrases that have become commonplaces. We could say, for instance, that the empirical temper of the British makes them shy away from any global explanations of life and history, such as Marxism claims to be, that it *ipso facto* makes all systems foreign to their way of thought. Like many commonplaces, this one contains an element of truth. But it is too crude for our purposes. For it is possible to reject Marxism as a global explanation, to have less than the degree of faith in it which an orthodox communist has, and yet to appreciate the importance and validity of its approach. And yet even this latter appreciation has been singularly absent in Britain. To illustrate the distinction, one might offer the comparison with Freudianism. Many believe that Freud's claims to explain human behaviour were too wide-ranging, but this has not prevented them from appreciating the fruitfulness of his basic ideas and from developing them further; and all in the spirit of the British 'empirical temper'. Why was the same courtesy never extended to Marx?

This may seem all the more surprising since this country was known at the turn of the century for the revival of Hegelian thought and the school of followers of Hegel which dominated its philosophical life. If Hegel, why not Marx? The answer is, of course, and this would be a good place to begin our analysis, that the Hegelian revival was itself only an interlude in a long tradition of philosophical empiricism. The movement began to be challenged by Russell at the turn of the century (not quite from an empiricist point of view, although Russell's epistemology has always been close to that of classical empiricism) and by Moore. In the 1930s and 1940s it was entirely swept aside by the loose-knit trend of thought known as linguistic analysis. This represented a return to an indigenous philosophical tradition, and a return which was also a reaction against Hegelianism. British philosophy since has tended not just to be non-Hegelian but to be anti-Hegelian. The form of its thought is such that it tends to find the whole language of Hegelianism meaningless, and therefore to find meaningless the language of Marxism as well. In this reaction against Hegelianism, which was a rediscovery and re-emphasis of certain parts of traditional British empiricism, we can find the obstacles to an easy acceptance of Marxism on to British intellectual soil. It is these, therefore, which we shall attempt to examine in the remainder of this article.

1. *Thought and Action*

The notion of 'obstacle' which we have introduced here is very difficult to elucidate without examples. What I am trying to drive at here is differences in the structure of thought, in ways in which fundamental concepts can be related, which make one way of thinking or school of philosophy quite opaque to another, which may make one seem to the other literally meaningless or at best confused. It would be best at this point to leave the realm of general description and look at the first example, the conception of thought and action.

One of the characteristic features of Marxist thought is its conception of thought and action and their relation to one another, a view which is, for instance, contained in the notion of *praxis*. For Marxists, the way men look at the world is conditioned by their activity in it, to such an extent that they would even claim that certain purely intellectual problems or philosophical problems cannot be solved until certain changes in the form of human activity have been achieved. Now there is much to question in this notion, and particularly in this latter claim, and there is no ground for surprise if many find difficulty with it. But with many British thinkers there has been an obstacle to its even receiving the consideration which most continental thinkers would agree was its due.

The essence of the Marxist notion seems to be that forms of activity are or include ways of looking at the world, that, to be more specific, different ways of economic life, of making and finding the means to life, incorporate different conceptual structures, different ways of classifying the environment and human life. Thus, the man of technological capitalist civilization has a different set of concepts than that of his ancestor or contemporary in feudal agricultural civilization. To say 'different set of concepts' is to say that the notions used to describe and account for certain ranges of reality in the language of one would have no counterpart in that of the other. Thus, the modern man's notion of the individual as the unit in society, his very notion of matter, these and many others would not correspond to their analogues in the speech of pre-modern men. These differences arise, according to Marxists, because of changes in the human condition over history. But, in Marxist terms, the human condition is defined at the most basic level by the forces of production (man's relation to nature) and the relations of production (man's relation to man); in other words, it is defined in terms of the type of economic activity which the conditions prevailing at the time make privileged. Man's condition is therefore defined for a given society by the way he deals with nature and the way he deals with his fellow man.

But man is a self-conscious being; he becomes conscious of his activity, and does so by elaborating a set of concepts by which he can account for the world around him and for his own life. But in each situation, that set of concepts will be developed which most adequately expresses the human condition, that is, the privileged forms of activity of the time. And since the latter changes through history, the former changes also.

Thus, in feudal society, the economy is based on subsistence agriculture. Now, for the subsistence farmer in a technologically primitive society, nature is a kind of partner; it is a living process which must be tended so that it may yield its fruit. Nature is seen as a source of activity, and the natural world tends to be thought of in teleological terms. In capitalist society, on the other hand, manufacture assumes greater and greater importance. But for the manufacturer, nature is simply a source of raw materials, it provides matter to be worked on and transformed; the natural world tends to be seen as 'dead matter', and the only source of activity is man himself.

To take another example, this time drawn from the field of social relations. The modern notion of the individual as prior in some sense to the society was bound to arise in our epoch because seeing oneself as an individual of this kind is a necessary part of the form of life of the entrepreneur in a régime of free enterprise. For the entrepreneur the rest of society is a set of individuals with whom he has to deal in such a way as to realize a profit, with whom he can enter into contractual relations or not depending on the advantage to be secured. Feudal society, on the other hand, where a man was held to a certain walk of life by status, and unfree to enter into new relations by contract, could never spawn such a notion. It would have been manifestly untrue to experience.

Essential to the Marxist notion, then, is the idea that forms of activity involve ways of looking at the world. Given this close link between the two, of course, it remains another question which is the dynamic factor, which is the lever of change, whether the form of activity, as Marxists think, or the manner of thought. This question which concerns human motivation is a crucial one to the Marxist theory of history. But before we can even pose this question we have to accept the conception of thought and action as being linked in the way mentioned above. And this is one of the obstacles as far as the British scene is concerned.

For this conception of thought and action is foreign to the re-discovered empiricist tradition. In order to make this point clearer we should refer back to traditional empiricism in the narrow sense, as a theory of knowledge. According to this theory the basis of human knowledge consists in the impressions received on the human mind from the outside world. This particular theory of knowledge was, of course, revived in this century with the return to the empiricist tradition. It has lost its popularity today. But it is still useful to refer back to it, because it is the cradle of a number of other views which have retained some currency, even when people have ceased to discuss the philosophical problems of perception in these terms.

For, on this view about knowledge, it is difficult to see what sense could be made of talk about different ways of seeing the world. In fact, if knowledge consists originally of impressions, then the type or form of impressions is fixed by human physiology or the nature of the human mind. They were generally thought to take the form of what was called in this century 'sense-data'. In any case, the form was the same for all people at all times. Our knowledge of the world, reflected in our talk about it, was entirely built up from our experience of such data, and their temporal and spatial relationships. All ways of looking at the world, or talking about it, must be reducible to one, that which designated the basic evidence, sense-data.

Or, to put the point in another way, any differences in outlook (i.e. conceptual differences, not just differences in the degree of knowledge) between men must arise from differences in the way the basic phenomena, alike the source of knowledge for all, were grouped. But since all concepts could be explicated in terms of a range of concepts designating the basic phenomena, all differences could be made completely transparent by giving the rule of translation for any language into the basic one. At once differences of conception become like differences of shorthand notation; they cannot be classified as more or less true, but only as more or less convenient.

The Marxist view, on the other hand, as implied in the thesis that men can only come to solve certain perennial intellectual problems through advances in *praxis*, that history is a progress towards truth, is that differences of conception are irreducible one to another. Indeed, the view that concepts dealing with global phenomena (e.g. societies, classes) can be explicated in concepts designating elements of these wholes (e.g. individuals) is itself an expression of a certain way of seeing the world, that which arises in bourgeois society, and is challenged in different ways, by the holistic conceptions of both feudal society (e.g. organic theories) and communism (e.g. theories of classes and history).

From an empiricist point of view, therefore, it is difficult to see what could be meant by talk about different ways of looking at the world, and *a fortiori* talk about the relation between these and forms of activity was bound to be opaque. But this latter was hard to understand for an additional reason which also arose out of the empiricist theory of knowledge. This theory essentially looked on knowledge as passive rather than active. Originally knowledge came through perception which was the reception of impressions on to the mind. This contrasts with an alternative theory of perception and knowledge, one which has mainly been put forward by idealist theories, to the effect that perception is a form of activity, that it essentially involves some structuring of the phenomena or interpretation. On this latter view, a way of looking at the world is a form of the perceiving or knowing activity which yields interpretations of a certain kind or structures the phenomena in a certain way. According to this conception therefore, since a way of looking at things is already a form of activity, it is more readily understandable how it could be linked with forms of economic and social activity. On the empiricist view, on the other hand, these forms of activity should have no effect on knowledge, unless it be a complex and indirect causal one, e.g. by making certain data less or more perceptible, the form of the data, however, remaining perennially the same.

In this way, the empiricist conception of the relation of thought to action, in which knowing is conceived as something quite distinct from activity, has made Marxism a closed book to many thinkers on the British scene, a doctrine which seemed too confused to be worthy of serious study. Concepts like *'praxis'* and 'ideology', which hang on the Marxian conception, could be given no clear meaning, and thus the main questions which Marxism was trying to answer couldn't be properly asked.

And this is not all. Other aspects of Marxist doctrine were affected in a similar way by the empiricist theory of knowledge. One of the key theses of Marxism is that human nature changes over history, that human motivation is not perennially the same, but that with the growth of consciousness, men seek new ends; their grosser needs become refined. Now empiricist theories have generally held that human motivation is always the same. Following the view that the mind is a bundle of impressions, they have seen motivation as arising from the fact that some of these are pleasant and others painful. Men seek to attain the first and avoid the second. Human beings are therefore always directed towards the same end. The progress of knowledge, by teaching man more about the rules governing natural events, makes him more capable in the search for pleasure, but it does not alter his goal. Once again the view is that thought and desire, just as it was the case above with thought and action, are to be clearly separated from one another, so that a change in one has no effect on the other. The result is that the Marxist discussion about the historical change of human nature becomes well-nigh incomprehensible.

2. *Holism and Historicism*

With this question of historical change, we come up against another set of obstacles to a discussion of the Marxist view of society and history created by the climate of empiricism. These, which are even more formidable than the ones discussed so far, relate to two central and related aspects of Marxist thought, its holism and its historicism. An examination of the first, which we shall now undertake, will lead us eventually to the second.

The problem of Marxist holism is this: Historical Materialism accounts for the course of history in terms of the interests and needs of classes and societies, in other words of human collectivities. The account is maintained even if there are no discernible individuals who have acted to affect the course of events with the needs and interests of the class concerned in mind. Marxism seems to speak, therefore, of a collective intention or purpose, where there is no corresponding individual intention or purpose. And this has always been a source of great perplexity among thinkers in Britain.

The sources of this misunderstanding go very deep into the two patterns of thought. Empiricism has always tended to be atomist in its leanings, and the temper has usually been inclined to account for social events in terms of a total of individual actions. Marxism insists on the contrary on certain global features and on the importance of structure in determining the course of a society's history. In part, the roots of this difference lie in what has been discussed above. If one accepts the importance of the way an individual looks at the world in determining his behaviour, and if one relates, as Marxism does, the social structure of a society and the outlook of its members, then one can readily see how certain global facts, such as the relations between classes, can be of decisive importance for the behaviour of the individuals and hence the course of events in the society. The chain linking social structure to individual action does not even require that the individuals have a clear conception of what is at stake. For instance, in the example cited in the preceding section, the entrepreneur may defend the régime of free enterprise, not because he has clearly realized that this is in his interest, but because the way of looking at things which goes along with his form of activity makes any other, more collective, mode of organization of society seem absurd and unrealizable. And yet it would not be stretching things to account for his behaviour, and that of his fellows, as a defence of this class's vital interest.

If this were all, the point would not have created the difficulty for non-Marxists which it has. But it is not all. It is one thing to say that, given a certain class structure, individuals will tend to act in a certain way, it is another thing to say that a certain type of class structure had to arise in order to fulfil a certain type of historical role. And yet Marxists do often talk in this second way, as though history takes the course that it does by some necessity. But then the problem of holism arises in a more acute form. For an explanation in terms of an historical role is a teleological explanation, and seems to imply a directing mind fitting the events of history as means to the end which is its consummation. For Hegelianism, with its notion of a world spirit, this concept of a directing mind was perfectly possible, but it is difficult to see what sense it can be given once this notion is abandoned. For then the subject of history remains simply the human race. But how can something be an action of the human race, and thus be in the realm of human action and be explicable on teleological grounds, when it is not the action of any individuals?

The question can be posed in another form. The events and changes in history are the result of myriads of individual actions. But the result need not be seen in terms of action or intention, it may be classed in the realm of pure accident. Thus, a stock market crash is certainly not willed or intended by any of the parties, who all stand to lose from it, but it results from the total of their individual actions in buying and selling. The atomistic view which is more natural to empiricism tends to look on history as analogous in this example to the stock market. The resulting course is the consequence of the individual actions, but is itself pure accident. Marxists, on the other hand, have tended to look on history as exhibiting a logic of its own, such that it should be possible to explain why things took the course that they did. Now up to a point this latter view is readily understandable. One can easily see how it may be the case that the behaviour of individuals at any one time is susceptible of explanation in terms of the class structure of their society. But what is not so easy to see is why the upshot of their actions over time should follow a meaningful pattern, why the change in the structure which is brought about by the struggle should not be in the realm of pure accident.

The problem, then, is this: Marxism seems to see history as following, as it were, a plan. History has a goal, the classless society, and the various periods in history represent stages to that goal which, incomplete as they are, represent the highest point attainable at the time. But to say that history follows a plan is to posit some subject of history, some directing mind. And yet Marxism excludes any extra-human subject from consideration.

The solution to the riddle in Marxist terms seems to be this: the subject of history is the human race as a whole, not just at this moment of time but over history. It is the human species in this general sense of whom one can say that they direct history to its goal; and this in a sense analogous to that in which we might say, for instance, that England fought the last war against Germany. But we can speak of a collectivity, 'England', fighting because most Englishmen were conscious of the goal in view, and let themselves be organized, taxed, inducted into the army, etc., to this end. But most men in history have hardly been conscious of its goal; can we then speak of them undertaking a collective action?

Marxists would claim that we could, for this reason: the goal to which history is moving is a society in which men at last have achieved control over nature, that is their environment, and their own destiny, that is, history. (For this reason Marx sometimes speaks of this as the dawn of history, and the earlier period as 'pre-history', but we shall continue to use 'history' in its usual sense here.) But the aim of controlling the environment and society (and, according to Marx, one cannot control one without the other) is not a new one. It is this that men have been attempting to do throughout history. Whatever else they have been doing this has been the main thing; that is, it is this problem which has really commanded attention, it is solutions to this problem which have come before solutions to all others, and therefore the dynamic element in history has been the changes wrought in the way men have tackled it.

At first, of course, men tackle this problem under the stress of imperious necessity to find the means to live. But they continue, even after immediate needs are met. And in so doing they form themselves as human beings and become more conscious of themselves as such. For it is just this striving for control over nature and history which differentiates man from other species of animal, from which, at the earlier stages, he is relatively indistinguishable.

Just because men are at the earlier stages relatively unconscious, they are not conscious of what they are seeking, or, rather, they seek it in disguised 'ideological' forms, as, for instance, the Pharaohs of Ancient Egypt who organized an immense productive machine in order to achieve, as they thought, personal immortality through the pyramids. In fact, this ideological consciousness is inescapable, since the goal cannot be reached in one step, and therefore men throughout most of history must bend their efforts to some approximation which will in some respects negate the goal (e.g. in being a form of class society), but which is necessary as a stage and cannot be by-passed. It is through the distortions of ideological consciousness that men can represent this as man's highest goal.

The different collective goals which societies have set themselves in history are therefore represented by Marxists as approximations to one final goal, as groping attempts to define it which have come as near as is possible in the conditions. But, it might be objected, history is made up not only of collective goals, but of the ambitions of individuals. What have these to do with the collective aims of the human race? Marxists at this point tend to make appeal to something like the Hegelian notion of the 'cunning of reason'. The ambition of powerful individuals is bound to serve the cause of general human advancement at the outset. But this concordance between private gain and public progress, left unexplained in Hegel, or, rather, put to the account of reason, is explained by Marx. The facts of the human condition are such that man can only increase his control over nature by collective action. The powerful individual can only increase his power by organizing men under him in a more effective way. He therefore contributes to progress. The Hegelian cunning of reason is replaced in Marxism by the thesis that man is powerless alone, that he can only increase his power through advances in social production. This radical view of man as a social animal we shall discuss later on.

But for the moment, we must answer the following objection: surely the ambition of some men would lead not to progress but to a reinforcement of outworn social forms. In the previous paragraph we seem only to have dealt with the ambitions of a rising class, but how about those of the feudality in the epoch of the rising bourgeoisie, of the possessing classes today and so on? The answer of Marxism is that this form of personal ambition will be unsuccessful. Precisely because it runs against the best that can be achieved in its epoch, it will be opposed by the most energetic and adventurous spirits, and ultimately by the greater part of the people. It will become uncertain of itself, unproductive, degenerate; and then it will fall before the onslaught of the rising forces.

In this way, the 'cunning of reason' operates also through the selection by history from among the ambitions of men of those which will lead to progress. But this selection is not operated by a mysterious spirit, but by the mass of men, conscious in some dim way that a higher stage is possible and desiring it. In this way, the collective endeavour always has the last word. And this is so because of the fact, which men dimly see, that collective endeavour is the only way to increase their control over their environment and society. Some men may be blinded by their connection with outmoded forms, which themselves receive their lustre from their erstwhile progressive nature, but the greater part sense the truth and pass on.

For this reason, it would be wrong to say that the ambitious members of a rising class are driven by purely personal motives. Private gain may be the form that the general human goal takes in an age where individual enterprise is the only possible form of economic advance. This dialectical unity between the particular desire and the general purpose may, of course, be unknown to the individual, but it is never entirely lost to sight. Many of the protagonists of the bourgeois epoch were conscious of serving a cause that was more than personal, and many in return were considered by their contemporaries as moral exemplars, even as heroes of their age (e.g. Robinson Crusoe).

For Marxism therefore, the broad movements of history are not to be classed in the realm of pure accident; they are to be classed, on the contrary, in something like the category of human activity. But the subject of this activity is the human species as a whole. To look at history in this way requires two assumptions: (1) a teleological assumption, that men are always moved by the same basic goal, to achieve control over nature and history, and (2) an assumption concerning the social nature of man, that man cannot achieve this, or indeed make any progress towards it at all, as individuals, but only in collective activity (social production).

Now, if this analysis is correct, then we do not have to look farther for the difficulties which Marxism has encountered in the empiricist climate of British thought. For an assumption like (1) runs clearly against the cast of empiricist thought which has always been hostile to explanations of a teleological sort. For it assumes some kind of essentialist theory of human nature as being bent towards the realization of certain goals. Empiricist thought has always been more inclined towards the mechanist type of explanation exemplified in Bentham's 'push-pull' theory: men are repelled by pain and attracted by pleasure. True, empiricism may stop short of a completely mechanistic explanation; it may leave room for a notion like 'desire', and make this the starting-point for its motivational theory (e.g. the desire for pleasure). But the desire itself is understood as an affect which colours an 'idea'; it is not seen as the consciousness, perhaps incomplete, of a tendency in the being concerned to seek this goal.

This latter is a teleological view in the strong sense of the term, where desires are explained by the purposes of the being; and it seems to be the form of teleology implicit in Marxism, which accounts, as we have seen, for conscious desire in terms of the basic goal and the prevailing conditions. Now this view requires that we give a sense to different ways of looking at the world, or in this case, different ways of conceiving the same goal; and this, as we have seen, empiricist thought does not accept. But apart from this, it has always been hostile to the notion of a purpose or tendency which can supposedly be identified separately from the conscious desires of the being concerned. For this conflicts with its mechanistic bent implicit from the beginning in the attempt to account for perception in terms of 'impressions' received from the outside world.

But if this teleological conception is swept aside, the Marxist view of history is literally incomprehensible. And so it has seemed to many empiricist thinkers. Since these tended to identify the goal sought in action with the conscious desire, they have tended to take the stock-market view of history; events come about, societies change by an accident which results from the compounded action of individuals. From this point of view the Marxist theory of history as tending towards a goal can at best be seen only as a refurbished form of Hegelianism, an attempt to smuggle in from outside the realm of particular human actions a mysterious directing mind. As such it can easily be brushed aside as confused or meaningless. And this is a temptation which many in this country have felt.

Marxist historicism is thus incomprehensible to the empiricist mind. And, as a result, Marxism has been seen as the protagonist of an inexplicable kind of holism as well. For in talking of the structural events of history, such as the rise of classes, as though they fell in the realm of human action, even though they did not represent the goal of any individual agent, they seem to be setting alongside the ordinary explanation through individual agents one which makes appeal to collective agents, such as classes, and thus to be endowing these strange entities with wills distinct from that of their members. For Marxism of course, the will of, say, the bourgeoisie is nothing mysterious, but is simply the commonly accepted aims of the bourgeois as seen in the historical context, and interpreted in the light of the basic human goal sought in historical action. This will not be perhaps the will of the bourgeois as they would recognize it. But this is not surprising, for they are only aware of the ends they seek in a distorted 'ideological' form. If, however, one wishes to maintain that a will can only have the content that it is conscious of having, that this type of 'interpretation', therefore, is without meaning, then, indeed, the will of a class becomes something mysterious added on to history, as it were, from the outside. The theory appears to be an odd kind of supernatural holism. And such has Marxism appeared to many in this country.

3. Individual and Society

We mentioned above two assumptions which underlie Marxist historicism, a teleological one and one concerning the social nature of man. The first, as we have seen, is hard to make clear on empiricist terms. But the second is as well. In saying that man is a social animal Marxists mean more than just the truism that men need the concurrence of others to control nature. Man's sociality is more than just a matter of physical weakness. He also needs other men to become human, to be a man at all.

As was mentioned above, man, in Marxist terms, becomes human over history in forging his human nature, that is, the nature of a free being who can control nature and himself. Men start off—Marx agrees with Rousseau—as clever animals. They become human only by developing the capacity to control their environment and society, a capacity which they develop in the attempt to practise it. But this means more than the development of technology; it means the development also of self-consciousness, and this in turn alters men's sensibility and emotions. In this way, man can be said to make his nature, or to re-make it in its specifically human guise.

Marxism holds, however, that this human nature is a social creation. The progress of the human spirit requires the elaboration of external forms of expression, music, art, literature, philosophy and so on, in which to embody itself; just as thought itself requires language. And, like language, these forms can only be developed by a human collectivity. Thus human nature is social, not just in that men experience a desire for each other's company, and not just in that they need each other's help but also in that their nature as human beings, all the developments which make them human, are themselves social creations. This is perhaps what Marx meant in the famous sixth Thesis on Feuerbach: 'the human essence is no abstraction inherent in each single individual. In its reality it is the ensemble of social relations.'

Now this conception is very foreign to the empiricist cast of thought. The conception of the progressive development of human nature here plainly implies once more a development in the way of looking at the world, which, we have seen, empiricism cannot accept. But beyond this, the whole notion of historical development in this sense is foreign to empiricist thought. Intellectual progress can only be understood as progress in human knowledge, the learning of connections between phenomena. But, although what is known may change, the manner of knowing is perennial. The human mind starts off as a tabula rasa which then is filled with information, valuable or valueless, correct or incorrect, but its way of coming to grips with reality is always the same, the gathering of information.

But since empiricism refuses the notion of an historical change in our manner of knowing, it also naturally refuses to see this as a social creation. Each individual is from the beginning capable of learning, and has all that he needs to learn. True, society by the division of labour can help us to learn more quickly; or by social control it can inculcate prejudice or ignorance. But the individual cannot be said to owe his intellect, his capacity for human knowledge, much less his sensibility, his capacity for human feeling, to society. On empiricist terms, such an affirmation would have little meaning.

But this affirmation is a central thesis of Marxism. Once again the two views pass each other by in the night of mutual incomprehension.

4. Fact and Value

The teleological assumption which we mentioned above is important in connection with another aspect of Marxist doctrine which has not encountered much understanding in England, the Marxist ethic. While rejecting traditional ethical language and traditional ethical judgements, Marxism has a definite standard of value, of higher and lower. The end of pre-history definitely brings a higher and better state for man than its beginning. The basis of this standard of value lies in the teleological notion of human nature: a stage or form of society is higher than another because it involves a greater realization of human goals.

Marxist values therefore repose, allegedly, on certain facts about human nature and the goals men strive to realize in history. In the intellectual climate of contemporary Britain, however, it is taken for granted by many that fact and value constitute separate logical universes. That is, one can never argue for a value from a fact; for given any fact, it is logically permissible to take a number of different attitudes to it. It would seem to follow that one can only argue for the acceptance of a value on the basis of a fact if one has already assumed a certain attitude towards that fact, and this attitude itself cannot be justified from that fact. The Marxist ethic comes up here against a brick wall of incomprehension, it is seen as a pure confusion.

The difference of view here, however, is really rooted in the respective place which the two ways of thought give to teleological explanation. If one accepts that the Marxist view of man and his fundamental goals is correct, then one can hardly deny the conclusion which follows, viz. that the classless society would be in some sense of the word a 'higher' or 'better' form of life than, say, slave society.

The question could, of course, arise whether 'better' and 'higher' are used here in a moral sense, and if one answered in the negative, one could perhaps claim to be following a precedent set by Marx himself. But this position would seem to be based more on a verbal than on a substantive point. Ethical views vary greatly among men and over history, and it is possible for the term 'moral' to become attached in current usage exclusively to some small sub-set of them. Thus, if 'morality' means the Kantian morality, whose foundation is the moral quality of the will, and which issues in injunctions binding without regard to time or circumstance, then clearly Marx is bound to reject 'morality'. But if we use the term in a less restricted way, if we mean by 'morality' a doctrine touching the fundamental human good and the way to

244

realize it, where 'fundamental' good is taken to mean a good which is inescapably and universally the good of man, then there can be no objection to speaking of a Marxist morality.

That the classless society is conceived by Marxists as a universal good in spite of their theory of history as determined by class conflict is clear from their belief that the average member of a classless society is more fully developed as a human being than the most powerful member of the ruling class in a class society. That it is an inescapable good, that, in other words, whatever men think, believe, choose or decide, it remains objectively a good for them, follows from the teleological notion of human nature itself. For the condition of a man's finding his highest fulfilment in classless society is simply the inescapable one that he be a member of the human race.

Thus, Marxist morality can be said to be founded on a fact or an alleged fact, viz. that the human essence is as Marx defines it. The inference is valid; but the argument is hardly likely to carry weight with philosophers steeped in the empiricist tradition, for, as we have seen, the notion of an essence of man defined in teleological terms is not easily acceptable or even readily understandable by thinkers in this tradition. Indeed, the alleged logical distinction between fact and value can only be considered valid if we hold that notions of this kind have no application. Once again, therefore, the teleological assumptions of Marxism represent a stumbling block to its naturalization on the British scene.

The misunderstanding concerning Marxian morality is therefore complete. Marxism is either seen as putting forward a logically confused ethic, based on a crude identification of what will be with what should be, or it is seen as rejecting all ethics out of hand. It must be pointed out that this latter misunderstanding is much more widespread, and was for long the generally accepted view about Marxism in Europe as well. But its persistence in Britain is due to the quite different view about ethics and its relation to the nature of man which prevails in that country.

Conclusion

We have been trying in this paper to give some account of the relative absence of Marxism from the British intellectual scene. But we have attacked the problem, as it were, from the side.

Instead of offering an historical explanation, we have tried to out-line some of the obstacles to the naturalization of Marxist thought in this country, obstacles which have to do with fundamental differences in the structure of thought. We have seen that the Marxist notion of a plurality of ways of looking at the world, its essential doctrines concerning historicism and holism, its reliance on teleological explanation, its conception of the social nature of man, and its view of the relation of fact and value, all find little resonance in Britain, and come up against formidable obstacles in the empiricist cast of thought which has been dominant in recent decades.

Now this is not an explanation; it does not tell us why these obstacles have arisen or why they have not been surmounted. But it may be the indispensable beginning to such an explanation, at least if we are Marxist enough to admit that the dominant cast of thought in a country cannot be unconnected with its social reality. One can perhaps see in the popularity of empiricist modes of thinking the continued resilience of the British liberal tradition, its distrust of mystique, its utilitarian bent and its emphasis on individualism.

But even if our study yields no fruit in this way, it may nevertheless have some utility. For, if correct, it can reveal the points at which serious study and thought could bring results in terms of mutual understanding. And this is a not unworthy goal.

11. ON THE THEORY OF DEMOCRACY

RICHARD WOLLHEIM

I

IT has been widely alleged that in the English-speaking world political philosophy is dead. And the responsibility for its death has been laid squarely at the door of analytical philosophy.

Now it is certainly true that since the mid-1930s, when the analytical idiom first began to achieve dominance in British and American philosophical circles, no major work of political philosophy has appeared. And it is no less true that many philosophers working in that idiom are of the belief, indeed of the expressed belief, that there is no room inside it for political philosophy as traditionally conceived.

The non-existence of work of a particular kind within a certain tradition should not be taken as conclusive, or even as strong, evidence for the impossibility of work of that kind being produced within the tradition. It might well be that an explanation is to be found among factors that lie outside the tradition: alternatively, the omission may be purely coincidental, and is something that will be rectified naturally in the course of time. Accordingly, the first of the two facts that I cite would not be very significant if it were not for the second. For it *is* surely indicative when the practitioners of a tradition disclaim the capacity to produce work of a specific kind within that tradition. What they say needs to be taken seriously.

It might therefore be thought that for someone who wished to challenge, or at any rate to re-examine, the view that analytical philosophy meant of necessity the extinction of political philosophy, these disclaimers would provide a natural starting-point.

For though, as I have said, they need to be taken seriously, it does not follow that they must be assumed to be reliable. It is easy to think of three ways in which they might go wrong:

(a) The reasoning might be invalid.

(b) The conception of analytical philosophy that figures in the premise might be too comprehensive in that it includes theses that are false or at any rate not intrinsic to analytical philosophy. So for instance, in *Language, Truth and Logic* [AYER (1)], A. J. Ayer's rejection of political philosophy was based on the assumption that the meaninglessness of all value-judgements was an essential thesis of analytical philosophy.

(c) The conception of political philosophy that figures in the conclusion might be too narrow in that it excludes certain activities or concerns that have been intrinsic to political philosophy. So, for instance, in *The Vocabulary of Politics* [WELDON], T. D. Weldon's argument that analytical techniques reveal the bankruptcy of 'classical' political philosophy, as he called it, was based upon the assumption that traditionally political philosophy was limited to the production of 'political foundations', i.e. demonstrative arguments proving the unconditional superiority of one particular form of government over all others.

However, the detailed examination of very general arguments like Ayer's and Weldon's runs the risk of being excessively programmatic.[1] Accordingly, in this essay I shall attempt to re-examine the relations that hold between analytical philosophy and political philosophy by means of a more oblique approach. I shall take up a topic that has traditionally been the concern of political philosophers, the nature of democracy, and limiting myself entirely to analytical techniques, I shall consider various ways in which the traditional inquiry might be advanced as well as other ways in which it may well have to be abandoned; and I shall leave the reader to draw what conclusions he wishes about the mutual exclusiveness of analytical and political philosophy.

II

1. It is an early theorem of analytical philosophy that a question of the form 'What is an x?' admits of two, and only two, interpre-

---

[1] For a more general treatment of this point, see WOLLHEIM (1).

tations. It may be asked as part of a scientific inquiry; in which case it is assumed that the question of how to identify an *x* has already been solved, and that what is now required is a list of the properties, or at any rate the more important properties, possessed by *x*'s. Alternatively, the question may be raised as a linguistic question: what is the meaning of the term '*x*'? In such cases it is of course *not* assumed that the problem of identifying *x*'s has been solved; indeed, one way (admittedly an unrefined way, but adequate for the present) of characterizing linguistic questions would be as questions about the range of phenomena that a certain word or phrase properly picks out. The question 'What is an *x*?' when asked within philosophy is always to be understood as a linguistic question; or, to put it another way, raised inside philosophy 'What is an *x*?' should be written as 'What is an "*x*"?' —the inverted commas showing that it is the term not the phenomenon that is the subject of our investigations.

If we accept this for the moment, then the question 'What is democracy?' raised as a question in political philosophy is equivalent to 'What is "democracy"?' It is a question, that is to say, about the term 'democracy'.

2. One ordinary or non-philosophical method of answering a question about the meaning of a word would be to look the word up in a dictionary; another method would be to examine what ordinary people naturally think the word means; and yet another method would be to examine the word's etymology. It is a general issue that has been raised more than once in this book: whether a philosophical inquiry into the meaning of a word is to be identified with, or to be conducted in the same manner as, a non-philosophical inquiry. Let us assume for the present that the two types of inquiry proceed in the same way, and adopt, for the word 'democracy', the third of my three methods. We shall then find that the word derives from the Greek words: *demos* = the people, *kratos* = power. This would suggest that the word 'democracy' denotes a form of government in which power resides with the people; a suggestion which, of course, totally coincides with the definition that would be found in any dictionary and also with what anyone conversant with the language would say.

But a somewhat closer look at the word's etymology, at both the prefix and the suffix of which it is constituted, will alert us to one aspect of its historical meaning which otherwise might be overlooked.[2] For the suffix *kratos* reminds us that the word 'democracy' was in origin one of a set of words, all of which have this same termination or another one identical in meaning to it deriving from the related word *arché* (= power). These words, which are variously translated as 'monarchy', 'aristocracy', 'plutocracy', 'ochlocracy', can be regarded conjointly as forming a disjunction exhaustive of all possible governments. All the elements in the set or disjunction have this in common, that they indicate a form of government in which one particular section of the population rules; each, however, differs from all the others in respect of which section it is that does rule. If we now turn to the prefix *demos*, we find that this means 'the people'; but the people, it must be observed, in the sense of the popular, or less privileged, section of the community. Aristotle, rejecting an earlier and less reflective tradition, argued that the necessary in contrast to some contingent mark of the *demos*, that which essentially distinguished it from the non-*demos*, was poverty rather than numerosity. But it is of course common both to his and the earlier interpretation that there is non-*demos* as well as *demos*; or, to put it another way, that the *demos* is a part, not the whole, of the community.

Reflecting on the structure of the word *demokratia* and on the meaning of the word '*demos*', we are led to the view that for the Greeks democracy was essentially a sectional form of government; democracy, that is, was government *by* one section of the community—though in their theory the Greeks were insistent (and probably this was borne out in fact) that government *by* a certain section did not necessarily mean government *for* that section. And certainly such evidence as we have (and it cannot be too often emphasized that this is both partial and biased) would seem to support such a view. Now, if this is so, it must be immediately apparent that what democracy meant to the Greeks differs markedly from what democracy means to us; so markedly, indeed, as to make it plausible to say that we have here two different senses of the word.

For there is no doubt that to the ordinary man today democracy is not a sectional form of government; on the contrary, it is essentially opposed to all sectional forms of government, whether by one man, by the best, by the rich or by the mob. For if it is

[2] See PAUL.

true, as we have seen, that democracy now, as it did in the past, means rule by the people, to the Moderns the people is identified, not as it was by the Ancients with one part of the population but with the people as a whole.

3. Our inquiry into the meaning of the word 'democracy' would appear to have brought us to an *impasse*. For taking our cue from one of the ways in which we might normally establish the meaning of a word, i.e. by examining its etymology, we were led to *a* particular conception of democracy, according to which democracy is identified with a specific form of sectional rule; taking another cue from another of the ways in which we might conduct such an inquiry, i.e. by considering what people would ordinarily say the word meant, we were led to a second conception of democracy according to which democracy is *par excellence* non-sectional government. These two conceptions of democracy are expressed by two different senses of the word 'democracy'. The question now arises, Are we simply to record the fact that there are these two different senses of the word, and leave it at that; or can we get beyond this point?

There exist, within analytical philosophy, two arguments that purport to show that we cannot go beyond this point; or that if we can, it is only at the expense of doing something very different from, and far less interesting than, that which we might think we were doing. One argument denies the possibility of all movement; the other concedes the possibility but denies it the name of progress.

K. R. Popper has argued that if we ask, in the linguistic mode, 'What is an "x"?' and we are given two different answers, 'An x is an a' and 'An x is a b', these two answers reflecting two different senses of the word 'x', then to go on to ask 'Which of these is really x?' or 'Are x's really a or b?' commits one to a belief in certain metaphysical entities called 'essences'. Aristotle believed in these entities, and he transmitted this pernicious belief, which accounts for most errors in philosophy, to his successors. Once we have liberated ourselves from it, we must see that there could not be an answer to these questions about what an x really is, or whether this or that is really an x. For if we do not believe that x has an essence $x$ness, about which we can legitimately ask whether it is identical with, or included in, $a$ness (or the essence of a) or $b$ness (or the essence of b), then we are forced to realize that 'x' the word is a mere token which can be used in this or that way, as we please, provided only that we make it clear which way we are using it: what we cannot ask is which is its 'correct' use, unless we mean by this, quite trivially, how it is used by those people whom we have arbitrarily picked out as its 'correct' users. To ask whether democracy is *really* government by the people in the sense of the poorer section of the population or government by the people in the sense of the whole population, is to ask an empty question; for we could use the word 'democracy' in either of these two ways, and nothing would hang by it—given, that is, that we make our usage clear and that we keep it consistent.

Another argument, which this time would allow us to debate about the real nature of, say, democracy, but at the price of radically re-interpreting what we would be doing, is one associated with the name of C. L. Stevenson. For Stevenson argued that many of the terms that are so hotly disputed in this way possess an emotive character: that is to say, when applied to objects they carry with them and impart to these objects an aura of a favourable (or unfavourable) kind. When we are uncertain in our own minds, or disagree with someone else, about the application of such terms, the dispute is in effect about which objects we would like to see these terms honour (or degrade). If 'x' has a favourable emotive character, to say 'x's are really *a*' is to be pro-*a*: to say 'x's are really *b*' is to be pro-*b* [cf. STEVENSON (3), 4]. Now, 'democracy' has most evidently, in the modern world at any rate, a favourable connotation. Accordingly, to express an opinion as to whether democracy is really a sectional form of government or whether it is really a non-sectional form of government would be simply to express a preference, probably in accordance with one's deepest attitudes, between these two modes of political rule; and the intensity with which one would resist any different application of the word would reflect one's dislike of seeing a form of government that one regards unfavourably, honoured by this honorific label.

4. There is, however, implicit in much contemporary analytical philosophy the view that not all decisions as to the proper usage of a word need be arbitrary; either in the sense implicit in Popper's argument, nor in the rather different one implicit in Stevenson's. For the suggestion of arbitrariness attaches to the decision, only in so far as the decision is conceived as being narrowly between

two or more definitions of the word; each fairly succinctly stated; and both baldly presented as rival candidates for adoption. But broaden the picture a little; take in the whole context in which the word is habitually used; consider, for instance, the arguments in which it normally figures, the meaning and usage of its various cognates and correlatives, the kind of situation in which it could never be employed without strain or incongruity, the objections that might typically be brought against the phenomena to which it is customary to apply it; place the decision in this wider setting, and the air of arbitrariness will tend to disappear. The rival definitions will now emerge more like rival theories about the word's functioning, each aiming to provide a comprehensive account of the role it fulfils in the language. And if the various candidates for this task are now likely to seem too crude or abbreviated to discharge it properly, it is also likely that the decision between them as to which is the more enlightening, or at any rate the least distorting, will appear as something governed by reason and evidence; and not either the totally fortuitous choice between equally permissible alternatives, or the arbitrary capture of an honorific word for the object of one's own preference, which had seemed according to the two preceding arguments to be the only possibilities.

Now, if we conceive the decision between the two senses of 'democracy' in this new way, there can be no doubt but that what I have called the modern sense provides the better account of the many ways in which it is used and the different purposes to which it is put. I have not here the opportunity to prove, but equally I imagine few would wish to dispute, that the word 'democracy' is widely used, both by those who are for and those who are against the thing, to mean government by the people where, in turn, 'the people' means the whole population.

But it will be apparent that if this is what 'democracy' means nowadays, then the contemporary concept of democracy has certain difficulties attached to it that did not arise with the concept that passed under the same name in classical times. For, first of all, we might ask, How can the population as a whole rule when the population of a modern democracy is likely to be numerous and diverse, and secondly, If the population as a whole rules, who is there left to be ruled over? These questions can, of course, also be raised in connection with the classical concept of democracy.

But they also can fairly readily be answered. For the *demos*, being a clearly demarcated section or class of the population, the attribution to it of an adequate degree of unanimity presents no special difficulty. And as to who is to be ruled over, the answer is the non-*demos*—parallel, that is, to the answer of the non-*aristos* in the case of aristocracy, or the non-*plutos* in the case of plutocracy, or the non-*ochlos* in the case of ochlocracy.

5. The formulation of these two questions allows us to organize a number of 'political theories', some of which have only been very imperfectly understood, into two broad categories; according to the type of solution that they propose to these questions. I shall call these two solutions the Idealist solution and the Liberal solution.

The Idealist solution has as its starting point a particular assumption about human nature, according to which every rational being, and hence every member of society, possesses two selves or wills: a 'true' or 'real' self or will, and an 'arbitrary' or 'fitful' self or will. Every true self is not merely coherent internally, in that all its manifestations are of a piece, but is also coherent with all the other true selves so that their joint activities display a harmony (*volonté générale* according to Rousseau); by contrast every arbitrary self is both internally discordant and also discordant with all the other arbitrary selves—or if, by chance, it does find itself in unison with them, this unison (Rousseau's *volonté de tous*) is purely coincidental and transient. On the basis of this para-psychological assumption, the two questions that I have suggested arise on a modern conception of democracy—or 'the paradox of self-government' as a thinker of this school, Bernard Bosanquet, called them—admit of a solution that is theoretically neat. For to the first question, "How can the people rule, being so many and so diverse?", the answer is returned that it is their true selves that rule and these are harmonious, not diverse; and diversity being denied, numbers are immaterial. And to the second question, "If the people rules, who is there left to be ruled over?", the answer is, simply, the arbitrary selves: in other words, though in a democracy the ruled are different from the rulers just as they are in a plutocracy or a theocracy, in a democracy they are different, not in being different people, but in being different parts of the same people.

It is true that for reasons that need not detain us here, the Idealist theory is not explicitly put forward as a theory of democracy. But I do not think that this need inhibit us from treating it as one. For, in the first place, it was certainly put forward as a theory of 'self-government', or, as Rousseau, its most notable exponent, put it, of 'a form of association . . . in which each, while uniting himself with all, may still obey himself alone'. And, secondly, the theory seems designed to furnish explicit answers to the two questions which it would be no exaggeration to say not merely pertain to but *characterize* the modern concept of democracy.

In contrast, Liberal solutions to these two questions, insist on admitting, rather than denying, the facts of diversity in human society, and yet say that it is possible for the people as a whole to rule. Indeed, most Liberal theories of democracy have attached to them a justification of democracy, which makes this diversity democracy's *raison d'être*: it is according to this argument precisely because people are diverse that democracy is the only tolerable form of government under which they can live.

6. Idealist theories provide, as we have seen, clear answers to the two questions that I have isolated as essential to the modern conception of democracy; but they do so only at the price of certain presuppositions that are totally unacceptable in themselves. For the entities to which the Idealist appeals in formulating his solution can have no proper place in an empiricist universe. At once lacking any experiential base and yet purporting to explain observable behaviour, concepts like 'the general will' or 'the real self' are bound to be rejected as meaningless by any analytical philosopher; even, that is, by one who no longer regards it as feasible or even desirable to try and fix the limit of meaningful language by means of a rigorous criterion, in the style of the old Verification Principle.

Moreover, to the majority of analytical philosophers—though no longer to all—these concepts, which are intrinsic to the Idealist scheme, would seem to have a further objectionable feature, over and above their absence of an empirical criterion. And that is that they seek to merge two linguistic functions that are in reality distinct. For they profess at one stroke to describe a certain state of affairs (if of a recondite or opaque kind) *and* to recommend a certain course of action. Once it has been established that something or other is what the people 'really want', then on the Idealist theory it follows that this something or other should be enacted.

Now, many analytical philosophers would maintain that analytical techniques had clarified what had long been supposed, by traditional philosophers, to be wrong with this kind of argument—even if they would concede that these techniques had not shown, with adequate rigour, exactly why it was wrong. Furthermore, it is worth observing that even those analytical philosophers who reject the 'is' 'ought' dichotomy would probably find unacceptable the particular way in which it is rejected within the Idealist solution. For though such philosophers might well argue that there is a valid route from, e.g., what people want to what should be done, they would not favour a concept in which the two notions of 'wanted by all' and 'ought to be done' were totally fused.

But if it is true that Idealist theories of democracy meet the challenge that any such theory has to meet, though at a price that is impossibly high, it is difficult to see how any Liberal theory can claim even such initial success. For if the citizens of a democracy are numerous and divergent in their views, as *ex hypothesi* any such theory concedes, how can they possibly co-operate as a body in the initiation and implementation of laws? It seems evident that they can't. Yet it is in terms of these two activities that the original theory of democracy and for that matter the original theories of aristocracy, oligarchy and plutocracy—distinguished the ruling section of the society from the section over which rule is exercised.

The answer is that whereas Idealist theory retains this interpretation of what it is to rule or be the ruling section in a society, Liberal theory can be distinguished by its rejection of it—just as the various different Liberal theories can be distinguished one from another by the interpretation that they would substitute for it. If we return to the phrase 'Democracy is a form of government where the people rule', we can now see that Idealist and Liberal theory agree (in contradistinction to classical theory) in the sense that they give to the phrase 'the people'; the Liberal theory disagrees with the interpretation that the Idealist theory would put upon the concept 'ruling'; and each Liberal theory disagrees with every other about the correct interpretation to be placed upon the concept.

Disagreement about the correct interpretation of the concept 'ruling' can, however, serve as more than a means of classifying Liberal theories; it can also be used to evaluate them. For we can think of them as being no more viable than the interpretation that they offer.

7. Typical Liberal theories of democracy would be those adduced by James Madison and John Locke. In Madisonian theory[3] the concept of ruling is so interpreted that it becomes correct to say that everyone rules when and only when, on the classical interpretation of the concept, it would be true that no one rules. In Lockean theory the concept is so interpreted that to say that a man rules is equivalent to saying that he has consented to the laws under which he lives. A third interpretation, which belongs to what I shall, non-committally, call 'contemporary' theory, would equate saying that a man rules to saying that he has chosen the laws under which he lives.

A question that now arises is why these various theories should be described as offering different interpretations of the same concept rather than as using the same term in different senses. Or, to put it another way, why could not, for example, the Lockean view of 'ruling' be said to stand to the Madisonian view as the classical view of 'democracy' does to the modern? What is this new distinction that occurs within Liberal theories?

There may be different ways of formulating the distinction, but as a preliminary move we might say that when a term 'x' is used in different senses a and b, though it is not, as we have seen, a matter of arbitrary *fiat* whether x is *really a* or *really b* but something that is determined by reasons, still the reasons relate solely to the question how the term 'x' is used within the language; whereas, when a and b are different interpretations of x, neither a nor b gives the whole sense of 'x'. Rather, 'x' has a residual meaning—let us call it m—which both those who subscribe to the a-interpretation and those who subscribe to the b-interpretation would accept. Indeed, the point of disagreement between these two groups is a matter of whether being a or being b is more likely to facilitate x in being m; the decision, Is x a or b, will be grounded in the judgement whether a or b is the better means to the instantiation of means to m. And this judgement will be a non-linguistic judgement; though, of course, it is a linguistic matter that m *is* part of the meaning of x.

Let us now consider the appropriateness of talking of interpretations in the present context. If one says that the people rule,

<hr />

[3] Madisonian theory has been rigorously formulated in DAHL.

one must mean something to the effect that the people have the supreme or ultimate power. But 'power' is an elusive and flexible notion, and precisely what it is to have power will vary vastly depending on who is said to have power, over whom they have it, what kind of power it is, and when.

Governments can be classified vaguely by saying that power rests with the people. In this sense democracy is a persistent concept, and all democracies form a true class. But the form that this power assumes can be so disparate that any theory of democracy must, if it is to achieve any degree of specificity, have attached to it some general characterization of the kind of power involved; in this way, different theories of democracy, while agreeing in the assertion that the people rule, provide their own interpretation of what it is to rule.

8. Of the various interpretations I have quoted of the concept 'ruling' as it appears in the formula 'Democracy is a form of government where the people rules', the most plausible would seem to be that contained in what I have called 'contemporary theory': i.e. that which would equate it with choosing the laws under which one lives. The adequacy of this interpretation might be expressed by saying that it is neither too weak nor too strong for its purposes. For it stands, on the one hand, in contrast to the Madisonian interpretation, which is clearly too weak—for a state of affairs merely in which 'tyranny' was avoided and a balance of sectional interests achieved (the Madisonian ideal) would not be generally acceptable as democracy—and, on the other hand, in contrast to the classical interpretation, which, as we have already seen, is too strong. As for the Lockean interpretation: taken *literally*, it is obviously too strong, for we cannot rightly expect individual consent before we concede the fact of universal rule; but as understood by Locke (according to whom 'tacit consent . . . reaches as far as the very being of any one within the territories of that government') it is obviously too weak, in that it would allow almost any government to enjoy universal consent and therefore to count as being democratic.

In might, however, seem far from evident that the 'contemporary' interpretation is not too strong. More specifically, it might be asked why it is less strong than the classical interpretation; why is the demand that people should choose the laws under which they live a weaker demand than that they should initiate and implement them? One can see that this is something which it is *an easier task* for a large group of people to perform; but that does not mean that it constitutes *a weaker interpretation* of ruling. It is, for instance, easier for a large body of people to rebel against a law than for them individually to express disapproval of it; but it does not follow from this that provoking rebellion would be a weaker interpretation of what it is for a law to be unpopular than exciting universal disapproval.

The important consideration here is that whereas to say that the people as a whole have initiated a certain set of laws entails that every single individual has initiated those laws, no parallel entailment holds in the case of the people's choosing a certain set of laws. The people as a whole may be said to choose laws A rather than laws B, C or D without its being true that A is the first choice of every single citizen.

And yet, of course, there must be some kind of correlation between the people's choice and the first choices of the individual citizens. And, furthermore, not any correlation will suffice. It could not, for instance, be said that the people as a whole had chosen laws A rather than B, C or D, when 90 per cent of the individuals concerned prefer either B, C or D to A. What, then, is an acceptable correlation?

One line of thought, which has been very audible recently among economists and political scientists, is that which would assimilate the relation between the people's choice and individual preferences to the kind of aggregation problem that arises within welfare economics.[4] On this view the people's choice is regarded as a function of the choices of the various individuals, and the problem is to formulate the exact rule which will permit one to derive the former from the latter.

But this approach is fraught with difficulty. For in the first place, it has been shown that if we mean by 'the choices' of the individual citizens merely their first choice and this is all that we aggregate, then any rule that we construct will in certain circumstances produce counter-intuitive results. Suppose that A, B and C are the alternatives, and 40 per cent have A as their first choice, 30 per cent B and 30 per cent C. Then any plausible rule would give A as the 'people's choice'; but if we assume that all those whose first choice is B would prefer C to A, and all those whose

4 See ARROW.

first choice is C would prefer B to A, the selection of A becomes unplausible.[5]

The natural thing to do, then, is to broaden our conception of the individual citizen's choice by taking into account their total ordering of all the alternatives before them. But if we do this, it has been shown that it is impossible to devise a rule for aggregating such preference scales that both satisfies certain intuitive requirements and also gives us in all cases a determinate answer. In other words, the intuitive requirements that we make of such a rule are inconsistent.[6]

9. It might be disputed whether either of these two arguments about the difficulties in the way of constructing a 'democratic function' (to use a phrase parallel to 'social welfare function') strictly falls within the scope of philosophy. But what clearly is a philosophical issue is the prior question of whether this is the right way to conceive of the relation between the people's choice and the individual citizen's choices. For if it is not necessary to find a rule which will allow us to go from the latter to the former, then the fact that no such rule, or no rule that is not hedged around with severe limitations, can be constructed, will have no consequences for democracy. But if it is necessary to find such a rule, then it follows that either democracy is impossible or some different interpretation of it is called for.

Various arguments to demonstrate that the assimilation of the people's choice to a mathematical aggregate of individual choices is mistaken could be put forward. One such demonstration might take the form of arguing that both the belief that there is a people's choice and the belief that a 'democratic function' cannot be constructed are better founded than the belief (which is clearly inconsistent with them) that the people's choice is determined by the 'democratic function'; therefore we can use the first two beliefs to disprove the third.

Another way of arguing the point would be to draw attention to the way we regard the actual process by which the citizens of a democratic country express their choice: that is to say, the voting procedure. For if we understood the people's choice as something determined by a democratic function, then we would surely regard the voting procedure, which would be the physical correlate of such a function, as something intrinsic to the concept of

---

[5] See BLACK, D., pp. 67–8   [6] See ARROW, Ch. V.

'the people's choice'. Yet it seems evident that this is not how we regard it. There are in existence a number of different voting procedures, which are used in different societies all of which are regarded with equal right as democratic. Which procedure is in fact employed in a given society is determined partly by pragmatic, partly by historical, considerations; in no case is it the result of a deduction from the nature of democracy.

The relation of electoral procedures to the people's choice might be characterized by saying that they provide the criteria for the people's choice; to be the winning candidate according to the procedure current in the particular society is the criterion by which a law or set of laws can be picked out as the people's choice.

What is meant here by talking of a 'criterion'? To say that X is the criterion of a is not to say that X is part of the meaning of a. On the contrary, it is to say that it is not part of the meaning of a. However, it is part of the meaning of a that it should have a criterion; furthermore, the range of possible or alternative criteria will be determined by the meaning of a. But which out of these possible criteria is the actual one, is a matter that is determined solely by considerations of practice and convenience.

An obvious and much cited example of a criterion is provided by the symptom of a disease. To talk of a disease is to talk of something that must express itself physically; but exactly what physical manifestation of the diseased body we take as a symptom will depend on such factors as its recognizability, its accessibility, its divergence from other symptoms, etc. It is markedly analogous considerations that determine what voting procedure we take as telling us which policy is the people's choice.

10. Democracy is a form of government in which the people's choice is (or is within certain limitations) law. Further, the people express their choice through an electoral procedure. But so far the discussion has been conducted as though the connection between these two propositions was closer than in fact it is. For in elections the people do not directly choose between a set of alternatives one of which will be law. For they do not choose between legislative programmes at all: they choose between candidates.

The introduction of this mediating link between the people and legislation finds expression in something virtually unknown to classical theory: the representative assembly. Now the representative assembly can be conceived as merely a transmitting link between the two terms that it relates: in the assembly, that is to say, the votes that the successful candidates have received are converted into votes that they in turn give to the legislative programme for which they stood. We may call this the Legislative Conception of the assembly.

But in modern democracy the representative assembly is not conceived of solely in this way. The fact that it is a place where speeches are made and listened to, where grievances are aired and issues debated, gives it an intrinsic as opposed to a merely instrumental value. One aspect of democracy is that it is 'government by discussion', and the central forum for this discussion is the representative assembly. It is therefore not surprising that a view should develop which would make this deliberative role the essential function of the assembly. We may call this the Deliberative Conception of the assembly.

The question now arises whether there is any conflict between these two conceptions. More specifically we might ask, first, Is the method that is most appropriate for constituting an assembly conceived of on the Legislative model necessarily the most appropriate for constituting an assembly conceived of on the Deliberative model? And secondly, Can an assembly that discharges the function appropriate to one model also discharge that appropriate to the other?[7]

In answer to the first question, it must be pointed out that in order for the assembly to function legislatively, it is necessary that the candidates who support the people's choice should occupy a position in the assembly somewhere between an absolute majority and a plurality. It is only an absolute majority that will guarantee that the people's choice is enacted, but, depending on how the minorities might unite against them,[8] various weaker positions might be occupied by the candidates favouring the people's choice, and the same result could with greater or lesser degree of certainty be achieved. Now every weakening of the majority in the assembly potentially at any rate brings it closer to the Deliberative model; because it increases the possibilities for the expression of the minority views. But, of course, it also increases the chances that the majority view or the people's choice will not be enacted. It is

[7] See WOLLHEIM (2).   [8] See DOWNS.

in the context of this issue—of how far can the deliberative function of the assembly be increased without imperilling its legislative function—that the issue of Proportional Representation coherently stated (which it seldom is) properly belongs. It has nothing to do with the assembly as a legislative machine; but on the assumption that the legislative role is secure, it aims at ensuring that the maximum diversity of opinion exists within the assembly. It is indicative that John Stuart Mill, its most distinguished advocate, should have conceived of the assembly as 'the nation's Committee of Grievances, and its Congress of Opinions'.

The second question might be put like this: If the discussion in the assembly is a genuine one, those taking part in it must be prepared to listen to it and accordingly to change their minds if convinced; but if they are prepared to change their minds, what guarantee is there that the people's choice will be enacted? If, on the other hand, the members of the assembly are not prepared to change their minds and so jeopardize the legislative prospects of the people's choice, in what sense could they be said to 'take part' in a debate at all? Various solutions to this dilemma have, implicitly at any rate, been proffered. One is that though the debate occurs within the representative assembly, its natural audience is the electorate, and the effect it aims at is therefore recorded not in the votes inside the assembly but in the votes cast at the subsequent election. Another solution is that it is only on some issues that the members of the assembly cannot change their minds: on others they legitimately can.

It would not be part of a philosophical examination of democracy to settle for one of these solutions rather than another, but a consideration of the solutions and of the problem that they purport to solve would be essential to what is certainly a philosophical inquiry—how democracy is best characterized and whether it can be characterized in a consistent fashion.

11. In discussing the voting procedure as the method of selecting one out of a set of alternatives offered to the electorate as the people's choice, it was pointed out that no procedure could be shown to be *the* 'correct' one in the sense of being derived from the nature of democracy. Yet it became clear in the course of discussing the legislative function of the assembly that in practice the choice of procedures lay between those which picked out the majority or plurality first preference—even if it can be

shown that theoretically this could lead to counter-intuitive results.

The question then arises, Are we not now back at the old classical conception of democracy as a sectional form of government? Or to go back to our discussion in §8, Has it not turned out that the 'contemporary' interpretation of 'ruling' and hence of 'popular rule' is after all too weak in that it permits one to say that the people (as a whole) rule when, in fact, only a part of the people rules?

The orthodox answer at this stage is to point out that if in one sense modern democracy is majority rule, this sense is innocuous; in that the majority is not a determinate section of the population as it was in classical theory but is rather a fluid proportion of the citizen body to which anyone at any moment might belong and which equally might crystallize round any point of view.[9]

But for this answer to be satisfactory, it is necessary to be somewhat clearer about the implications of 'might belong' or 'might crystallize'. In a society, which was divided into two classes, one very rich and small, the other very big and poor, and where the issues on which the electorate was asked to choose were invariably 'class' issues, could we plausibly say that we here had anything but sectional rule—even though the theoretical possibility existed that the poor might in large numbers be converted to the views of the rich.

Reflection on such cases suggests that for a modern democracy to exist, there must be an absence of factors that create permanent divisions of political opinion among the electorate. For as long as these factors exist, to talk of the majority as a fluid fraction of the population rather than as a ruling section is empty.

From this it might be argued that democracy is impossible in particular kinds of rigidly inegalitarian society. The exact degree of equality and social mobility that democracy requires is an empirical question, but it would look as though there is an *a priori* argument to show that some degree is necessary. This conclusion might seem surprising to many.

12. What are the ideal conditions for democracy? or, alternatively, What conditions does democracy require to survive? are questions that political philosophers have often discussed; but it is arguable that properly speaking, they do not belong to political

[9] For this view, see, e. g., BENN and PETERS, Ch. 15., and MAYO, Ch. 8.

philosophy at all, since the first is an ethical question and the second an empirical question. But both these questions presuppose, or answers to them invoke, an issue that is definitely of philosophical concern; and that is how we are to distinguish between the *logical* conditions of democracy or the conditions whose instantiation is entailed by the existence of democracy, and the *natural* conditions of democracy or the conditions that democracy requires for its survival or success.

The distinction is of importance because those who advocate and those who reject democracy should be aware of what it is to which they are necessarily committed (or opposed) and what it is to which they are only contingently committed (or opposed). And it is noticeable that many of the current unreflecting views on this subject do not stand up to critical examination.

For instance, it is often assumed that a belief in democracy on the part of the citizens is a necessary condition of democracy. But if we mean by 'belief' in this context more than the disposition to operate the democratic machine, it seems unlikely that such a connection holds or that, if it does hold, it is more than an empirical link. On the other hand, it seems that many of the political phenomena and institutions that are argued for, often rather tentatively, by supporters of democracy as merely desirable appendages are in fact intrinsic to democracy.

The core of the matter is the intimate connection that we have seen exists between democratic rule and popular choice. For if democratic rule is to be a reality, the choice made by the people must be a genuine choice. Now this requires: first, that the electorate should have a wide range of alternatives from which to make its choice; secondly, that it should be confident that the policy it chooses will be put in practice; and thirdly, that the choice should be based upon a reflective and informed assessment of the alternatives.

The first of these conditions (and also the second) requires that there should be a developed party system. The parties must represent all the major opinions existing in the society, and these opinions must not be arbitrarily linked in such a way that a citizen might easily find his more important views evenly distributed between the parties. The second condition requires that each party should be linked to its opinions in a particular relation that is expressed by talking of the 'mandate': that is to say, these opinions should be produced in the form of a policy and the production of this policy should be regarded as a pledge as to what the party will do if it is elected.

The third condition requires both that the electorate should be able to understand the issues between which it is asked to choose and also that it should have access to all ideas that relate to these issues. In other words, both Education and Toleration are essential not accidental attributes of a democracy.

III

This essay purports to be no more than the briefest prospectus of what a philosophical inquiry into democracy, that restricts itself to purely analytical techniques, might achieve. Every argument that has been adduced deals either with strict logical relations, like entailment, or else with quasi-logical relations, like 'interpretation of' or 'criterion of'. Yet it will be apparent, even from this survey, that these techniques, so far from always giving 'negative' results, can also establish on a firm basis connections that are ordinarily thought to be tentative or the result of purely subjective opinion. This same point might be put, perhaps rather more effectively, by saying that to be negative can include being destructive of ill-founded scepticism as well as of ill-founded speculation.

12. HISTORICAL UNDERSTANDING AND THE EMPIRICIST TRADITION

PATRICK GARDINER

CONTRASTS are often drawn between, on the one hand, the conception of philosophical inquiry widely accepted and followed in the English-speaking world and, on the other, philosophy as it is understood and practised in 'Continental' countries, by which is meant (principally) Italy, France and Germany. Those who like to draw such contrasts may intend them to apply specifically to the contemporary scene, but they are none the less often put forward with the accompanying suggestion that the divisions alluded to have deep roots in the past, reaching back at least to the seventeenth century. Undoubtedly, in insisting upon the existence of sweeping divergences of this kind, there is almost inevitably a danger of exaggeration and over-simplification, and of highlighting points of difference in a manner likely to obscure the presence of various parallels and connections that are in fact equally well-founded and important. But it is not my purpose in this essay to discuss the validity or fruitfulness of such contrasts in general. Instead, I wish chiefly to concentrate attention upon one particular feature of the development of English philosophy which, if comparisons are to be made at all, seems to be of obvious relevance. This concerns the attitude adopted towards historical knowledge and understanding.

It would certainly be idle to pretend that the study of history is a subject which, from a theoretical point of view, has traditionally excited the interest of British philosophers. The great empiricists of the seventeenth and eighteenth centuries—Locke, Berkeley and

267

Hume—were, of course, profoundly occupied with the general problem of determining the nature and scope of human knowledge. At the same time, however, the manner in which they approached this problem reflected a concern with, and emphasis upon, certain specific domains of experience and inquiry; and it was these domains, to the exclusion of others that might have attracted their attention, which remained constantly at the centre of their field of vision. First and foremost, there was their preoccupation with the question of accounting for and attempting to justify the type of knowledge we claim to have at the level of our everyday sensory perception—the knowledge that is embodied in our ordinary commonsense judgements concerning the world around us. But they did not stop there. They also applied themselves to the consideration of some of the more specialized branches of inquiry which play a cardinal role in our thought about our environment. On the one hand, there were the formal disciplines of logic and mathematics, disciplines in which the results, arrived at purely *a priori*, seemed to possess a certainty exceeding any obtainable by the experimental or observational methods employed elsewhere. On the other, there were the interpretations of reality, indubitably based upon observation and yet apparently far removed from the crude approximations of common sense, which had been provided in the theories and hypotheses of natural scientists like Galileo and Newton. The latter in particular exercised, though in different ways, a pervasive influence over the philosophers in question.

This was true above all of Hume. In his eyes, the exploration of the ways in which human beings typically reason about and interpret their experience was seen as forming part of a wider investigation whose subject-matter was human nature itself. Furthermore, he believed it impossible to form any adequate notion of the human character 'otherwise than from careful and exact experiments, and the observation of those particular effects, which result from its different circumstances and situations'. In other words, Hume had in view a 'science of man' which would involve the application to psychological phenomena of methods similar in form to those used in the scientific study of the non-human or 'natural' realm. It had, furthermore, a similar object, inasmuch as Hume thought that it would be possible to arrive in this way at 'universal principles' comparable in explanatory power to the

268

Newtonian principle of gravitational attraction; when referring, for example, to the famous principle of 'the association of ideas', he spoke of 'a kind of *Attraction*, which in the mental world will be found to have as extraordinary effects as in the natural, and to show itself in as many and as various forms'. Hume's general picture of the mind seems, in fact, to have been largely that of a quasi-mechanical system, in which atomistically conceived impressions and ideas follow one another and combine according to laws and regularities; these laws and regularities were held to be ascertainable by careful observation and introspective attention. He frequently spoke, too, as if the kind of influence exerted by the mind upon the body conformed to a similar pattern, particular 'passions' and 'volitions' being discovered through experience to give rise to subsequent physical actions in a regular manner. It was the task of the philosopher as far as possible to discover and systematize such uniformities, thereby arriving at verifiable hypotheses which would stand in marked contrast to empty untestable theorizing of the sort that traditionally went by the name of 'metaphysics'.

Thus empiricism, as it emerges in Hume, has a number of significant aspects. While on the epistemological side it appears partly orientated towards meeting, if not solving, theoretical difficulties arising from a consideration of basic assumptions underlying the procedures of natural science, in a more general way it is heavily impregnated with the belief that natural science itself provides the standards in accordance with which philosophy should seek to determine its own methods and aims. And it further involves the postulation of an interpretative framework, also closely modelled on current scientific conceptions, in terms of which human psychology and the phenomena of consciousness are to be portrayed and understood. Though they did not go uncriticized, these Humean ideas and preoccupations nevertheless struck deep roots, exercising a radical long-term influence on the subsequent evolution of British thought and speculation. Thus, Hume's view that all our experience, including the experience we have of ourselves as persons, may ultimately be analysed into a stream of distinct 'ideas and impressions', together with his belief in the operation of fundamental 'associative' laws, found ready and widespread acceptance among nineteenth-century thinkers, philosophers and psychologists alike, and infected, not only the accounts that were provided of human emotion and the springs of action but also, in the case of certain writers, the treatment accorded to crucial issues in logic and methodology. Again, the suggestion that philosophical inquiry is, or should be made, 'scientific' is one that has retained a certain hold upon the imagination of English philosophers: Russell, to give only one contemporary instance, has insistently maintained that philosophy is in some sense a science, though the precise sense in which he believes this to be true has not always been entirely clear. And such claims can, I think, be seen in turn to be symptomatic of something deeper and more permanently important. Since the time of Hume, and with only comparatively brief interruptions, the climate of philosophical opinion has been largely dominated by a profound regard for the criteria of truth and intelligibility accepted and applied in the various natural sciences. Even in the nineteenth century there was a tendency to assimilate knowledge (in the 'strict' sense) to scientific knowledge; though this tendency was perhaps more marked in the writings of American 'pragmatists' than in those of empiricists working in Britain. Likewise, there was a proneness to identify genuine issues, as opposed to those deemed spurious or unreal, according to whether they were decidable by reference to standards assumed to be characteristic of scientific thinking—an approach which the Utilitarians adopted with dramatic effect in the fields of morals, politics and law. And two of the most influential books in philosophy of the time— Mill's *A System of Logic* [MILL] and Whewell's *The Philosophy of the Inductive Sciences* [WHEWELL]—were largely or wholly taken up with problems in the theory of science. Such deference to the claims of science was not, as I have already implied, universally manifested; indeed, in the period towards the end of the century when the school of Absolute Idealism was in the ascendant, it was notably in abeyance, although even then the advances in biology initiated by Darwin had done much to reinforce the prestige of science, and it is worth remembering that the age of F. H. Bradley was also the age of Herbert Spencer with his curious brand of evolutionary naturalism. Moreover, the Idealist period was no more than an interlude, and a comparatively brief one: by the end of the first decade of the present century a reaction against monistic metaphysics had already set in, and it was accompanied by a revival of interest in Hume. It was, however, the subsequent impact of positivistic doctrines stemming from the Vienna Circle that perhaps did most to bring about a renewed concentration of attention upon scientific procedures and aims on the part of philosophers. In retrospect this appears scarcely surprising. The inspiration of Logical Positivism in its original purity was largely founded on an extreme respect for scientific achievement, and while this did not lead to the demand that philosophy should seek to attain the status of a science in its own right, it exhibited itself in a number of other ways: for instance, in the stress laid on the connection of meaning with empirical verification and in the claim that the prime object of philosophical investigation was the clarification of propositions and concepts proper to science. As a consequence philosophers in Britain and the United States who were influenced by positivism tended almost inevitably to approach their problems in a manner that reflected scientific interests. Admittedly, psychological inquiries and the provision of genetic explanations were expressly eschewed in favour of linguistic or conceptual analyses; in this regard they diverged significantly from their nineteenth-century predecessors. But in the forms of thought and discourse principally selected for consideration, as well as in the kinds of elucidation offered, a comparable preoccupation with natural science was—for a time, at least—plainly manifest in their work. Even if there was no systematic attempt to 'reduce' all purportedly informative statements to one preferred type, the suggestion that at least scientific assertions represented a sort of paradigm or model in terms of which other forms of language and communication could finally be judged and appraised underlay much that was written.

In the light of this necessarily somewhat bald outline it is perhaps possible to appreciate the reasons for the comparative neglect which history, considered as an independent field of inquiry, has suffered at the hands of English philosophers. In part, such neglect might be thought to derive from the fact that history, by contrast with the natural sciences, has been late in attaining the status of a clearly demarcated branch of knowledge, with its own determinate procedures and accepted standards of accuracy and interpretative exactitude. The contempt expressed for historical writing by Descartes had some justification in the early seventeenth century, and it might be argued that this situation had not appreciably changed at the time when the foundations of British empiricism came to be laid. Such an explanation, none the less, has obvious limits as it stands. Even at the time when Locke was writing any excuse there might previously have been for treating historical narrative as little more than an unco-ordinated, if entertaining, jumble of ill-attested conjectures, traveller's tales and shots in the dark was wearing decidedly thin; while, so far as Hume was concerned, such a conception must surely have appeared totally absurd. For Hume was himself a practising historian, to whom the marshalling and criticism of evidence and the use of such evidence to support statements of historical fact presented itself, not merely as a theoretical possibility, but as a practical necessity, nor was he in any doubt about the need to distinguish history proper from stories containing wildly improbable human happenings and deeds—these would be no better from a historical standpoint than those in which the author 'stuffed his narration with stories of centaurs and dragons, miracles and prodigies'. 'What,' he asks in his *Inquiry Concerning the Human Understanding* [HUME (2)], 'would become of history had we not a dependence on the veracity of the historian according to the experience which we have had of mankind?' Yet the fact remains that references to history in Hume's philosophical works are scattered and cursory, and are usually introduced only to illustrate some point in the context of a more general argument which has no specific relation to history as such. And here perhaps lies the main clue to the lack of philosophical interest in history which both Hume and a number of his empiricist successors conspicuously showed. For Hume habitually speaks of historical reasoning as if it were no more than a particular application of inductive reasoning in general, and as if it were subject to the same general canons which apply universally throughout the entire domain of empirical inference and explanation. There could therefore be no justification, epistemological or logical, for undertaking a philosophical examination of historical thinking in isolation from other forms of empirical inquiry, since all share the same essential features; in particular, there could be no reason for according to history a treatment separate from that accorded to the natural sciences. This is made apparent by Hume both when he is speaking of the manner in which historical accounts are validated and when he discusses the final aims and purposes of historical inquiry. On the first point he claims that the reliance of the historian upon the evidence at his disposal and the conclusions he draws from that evidence are wholly founded upon inductive principles; it is our general knowledge of causes and effects and of the regularities governing human behaviour, all of which derives from past experience, that makes the interpretation of documents possible and leads us to infer that they provide trustworthy accounts of the events they purport to describe. And, on the second point, he claims that the 'chief use' of history 'is only to discover the constant and universal principles of human nature . . . furnishing us with materials from which we may . . . become acquainted with the regular springs of human action and behaviour'. Thus, it must be absurd to *oppose* history to science. Not only does it achieve its results by means of a type of reasoning that is common to all branches of scientific inquiry; these results are themselves to be seen as contributing in an essential way to the development of what is (Hume thinks) the most fundamental science of all—the science of man.

The denial that any radical differences separate the fields of historical and scientific knowledge, and the connected belief that no philosophically important issues belong to the first that are not equally comprehended within the scope of the second, represent assumptions which have remained largely unchallenged by much subsequent empiricist thought. True, there have been divergences in the manner in which these assumptions have been interpreted. It has been argued, for instance, that the inferences and explanations characteristically made or given by historians lack the precision and finality of those attainable in other, more 'exact', sciences; that there is nothing in history which corresponds to the body of systematic and complex theories, deductively organized and experimentally established, exemplified in highly developed natural sciences like physics or chemistry; that the focus of the historian's attention is in any case different from that of workers in other scientific fields, inasmuch as his interest is primarily (*pace* Hume) one of describing and explaining particular events or sequences of events that happened in the past, rather than of framing universal laws or hypotheses which obtain irrespective of time and place and which can be used for purposes of predicting or controlling the future course of things. Qualifications of this sort have not, however, been thought to entail the conclusion that history has some kind of unique epistemological status. Instead, it has sometimes been suggested that they show merely the limitations of historical thinking when set beside the achievements of more successful branches of inductive inquiry, the crude or makeshift character of its procedures when compared with those of more advanced or refined empirical disciplines and the relative modesty of its aims; if any philosophical moral is to be drawn from this, it is that history should attempt to approximate more closely to the standards set in other domains rather than that it enjoys some position of privilege which mysteriously puts it beyond criticism.

Whatever degree of acceptance such conceptions of historical inquiry may have found among English philosophers, Italian readers will not need reminding that it is precisely notions like these which have been the target of the attacks of a long line of Continental thinkers, attacks based upon a quite distinct view of the nature and significance of historical knowledge. It was, perhaps, the principal achievement of R. G. Collingwood (1889–1943) to have interpreted the implications of this type of criticism in such a manner that they could no longer be reasonably ignored by his philosophical contemporaries. Collingwood himself was under no illusions concerning what he felt to be the prevailing climate of philosophical opinion in England; when, for instance, he read the works of his compatriots, he described himself as being constantly 'haunted by the thought that their accounts of knowledge, based as they seem to be on the study of perception and scientific thinking, not only ignore historical thinking but are actually inconsistent with there being such a thing'. And in his writings on the subject, particularly in his book *The Idea of History* [COLLINGWOOD], he made a determined effort to examine the presuppositions of genuine historical inquiry in a manner that would establish, clearly and conclusively, the autonomy of history as a discipline with its own specific methods and procedures—as 'a self-dependent, self-determining and self-justifying form of thought'. In attempting this task Collingwood, like Croce to whom he owed so much, totally rejected the 'naturalistic' interpretations which had, in his view, been falsely put upon the historian's activity by positivistically minded theorists; these interpretations showed only too evidently that their proponents lacked any real understanding of the nature of the historian's approach to his material and subject-matter.

In what did this lack of understanding consist? For Collingwood it may broadly be said to have lain in a failure to appreciate,
and inattention to, certain special problems which arise when the
subject of study is the human mind and intellect. There is a recurrent temptation to carry over into the investigation of human
thought and personality categories and explanatory schemes which
are essentially adapted to rendering intelligible processes and
events in inanimate nature; attempts to do this are, however,
necessarily misconceived. The mind, at any rate so far as its
rational, reflective activities are concerned, is not susceptible to an
analysis such as Hume and his successors tried to provide, and it
is precisely for this reason that history cannot be conceived on the
model of the natural sciences: for the events with which the
historian is concerned are human actions, and actions are the out-
ward expression of thought; neither actions nor the thinking processes of which they are the direct embodiment are explicable in
terms of observed correlations between occurrences of the type
that underlie the scientist's explanations of events in unthinking
nature. It was on these general grounds that Collingwood denied
that the concept of cause had the same force when employed in
historical contexts as it had elsewhere, insisting that the historian
used it in a 'special sense' and that his so using it pointed to a decisive difference in his mode of interpreting the phenomena with
which he had to do. Thus, the historian certainly endeavours in
his narrative to show why certain things happened, why certain
things were done; if he did not, his narrative would not be history
at all, but mere 'chronicle', a list of happenings without coherence
or intelligibility. But showing why the events occurred as they
did is essentially a matter of grasping and making transparent their
'inner side', namely, the thought of which they are the overt manifestation as the actions of rational agents confronted with certain
practical problems. Moreover, it would be a mistake to represent
this interior side to action as comprising what Hume referred to as
'internal impressions'—feelings or sensations connected together
by determinate psychological laws. For a historian to be able to
understand for himself, and so be in a position to explain to others,
the behaviour of some given historical figure in a particular
situation, he must 're-enact' in his own mind the selfsame process
of thinking that originally found expression in that behaviour and
gave it significance and point; and this, Collingwood suggested,

would be quite impossible if acts of thought were mere perishing sensations or states of feeling. The latter cannot in the requisite sense be re-experienced on a later occasion; we can at best have subsequent experiences which we recognize to be qualitatively similar to them, for they themselves have been carried away on the stream of time and are irrecoverable. And this illustrates a difference of type or category of central importance to a correct appreciation of historical thinking: unlike a sensation, say, or an emotion, 'one and the same act of thought may endure through a lapse of time and revive after a time when it has been in abeyance', the possibility of such revival constituting a fundamental presupposition of the historian's procedure. Thus, Collingwood believed that he had extracted what was implicit in the Crocean dictum that 'all history is contemporary history', giving it a clear and intelligible sense: past actions, if they are to be historically known, must be re-lived in the historian's mind in the way described, such 'inward' re-creation standing at the opposite pole from the 'external', purely observational approach which the natural scientist adopts towards his material.

It must, I think, be admitted that the manner in which Collingwood tended to formulate his thesis of history as the re-enactment of past thinking was not entirely fortunate. He sometimes gives the impression of regarding the historian's procedure as implying the existence of a unique power of self-certifying intuition, and again of supposing the historian to be in some way endowed with a capacity for identifying himself with those about whom he writes which transcends temporal intervals and overcomes the barriers normally thought to separate the consciousness of one individual from that of another. Such contentions seem to raise profound logical, as well as epistemological, difficulties, and a number of modern critics have not been slow to point these out. They have argued, too, on more general grounds that Collingwood confused the question of how a historian may be led to propound a certain hypothesis—which may possibly involve 'insight' or 'empathetic understanding' in some sense of these not very clear notions—and the question of what it is for a hypothesis to be substantiated or confirmed; it is useless for a historian to say that he knows a certain interpretation of what somebody did to be correct because he has 'revived' the thought of the agent in his own mind, for this leaves unanswered the problem of whether the thought he claims to have revived can in fact be validly attributed to the agent in question. Suppose that two historians differ in the interpretations they put forward, each claiming that they have re-enacted the agent's calculations and reasons: how is one to choose between their divergent accounts if not by reference to objective criteria which necessarily take one beyond the narrow circle of subjective conviction and certitude?

The force of these objections and of others like them may be granted. None the less, it is arguable that they rest upon a too restricted view of the kind of position Collingwood, together with those of his Continental predecessors who similarly insisted upon the autonomous character of historical thinking, wished to maintain, and that they obscure features of his account which, properly understood, throw into prominence certain important defects in traditional empiricist conceptions of knowledge and explanation. For what, among other things, Collingwood did was to focus attention upon the concept of *action*, regarded as a funda-mental and ineliminable category of human thought which plays a far more pervasive and complex role in the interpretation of behaviour than many philosophers, imbued with the belief that everything can be represented in language appropriate to the de-scription of physical processes and events, have been prepared to recognize. When, as is the case in history, we are dealing with human beings, our essential concern is with agents and their activities. What takes place is then seen, first and foremost, as something *done*, and to see what happens in this way is to see it as more than a mere observable occurrence, a bare 'fact of nature' to be explained simply by subsuming it beneath empirically ascer-tainable laws and uniformities. The German writer, Wilhelm Dilthey, to whom Collingwood was already indebted, denied that the historian could treat what happened in history as 'spectacles to be watched'—this was falsely to assimilate history to what he called 'natural-scientific knowledge'; instead, it must be under-stood as the overt expression in 'living utterances' of states of mind and feeling which the historian can enter into and share. Such a judgement need not be interpreted in a manner that re-quires us to suppose that it ascribes to the historian some recon-dite or 'mystical' mode of cognition which is denied to investi-gators in other domains; although Dilthey, like Collingwood, admittedly sometimes writes as if this were so. Instead, it may be regarded as primarily making a point about the kind of conceptual framework to which we commit ourselves when we refer to an event as a human action, such reference carrying certain special—though by no means unfamiliar or out-of-the-way—implications concerning the fashion in which what is referred to can be appropriately characterized and understood. A whole range of notions that would be simply out of place in some contexts are here seen to be relevant, not merely to the type of explanation which may be provided of what has occurred but also to the very manner in which that occurrence may be identified and described. Occupying a central place among such notions are those of intention, motive, purpose, reason and belief. Thus, we do not, for example, raise questions involving plans or aims when trying to understand events of inanimate nature, nor—other than in a way that is more or less explicitly metaphorical—do our descriptions of such events tacitly ascribe intentions to the phenomena concerned. By contrast, the discussion of human conduct necessarily brings ideas like these into play, which may indeed be said to be to a large extent built into the terms and concepts we typically employ to pick out and characterize the things people do. For description and explanation are in this area tightly interwoven: the choice of one word or expression to describe a person's action in preference to another which, from the point of view purely of the 'observed facts', may seem equally applicable is frequently of the utmost significance when the question is one of understanding or appraising what has been done. And this is not surprising. For what a man believes himself to be about, what ends, for instance, he has in view or what description he would accept of his action in relation to his situation as he conceives it to be, are to a considerable extent actually constitutive of what he is doing; they cannot be treated as mere extrinsic accompaniments, determinable independently of his action as it really is 'in itself' and irrelevant to its true nature.

Such considerations, if correct, have an obvious bearing upon the problem of historical knowledge. Not only does the provision of historical explanations presuppose a general understanding of what it is to think and behave as a purposive agent with the ability to apply and conform to rules or principles of action and to pursue objectives in the light of practical calculations or reasons. There is a further, and crucially important, sense in which the just characterization and interpretation of particular historical events is logically dependent upon a capacity to appreciate the significance of these events from the standpoint of those who participated in them. For to portray what these participants did, to exhibit accurately and intelligibly the role they played, it is necessary for the historian to reconstruct, in addition to the individual intentions, hopes, fears and so forth that informed their activities, the wider setting of accepted belief and social convention which (very often) gave point and meaning to their behaviour; the beliefs they held, the conventions they observed and followed, may diverge profoundly from those with which the historian is familiar in the context of his own life and society, finding expression in quite different systems of classification and evaluation, and it may demand great imaginative effort, as well as extensive research, for him to achieve the kind of comprehension requisite in such a case. Dilthey employed the notion of 'objective mind' to refer to factors of the latter type, and he was perhaps more sensitive than Collingwood, whose approach was in general highly individualistic, to their importance for historical understanding and exegesis. But in the case of Collingwood also one can perceive the relevance of some of the points that have been made, particularly in connection with his claim that actions have an 'inner side' which it is the task of the historian to uncover and 'revive' within his own mind. Collingwood has often been criticized for excessive intellectualism, for assuming too easily that the only activities which can engage the interest of the historian *qua* historian are those involving some definite process of deliberative ratiocination: it is pointed out that such assumption is simply not true to actual historical practice, and that the conclusion drawn —that all history is really the history of thought—is therefore unjustified. Certainly Collingwood's criteria for calling something an action and his conception of what it is for actions to involve thinking seem too narrow; there are, for instance, surely many cases where we should be said to have acted intelligently or for a reason, but where what we did was not preceded by any process of calculation or planning; it would be sufficient that we should have been able to give an account of what we were doing and why if we had been asked. It will, even so, still remain true that the historian's understanding or misunderstanding of what men have done in the past is intimately bound up with the ability to interpret and describe their conduct in terms which the agents themselves would have found comprehensible and applicable; in this sense the claim that historical events must be grasped 'from within' and cannot be looked at purely 'externally' represents not so much a gratuitous piece of obscurantist metaphysics as the recognition of an indispensable feature of historical procedure.

Seen in this light the ideas advanced by Collingwood and others regarding the status of historical knowledge and explanation have interesting points of connection with certain recent developments in analytical philosophy of the kind now practised in Britain and the United States. Generally speaking, British philosophers no longer subscribe to the restrictive tenets of logical positivism mentioned earlier, and the somewhat puritanical tendency to treat the concepts and propositions of natural science as paradigm instances of significance has lost much of its previous hold. One symptom of the shift in the philosophical climate which has taken place during the last decade or so has been a greater readiness to give serious attention to the problems presented by the human studies. Thus, topics specifically relating to the philosophy of mind and conduct have moved to the centre of much contemporary discussion; chief among these have been notions like that of intention, and the part they play in the description and explanation of actions. Moreover, the type of analysis accorded to such concepts has been in the direction of showing the difficulties that arise if attempts are made to interpret them according to the conception of mental operations favoured by traditional empiricist theory; the Humean picture of mental life, for example, as a succession of 'impressions and ideas', some of which—in the shape of 'volitions' or 'motives'—causally produce bodily movements, has been subjected to a variety of criticisms designed to expose its logical inadequacy and incoherence.[1] This is not the place to try to examine and evaluate the force of the arguments adduced, which are often subtle and complex; but it is at least clear that they have important consequences so far as the philosophical analysis of history is concerned. For, apart from anything else, many of them constitute a challenge to a basic assumption which has lain at the root of a great deal of empiricist thought about history: namely, the belief that all explanations, including those of human behaviour, conform without exception to a single pattern

[1] See, e.g., RYLE (2); WITTGENSTEIN (3, 4); ANSCOMBE; HAMPSHIRE (2).

—to explain something must always and necessarily be a matter of subsuming it beneath a causal uniformity or law correlating discrete events. Despite his very different general standpoint and aims, Collingwood also, as we have seen, attacked this assumption, his final position being that causal explanations in the Humean sense had no place in history considered as the study of what men have thought and done. Whether the latter conclusion is justified is far from clear: even if it is true that some explanations of human behaviour cannot be satisfactorily elucidated in such terms, it does not follow that none can; and, in any case, it seems difficult to see how historians could altogether dispense with generalizations, however indirect their reference to these may be, in their attempts to make the past intelligible. Nevertheless, it is to Collingwood's credit that he drew attention to some of the problems surrounding the interpretation of human action, recognizing their relevance to the philosophy of history; and the very fact that these problems are now the subject of detailed and serious discussion permits the hope that history may, as he believed it should, come to be accorded a less summary treatment than it has been wont to receive at the hands of British philosophers.

There are, indeed, indications that such a change in attitude may already be in progress. During the last few years there has been a notable increase in the number of books and articles published on the subject of historical understanding and interpretation. If few of their authors would subscribe unreservedly to Collingwood's claim that 'the chief business of twentieth-century philosophy is to reckon with twentieth-century history', there is at least general agreement among them that history presents problems for the philosopher which merit more attention than has hitherto been granted. And it is perhaps significant that, in the comparisons they have made between historical and scientific modes of thought and inquiry, it is the differences rather than the resemblances which have tended increasingly to be emphasized.

Recent discussions in the philosophy of history have in fact centred round a number of distinct focal points or topics, though most of these can be seen in the end to involve questions concerning the relation of the historical to the scientific disciplines. One such topic, interest in which was partly stimulated by the publication of A. J. Toynbee's controversial *A Study of History*

[TOYNBEE], has been the status and validity of allegedly scientific systems or projects purporting to show that the historical process as a whole conforms to some unifying pattern or that it is subject to certain discoverable 'laws of development'. It has been argued from a number of directions, for instance, that theories of this general type exhibit important confusions and misconceptions: not merely (as Professor Popper, among others, has trenchantly maintained in POPPER (3)) are their proponents apt to presuppose radically mistaken notions of the nature and methods of scientific inquiry as this is actually carried on; it has been claimed from the other side that they betray an equally serious inability to comprehend the distinctive character of historical thinking, the categories and aims of which are irreducible to those of the kind typically found in the natural sciences—'the attempt to construct a discipline which would stand to concrete history as pure to applied, is not a vain hope for something beyond human powers, but a chimera, born of a profound incapacity to grasp the nature of natural science, or of history, or of both'.[2] Such considerations have in turn been thought to bear upon another issue which has also attracted the attention of philosophers; namely, the thesis of historical determinism and the implications of that thesis for the ascription of responsibility to individual historical agents. Thus, the claim that historical events are ultimately the product of impersonal forces and of circumstances beyond human control, and the accompanying suggestion that evaluative judgements of praise and blame are unjustified and out of place in history, have been examined in relation to the actual practice and presuppositions of historical study; and here likewise it has been argued by some that the position in question conflicts (necessarily and to an extent not sufficiently recognized by its adherents) with much that is fundamental to the very notion of historical understanding and inquiry as ordinarily conceived. It is, however, to the central problem of what constitutes historical explanation and of how such explanation may be characterized and elucidated that, perhaps inevitably, contemporary writers have chiefly addressed themselves.

Much that has been written on this subject has been prompted in the first instance by reflection upon an analysis of historical explanation offered by Professor C. G. Hempel [HEMPEL (1)].

[2] BERLIN (2). See also BERLIN (1).

According to this analysis, which is basically of a Humean type, there is no essential difference in logical structure between scientific explanation and explanation of the kind used by historians: crudely speaking, in both cases the explanation of a given event presupposes general laws or 'regularities' in terms of which the event in question is correlated with other events or circumstances that represent its 'determining conditions' or 'causes'. Such an account has initial plausibility, particularly for empiricists anxious to avoid (in history as elsewhere) any view savouring of mysterious 'intuitable' connections between phenomena; nevertheless, subsequent discussion has on the whole been critical of Hempel's suggestion. To begin with, it involves the questionable assumption, to which attention has already been drawn, that all authentic explanation conforms to a single uniform pattern; and it has been contended that, even if some of the explanations historians characteristically provide can broadly be interpreted (granted certain qualifications and amendments) along the proposed lines, there are others—notably those specifically concerned with the motives and reasons of individual agents—which are resistant to such an analysis and demand different treatment.[3] Some writers, however, have wished to go farther than this, arguing that in the context of history what has been termed the 'covering law model' of analysis is wholly, and not merely partially, inappropriate; more particularly, they have claimed that attempts to state and to render explicit the laws allegedly presupposed by historical explanations result in formulations that are either hopelessly vague or suicidally over-specific. And in place of such an approach it has been suggested, among other things, that a closer examination of what is referred to as 'the historian's judgement in the particular case' is required—though how exactly such judgement may be exercised in the absence of any reference to general laws or uniformities has not always been made as clear as might be wished.

Views of this kind, at least in their negative aspects, appear to share obvious features in common with the conception of history as an autonomous discipline advanced by Croce and Collingwood; moreover, Professor Dray (to give only one instance) has, in his own interesting discussion of problems raised by historical explanations of individual actions, also shown qualified sympathy

[3] See, e.g., GARDINER, Part 3.

with the positive thesis of history as the re-enactment of past thinking and experience [DRAY, Ch. 5]. Even so, it remains important not to exaggerate the similarities. Recent philosophers have certainly not shared the idealist metaphysic which underlay earlier endeavours to vindicate the autonomy of history; nor have they hesitated to criticize, often very severely, the quasi-psychological manner in which these vindications were sometimes expressed. Instead, their inquiries have tended to be of a strictly conceptual or 'logical' character, and have been undertaken with the aim of providing a careful analysis of historical statements as these are actually made and understood. The guiding purpose has not been to refashion history after an alien image or to try to fit it into some preconceived framework of knowledge; rather it has been to show, through an unprejudiced attention to the ways in which historians customarily speak and argue, the nature of historical thinking as it is in fact accepted and practised.

There are, I believe, considerable merits in such an approach; not least, it may help to extend the boundaries within which philosophy in the English-speaking world has perhaps been for too long confined. But there is also a possible danger involved, which in concluding may briefly be mentioned. History—the study of history—itself has a history; it has not always taken the shape in which we now know it. And the course of its development has to some extent been influenced by the work of Continental philosophers and theorists who, dissatisfied with the state of the subject as they found it, offered revolutionary proposals for its reform and re-orientation. Some of their suggestions now lie fossilized in great systems of the kind which in modern times have been the object of intensive, and to a large degree justified, attack; others, on the other hand, proved to be of far-reaching consequence and importance for the subsequent evolution of history and the humane disciplines generally. It would be unfortunate if too great a respect for the manner in which historians at present proceed were to prevent philosophers from engaging in the type of critical reflection and appraisal it has been traditionally part of their function to provide.

13. CONTEMPORARY AESTHETICS AND THE NEGLECT OF NATURAL BEAUTY

R. W. HEPBURN

OPEN an eighteenth-century work on aesthetics, and the odds are that it will contain a substantial treatment of the beautiful, the sublime, the picturesque in nature.[1] Its treatment of art may be secondary and derivative, not its primary concern. Although the nineteenth century could not be said to repeat these same emphases, they certainly reappear in some impressive places, in Ruskin's *Modern Painters*, for instance—a work that might have been entitled, no less accurately, 'How to look at nature and enjoy it aesthetically.' In our own day, however, writings on aesthetics attend almost exclusively to the arts and very rarely indeed to natural beauty, or only in the most perfunctory manner. Aesthetics is even *defined* by some mid-century writers as 'the philosophy of art', 'the philosophy of criticism', analysis of the language and concepts used in describing and appraising art-objects. Two much-quoted anthologies of aesthetics (Elton's in this country, Vivas and Krieger's in America) contain not a single study of natural beauty.[2]

---

[1] By 'nature' I shall mean all objects that are not human artefacts. This will of course include living creatures. I can afford to ignore for the purposes of this study the many possible disputes over natural objects that have received a marked, though limited, transformation at man's hands.

[2] ELTON; VIVAS–KRIEGER. Compare also OSBORNE, which likewise confines its investigation to art-experience. BEARDSLEY is sub-titled *Problems in the Philosophy of Criticism*.

Obsorne defines beauty as the 'characteristic and peculiar excellence of works of

Why has this curious shift come about? For part of the answer we have to look not to philosophers' theories but to some general shifts in aesthetic taste itself. This is a legitimate procedure, since, despite the difference of logical level between them, judgements of taste and the theorizings of aesthetics exert unmistakable influences upon one another. Relevant facts, then, are these: that—for all the cult of the open air, the caravans, camps and excursions in the family car—serious aesthetic concern with nature is today rather a rare phenomenon. If we regard the Wordsworthian vision as the great peak in the recent history of the subject, then we have to say that the ground declined very sharply indeed from that extraordinary summit, and that today we survey it from far below. In one direction it quickly declined to the deeps of the romantics' own 'dejection' experiences, and in another to the forced ecstasies and hypocrisies of a fashionable and trivialized nature-cult. At its most deeply felt the Wordsworthian experience brought a re-kindling of religious imagination for some who found it no longer sustained by the traditional dogmas. But a still more radical loss of religious confidence came to undermine the undogmatic Wordsworthian experience itself.

The vanishing of the sense that nature is man's 'educator', that its beauties communicate more or less specific morally ennobling messages, this is only one aspect of the general (and much anatomized) disappearance of a rationalist faith in nature's thorough-going intelligibility and in its ultimate endorsement of human visions and aspirations. The characteristic image of contemporary man, as we all know, is that of a 'stranger', encompassed by a nature, which is indifferent, unmeaning and 'absurd'.

The work of the sciences, too, has tended to increase bewilderment and loss of nerve over the aesthetic interpretation of nature. Microscope and telescope have added vastly to our perceptual data; the forms of the ordinary landscape, ordinarily interpreted, are shown up as only a selection from countless different scales.

It is not surprising that (with a few exceptions) the artists themselves have turned from imitation and representation to the sheer creation of new objects, rewarding to contemplate in their own right. If they are expressive of more than purely formal relation-

---

art'. Beardsley's opening sentence reads: 'There would be no problems of aesthetics, in the sense in which I propose to mark out this field of study, if no one ever talked about works of art.

ships, then that 'more' tends to be not the alien external landscape but the inner landscape of the human psyche.

On the theoretical level, there are other and distinctive reasons for the neglect of natural beauty in aesthetics itself, especially in an aesthetics that seeks to make itself increasingly rigorous. One such reason is that if we are aiming at an entirely general account of aesthetic excellence, this account cannot make essential reference to experience of (or imitation of) nature; since there are arts like music which are devoid of any such reference. Some writers have been impressed by the fact that certain crucial features of aesthetic experience are quite unobtainable in nature—a landscape does not minutely control the spectator's response to it as does a successful work of art; it is an unframed ordinary object, in contrast to the framed, 'esoteric', 'illusory' or 'virtual' character of the art-object. And so the artefact is taken as the aesthetic object *par excellence*, and the proper focus of study.

Although it is now very much in eclipse, the last widely accepted unified aesthetic system was the expression theory. No single new system has taken its place; and some of its influences are still with us. The expression theory is a *communication*-theory: it must represent aesthetic experience of nature either as communication from the Author of Nature, which it rarely does, or else (rather awkwardly) as the discovery that nature's shapes and colours can with luck serve as expressive vehicles of human feeling, although never constructed for that end.[3] The theory most readily copes with artefacts, not natural objects; with successful interpersonal communication, not the contemplation of sheer entities *as* entities. Although some very recent aesthetic analyses provide instruments that could be used to redress the lopsidedness of these emphases, they have not yet been applied extensively to this task.[4]

We may note, finally, that linguistic or conceptual analysts have been understandably tempted to apply their techniques first and

[3] For Croce's view, see CROCE, Part I, Ch. 13.

[4] I am thinking, for example, of the recent insistence that even the art-object is primarily *object*, that it must not be approached simply as a clue to its creator's states of mind. See BEARDSLEY *passim*, especially the earlier sections. I discuss some aspects of this 'anti-intentionalism' later in this paper.

(It should be mentioned that Beardsley's book contains an exceptionally rich bibliography of recent English and American writing in aesthetics. A reader who follows up the references given in his notes and discussions (appended to each chapter of the book) is given a very full survey of current argument and opinion.)

foremost to the arguments, counter-arguments and manifestoes lying to hand in the writings of critics of the arts. In the case of natural beauty, however, such a polemical critical literature scarcely exists. The philosopher must first work out his own detailed and systematic account of the aesthetic enjoyment of nature. And this he has so far been slow, or reluctant, to do.

Having outlined the situation, the neglect of the study of natural beauty, I now want to argue that the neglect is a very bad thing: bad, because aesthetics is thereby steered off from examining an important and richly complex set of relevant data; and bad because when a set of human experiences is ignored in a theory relevant to them, they tend to be rendered less readily available as experiences. If we cannot find sensible-sounding language in which to describe them—language of a piece with the rest of our aesthetic talk, the experiences are felt, in an embarrassed way, as off-the-map; and, since off the map, seldom visited. This result is specially unfortunate, if for other reasons the experiences are already hard to achieve—in some of their varieties at least. What, then, can contemporary aesthetics say on the topic of natural beauty?

In a one-chapter study like this the whole problem (or tangle of problems) cannot be teased out minutely. There must be drastic selecting among possible themes. Bearing in mind the general aims of this book, I have tried in what follows to strike a reasonable compromise. On the one hand, the reader needs some surveying of the philosophical situation, some indicating of the main patterns of current argument and opinion; and on the other hand (knowing how much emphasis is put upon minute logical analysis in British philosophy), he must be provided with some samples of that—brief and tentative though they will have to be. This essay has begun with some very general remarks indeed: it will move gradually towards discussing more specific and limited issues, and its last topic of all will be its most highly particularized one. These various topics are not so intimately related as to be links in a single chain of argument. But the later discussions make frequent and essential reference back to points made earlier. I call this in one sense a compromise (in that neither the survey nor the analysis is more than a sketch); but in another sense it tries to exhibit what are always legitimate, indeed necessary, tasks for the writer on aesthetics. He is ill-advised to do *nothing but* general surveying, or his work would be too loosely and remotely related to the particularities of actual aesthetic experiences. But a monomaniacal concern with analysis alone can be equally unfortunate. It may prevent even an intelligent choosing of cruces for the analysis itself, and make it impossible to see the bearing of the analyses upon the inquiry as a whole, far less upon the related fields of ethics and the philosophy of mind.

If I am right that systematic description is one main lack in the treatment of our subject, my first obligation may well be to supply some account of the varieties of aesthetic experience of nature. But their variety is immense, and mere cataloguing would be tedious. I shall suggest, therefore, two principles of selection that may throw together some samples interesting in themselves and useful for our subsequent arguments.

First, we have already remarked that art-objects have a number of general characteristics not shared by objects in nature. It would be useful if we could show (and I think we can) that the absence of certain of these features is not merely negative or privative in its effect, but can contribute positively and valuably to the aesthetic experience of nature. A good specimen is the degree to which the spectator can be involved in the natural aesthetic situation itself. On occasion, he may confront natural objects as a static, disengaged observer; but far more typically the objects envelop him on all sides. In a forest, trees surround him; he is ringed by hills, or he stands in the midst of a plain. If there is movement in the scene, the spectator may himself be in motion, and his motion may be an important element in his aesthetic experience. Think, for instance, of a glider-pilot, delighting in a sense of buoyancy, in the balancing of the air-currents that hold him aloft. This sort of involvement is well expressed by Barbara Hepworth:

> What a different shape and 'being' one becomes lying on the sand with the sea almost above from when standing against the wind on a sheer high cliff with seabirds circling patterns below one. [HEPWORTH, Ch. 4]

We have not only a mutual involvement of spectator and object, but also a reflexive effect by which the spectator experiences *himself* in an unusual and vivid way; and this difference is not merely noted, but dwelt upon aesthetically. The effect is not unknown to art, especially architecture. But it is both more intensely realized and pervasive in nature-experience—for we are *in* nature and a part *of* nature; we do not stand over against it as over against a painting on a wall.

If this study were on a larger scale, we should have to analyse in detail the various senses of 'detachment' and 'involvement' that are relevant here. This would prove a more slippery investigation than in the case of art-appreciation; but a rewarding one. Some sort of detachment there certainly is, in the sense that I am not *using* nature, manipulating it or calculating how to manipulate it. But I am both actor and spectator, ingredient in the landscape and lingering upon the sensations of being thus ingredient, rejoicing in their multifariousness, playing actively with nature, and letting nature, as it were, play with me and my sense of myself.

My second specimen is very similar, though, I think, worth listing separately. Though by no means all art-objects have frames or pedestals, they share a common character in being *set apart* from their environment, and set apart in a distinctive way. We might use the words 'frame' and 'framed' in an extended sense, to cover not only the physical boundaries of pictures but all the various devices employed in the different arts to prevent the art-object being mistaken for a natural object or for an artefact without aesthetic interest. Our list of frames, in this wide sense, would include the division between stage-area and audience-area in the theatre, the concert-convention that the only aesthetically relevant sounds are those made by the performers, the layout of a page in a book of poems, where typography and spacing set the poem apart from titles, page-numbers, critical apparatus and footnotes. Such devices are best thought of as aids to the recognition of the formal *completeness* of the art-objects themselves, their ability to sustain aesthetic interest, an interest that is not crucially dependent upon the relationships between the object and its general environment. Certainly, its environment may enhance or weaken its effect; and we may even see parts of the environment in a new way as a result of contemplating an art-object. But this does not affect the central point, that these works of art are first and foremost bounded objects, that their aesthetic characteristics are determined by their internal structure, the interplay of their elements.

In contrast, natural objects are 'frameless'. This is in some ways a disadvantage aesthetically; but there are some remarkable compensating advantages. Whatever lies beyond the frame of an art-object cannot normally become part of the aesthetic experience relevant to it. A chance train-whistle cannot be integrated into the music of a string quartet; it merely interferes with its appreciation. But where there is no frame, and where nature is our aesthetic object, a sound or a visible intrusion from beyond the original boundaries of our attention can challenge us to integrate it in our overall experience, to modify that experience so as to make room for it. This, of course, *need* not occur; we may shut it out by effort of will, if it seems quite unassimilable. At any rate, our creativity is challenged, set a task; and when things go well with us, we experience a sudden expansion of imagination that can be memorable in its own right.

> 'And, when there came a pause
> Of silence such as baffled his best skill:
> Then sometimes, in that silence, while he hung
> Listening, a gentle shock of mild surprise
> Has carried far into his heart the voice
> Of mountain-torrents'; Wordsworth: *There Was a Boy*

If the absence of 'frame' precludes full determinateness and stability in the natural aesthetic object, it at least offers in return such unpredictable perceptual surprises; and their mere possibility imparts to the contemplation of nature a sense of adventurous openness.[5]

Something more definite can be said on the determinate and indeterminate in this connection. In, say, a painting, the frame ensures that each element of the work is determined in its perceived qualities (including emotional qualities) by a limited and definite context. Colour modifies colour and form modifies form; yet the frame supplies a boundary to all relevant modifiers, and,

[5] Unrestricted generalizations in aesthetics are usually precarious in proportion to their attractiveness. I have taken care not to set out the above contrast between 'framed' and 'unframed' as a contrast between *all* art-objects and *all* natural objects considered aesthetically; for not every art-object has a frame, even in the extended sense I have used above. Works of architecture, for instance, are like natural objects, in that we can set no limits to the viewpoints from which they can properly be regarded, nor can we decree where the aesthetically relevant context of a building ends. A church or castle, seen from several miles away, may dominate, and determine how we see a whole landscape. The contrast between framed and frameless can none the less be made for very many types of aesthetic object—far enough at least to justify the general points made in the text.

thus, any given colour or shape can be seen in a successful painting, to have a determinate, contextually controlled character. Obviously, this is one kind of determinateness that cannot be achieved with natural objects; and that for several reasons. To consider only one of them: the aesthetic impact made upon us by, say, a tree, is part-determined by the context we include in our view of it. A tree growing on a steep hill-slope, bent far over by the winds, may strike us as tenacious, grim, strained. But from a greater distance, when the view includes numerous similar trees on the hillside, the striking thing may be a delightful, stippled, patterned slope, with quite different emotional quality—quixotic or cheery.[6] So with any aesthetic quality in nature; it is always provisional, correctible by reference to a different, perhaps wider context, or to a narrower one realized in greater detail. 'An idyllic scene? But you haven't noticed that advancing, though still distant, thundercloud. Now you have noticed it, and the whole scene takes on a new, threatened, ominous look.' In positive terms this provisional and elusive character of aesthetic qualities in nature creates a restlessness, an alertness, a search for ever new standpoints, and for more comprehensive gestalts. Of this restlessness and of this search I shall, very shortly, have more to say.

My last point on the present topic is this. We can distinguish, in a rough and ready way, between the particular aesthetic impact of an object, whether natural or artefact, and certain general 'background' experiences, that are common to a great many aesthetic situations and are of aesthetic value in themselves. With an art-object, there is the exhilarating activity of coming to grasp its intelligibility as a perceptual whole. We find built-in guides to interpretation, and contextual controls for our response. We are aware of these features as having been expressly put there by its creator. Now I think that we can locate a nearly parallel but interestingly different background experience when our object is not an artefact but a natural one. Again, it is a kind of exhilaration, in this case a delight in the fact that the forms of the natural world *offer scope* for the exercise of the imagination, that leaf pattern chimes with vein or pattern, cloud form with mountain form and mountain form with human form. On a theistic view this begets a distinctive sort of wonderment at the 'artistry' of God. On a naturalistic view it can beget at least no less wonderment at this

[6] On emotional qualities I have written elsewhere. [HEPBURN]

uncontrived adaptation. Indeed, when nature is pronounced to be 'beautiful'—not in the narrower sense of that word, which contrasts 'beautiful' with 'picturesque' or 'comic', but in the wide sense equivalent to 'aesthetically excellent'—an important part of our meaning is just this, that nature's forms do provide this scope for imaginative play. For that is surely not analystically true; it might have been otherwise.

I have been arguing that certain important differences between natural objects and art-objects should not be seen as entailing the aesthetic unimportance of the former, that (on the contrary) several of these differences furnish grounds for distinctive and valuable types of aesthetic experience of nature. These are types of experience that art cannot provide to the same extent as nature, and which in some cases it cannot provide at all.

Supposing that a person's aesthetic education fails to reckon with these differences, supposing it instils in him the attitudes, the tactics of approach, the expectations proper to the appreciation of art-works only, we may be sure that such a person will either pay very little aesthetic heed to natural objects, or else will heed them in the wrong way. He will look—and of course look in vain—for what can be found and enjoyed only in art. Furthermore, one cannot be at all certain that he will seriously ask himself whether there might be other tactics, other attitudes and expectations more proper and more fruitful for the aesthetic appreciation of nature. My sampling of these 'differences', therefore, is not a merely introductory exercise in distinction-making. It has the polemical purpose of showing that unless these distinctions are reckoned with both in aesthetic education and theorizing, one can neither intelligently pursue nor adequately comprehend experience of natural beauty, save only in its most rudimentary forms.

So much for the listing of neglects and omissions. I want now to turn to something more constructive, and to take as a starting-point certain recurrent and *prima facie* attractive ways in which natural beauty has in fact been attended to and described, both in the past and present. I say 'as a starting-point', because I do not plan to examine in detail specific philosophical theories that have incorporated them. Rather, we shall take note of those approaches, the characteristic vocabulary that goes with them, and inquire how far (if at all) they point to an aesthetic of natural beauty that could be viable today.

Accounts of natural beauty sometimes focus upon the contemplating of single natural objects in their individuality and uniqueness (for an example—Pepita Haezrahi's analysis of the aesthetic contemplation of a single falling leaf [HAEZRAHI, Ch. 2]. Other writers, with greater metaphysical daring—or rashness—speak of the enjoyment of natural beauty as tending towards an ideal of 'oneness with nature' or as leading to the disclosure of 'unity' in nature. The formulations vary greatly and substantially among themselves; but the vocabulary of unity, oneness as the key aesthetic principle, is the recurrent theme. (On this point see terminal Note, p. 308.)

There are strong influences in contemporary British philosophy that prompt one to have the fullest sympathy with a particularist approach to natural beauty—as the contemplation of individual objects with their aesthetically interesting perceptual qualities; and to have very little sympathy for the more grandiose, speculative and quasi-mystical language of 'oneness with or in nature'. Yet it seems to me that we do not have here one good and one bad aesthetic approach, the first sane and the second absurd. Rather, we have two poles or well-separated landmarks between which lies a range of aesthetic possibilities; and in the mapping of this range those landmarks will play a valuable, perhaps a necessary role.

We must begin by bluntly denying the universal need for unity, unity of form, quality, structure or of anything else. We can take aesthetic pleasure in sheer plurality, in the stars of the night sky, in a birdsong without beginning, middle or end.[7]

And yet to make unity, in some sense, one's key concept need not be simply wrong-headed or obscurantist. Nor do we have to say, rather limply, that there are two distinct and unrelated types of aesthetic excellence, one that contemplates individual uniqueness and the other—no better or worse—that aims at some grand synthesis. I want to argue that there are certain incompletenesses in the experience of the isolated particular, that produce a *nisus* towards the other pole, the pole of unity. Accuracy, however, will require us to deny that there is a single type of unification or union; there are several notions to be distinguished within the ideal, and the relations between them are quite complex.

One such direction of development we have already noted;

[7] Compare MONTEFIORE (2).

namely, the *nisus* towards more and more comprehensive or adequate survey of the context that determines the perceived qualities of a natural object or scene. Our motives are, in part, the desire for a certain integrity or 'truth' in our aesthetic experience of nature; and of this more shortly. In part also we are prompted by our awareness that in all aesthetic experience it is contextual complexity that, more than any other single factor, makes possible the minute discrimination of emotional qualities; and such discrimination is accorded high aesthetic value. It is largely the pursuit of such value that moves us to accept what I called 'the challenge to integrate'—to take notice of and to accept as aesthetically relevant some shape or sound that initially lies outside the limit of our attention. 'Challenge' was not, I think, an overdramatic word to use. For we can contrast the stereotyped experiences of the aesthetically apathetic and unadventurous person with the richly and subtly diversified experiences of the aesthetically courageous person. His courage consists in his refusal to heed only those features of a natural object or scene that most readily come together in a familiar pattern or which yield a comfortingly generalized emotional quality. It also involves taking the repeated risk of drawing a blank, of finding oneself unable to hold the various elements together as a single object of contemplation, or to elicit any significant aesthetic experience from them at all.

The expansion of context may be a spatial expansion, but it does not have to be spatial. What else can it be? When we contemplate a natural object, we may see it not as sand-dune or rock but simply as a coloured shape. If this is difficult, we can look at the world upside down, with our head between our legs. But although an aesthetic view of an object will strive to shake free from conventional and deadening conceptualizings, that is not to say that *all* interpretings, all 'seeings as . . .' are lapses to the non-aesthetic. We ought not to accept a dichotomy of 'pure aesthetic contemplation'—'impure admixture of associations'. Suppose I am walking over a wide expanse of sand and mud. The quality of the scene is perhaps that of wild, glad emptiness. But suppose that I bring to bear upon the scene my knowledge that this is a tidal basin, the tide being out. The realization is not aesthetically irrelevant. I see myself now as virtually walking on what is for half the day sea-bed. The wild glad emptiness may be tempered by a disturbing weirdness.

This sort of experience can readily be related to the movement we were examining, the movement towards more complex and comprehensive synopses. In addition to spatial extension (or sometimes instead of it), we may aim at enriching the interpretative element, taking this not as theoretical 'knowledge about' the object or scene, but as helping to determine the aesthetic impact it makes upon us. 'Unity' here plays a purely 'regulative' role. Nature is not a 'given whole', nor indeed is knowledge about it. But in any case, there are practical, psychological limits to the expansion process; a degree of complexity is reached, beyond which there will be no increase in discrimination of perceptual or emotional qualities: rather the reverse.

A second movement away from contemplation of uninterpreted particulars is sometimes known as the 'humanizing' or the 'spiritualizing' of nature. I shall merely note its existence and relevance here, for there have been a good many accounts of it in the history of aesthetics. Coleridge said that 'Art is . . . the power of humanizing nature, of infusing the thoughts and passions of man into every thing which is the object of his contemplation' [COLERIDGE, Vol. II]. And Hegel, that the aim of art is 'to strip the outer world of its stubborn foreignness' [HEGEL, Introduction]. What is here said about art is no less true of aesthetic experience of nature itself. Imaginative activity is working for a *rapprochement* between the spectator and his aesthetic object: unity is again a regulative notion, a symbol of the unattainable complete transmutation of brute external nature into a mirror of the mind.

By developing and qualifying the 'humanization' ideal we can come to see yet a third aspect of the *nisus* towards unity. A person who contemplates natural objects aesthetically may sometimes find that their emotional quality is describable in the vocabulary of ordinary human moods and feelings—melancholy, exuberance, placidity. In many cases, however, he will find that they are not at all accurately describable in such terms. A particular emotional quality can be roughly *analogous* to some nameable human emotion, desolation for instance; but the precise quality of desolation revealed in some waste or desert in nature may be quite distinctive in timbre and intensity. To put this another way: one may go to nature to find shapes and sounds that can be taken as the embodiment of human emotion, and in so far as this occurs, nature is felt to be humanized. But instead of nature being humanized, the reverse may happen. Aesthetic experience of nature may be experience of a range of emotion that the human scene, by itself, untutored and unsupplemented, could not evoke. To extend the scope of these remarks, recall once again our quotation from Barbara Hepworth (p. 8). To be 'one' with nature in that sense was to realize vividly one's place in the landscape, as a form among its forms. And this is not to have nature's 'foreignness' or otherness overcome, but in contrast, to allow that otherness free play in the modifying of one's everyday sense of one's own being.

In this domain, again, we need not confine ourselves to the contemplating of naked, uninterpreted particulars. In a leaf-pattern I may 'see' also blood-vessel patterns, or the patterns of branching, forked lightning: or all of these. In a spiral nebula pattern I may see the pattern of swirling waters or whirling dust. I may be aware of a network of affinities, of analogous forms, that spans the inorganic or the organic world, or both. My experience has a quality of *multum in parvo*.[8] This is not necessarily a 'human-izing' of nature; it may be more like a 'naturizing' of the human observer. If, with Mr Eliot, one sees 'The dance along the artery/ The circulation of the lymph' as 'figured in the drift of stars', something of the aesthetic qualities of the latter (as we perceive them) may come to be transferred to the former. Supposing that by this kind of aesthetic experience nature is felt to lose some of its 'foreignness', that may be because we have ourselves become foreign to our everyday, unexamined notion of ourselves, and not through any assimilation of nature's forms to pre-existent notions, images or perceptions.

A fourth class of approaches to the ideals of 'unity' is itself rather heterogeneous; but we can characterize its members as follows. They are, once again, concerned less with the specific content of particular aesthetic experiences than with what we have called the 'background' quality of emotions and attitudes, common to a great many individual experiences. In their case the background is a sense of reconciliation, suspension of conflict, and of being in that sense at one with the aesthetic object. This particular sort of 'at-one-ness' could hardly be present in art-experience, since it requires that the aesthetic object should be at the same time the natural environment or some part of it. This is the same environment from which we wrest our food, from which

---

[8] See KEPES *passim*, on such analogies and affinities among natural forms.

we have to protect ourselves in order to live, which refuses to sustain our individual lives beyond a limited term, and to which we are finally 'united' in a manner far different from those envisaged in the aesthetic ideals of 'unity': 'Rolled round in earth's diurnal course With rocks and stones and trees.' To attain, and sustain, the relevant detachment from such an environment in order to savour it aesthetically is in itself a fair achievement, an achievement which suffuses the aesthetic experiences themselves with that sense of reconciliation. A cease-fire has been negotiated in our struggle with nature.

There is immense variety in the ways in which this can manifest itself in individual experience. The objects of nature may look to us as if their *raison d'etre* were precisely that we should celebrate their beauty. As Rilke put it: 'Everything beckons to us to perceive it.' Or, the dominant stance may be that of benediction: the Ancient Mariner 'blesses' the watersnakes at his moment of reconciliation.

The fourth type of unity-ideal is notably different from our first three specimens. The first three quest after unity in the particular aesthetic perception itself: the attainment of complex unified synopses, the grasping of webs of affinities and so on. The fourth, however, could arise in the contemplation of what is itself quite *un*-unified in the above senses, the night sky again, or a mass of hills with no detectable pattern to unite them. It is more strictly a concomitant, or a by-product of an aesthetic experience that we are already enjoying, an experience in which there may have been no synoptic grasping of patterns, relating of forms or any other sort of unifying.

I suspect that someone who tried to construct a comprehensive aesthetic theory with 'unity' as its sole key concept would obtain his comprehensiveness only by equivocating or punning over the meaning of the key expression, only by sliding and slithering from one of its many senses to another. When one sense is not applicable, another may well be. The fourth sense in particular can be relevant to vivid aesthetic experience of any natural object or collection of objects whatever.

So much the worse, we may conclude, for such a theory *qua* monolithic. But to say that is not to imply that our study has yielded only negative results. This is only one of several areas in aesthetics where we have to resist the temptation to work with a single supreme concept and must replace it by a *cluster* of related key concepts. Yet, in searching out the relevant key-concepts, the displaced pseudo-concept may yet be a useful guide—as it is in the present case. We should be ill-advised, however, to take this cluster of unity-concepts as by itself adequate for all explanatory purposes. Our analysis started with the stark contemplation of the uninterpreted, unrelated natural object in all its particularity and individual distinctness. This was not a mere starting-point, to be left behind in our pursuit of the 'unities'. On the contrary, aesthetic experience remains tethered to that concern with the particular, even if on a long rope. The rope is there, although the development and vitality of that experience demand that it be stretched to the full. The pull of the rope is felt, when the expanding and complicating of our synopses reaches the point beyond which we shall have not more but less fine discrimination of perceptual quality. It is felt again, when we risk the blurring and negating of natural forms as we really perceive them, in an anxious attempt to limit our experience of nature to the savouring of stereotyped and well-domesticated emotional qualities. It is even relevant to our fourth type of unity-ideal: for the sense of reconciliation is not an independent and autonomous aesthetic experience, but hangs entirely upon the occurrence of particular experiences of particular aesthetically interesting natural objects.

Up to this point my aim has been chiefly to describe some varieties of aesthetic experience of nature. From these we may make the following inferences. (i) Although some important features of art-experience are unattainable in nature, that by no means entitles the aesthetician to confine his studies to art; for even these points of apparent privation can yield types of aesthetic experience that are well worth analysis. (ii) Accounts of natural beauty that take 'unity' as their central concept are often metaphysically extravagant, and are chronically unperceptive of ambiguities in their claims. Nevertheless, a cautious aesthetician would be unwise to let this extravagance deflect him from patiently teasing out the numerous and important strands of experience that originally prompted these accounts.

I turn now to a second main topic. Although recent aesthetics has been little concerned with natural beauty as such, yet in the course of its analysis of *art*-experience, it has frequently made comparisons between our aesthetic approach to art-objects and to objects in nature. It has made these comparisons at crucial points in argument, and in several different sorts of context. But what has not been asked—or adequately answered—is whether the comparing has been fairly done; whether, in particular, the account of nature-experience, given or presupposed, is an adequate or a distorted account. Our discussion of some 'varieties' may have furnished us with useful data.

A substantial part of recent aesthetics has been the criticism of the expression theory of art. Right at the centre of this criticism is the denial that we need concern ourselves with discovering the intention or the actual feelings or intuitions of the artist, when we try to appreciate or to appraise his artefact. The expression theory saw the artefact as the middle link in a communication from artist to spectator; the critics of the theory see the artefact first and foremost as an object with certain properties, properties which are, or should be, aesthetically interesting, worth contemplating, and which in their totality control and guide the spectator's response. This change of emphasis chimes in well with the desire for a 'scientific' criticism (the properties are *there* in the artefact, the object), and with the anti-psychologistic mood of current British and American philosophy (the work of art is not an 'imaginary' one: and we are not probing behind it to its creator's states of soul).

Clearly this is an aesthetic approach that reduces the gulf between art-object and natural object. Both are to be approached primarily as individual, self-contained entities, exciting to contemplate by virtue of the objective properties they can be seen to possess.[9] But, let us ask, how far can we accept this comparison? Critics of the critics have pointed out some deficiencies. They have insisted, for instance, upon the irreducible relevance of linguistic, social and cultural context to the interpretation of a poem. The identical words might constitute *two* poems, not one, if we read them in two different contexts.[10] We could extend this criticism

[9] This account is highly general and schematic. I have said nothing about the basic differences among the arts themselves, which make the 'aesthetic object' in (say) music so unlike that in literature or that again in architecture. My account as it stands is most immediately relevant to the visual arts, especially sculpture; but what is said about overall trends and emphases has extension beyond those.

[10] H. S. Eveling argues [EVELING] that we should have a clash of competing criteria in such a situation. We should want to say 'same words, same poem': but, knowing how differently we shall interpret the words, according to the context in which we read them, we also want to say, 'one set of words but two poems'.

as follows. Suppose we have two perceptually identical objects, one an artefact and the other natural. They might be a 'carved stone' of Arp and a naturally smoothed stone; a carving in wood and a piece of fallen timber. Or they might be identical in pattern, though not in material; for example, a rock face with a particular texture and markings, and an abstract expressionist painting with the same texture and the same markings. If we made the most of the *rapprochement*, we should have to say that we had in each of these cases essentially *one* aesthetic object. (Although numerically two, the pair would be no more aesthetically different from one another than two engravings from the same block.) Yet this would be a misleading conclusion. If we knew them for what they are—as artefact or natural object—we should certainly attend differently to them, and respond differently to them. As we look at the rock face in nature, we may realize imaginatively the geological pressures and turmoils that produced its pattern. The realizing of these need not be a piece of extra-aesthetic reflection: it may determine for us how we see and respond to the object itself. If we interpreted and responded to the abstract painting in the same way (assuming, of course, that it is a thoroughgoing abstract and not the representation of a rock face!), our interpretation would this time be merely whimsical, no more controlled or stabilised than a seeing of faces in the fire.[11] If we arbitrarily restricted aesthetic experience both of nature and art to the contemplating of uninterpreted shapes and patterns, we could, of course, have the *rapprochement*. But we have seen good reason for refusing so to restrict it in the case of nature-experience, whatever be the case with art.

Take another example. Through the eye-piece of a telescope I see the spiral nebula in Andromeda. I look next at an abstract painting in a circular frame that contains the identical visual pattern. My responses are not alike, even if each is indisputably aesthetic. My awareness that the first shapes are of enormous and remote masses of matter in motion imparts to my response a strangeness and solemnity that are not generated by the pattern

[11] It is a weakness of some abstract painting that it sacrifices almost all the devices by which the spectator's response can be controlled and given determinateness. In the case of natural objects one is free to rely upon 'controls' external to the object—as in the present example. But even if the artist makes his artefacts very like natural objects, our knowledge that they are in fact artificial and 'framed' prevents us relying, in their case, upon such external controls.

alone. The abstract pattern may indeed impress by reminding me of various wheeling and swirling patterns in nature. But there is a difference between taking the pattern as that sort of reminder, and, on the other hand, brooding on this impressive instantiation of it in the nebula. Furthermore, a point already made about the emotive 'background' to aesthetic experience is relevant here again. Where we confront what we know to be a human artefact— say a painting—we have no special shock of surprise at the mere discovery that there are patterns here which delight perception; we know that they have been put there, though certainly we may be astonished at their particular aesthetic excellences. With a natural object, however, such surprise can figure importantly in our overall response, a surprise that is probably the greater the more remote the object from our everyday environment.

A more lighthearted but helpful way of bringing out these points is to suppose ourselves confronted by a small object, which, for all we know, may be natural or may be an artefact. We are set the task of regarding it aesthetically. I suppose that we might cast upon it an uneasy and embarrassed eye. How shall we approach it? Shall we, for instance, see in its smoothness the slow mindless grinding of centuries of tides, or the swifter and mindful operations of the sculptor's tools? Certainly, we can enjoy something of its purely formal qualities on either reckoning; but even the savouring of these is affected by non-formal factors that diverge according to the judgement we make about its origin.

To sum up this argument. On the rebound from a view of art as expression, as language, and the work of art as the medium of communication between artist and spectator, some recent aesthetics has been urging that the artefact is, first and foremost, an object among objects. The study of art is primarily the study of such objects, their observable qualities, their organization. This swing from intention to object has been healthful on the whole, delivering aesthetics and criticism from a great deal of misdirected labour. But it has countered the paradoxes of expressionism with paradoxes, or illuminating exaggerations, of its own. Differences between object and object need to be reaffirmed: indiscernibly different poems or carvings become discernibly different when we reckon with their aesthetically relevant cultural contexts; and the contextual controls that determine how we contemplate an object in nature are different from those that shape our experience of art. In other words, we have here a central current issue in aesthetics that cannot be properly tackled without a full-scale discussion of natural beauty.

That, however, is not the only current issue about which the same can be said. It can be said also (and this introduces our final topic) about the analysis of such expressions as 'true', 'false', 'profound', 'shallow', 'superficial', as terms of aesthetic appraisal. These have been studied in their application to art-objects, but scarcely at all in connection with nature.[12] It might indeed be contested whether they have *any* meaningful use in the latter connection. I should readily admit that ordinary language can give very little help here; but I am equally sure that a use or uses can be *given* to these expressions in that context, and that such uses would be closely related to the more familiar uses in talk about art. But would this not constitute a merely arbitrary and pointless extension of a vocabulary useful only in art-criticism? Not really: it would rather be to give comprehensiveness to a set of discriminations important throughout aesthetic experience, but which has tended, for various understandable reasons, to be worked out in detail only with respect to art.

Where then, in the aesthetic experience of nature, is there any room for talking of 'truth', 'depth', 'triviality'? We can best approach an answer by way of some analysis of an expression which we have used once or twice already but not explained. It is a sense of the word 'realize'. Here are some examples of the use. 'I had long *known* that the earth was not flat, but I had never before *realized* its curvature till I watched that ship disappear on the horizon.' 'I had seen from the map that this was a deserted moor, but not till I stood in the middle of it did I realize its desolation.' Here 'realize' involves making, or becoming, vivid to perception, or to the imagination. If I suddenly realize the height of a cumulo-nimbus cloud I am not simply *taking note* of the height, but imagining myself climbing into the cloud in an aeroplane or falling through it, or I am superimposing upon it an image of a mountain of known vastness, or . . . or . . . Auxiliary imagings may likewise attend my realizing of the earth's curvature, the image of my arms

---

[12] On art, see HOSPERS.

stretched out, fingers reaching round the sphere; and the realization of loneliness may involve imagining myself shouting but
being unheard, needing help but getting none. In some senses, to
realize something is simply to 'know' or 'understand', where
'know' and 'understand' are analysable in dispositional terms. But
our present sense of 'realize' has an essential episodic component:
it is a coming-to-be-aware, a 'clock-able' experience. In the aesthetic setting that interests us, it is an experience accompanying
and arising out of perceptions—perceptions upon which we
dwell and linger: I am gazing at the cumulo-nimbus cloud, when I
realize its height. We do not discard, or pass beyond, the experience, as if we were judging the height of the cloud in flight-
navigation, or the loneliness of the moor in planning a murder.
Realizing, in our sense, is not estimating or calculating. When I
am told that the moon is a solid spherical body, 200,000 miles
from the earth, I may go outside and look up at it and try, in the
aesthetically relevant sense, to realize its solidity and its distance.
Reference to perception can again be made obvious. We could not
seriously ask ourselves 'Am I, in fact, accurately realizing its
distance at 200,000 miles, or am I mistakenly imagining it as
190,000?' Such discriminations cannot be made perceptually: they
can only be calculated.

Though we have no room to multiply examples, it should be
obvious that this sort of realizing is one of our chief activities in
the aesthetic experiencing of nature. It has been central in earlier
illustrations, the contemplation of the rock face, the spiral nebula,
the ocean-smoothed stone.

But my suggestion that realizing is 'episodic', occurrent, may
properly be challenged. Suppose that I am realizing the utter
loneliness of the moor, when suddenly I discover that behind
sundry bits of cover are a great many soldiers taking part in a
field-exercise. Could I, without illogic, maintain that I had been
realizing what was not in fact the case? Hardly. 'Realize' contains
a built-in reference to truth. It may have episodic components, but
it cannot be exhaustively analysed in that way. I cannot be said
to have realized the strength and hardness of a tall tree-trunk, if,
when I then approach it, it crumbles rotten at a touch. But surely
I was doing *something*: my experience did occur; and nothing that
subsequently occurs can alter it.

Now, this experience was, of course, the aesthetic contemplation of apparent properties. That they turn out not to be also actual properties may disturb the spectator, or it may not. For some people aesthetic experience is interested not at all in actuality —only in looks, seemings: indifference to truth may be part of their definition of the aesthetic. If the soldiers appear or the tree crumbles, the aesthetic value of the prior experiences is (to those people) not in the least affected.

But it is possible to take a rather different view. One could agree that a large range of aesthetic experience is not concerned about truth; but yet attach a peculiar importance to the range that is. I am not sure that the gulf between this and the contrasted view is wholly bridgeable by argument; but some reflections can be offered along the following lines.

If we want our aesthetic experiences to be repeatable and to have stability, we shall try to ensure that new information or subsequent experimentation will not reveal the 'seemings' as illusions, will not make a mock, as it were, of our first experience. If I know that the tree is rotten, I shall not be able again to savour its seeming-strength. I could, no doubt, savour its 'deceptively strong appearance'; but that would be a quite different experience from the first, and one that accepted and integrated the truth about the tree's actual rottenness.

Suppose the outline of our cumulo-nimbus cloud resembles that of a basket of washing, and we amuse ourselves in dwelling upon this resemblance. Suppose that on another occasion we dwell, not upon such freakish (or in Coleridge's sense 'fanciful') aspects, but try instead to realize the inner turbulence of the cloud, the winds sweeping up within and around it, determining its structure and visible form. Should we not be ready to say that this latter experience was less superficial or contrived than the other, that it was truer to nature, and for that reason more worth having? Or, compare again the realizing of the pressures, thrustings and great age of the rock before us, with merely chuckling over the likeness of its markings to a funny face. If there can be a passage, in art, from easy beauty to difficult and more serious beauty, there can also be such passage in aesthetic contemplation of nature.

If there were not a strong *nisus* in that direction, how could we account for the sense of bewilderment people express over how to bring their aesthetic view of nature into accord with the discoveries of recent science? Because of these discoveries (as Sir

Kenneth Clark puts it), 'the snug, sensible nature which we can see with our own eyes has ceased to satisfy our imaginations.[13]

If the aesthetic enjoyment of nature were no more than the contemplation of particular shapes and colours and movements, these discoveries could not possibly disturb it. But they do: they set the imagination a task in 'realizing'.

An objector may still insist that reference to truth (whether in nature or art) is aesthetically irrelevant. To him the only relevant factors are the savouring of perceptual qualities and formal organization. Can anything be said in reply to his claim? The formalist might at least be reminded that a major element in his own enjoyment is the synoptic grasping of complexities. A particular colour-patch may be seen as part of an object, as modifying the colour of adjacent patches, and as contributing to the total perceived pattern—all simultaneously. One could argue that reference to truth—the striving to 'realize'—should be taken as adding one more level of complexity, a further challenge to our powers of synopsis, and that for the *exclusion* of it no good reason could be given.

But a more searching anxiety might be expressed, in these terms. Sometimes, indeed, such realizings may enhance an aesthetic experience, but may they not on other occasions destroy it? If, for example, you see the full moon rising behind the silhouetted branches of winter trees, you may judge that the scene is more beautiful if you think of the moon simply as a silvery flat disc at no great distance from the trees on the skyline. Why should you have your enjoyment spoiled by someone who tells you that you ought to be realizing the moon's actual shape, size and distance? Why indeed? There may be cases where I have to choose between, on the one hand, an aesthetic experience available only if I inhibit my realizing, and, on the other hand, a different aesthetic experience, available if I do some realizing. In our example, the first experience is of beauty (in the narrow sense), and we could not count on the alternative experience being also one of beauty, in the same sense. It might, of course, be still aesthetically exciting, that is, of beauty in the wider sense, the commoner sense in aesthetics. But, the objector might still press, there is no guaran-

---

[13] CLARK, p. 150. Sir Kenneth Clark is writing of art and artists, but his points are no less relevant to a contemplation of nature that never passes into the constructing of art-objects.

teeing even this latter possibility for *all* cases where we attempt to realize the nature of the objects contemplated. And this is exactly the difficulty we feel with regard to the bearing of present-day science on our vision of the natural world. Sometimes our attempts at realizing fail altogether, as with some versions of cosmologies and cosmogonies; or if they do succeed, they may be aesthetically bleak and unrewarding. Compromises, the balancing of one aesthetic requirement against another, are frequent enough, and may well be inevitable. One may say in a particular case— 'This is the nearest I can come to making imaginatively vivid what I know about that object. My realizing is still not quite adequate to my knowledge; but if I were to go any farther in that direction I should lose touch altogether with the sights, sounds and movements of the visible world, seen from the human point of view. And that would impoverish, not enrich my total aesthetic experience.' What we should be feeling, (need I say?), is the tug of that rope—the rope that tethers aesthetic experience to the perception of the particular object and its perceived individuality.

To be able to say anything more confident about this problem, one would need to hold a metaphysical and religious view of nature and science, which denied that the imaginative assimilating of scientific knowledge could ultimately lead to aesthetic impoverishment. Probably Christian theism is one such view; and Goethe's philosophy of nature seems to have been another. These possibilities we can only take note of in this essay, without being able to explore them.

We may recall at the same time, and in conclusion, that the 'unitary' accounts of natural beauty have, historically, been closely allied with various sorts of pantheism and nature-mysticism. I have argued that there are, in fact, not one but several unity-ideals; that it is most unlikely that any single aesthetic experience can fully and simultaneously realize them all; and I believe that with certain of them the notion of full realization makes dubious sense. Nevertheless, it does not follow that the idea of their ever more intense and comprehensive realization is without value, nor that the link with nature-mystical experiences must be severed.[14]

Although I can only hazard this suggestion in the most tentative way, I suspect that no more materials are required than those with which we are already furnished, in order to render available

[14] See HOUGH, p. 174 *seq.*

certain limited varieties of mystical experience, and logically to map them. Those materials provide us, not with affirmations about a transcendent being or realm but with a *focus imaginarius*, that can play a regulative and practical role in the aesthetic contemplation of nature. It sees that contemplation as grounded, first and last, in particular perceptions, but as reaching out so as to relate the forms of the objects perceived to the pervasive and basic forms of nature; relating it also to the observer's own stance and setting, as himself one item in nature—a nature with whose forces he feels in harmony through the very success of this contemplative activity itself.

But even if something of the intensity and momentousness of mystical experience can be reached along such lines, this would be —for all I have said or shall say—a mysticism without a God. And surely the absence of belief in transcendence would make this quite different from a mysticism that admits it and centres upon it. Different, indeed, in the quality of available experience and in expectations aroused both for the here-and-now and the hereafter; but not so radically different as to make 'mysticism' a misnomer for the former. Belief in a transcendent being means that, for the believer, the 'focus' is not imaginary but actual—in God; and it is doubtless psychologically easier to work towards a goal one believes to be fully realizable than towards a focus one believes, or suspects, to be imaginary. Rather similarly, in ethics a student may exercise a check to his practical moral confidence, when he discovers that 'oughts' cannot be grounded in 'is's'. Yet it is seldom that he indulges for this reason in a permanent moral sulk. Perhaps, if I am right, it is no more reasonable to indulge gratuitously in a nature-mystical sulk. But I begin to moralize: a sign that this paper has come to its proper end.

NOTE TO PAGE 294

(*a*) Graham Hough's *Image and Experience* (1960) contains some suggestive reflections stemming from his discussion of Ruskin and Roger Fry.

> By intense contemplation of . . . experiences of form and space we become conscious of the unity between ourselves and the natural world. [HOUGH, p. 175]

> It is Ruskin's special distinction to show . . . how the experience of the senses can lead directly to that unified apprehension of nature, and of ourselves as a part of nature, which can fairly constantly be

recognized, under various mythological disguises, not only as that which gives value to aesthetic experience but also as one of the major consolations of philosophy. [HOUGH, p. 176]

(*b*) We have quoted (p. 289) Barbara Hepworth on the mutual involvement of the spectator and natural aesthetic object, the changes in the sense of one's own being, according to one's position in the landscape. She goes on, in the same autobiographical sketch, to call this a 'transmutation of essential unity with land and seascape, which derives from all the sensibilities . . .'

(*c*) The nature-mystical interpretation of the experience of unity-with-nature is briefly stated by Evelyn Underhill in her *Mysticism*. In moments of intense love for the natural world, 'hints of a marvellous truth, a unity whose note is ineffable peace, shine in created things' [UNDERHILL, p. 87].

W. T. Stace, listing the common characteristics of 'extrovertive mysticism' (to which nature-mysticism belongs), includes the following. 'The One is . . . perceived through the physical senses, in or through the multiplicity of objects.' Also: 'The One is apprehended more concretely as being an inner subjectivity in all things, described variously as life, or consciousness, or a living Presence.' He adds: 'There are underground connections between the mystical and the aesthetic . . . which are at present obscure and unexplained' [STACE, pp. 79, 81].

(*d*) On Coleridge, see WILLEY, Ch. 1 generally, especially Sects. III and IV. Coleridge wrote:

The groundwork . . . of all true philosophy is the full apprehension of the difference between the contemplation of reason, namely that intuition of things which arises when we possess ourselves as one with the whole . . . and that which presents itself when . . . we think of ourselves as separated beings, and place nature in antithesis to the mind, as object to subject, thing to thought, death to life. [*The Friend*, Bohn Ed., p. 366; quoted WILLEY, pp. 29 f.]

Coleridge's statement has, of course, a much wider application than the topic of natural beauty; but he certainly applied it there.

(*e*) See also Wordsworth, *The Prelude*, Bk. VI, lines 624–40, and *Tintern Abbey*, lines 88–102.

If this were primarily a historical study, we should have had to trace systematically the development of those conceptions (nature—mystical, Platonic, romantic, etc., etc.) that are behind the vocabulary of 'unity with nature'. What we are asking here, however, is how far these ideas could be of help to someone trying to make sense of natural aesthetic experience at the present time. Thus these brief quotations and references, culled from a fairly wide field, may suffice to show at least the existence of the tendencies with which we shall be chiefly concerned.

14. THE POSSIBILITY OF
A DIALOGUE

ISTVÁN MÉZÁROS

[MR MÉZÁROS' paper was written from a position notably
different, both personally and philosophically, from those of the
other contributors to this volume, and has, accordingly, a rather
different purpose which some biographical remarks may help to
make clear. Mr Mézáros first studied philosophy in Hungary and
subsequently worked under Professor Lukács at the University
of Budapest. He then moved to Italy, coming from there to do
research at Bedford College in the University of London. He now
holds the position of Lecturer in Philosophy at the University of
St Andrews, Scotland. He is thus in the unusual position of having
acquired some first-hand experience of contemporary British
philosophy after having had his original philosophic formation in
the traditions of the Continent. (He has, indeed, already published
works in Hungarian, Italian and German.) In this paper he offers
some selected impressions of certain features of British philosophy
which he has found to present particular difficulties to one coming, as he does, from the very different philosophical background
of the Continent. Mr Mézáros here concentrates his attention on
those aspects of British philosophy which he believes to be most
in need of criticism, in the hope that his expression of these
criticisms will help to clarify some of the difficulties which hinder
understanding between British and other philosophers. It may be
found helpful to read Mr Mézáros' criticisms in close conjunction
with those other chapters of this volume which deal with the topics
with which he is concerned, in particular, the chapter by Mr
Pears on Wittgenstein and Austin.—EDITORIAL NOTE]

A few years ago a philosophical conference was held at Royaumont. Its records were published with the title *La Philosophie Analytique*,[1] and a reviewer wrote about it:

> This is the record of a dialogue that didn't come off, a *dialogue de sourds*. . . . The will to dialogue seemed to be absent with some of the 'Oxonians'. This may well have been due to the contempt in which 'Continental' philosophers are often held at Oxford, which hardly accords them the status of worthy interlocutors. But, except for one case, this cannot really provide the explanation. The root of this reluctance seems to lie more in the fact that the Continental questioners wished to discuss matters which are rarely discussed in Oxford and usually thought to be a waste of time. . . . The questioners naturally wanted to bring the discussion to matters of *methodology* to the philosophical justification of the procedures of the school. And this is not a popular subject of discussion at Oxford. Indeed, it rarely needs to be raised, since Oxford has lived for so long in a state of cultural solipsism, out of communication with rival schools, that it rarely meets a challenge which would require clarification.[2]

Are the chances of a successful dialogue any better today than at the time of the Royaumont conference? If not, then this volume is bound to fail. This means that our answer to this question must be at least a conditional yes, otherwise one would hardly be justified in publishing this volume. But if the answer is yes, we cannot leave the question at simply asserting the existence of a more optimistic attitude to philosophical problems as it is done in the introduction of a fairly recent collection of essays on political philosophy from which we learn that '*the mood is very different and very much more favourable than it was six years ago*'.[3] Changes of this kind need explanation and the explanation is certainly not given in stating that 'we don't believe any more that political philosophy is dead' because it remains to be answered: 'why did you believe it in the first place?' If questions of this kind are not answered the doubt may persist that the changes we can point at are only manifestations of a passing mood. And it would be foolish to base hopes for the success of a dialogue on a passing mood.

On the following pages I'll try to review those problems which

---

[1] 'Cahiers de Royaumont', *Philosophie No. IV*. Referred to in this article, and in the Bibliography, as CRP IV.

[2] TAYLOR. [3] LASLETT and RUNCIMAN, p. vii.

occupied me in the course of teaching philosophy in Britain as I came into close contact with contemporary British philosophy. For these problems are likely to cause much headache to all those who were not brought up in the school which dominated British philosophical thinking during the past two decades.

Unrecognized Preferences

The first questions the outsiders are likely to ask may sound something like this: what are the main characteristics and the origins of contemporary British philosophy? They will find, no doubt with disappointment, that the number of writings dealing directly with these questions is rather small. Most often they will be advised by British philosophers to read the originals and find out for themselves what these characteristics are.

The relative justification for such advice is, of course, that on the Continent there are too many school textbook-like generalizations which enable the student to avoid reading the originals and to acquire a rather superficial knowledge of names and skeleton systems without grasping the spirit of the various philosophical schools he is forced to race through.

But why should one assume that there can be no other way beside these two extremes? After all, one isn't necessarily hindered by a map if one wants to find places of importance in an unknown land. No one could dispute that by learning all the names on a map one would hardly know anything about the land itself. But from this it doesn't follow that maps are to be disposed of.

As far as the history of philosophy is concerned, British philosophy is mainly centred upon the less systematic heritage of Plato, Hume, John Stuart Mill, G. E. Moore and Wittgenstein. This set of preferences is, however, presented as the *natural choice* which needs no justification whatsoever. That Aristotle as a systematizer is neglected, that great philosophers like Diderot are completely ignored, that Hegel only appears as a kind of evil spirit, that there is little inclination to deal with or even to recognize problems raised by Marx, and that existentialism is hardly taken notice of, all this cannot matter if you believe that your orientation is so natural and unbiased that it shouldn't even be called a choice. Thus, rival claims must be dismissed not with concrete arguments but *en bloc* as manifestations of the 'metaphysical muddle' that keeps one from recognizing the natural choice.

In this way, if you ask for the justification of a set of preferences, the answer is that your demand is the proof of how muddled you are. Needless to say that there can be no dialogue on a similar basis. Arguing in this manner is circular because it takes as evidence for its own wisdom the rejection of alternative approaches, while both self-approval and the rejection of alternatives would need separate justification.

The elementary condition of a fruitful dialogue is, naturally, not the readiness to give up existing preferences, but the sober recognition that these preferences *are preferences*, however justified they may be. In this context one should recognize that one of the main characteristics of contemporary British philosophy, the refusal to discuss issues of a comprehensive character, is one of the possible, and in this way certainly significant, approaches to the contemporary world, and not '*the* revolution in philosophy' as the partisans of this approach called it a few years ago.[4]

It would be an important task to investigate why British philosophy took the turn it did. Here we may refer to Gilbert Ryle's attempt at explaining the analytic character of British philosophy. He writes in the Introduction to *The Revolution in Philosophy*:

> Philosophy developed into a *separate academic subject*, partly detached from classical scholarship, from theology, from economics, and last of all from psychology. The teachers of philosophy of a university came to constitute a faculty, and they organized their own discussion-groups. From 1876 there existed the quarterly journal *Mind*, and not very much later there was formed the Aristotelian Society, at the meetings of which were read and discussed papers that were subsequently printed in the Society's annual proceedings. . . . *This new professional practice of submitting problems and arguments to the expert criticism of fellow craftsmen led to a growing concern with questions of philosophical technique and a growing passion for ratiocinative rigour.* . . . *Philosophers had now to be philosophers' philosophers*; . . .[5]

This analysis is revealing in more than one respect. First of all because, to borrow a comparison, it is like trying to explain the origin of evil by the fall of man. Ryle here undertakes to find an

---

[4] RYLE (3).   [5] Ib., pp. 3–4.

explanation for the highly professionalized analytic character (what he optimistically calls 'the sophistication of the virtuoso') of British philosophy. He does, of course, stress the influence of the natural sciences on the general temper of British philosophy. Nevertheless, he finds an important part of his explanation in that philosophy has become 'a separate academic subject'. He undertakes to find out why British philosophers have become 'more technical in their discourse', i.e. philosophers' philosophers, and finds that it was because 'Philosophers had now to be philosophers' philosophers.' To this extent his explanation is given in a circular reference to facts which themselves badly need explanation.

Or do they? Obviously not, if you are convinced that the present state of philosophy is the *ideal* one. In this case, everything that preceded *the* revolution in philosophy will appear as a subordinated moment of this ultimate climax. And the implicit rejection of the possibility that it *could* be (now and tomorrow) otherwise carries with itself the extremely problematic tendency of treating historical facts with the greatest liberality, onesidedly emphasizing in the past, quite out of proportion, practices which seem to resemble current ones, neglecting all contrasting features, in order to be able to reach the well-known uncritical conclusions.

The attitude of those who are not happy with the state of affairs optimistically described by Ryle—and there are quite a few of them among British philosophers, although, for understandable reasons, this is hardly known on the Continent where British philosophy is generally treated as a homogeneous entity—will be significantly different. As soon as they realize that, for instance, 'One of the consequences of treating ethics as the analysis of ethical language is that it leads to the increasing triviality of the subject',[6] they will be prepared to state their preferences as preferences and enter on this basis into a dialogue with other trends.

Ryle's approach not only fails to give an explanation but also neglects or obscures important facts which are essential to a plausible explanation. It lays too much emphasis on all this being a specifically British phenomenon. Yet the truth is that:

(1) Analytic philosophy didn't originate in Britain, but on the Continent. Frege deeply influenced not only Wittgenstein but

---

[6] H. M. WARNOCK (2), p. 202.

also Bertrand Russell and, mainly in its Russellian version, G. E. Moore as well. Even in the later development of British analytic philosophy the vital stimulus came essentially from Austria ('Viennese School', Wittgenstein), although at this stage one can detect of course a certain amount of reciprocal influence in the affinity between G. E. Moore and the later Wittgenstein.

(2) It is characteristic of the culture of our century to concentrate on the straightforward description and analysis of different types of experience. This tendency embraces the majority of social sciences and a variety of artistic trends, and it is by no means confined to philosophy, let alone to British philosophy.

In these contexts the attempted explanation in the form of the reference to the fact that British philosophers had to publish short articles in *Mind* and in the *Proceedings of the Aristotelian Society* must seem trivial and utterly irrelevant. Even if it were true that 'the span of an article or a discussion paper' is not 'broad enough to admit of a crusade against, or a crusade on behalf of, any massive "Ism" ',[7] this couldn't be said about the numerous long books British philosophers went on publishing just as much as their Continental colleagues. Here one needs first to try and explain a European phenomenon, in its broadest contexts, in its proper framework and on a European scale.

The most important questions to explain are why these analytic trends couldn't become *dominating* in their place of origin, on the Continent, and why they were able to conquer the British philosophical stage. And why British philosophy became virtually exclusively analytic in character *after the Second World War*. For, despite the impression one might get from reading *The Revolution in Philosophy*, before and also during the Second World War 'analytic philosophy' was only one of several trends in Britain, and Gilbert Ryle himself wrote in the early thirties in an idiom considerably different from that of *The Concept of Mind*.

These questions are important because unless one can point to phenomena which indicate the weakening of these factors that resulted after the Second World War in the domination of an *exclusivistic* attitude to philosophy, either stigmatizing every other approach as 'metaphysical nonsense' or 'conceptual confusion' or

7 RYLE (3), p. 4.

at best giving them the polite cold shoulder of effective non-recognition, there can be no hope whatsoever for fruitful discussions on the basis of mutual understanding. The Royaumont conference was bound to fail because the participants showed no signs of being prepared to reconsider the foundations of these exclusivistic attitudes. As R. P. Van Breda put it:

> Quite often, one was given to understand: 'You are doing, no doubt, something different; go on, if it interests you. Well and good.' I believe, for my part, that there is an implicit value judgement here, and that it exists on both sides. When we meet you, we are sometimes too polite and not honest enough. *It is the pure and simple truth, I believe, to say that there are many continental philosophers who are not in the least interested in your philosophy. And I dare say that it is the same with you so far as continental philosophers are concerned.*[8]

Such attitudes cannot but lead to a 'dialogue de sourds'. This is why the first step towards a fruitful communication of ideas must be the recognition of existing preferences and, by implication, a change in attitude from exclusivism to mutual understanding.

Inconsistencies

At the Joint Session of the Aristotelian Society and The Mind Association A. E. Teale complained in 1957, in his inaugural address, about 'the many prohibitions issued by philosophers who first tell us that it lies beyond the province of a philosopher to determine empirical facts, and then proceed to inform us that, e.g., "remorse does not differ in any morally significant way from embarrassment", or that "our consciences are the product of the principles which our early training has indelibly planted in us" '.[9]

These prohibitions are, of course, closely linked with a general conception of philosophy which we shall have to discuss later on. Now we are concerned with the bewildering experience of seeing a principle contradicted often in the same article and sometimes only a few lines away from its positive assertion. A case in point may be the very influential late J. L. Austin's discussion of 'Truth'. He states his opinion that 'We become obsessed with "truth" when discussing statements, just as we become obsessed with "freedom" when discussing conduct.' Then he proposes to

---

[8] CRP IV, p. 344.   [9] TEALE, p. 6.

do away with the discussion of problems like freedom and truth (or of something being done freely or not freely) and to concentrate, in their stead, on adverbs like 'accidentally', 'unwillingly', 'inadvertently', because in this way *'no concluding inference is required'*. But curiously enough in the next sentence he says *'Like freedom, truth is a bare minimum or an illusory ideal'*,[10] and nothing could have the character of a more concluding statement than this, whatever it might mean. Of course, it is not a concluding *inference*: nothing has warranted it to be drawn from what has been previously said. It is a categorical assertion without the slightest attempt at finding supporting arguments. But what is more important, the author advises us to get away from the problems of truth and freedom, not to make generalizations about them but to stick to adverbial cases of a far more particularized character, then dogmatically makes a generalization of the highest order, expressing his own highly sceptical preferences.

There are many who would deny that we become obsessed with truth when discussing statements and with freedom when discussing conduct. These 'obsessions' are, in fact, far more ancient than discussions of this kind or of any other kind.

If there is anything obvious about the sources of what Austin calls philosophical mistakes, it is that they are manifold and far more persistent than one might wish. Therefore, it is misleading to reduce this complexity of causes to alleged linguistic confusions. One of the major difficulties in philosophical discussions is that what one trend refers to as mistakes the other might praise as achievements, and vice versa. In such a situation it is extremely doubtful whether the emotional use of adjectives like 'obvious' and 'notorious', etc., or indeed the peculiar use of inverted commas with which Austin's writings are so full, could help at all.[11] And

---

[10] AUSTIN (2), p. 98.

[11] 'Mistakes in philosophy notoriously arise through thinking that what holds of "ordinary" words like "red" or "growls" must also hold of extraordinary words like "real" or "exists". But that "true" is just such another extraordinary word is obvious' (*Id.*, pp. 95–6). One should note here not only the absence of any attempt at substantiating these far from obvious assertions but also the peculiar use of inverted commas in contrasting 'ordinary' (i.e. not quite ordinary) with the allegedly extraordinary (without inverted commas). To establish that there is a philosophically useful class of what are called extraordinary words, and that the quite commonly used word *true* belongs to it, more would be needed than the inconsistent omission of the inverted commas in one of the two contrasted classes and the dismissal of doubts that might arise by means of the adjective *obvious*.

when the unsupported, categorical statements are coupled with inconsistencies, or when prohibitions are violated by those who issued them, one can hardly expect anything but a hardening of the other side's position. After all, it is a basic condition of any dialogue that the same criteria of judgement should be applied by the participants to the assessment of the arguments of *both* sides.

The Analogy of Natural Science

At the Royaumont conference when Austin, Ayer and Ryle were pressed to define their philosophical methodology, in one way or in another they all referred to Natural Science.[12] Austin, for instance, emphasized that the way in which one ought to proceed in philosophy is *'Comme en Physique ou en sciences naturelles'*, and even said that: *'Il n'y a pas d'autre manière de procéder.'* [13]

The reason behind this attitude was clearly expressed by Austin in the same discussion, and for its importance we have to quote it at greater length. He was asked the question: what are the criteria of a good analysis? He answered it in this way:

Pour moi la chose essentielle au départ est d'arriver à un accord sur la question 'Qu'est-ce qu'on dirait quand?' ('What we should say when'). A mon sens, l'expérience prouve amplement que l'on arrive à se mettre d'accord sur le 'Qu'est-ce qu'on dirait quand?' (sur telle ou telle chose), bien que je vous concède que ce soit souvent long et difficile. Si longtemps que cela prenne, on peut y arriver néammoins; et sur la base de cet accord, sur ce donné, sur cet acquis, nous pouvons commencer à défricher notre petit coin de jardin. J'ajoute que *trop souvent c'est ce qui manque en philosophie: un 'datum' préalable sur lequel l'accord puisse se faire au départ.* Je ne dis pas qu'on puisse espérer partir, dans tous les cas, d'une donnée considérée par tous comme acquise. *Nous sommes tous d'accord pour penser au moins que c'est souhaitable.* Et j'irai jusqu'á dire que *quelques-unes des sciences expérimentales ont découvert leur point de départ initial et la bonne direction à suivre, précisément de cette manière*: en se mettant d'accord sur la façon de déterminer une certaine donnée. Dans le cas de la physique, par l'utilisation de la méthode expérimentale; dans notre cas, par *la recherche impartiale* d'un 'Qu'est-ce qu'on

---

[12] Cf. CRP IV, pp. 330–80.

[13] To avoid misunderstanding I quote Austin's text in the French original and give the translation in the footnotes. *'As in Physics or in Natural Sciences'*, *'There is no other way to proceed'* (*Id.*, p. 350).

dirait quand?'. Cela nous donne un point de départ, parce que, comme je l'ai déjà souligné, *un accord sur le 'Qu'est-ce qu'on dirait quand?' entraîne, constitue déjà, un accord sur une certaine manière, une, de décrire et de saisir les faits.*[14]

As we can see, Austin, like some of his predecessors, advocates proceeding on the lines of experimental science in order to find a basis of departure about which everyone concerned could agree. The ideal is what he calls 'la recherche impartiale', i.e. the elimination of ideological bias. But is this programme realistic? Isn't 'la recherche impartiale' in philosophy 'a bare minimum or an illusory ideal'?

The first difficulty which arises in this context is that the datum of departure is necessarily *selective* (as indeed everything is wherever human knowledge is involved) and therefore disagreements may always arise, if the basic philosophical positions differ. The analogy with natural science does not seem to exist here, since selectiveness is just as much present in experimental sciences as in philosophy and yet it doesn't result there in irreconcilable oppositions concerning the point of departure and the criteria of selection (presumably because alternatives can be tested and the outcome of testing is an unassailable practical judgement). In physics, for instance, the point of departure is generally agreed because a certain type of limitation imposed upon its inquiries through centuries resulted in practical conclusions that simply were bound to be incorporated in the formulations of successive generations of physicists if they wanted to advance their science. If physicists

---

[14] 'For me the essential thing in the first place is to reach an agreement on the question "what we should say when". In my view, experience amply proves that one reaches agreement about the question "what we should say when" (on this or that), although I concede that to reach such an agreement is often difficult and takes a long time. No matter how long it takes, one can succeed all the same; and on the basis of this agreement, this datum, this acquisition, we can start to clean up our small corner of the garden. I add that *too often what is lacking in philosophy is a preliminary "datum" on the basis of which one could reach an agreement to start with.* I don't say that in all cases one could hope to set out from a datum considered by all as established. *We all concur in thinking at least that such an agreement is desirable.* And I would go as far as to say that *some of the experimental sciences have discovered their initial point of departure and the right direction to follow precisely in this way:* by reaching an agreement on the manner of determining a particular datum. In the case of physics by utilizing the experimental method; in our case, by means of *impartial research* as to "what we should say when". This gives us a point of departure, because, as I have already underlined, *an agreement on the "what we should say when" entails, constitutes already, an agreement on a certain way, one particular way, of describing and grasping the facts'* (*Id.*, p. 334).

always started from nothing they would inevitably end up with nothing, and therefore if someone sets out to question the practically established point of departure and the criteria of selection of this particular science, he would put himself outside the framework of physics. In philosophy, however, questioning the alternative points of departure as well as the criteria of selection in view of finding *justification* for the one a particular philosopher proposes to adopt, is not only legitimate but also inevitable. Consequently, if one is aiming at a general agreement concerning the points of departure, one either has to do away with selectiveness (which is impossible) or to face up to those factors that result in those antagonistic oppositions that are absent from natural science.

Obviously, Austin cannot take the second alternative because this would amount to admitting that the analogy with natural science does not hold (as we have seen the situation in philosophy is not analogous but contrasting with that of Natural Science), and thus the illusions connected with the conception modelling itself on the natural science ought to be given up. Therefore, he must try to do away with selectiveness. The result is an inconsistent wavering between claims of *completeness* and the admission that what he puts forward is a *choice*. First he says that one must '*s'assurer que l'inventaire est bien complet*' and therefore one must prepare 'une liste de *tout* ce qui se rapporte, dans le langage, au sujet que nous examinons: *de tous les mots* que nous emploierions, de *toutes les expressions* dans lesquelles ces mots rentreraient' (which is not only an empirical but also a logical impossibility). But in the next sentence he says that 'Il est essentiel que *ce choix* soit assez *représentatif.*' Austin sees that the programme of completeness would only have the plausibility of being realized if one can 'prendre un problème qui porte sur un point suffisemment limité'.[15] But how could one even hope for a general agreement— the aim of the whole exercise—when both representativeness and 'sufficient limitation' are involved?

And this brings us to the second, far more important difficulty. The question arises how limited a problem should be to qualify as

---

[15] '*Make sure that the inventory is quite complete*'; 'a list of *everything* that is in connection, in the language, with the subject we are examining: of *all the words* that we would employ, of *all the expressions* these words would go in'; 'It is essential that *this choice* be *representative* enough'; 'take a problem that bears on a *sufficiently limited* point' (*Id.*, p. 332).

'sufficiently limited' and thus enable us to achieve completeness and general agreement. Suppose we obtained general agreement about a sufficiently limited subject, the question that really matters is whether the subject so limited is *philosophically important* or not. If one limits and restricts problems to the extent that is deemed necessary for achieving completeness and general agreement, doesn't one also confine oneself to trivialities? (like 'we aren't asking for the truth, the whole truth and nothing but the truth when inquiring about the battle of Waterloo'—but who on earth thought we were?). It is highly significant that Bertrand Russell, who in many ways shares the goals of a philosophy aiming at a general agreement to be reached through procedures similar to Natural Science, rejects the linguistic approach of 'Qu'est-ce qu'on dirait quand.' If disagreements are so strong between philosophers who, however differently, yet share this over-all aim, how can one realistically hope for a *general agreement* on anything of philosophical importance?

In fact, all the evidence Austin puts forward in the Royaumont discussion for his thesis is the categorical '*l'expérience prouve amplement* que l'on arrive à se mettre d'accord', etc. One might ask: *whose experience*? What we are expected to accept is not only the very doubtful statement according to which on the basis of impartial linguistic research—the supposed philosophical equivalent of experimental methodology—it is possible to achieve general agreement, but also that this kind of approach is a necessary requisite of all philosophy that wants to emancipate itself from 'daydreaming' (Austin's expression).

No one would dispute that 'un accord sur le "Qu'est-ce qu'on dirait quand?" (e.g. what Austin puts forward as a *necessary condition* of fruitful philosophical proceedings) entraîne, constitue déjà, un accord sur une certaine manière, *une*, de décrire et de saisir les faits'. But precisely for this reason only those can insist on the philosophical importance of agreements of this linguistic kind who are *already* committed to the positions of linguistic philosophy. Others will go on saying what T. M. Knox wrote: 'Much that these linguistic writers say seems to me to be true, but even so, it does not *matter*.'[16]

Wouldn't it be far more fruitful if instead of pursuing the frustrated aims of scientifically modelled 'unbiased philosophy' one

[16] KNOX, p. 291. Knox's italics.

admitted the existing difficulties. The desire to do away with all bias in philosophy in a way which 'entraîne, constitue déjà un accord', i.e. the acceptance of the *linguistic philosophical bias*, can only result in inconsistencies because the aims of this kind are self-contradictory.

The neopositivistic–linguistic bias also means that all approaches that are not 'sufficiently limited' are dismissed—again, not with argument, but with the authority of a presumed analogy with science. This can be illustrated with another quotation from J. L. Austin who said in the same discussion:

> *Nous devons aller chercher nos sujets dans les régions moins septiques, moins âprement disputées.* J'y vois pour ma part trois bonnes raisons : en premier lieu, nous nous y ferons la main, sans trop nous échauffer; en second lieu, les grands problèmes qui ont résisté à tous les assauts de front, peuvent céder si nous les attaquons par un biais; en troisième lieu, et ceci me paraît de beaucoup le plus important, n'y a-t-il pas quelque risque à *prétendre à savoir à l'avance quels sont les problèmes les plus importants*, à supposer même, ce qui est encore à voir, que nous puissions *prétendre connaître la meilleure méthode d'approche pour les attaquer?* Je crois qu'en prenant du recul, nous aurons plus de chance de voir se profiler les sommets, et de trouver la bonne voie, chemin faisant. L'exemple de la physique est ici encore, instructif. En bricolant, de droite et de gauche, avec ses instruments, comme le faisait Faraday, on a plus de *chance de tomber sur quelque chose de vraiment important* qu'en se disant un beau jour : '*Attaquons-nous à quelque grand problème : demandons-nous, par example, de quoi est fait notre univers?*'[17]

As we can see, Austin puts his faith into the pure *chance* of happening on something 'vraiment important'. In the second place he also contradicts himself by first saying that it is idle to

[17] '*We have to look for our subjects in the less septic regions, those that are less bitterly disputed.* For this I see three good reasons: in the first place, we can try our hand without getting too heated; in the second place, the big problems that have resisted all assaults from the front might yield if we attack them from the side; in the third place, and this seems to me by far the most important, isn't it risky *to claim to know in advance which are the most important problems*, or even to suppose, what remains to be seen, that we could *claim to know the best method of approach for attacking them*? I believe that by falling back we shall have a better chance of seeing the peaks standing out, and of finding a good route, as we go along. The example of physics is again instructive. By pottering about on one side and another with one's instruments as Faraday did, one has *a better chance of happening on something really important* than by saying one fine day: *let's attack some great problem; let's ask, for instance, what our universe is made of.*' (CRP IV, p. 350).

pretend to know 'la meilleure méthode d'approche', and then by declaring that the best thing to do is to adopt the instructive method of physics. And we can detect a significant bias as well which consists in this, that when he wanted to justify the linguistic approach he appealed to the fact that certain linguistic distinctions were perpetuated in the written and spoken language throughout history,[18] now he is determined not to apply the same considerations to decide which are the important philosophical problems. On the contrary, in this latter regard the fact that certain philosophical problems were perpetuated throughout history counts as an evidence for the denial that they are important and for the assertion according to which they only demonstrate that until recently philosophy was in a *cul de sac*. Thus, when it suits the linguistic bias, history does exist, when it would go against this bias, it doesn't.

The bias is present not only in the sarcastic rejection of inquiries of a *comprehensive* character, at the end of our quotation, but also in the *misleading description* (in Austin's vocabulary: 'impartial research') of science as being confined to little things and advancing *by chance*. Chance, of course, plays an important part in the development of science, just as much as in life in general. But if we are to have an important scientific achievement, there must be more to it than just 'bricoler, de droite et de gauche, avec des instruments'. And this something more is: relating the *limited* problems of detail to the most *comprehensive* ones. Without wishing to minimize in the least the importance of Faraday's results one must emphasize that the Faradays operate in a general framework created by the Galileos, Newtons and Einsteins. These great *scientists* have plenty of concern with those comprehensive issues that are eagerly dismissed with misplaced irony *in the name of science*, and such a concern is an integral part—in fact, synthesizing force—of their epoch-making achievements.

Here we can see that even the scientific myth is imposed upon

[18] 'si une langue s'est perpétuée sur les lèvres et sous la plume d'hommes civilisés, si elle a pu servir dans toutes les circonstances de leur vie, au cours des âges, il est probable que les distinctions qu'elle marque, comme les rapprochements qu'elle fait, dans ses multiples tournures, ne sont pas tout à fait sans valeur' ('if a language has perpetuated itself on the lips and under the pen of civilized men, if it could serve them in all the circumstances of their life, throughout ages, it is likely that the distinctions it marks, as well as the assimilations it makes, in its manifold turns of phrase, aren't altogether without value') (*Id.*, p. 335).

philosophy only by means of a misrepresentation of science, because actual scientific proceedings don't exclude comprehensive generalizations but are based upon them. What lies at the roots of approaches of this kind is the desire to escape from comprehensive issues, to minimize their importance, to deny their philosophical legitimacy and often [19] even their existence. (Significantly enough the achievements of British philosophy which followed the phase of *The Revolution in Philosophy*—Hampshire's *Thought and Action*, Strawson's *Individuals* (*Essay in Descriptive Metaphysics*), etc., are concerned with more comprehensive issues.) It is this desire to escape from comprehensive issues that results in unsustained sceptical declarations of the kind 'Like freedom, truth is a bare minimum or an illusory ideal' just as much as in the idealization of a non-existing Natural Science.

The Stumbling-block of Aesthetics

The Continental reader who is interested in the position of linguistic philosophy on aesthetic issues will find with great disappointment that British philosophical periodicals dedicate extremely little space for the discussion of such topics. And he will find with even greater disappointment that most of what appears on aesthetic problems is highly irrelevant, because it hardly ever asks the question: how will the solution of these problems help in a better evaluation of artistic creations? Linguistic philosophers would in fact deny that such questions are philosophically relevant.

To a certain extent it is understandable that British philosophers should feel aversion towards often uncritically accepted aesthetic formulations. William Elton, editor of the volume entitled *Aesthetics and Language*, quotes in his Introduction with justifiable indignation this passage: 'the music of Lourié is an ontological music; in the Kierkegaardian style, one would also say "existential". It is born in the singular roots of being, the nearest possible juncture of the soul and spirit';[20] and there are undoubtedly a great deal of similar generalizations, i.e. empty word-clouds, in aesthetic writings.

But the existence of nonsensical aesthetic articles is no reason

[19] Whenever they are summarily disposed of as 'conceptual confusions'.
[20] ELTON, p. 2.

for turning one's back on the *problems themselves*. For what could be more unrewarding than an alternative of this kind which we can read in *Aesthetics and Language* as a summing up of the essay entitled *The Expression Theory of Art*: 'Some music has some of the characteristics of people who are sad. It will be slow, not tripping: it will be low, not tinkling. People who are sad move more slowly, and when they speak, they speak softly and low. Associations of this sort may, of course, be multiplied indefinitely. And this now is the kitten in whose interest we made so much fuss about the bag. The kitten has, I think, turned out to be a scrawny little creature, not worth much. But the bag was worth it.'[21] What is not utterly trivial in all this is just plain nonsense, the result of ignoring the great varieties of musical expression. But what is even more disturbing in this quotation is the implicit suggestion that problems don't matter, only the form in which they are presented, i.e. the display of cleverness that is designed to create the impression that the issues with which the expression theory of art is struggling don't really exist.

If linguistic philosophers want to be true to their own programme of taking into account all the expressions (or more realistically all types of expressions) in which the problem-word of their inquiries occurs, they cannot leave out, as they have so far, the problems connected with *artistic language*. In fact, Austin was prepared to admit this when he said at Royaumont: 'Loin de moi le désir de les exclure du champ de nos recherches. *Leur heure viendra*. Je ne me sens pas de taille à les attaquer pour l'instant, voilà tout. Je sais tout ce que cette réponse peut avoir d'insatis-faisant.'[22]

It is a fact that the problems of artistic language were completely ignored during the whole history of linguistic philosophy. And considering the self-imposed limitations of linguistic philosophy

[21] *Id.*, p. 99.
[22] 'It is far from me to desire to exclude them from the field of our researches. *Their time will come.* I don't feel quite able to tackle them for the moment, that's all. I fully realize that this answer may sound unsatisfactory.' CRP IV, p. 350. In this context one can see again the inconsistency when Austin first says that in tackling the problems of artistic language one ought to proceed '*Comme en Physique, ou en Sciences naturelles* ... *Il n'y a pas d'autre manière de procéder.*' ('*As in Physics or in Natural Sciences* ... *There is no other way to proceed.*') Then, apparently forgetting about this, in the next sentence he goes on to say: '*Je suis sûr, en tout cas, qu'on ne peut rien en dire à l'avance.*' ('*I am sure, in any case, that one can say nothing in advance.*') But he has just said something 'à l'avance', something quite categorical too.

one must doubt whether they make it *possible* to tackle these problems. It is, indeed, very unsatisfactory to answer a criticism formulated on these lines by simply saying that their time *will* come. If the neglect of certain types of problems is as complete as this, there is usually more to it than just lack of time, or personal failure.

In this sense the state of these problems is revealing about linguistic philosophy in general. As a matter of fact I wouldn't hesitate to say that their time will never come within the methods of linguistic philosophy. Let us take three examples—three different types of use of artistic language—to see why not.

(1) 'Beauty is truth, truth is beauty.'

(2) 'C'est la chaude loi des hommes', 'C'est la dure loi des hommes', 'C'est la douce loi des hommes.'

(3) 'Sul ramo del nulla siede il mio cuore.'

What could the linguistic philosopher say about the first example, provided he is prepared to say anything other than what I've heard in discussions, that 'it doesn't make sense at all'? Considering his utterances about truth, etc., elsewhere, he might perhaps suggest that it is more profitable to dispose of abstract nouns and to take the adverbial form. But the trouble with this kind of approach is that it completely misses the whole point: that in poetry—because of the unity of content and form—one can't change anything at all, without changing the poetical content itself. One can more often than not reformulate, or 'translate' as it were, the expressions of common language. But one can *never* do this to poetry, because the change that had been introduced would mean that the analyst was talking about his own version and not about the poem he intended to talk about. Adverbial translation or anything of the kind is therefore quite out of the question as far as the problems of artistic language are concerned. Thus, if Keats writes: ' "*Beauty is truth, truth is beauty*" —*that is all/Ye know on earth, and all Ye need to know*', the philosopher must talk about *beauty* and *truth* as they are represented in this particular poem.

Taking the second example, the situation is even worse. Referring to the measuring rod of common language, expressions like 'warm law of men', 'hard law of men' and 'tender law of men' appear as most peculiar. And in any case, taken by themselves, it is not clear at all what they mean (if anything). Therefore, if our philosopher is prepared to give the benefit of doubt to the poet, he won't readily dismiss them as 'collection of words devoid of sense' but will say that they are 'idiosyncratic expressions' and of no philosophical interest. But *all* truly poetic expressions are, by definition, 'idiosyncratic'. And the solution of the problems connected with the specific character of poetry (or more broadly speaking of art in general)—the problems of artistic idiosyncrasy—is of the highest philosophical importance. (For instance, in relation to epistemology.)

About the third example, of course, there can be no doubt that it is the worst kind of 'conceptual confusion'. For how could my heart be sitting 'on the branch of nothing'? If it is nothing it surely cannot have branches and even if hearts could be imagined in a sitting position, they couldn't possibly sit where the poet says, because nothing can possibly sit on a non-existing branch of nothing. But objections of this kind, again, completely miss the whole point. The poet, fortunately, is not in the least worried about safeguarding himself against the possibility of similar objections at the price of communicating practically worthless conceptual commonplaces. He wants to convey, in a poem entitled *Without Hope*, the feelings of someone who is desperately isolated, and how magnificently he achieves this through these images:

> Sul ramo del nulla siede il mio cuore
> il suo piccolo corpo, muto, rabbrividisce,
> gli si raccolgono intorno teneramente
> e lo guardano, guardano le stelle.

Linguistic philosophy was always concerned with the meaning of expressions that can be reformulated or 'translated'. Consequently, it couldn't possibly take any notice of *literary meaning*. (This is why in aesthetic matters only those questions were discussed which could be formulated within the limitations imposed by an exclusive concern with literal meaning: i.e. questions about what the *critic* means when he uses terms like beautiful, original, etc.)

Artistic language eluded linguistic philosophy, because its problems cannot be tackled with the method of listing *atomistic units*, however numerous they might be. We can't possibly become wiser as to the meaning of the expression 'tender law of men', even by a *complete* list (a practical impossibility) of the sentences in which the words 'tender' and 'law' occur, but only by considering the poem as an *organic whole* where we read:

> C'est la douce loi des hommes
> De changer l'eau en lumière
> Le rêve en réalité
> Et les ennemis en frères

In a poem no word (or expression) has an isolated meaning, but only a meaning interrelated with all the other constitutive parts (words, expressions) of the given poem. In so far as words or expressions can be isolated from the poem (having a meaning of their own), they don't possess the meaning they carry in the poem through this manifold interrelation with all the parts of the poem as a whole, but only a meaning they have in the *common language* from which they have been taken (then adopted and transformed) by the poet.

If we are interested in the *poetic meaning*—as we must be in the analysis of artistic language—we must preserve the specific character of this part–whole relation, instead of destroying it by dissolving the manifold varieties of poetic expressions into their aesthetically irrelevant atomistic elements. When we talk about these isolated elements, we are no more talking about parts of a work of art, and it is an illusion to think that in the end this talk may add up to an aesthetically relevant picture. This is like expecting that the separate examination of every single particle of a mosaic will add up to an aesthetic assessment of that mosaic as a work of art. Particles of a mosaic taken by themselves are only coloured stones and not constitutive parts of a work of art, as isolated expressions taken from poems are just sentences (more often than not apparently quite meaningless sentences) which acquire their poetic meaning only by virtue of being in unchangeable interrelation with all the other parts of the poem as an organic whole.

It is a well-known fact that analytic philosophy, despite a growing interest in the contextual features of language, retains many of the atomistic presuppositions which were most conspicuous in positivism. This is why it is safe to say that one cannot expect a change in the situation, as far as artistic language is concerned, without changes deeply involving the particular atomistic pre-suppositions of linguistic philosophy. If, however, these changes occur, linguistic philosophy will be very different from the form in which we know it at present.

Dialogue—for What?

What are then the reasons for believing that, despite all the existing differences and difficulties, a dialogue beneficial for all concerned is possible?

The first of them is the fact that it was possible to make this volume. When we started to plan and to organize this volume a few years ago, we were convinced that the undertaking would succeed, because a major obstacle to dialogue is the refusal to talk sincerely about the persisting differences. In such a situation it would take a miracle to make the competing positions any less rigid. If, however, there is a will to *dialogue*—instead of *categorically stating* exclusivistic positions, as at Royaumont—and the parties involved are prepared to *listen to* the other side's arguments, a positive outcome is half assured.

British philosophers in the post-war period were used to addressing themselves to themselves, i.e. to a public that did not need to be *convinced*, except possibly in matters of detail, and therefore could satisfy with a rather one-sided, complacent exposition of their own arguments as well as with an almost caricaturistic over-simplification of all other types of position. This is obviously impossible in a dialogue, where arguments have to be formulated for the 'non-believers', and factual inaccuracies in relation to the opponents' position can be immediately scrutinized and refuted by the opponent in question. This is why dialogue is the most rewarding framework of discussion, and thus it is bound to produce positive results if there really exists a will to dialogue.

One might ask: isn't all this a one-sided effort? (It takes at least two to have a dialogue.) The answer is: definitely not, because there is evidence of an increasing interest on the Continent towards the problems tackled by British philosophers and towards the ways in which they are tackled. Again, one shouldn't forget the fact that this volume was prepared originally for an *Italian* publisher.

This interest on the Continent is not confined to philosophical trends that show affinities with neopositivism. The Italian critic and philosopher Cesare Cases, wrote years ago: 'Such a dialogue could be very useful to both groups in so far as the dialectical materialists should face up to attitudes and developments of thought usually ignored by them, and the neopositivists should be induced to get away from their interest in methodology for methodology's sake and to get to grips with particular exemplifications.'[23] One may add to this, that the interest is not even confined to Western countries, but exists in Eastern Europe as well. The Polish philosopher, Adam Schaff, in an article energetically criticized Stalinist philosophical isolationism and restrictive practices in this way:

> This policy, besides, is dangerous for those who practise it, because it deprives them of a real problem, of an impulse for their ideas, because it *impoverishes* their ideas. Assuredly, if one denies the existence of a problem only because it was put forward by an ideological adversary, one drops it practically from one's own theoretical baggage and blocks for oneself the road of development that leads to these problems. And what happens if these problems are really important? By barring the road that could lead to them, one restricts one's own field of vision and puts a brake on one's own theoretical development.

And as an example he gave linguistic philosophy that formulated

> *the extremely important problem of the active role of the language in the process of cognition.* Who was helped by the fact that all the problems raised by this philosophy have become *taboos,* because they started from false principles? Not us, to be sure. And at present *we are in the position of having to overcome the big delay in semantic researches in the field of logic, philosophy and sociology.*[24]

As far as contemporary British philosophy is concerned, the Continental reader has to realize that it isn't something static. On the contrary, thinking of the last few years one may confidently say that it is in a state of transformation that has far-reaching implications.

It is impossible to discuss in this context what sort of situation was reflected by the earlier phase of British philosophy (i.e. of the period around the year 1950), and what are the new needs that

[23] CASES p. 8. [24] SCHAFF, pp. 414–15.

underlie more recent developments. It is, however, necessary to point at a few characteristics of recent philosophical discussions.

I have already quoted Mary Warnock's condemnation of treating ethics as the analysis of ethical language because 'it leads to the increasing triviality of the subject'. Others point out similar things in relation to political philosophy, and others again express the opinion that philosophers of the past were too hurriedly labelled as worthless metaphysicians and insist on the need for a reinterpretation.

In general, there is the feeling that linguistic philosophy didn't fufil its claims and promises. As someone has put it: the sharpening of the knife (i.e. what the Italian philosopher calls 'the tendency towards methodology for methodology's sake') is not enough, one should try to use it for cutting. Only the act of cutting can, in fact, demonstrate the excellences or inadequacies of any knife.

Logical positivism had great hopes for the effectiveness of its own principles of verification, and these hopes were retained later on, although in different form, by linguistic philosophers as well. These hopes were greatly disappointed. The appeal to this principle didn't convert a single 'metaphysician' and it wasn't able to create a climate of opinion in which metaphysical theories couldn't flourish. A. J. Ayer recognized this when he wrote in the Introduction to the revised edition of his *Language, Truth and Logic* (1946): 'I confess, however, that *it now seems to me unlikely that any metaphysician would yield to a claim of this kind*;'. And yet he went on to say: 'although I should still defend the use of the criterion of verifiability as a methodological principle, I realize that *for the effective elimination of metaphysics it needs to be supported by detailed analyses of particular metaphysical arguments.*'[25]

Linguistic philosophy entertained this programme for eliminating speculative metaphysics by means of detailed analyses of particular metaphysical arguments. But even the most fervent supporters of this approach could not say that it succeeded in doing so.

Did it ever have the chance of succeeding? Hardly: Ayer's dictum suggests that a detailed application of the verification principle would be effective in eliminating metaphysics. But this could only be the case if it were true that it is an obviously mistaken kind of reasoning which gives rise to what is called a meta-

[25] AYER (1), p. 16.

physical argument. And in this way even the revised version of Ayer's philosophy still implies that all that is to be reckoned with is simply 'conceptual confusion' and that there are no other factors worth taking into account.

At this point the deadlock seems to be complete. And no wonder. For how can one entertain even for a moment the idea of a dialogue if one's approach implies—however politely this may be put—that everyone else is conceptually confused. There are many other factors than simply conceptual confusion which give rise to serious philosophical disagreement. And whereas in the case of conceptual confusions the only rational proceeding is to give up conceptually confused positions and to adopt the opponent's views, which are free from such confusions (i.e. an entirely *one-way* communication, in the spirit of many a platonic dialogue where the characters say things that are necessary for the easy triumph of Socratic inconclusiveness), in cases when those other factors are involved, and this is mutually recognized, real-life dialogue becomes possible, on the basis of the understanding that there are no easy, and certainly no automatic, solutions.

This is why I believe that the most promising recent developments in British philosophy are those which try to overcome the earlier deadlock. When a British philosopher strongly argues that the assessment of ethical rationality shouldn't be confined to the discussion of *how* one applies one's moral principles (i.e. the question of formal consistency in relation to the basic presuppositions of a given system) but should embrace the question of *what* one believes in (i.e. the evaluation of the presuppositions themselves), he is working on these lines. And when another philosopher formulates the question: '*how might one choose between one framework and another?*', he gets to grips, in a comprehensive way, with a fundamental issue about which all existing philosophical trends must have something to say, otherwise they could hardly find justification for themselves. This is *par excellence* a question of dialogue, and through its being linked with *ideological* considerations it becomes possible to provide a safeguard against formalistic oversimplifications.

Premature burial is one of the salient features of philosophical development, no doubt due to the wishful thinking associated with the death of the presumed enemy. Twentieth-century treatment of ideology is an outstanding example of premature burial.

What is often forgotten during the attempts at this burial, so characteristic of our times, is that an anti-ideological position is by no means necessarily less ideological than a more or less openly ideological one. The Neopositivist programme was to bring to an end ideological approaches to philosophical problems. Ironically, what it achieved was to create a powerful case for their resurrection.

The programme of achieving common understanding in philosophy by means of *explaining away* the ideologically affected issues didn't live up to the expectations of those who believed in it. It only succeeded in creating a situation in which all *other* views were stigmatized and summarily dismissed as ideological, and in this way it managed to rule out the possibility of mutual understanding. Therefore a more realistic reappraisal of the ideological complexities of contemporary philosophical discussions can produce nothing but good at the present stage.

One may ask at this point: won't the attitude we are advocating result in philosophical relativism and disorientation? If we are prepared to learn from the not so distant past, the answer is clearly no. Indeed, it is much more likely that disappointed expectations of a philosophy modelled on natural science should lead to disorientation and relativism than to the proper recognition of the limitations of the framework in which one is compelled to operate. Indeed, in view of the nature of all philosophical enterprise in general, and the specific characteristics and potentialities of given historical situations, we can understand that philosophical problems can never be solved for ever, but must again and again be reformulated with challenging new question marks.

ISTVÁN MÉZÁROS

BIBLIOGRAPHY

THE Bibliography that follows contains all the books and articles referred to in the essays of this collection. It does not aim to offer a comprehensive bibliography of analytical philosophy; for a very thorough guide to the literature (up to 1959), the reader should consult the Bibliography at the end of A. J. Ayer's collection, *Logical Positivism* [AYER (7)].

The following is a brief selection from the works listed in the Bibliography, which may be helpful as general introductions to analytical philosophy; details of publication will be found by looking them up in their place in the Bibliography:

Ayer, A. J. (ed.) *Logical Positivism* [AYER (7)].
'Cahiers de Royaumont', *Philosophie No. IV: La Philosophie Analytique* [CRP IV].
Flew, A. G. N. (ed.) *Logic and Language. First and Second Series* [FLEW (1) and (2)].
Ryle, G. (ed.) *The Revolution in Philosophy* [RYLE (3)].

The following, not contained in the Bibliography, may also be useful:
Hospers, J. *An Introduction to Philosophical Analysis*. London: Routledge & Kegan Paul, 1956.
Passmore, J. A. *A Hundred Years of Philosophy*. London: Duckworth, 1957.
Pears, D. F. (ed.) *The Nature of Metaphysics*. London: Macmillan, 1957.

Such histories, surveys and collections of essays, however, although they can be very helpful, are obviously no substitute for the works of leading philosophers themselves; notably of those who have most fundamentally influenced these philosophical developments, Moore, Russell and Wittgenstein, and also of such writers as Austin, Ayer, Hampshire, Popper, Ryle and Strawson.

The titles of those periodicals most frequently referred to have been abbreviated in the Bibliography. They are as follows:
BJPS   *British Journal for the Philosophy of Science*. Edinburgh: Nelson.

JP   *The Journal of Philosophy*. New York: Science Press.
PAS   *Proceedings of the Aristotelian Society*. London.
PAS SV   *Proceedings of the Aristotelian Society*. Supplementary
          Volume.
Phil.   *Philosophy*. Journal of the Royal Institute of Philosophy.
          London.
PPR   *Philosophy and Phenomenological Research*. Buffalo, N.Y.
PQ   *Philosophical Quarterly*. St Andrews.
PR   *Philosophical Review*. Ithaca, N.Y.: Cornell U.P.
RIP   *Revue Internationale de Philosophie*. Brussels.

Two others that frequently occur are *Mind* and *Analysis*; *Mind* is published by Nelson, Edinburgh, and *Analysis* by Blackwell, Oxford.

AGASSI, J. 'Corroboration Versus Induction.' *BJPS*, IX (1959), pp. 311–17.

ANSCOMBE, G. E. M. *Intention*. Oxford: Blackwell, 1957.

ANSCOMBE, G. E. M., and GEACH, P. T. *Three Philosophers*. Oxford: Blackwell, 1961.

AQUINAS, T. *Summa Theologica*. Rome: Marietti, 1948. English tr. by the Fathers of the English Dominican Province, New York: Benziger, 1947.

ARROW, K. J. *Social Choice and Individual Values*. New York: Wiley, 1951.

ATKINSON, R. F., and MONTEFIORE, A. C. '"Ought" and "Is".' *Phil.* XXXIII (1958), pp. 29–49.

AUSTIN, J. L. (1) 'Truth.' *PAS*, SV, XXIV (1950), pp. 111–28; reprinted in AUSTIN (2).

(2) *Philosophical Papers*. Eds. J. O. Urmson and G. J. Warnock. Oxford: Clarendon Press, 1961.

(3) *Sense and Sensibilia*. Ed. G. J. Warnock. Oxford: Clarendon Press, 1962.

(4) *How to Do Things with Words*. Ed. J. O. Urmson. Oxford: Clarendon Press, 1962.

AYER, A. J. (1) *Language, Truth and Logic*. London: Gollancz, 1936; 2nd edition, 1946.

(2) *The Foundations of Empirical Knowledge*. London: Macmillan, 1940.

(3) 'The Analysis of Moral Judgements.' *Horizon*, XX (1949), pp. 171–84; reprinted in AYER (6).

(4) 'Basic Propositions.' In BLACK, M.

(5) 'Truth.' *RIP*, VII (1953), pp. 183–200; reprinted in AYER (6).

(6) *Philosophical Essays*. London: Macmillan, 1954.

(7) (ed.). *Logical Positivism*. Glencoe, Illinois: The Free Press, 1959.

BAIER, K. *The Moral Point of View*. Ithaca: Cornell Univ. Press, 1958.

BARKER, S. F. *Induction and Hypothesis*. Ithaca: Cornell Univ. Press, 1957.

BEARDSLEY, M. C. *Aesthetics*. New York: Harcourt Brace, 1958.

BENJAMIN, B. S. 'Remembering.' *Mind*, LXV (1956), pp. 312–31.

BENN, S. I., and PETERS, R. S. *Social Principles and the Democratic State*. London: Allen and Unwin, 1959.

BERKELEY, G. *The Principles of Human Knowledge*. Ed. T. E. Jessop. London: Nelson, 1945.

BERLIN, I. (1) *Historical Inevitability*. London: Oxford Univ. Press, 1954.

(2) 'The Concept of Scientific History.' *History and Theory* 1 (1960), pp. 1–31.

BLACK, D. *The Theory of Committees and Elections*. Cambridge Univ. Press, 1958.

BLACK, M. (ed.). *Philosophical Analysis*. Ithaca: Cornell Univ. Press, 1950. See also GEACH, P. T.

BRAITHWAITE, R. B. *An Empiricist's View of the Nature of Religious Belief*. Cambridge Univ. Press, 1955.

CARNAP, R. *Der Logische Aufbau der Welt*. Berlin: Weltkreis-Verlag, 1928.

CASES, C. *Marxismo e Neopositivismo*. Torino: Einaudi, 1958.

CAVELL, S. 'Must We Mean What We Say?' *Inquiry*, 1 (1958), pp. 172–212.

CHURCH, A. *Introduction to Mathematical Logic*. 2nd edn. Princeton Univ. Press, 1956.

CLARK, K. *Landscape into Art*. London: Murray, 1949; London: Pelican Books, 1956.

COHEN, L. J. *The Diversity of Meaning*. London: Methuen, 1962.

COLERIDGE, S. T. *Biographia Literaria*. London: Fenner, 1817.

COLLINGWOOD, R. G. *The Idea of History*. Oxford: Clarendon Press, 1946.

CROCE, B. *Estetica come scienza dell'espressione e linguistica generale*. Milan: 1902; English tr. (*Aesthetic as Science of Expression and General Linguistic*) by D. Ainslie. London: Macmillan, 1922.

CROMBIE, I. M. 'Theology and Falsification.' In F-M.

CRP IV 'Cahiers de Royaumont', *Philosophie No. IV*. Paris: Editions de Minuit, 1962.

DAHL, R. A. *A Preface to Democratic Theory*. Chicago Univ. Press, 1956.

DEMOS, R. 'The Meaningfulness of Religious Language.' *PPR*, XVIII (1957), pp. 96–106.

DOWNS, A. *An Economic Theory of Democracy*. New York: Harper, 1957.

DRAY, W. *Laws and Explanation in History*. London: Oxford Univ. Press, 1957.

EDWARDS, P. 'Bertrand Russell's Doubts About Induction.' In FLEW (i).

ELTON, W. (ed.). *Aesthetics and Language*. Oxford; Blackwell 1954.

EVELING, H. S. 'Composition and Criticism.' *PAS*, LIX (1959), pp. 213–32.

EWING, A. C. 'The Justification of Emotions.' *PAS*, SV, XXXI (1957), pp. 59–75.

FINDLAY, J. N. (1) 'Can God's Existence be Disproved?' *Mind*, LVII (1948), pp. 176–83; reprinted in F-M.

(2) 'God's Non-Existence.' *Mind*, LVIII (1949), pp. 352–54; reprinted in F-M.

(3) *Values and Intentions*. London: Allen and Unwin, 1961.

FLEW, A. G. N. (1) (ed.). *Logic and Language*, First Series. Oxford: Blackwell, 1951.

(2) (ed.). *Logic and Language*, Second Series. Oxford: Blackwell, 1955.

FLEW, A. G. N., and MACINTYRE, A. (eds.) (F-M). *New Essays in Philosophical Theology*. London: SCM Press, 1955.

FOOT, P. (1) 'When is a Principle a Moral Principle?' *PAS*, SV, XXVIII (1954), pp. 95–110.

(2) 'Moral Arguments.' *Mind*, LXVII (1958), pp. 502–13.

(3) 'Moral Beliefs.' *PAS*, LIX (1959), pp. 83–104.

(4) 'Goodness and Choice.' *PAS*, SV, XXXV (1961), pp. 45–61.

FREGE, G. (1) 'Ueber Sinn und Bedeutung.' *Zeitschrift fuer Philosophie und Philosophische Kritik*, C (1892), pp. 25–50; English tr. ('On Sense and Reference') in GEACH–BLACK, pp. 56–78.

(2) 'Die Gedanke.' In *Beiträge zur Philosophie des Deutschen Idealismus* (1919); English tr. ('The Thought: A Logical Inquiry') by A. and M. Quinton, *Mind*, LXV (1956), pp. 289–311.

GALLIE, W. B. 'Liberal Morality and Socialist Morality.' *Phil.*, XXIV (1949), pp. 318–34; reprinted in LASLETT.

GARDINER, P. *The Nature of Historical Explanation*. London: Oxford Univ. Press, 1952.

GEACH, P. T. (1) 'Form and Existence.' *PAS*, LV (1955), pp. 251–72.

(2) 'Good and Evil.' *Analysis*, XVII (1957), pp. 33–42.

(3) 'Causality and Creation.' *Sophia*, 1 (1962), pp. 1–8.

See also ANSCOMBE, G. E. M.

GEACH, P. T., and BLACK, M. *Translations from the Philosophical Writings of Gottlob Frege*. Oxford: Blackwell, 1952.

GOODMAN, N. *The Structure of Appearance*. Cambridge, Mass.: Harvard Univ. Press, 1951.

GRAVE, S. A. 'The Ontological Argument of St Anselm.' *Phil.*, XXVII (1952), pp. 30–8.

HAEZRAHI, P. *The Contemplative Activity*. London: Allen and Unwin, 1954.

HAMPSHIRE, S. N. (1) 'Self-Knowledge and the Will.' *RIP*, VII (1953), pp. 230–45.

(2) *Thought and Action*. London: Chatto and Windus, 1959.

HARE, R. M. (1) *The Language of Morals*. Oxford: Clarendon Press, 1952.

(2) 'Geach on Good and Evil.' *Analysis*, XVII (1957), pp. 103–11.

(3) *Freedom and Reason*. Oxford: Clarendon Press, 1963.

HARRÉ, R. *Introduction to the Logic of the Sciences*. London: Macmillan, 1960.

HART, H. L. A., and HONORÉ, A. M. *Causation in the Law*. Oxford: Clarendon Press, 1959.

HEGEL, G. W. F. *Ästhetik*. Berlin: Aufbau-Verlag, 1955; English tr. (*The Philosophy of Fine Art*) by F. P. S. Osmaston. London: Bell, 1920.

HEIDEGGER, M. *Sein und Zeit*. Halle a.d.S.: Niemeyer, 1935. English tr. (*Being and Time*) by J. Macquarrie and E. Robinson. London: SCM Press, 1962.

HEMPEL, C. G. (1) 'The Function of General Laws in History.' *JP* XXXIX (1942), pp. 35–48.

(2) 'Studies in the Logic of Confirmation.' *Mind*, LIV (1945), pp. 1–26 and 97–121.

HEPBURN, R. W. 'Emotions and Emotional Qualities.' *British Journal of Aesthetics*, 1 (1961), pp. 255–65.

HEPBURN, R. W., TOULMIN, S. E., and MACINTYRE, A. C. *Metaphysical Beliefs*. London: SCM Press, 1957.

HEPWORTH, B. *Carvings and Drawings*. London: Lund Humphries, 1952.

HOBBES, T. *Leviathan*. Ed. M. Oakeshott. Oxford: Blackwell, 1946.

HONORÉ, A. M. See HART.

HOSPERS, J. *Meaning and Truth in the Arts*. Chapel Hill: Univ. of North Carolina Press, 1946.

HOUGH, G. *Image and Experience*. London: Duckworth, 1960.

HUGHES, G. E. 'Has God's Existence Been Disproved?' *Mind*, LVIII (1949), pp. 67–74; reprinted in F-M.

HUME, D. (1) *A Treatise of Human Nature*. Ed. L. A. Selby-Bigge. Oxford: Clarendon Press, 1866.

(2) *An Inquiry into Human Understanding*. Ed. L. A. Selby-Bigge. Oxford: Clarendon Press, 1894.

JEFFREYS, H. *Scientific Inference*. Cambridge Univ. Press, 1937.

JOSEPH, H. W. B. *An Introduction to Logic*. Oxford: Clarendon Press, 1906.

KANT, I. *Grundlegung der Metaphysik der Sitten*. Ed. R. Otto. Gotha: Klotz, 1930; English tr. (*Fundamental Principles of the Metaphysic of Ethics*) by T. K. Abbott, London: Longmans, 1949.

KENNY, A. 'Necessary Being.' *Sophia*, 1 (1962).

KEPES, G. *The New Landscape in Art and Science*. Chicago: Theobald, 1956.

KNEALE, W. and M. *The Development of Logic*. Oxford: Clarendon Press, 1962.

KNOX, T. M. 'Two Conceptions of Philosophy.' *Phil.*, XXXVI (1961), pp. 289–308.

KRIEGER, M. See VIVAS.

LASLETT, P. (ed.). *Philosophy, Politics and Society 1*. Oxford: Blackwell, 1956.

LASLETT, P., and RUNCIMAN, W. G. (eds.). *Philosophy, Politics and Society II*. Oxford: Blackwell, 1962.

LEWIS, C. I. (1) *Mind and the World Order*. New York: Scribner, 1929.
  (2) *An Analysis of Knowledge and Valuation*. La Salle: Open Court, 1946.

LEWIS, H. D. 'The Philosophy of Religion.' *PQ*, IV (1954), pp. 166–81 and 262–74.

MACINTYRE, A. C. See FLEW, A. G. N.; HEPBURN, R. W.

MAYO, H. B. *An Introduction to Democratic Theory*. London: Oxford Univ. Press, 1960.

MELDEN, A. I. (1) 'Willing.' *PR*, LXIX (1960), pp. 475–84.
  (2) *Free Action*. London: Routledge, 1961.

MILL, J. S. *A System of Logic*. London: Parker, 1843.

MITCHELL, B. (ed.). *Faith and Logic*. London: Allen and Unwin, 1957.

MITCHELL, D. *Introduction to Logic*. London: Hutchinson, 1962.

MONTEFIORE, A. C. (1) *A Modern Introduction to Moral Philosophy*. London: Routledge, 1958.
  (2) Review of 'The Meaning and Purpose of Art'. *Mind*, LXVIII (1959), pp. 563–64.
  See also Atkinson R. F.

MOORE, G. E. (1) *Principia Ethica*. Cambridge Univ. Press, 1903.
  (2) *Ethics*. London: Williams and Norgate, 1912.
  (3) *Philosophical Studies*. London: Kegan Paul, 1922.
  (4) *Philosophical Papers*. London: Allen and Unwin, 1959.

NOWELL-SMITH, P. H. (1) *Ethics*. London: Pelican Books 1954; Oxford: Blackwell, 1957.
  (2) 'Contextual Implication.' *PAS*, SV, XXXVI (1962), pp. 1–18.

OSBORNE, H. *The Theory of Beauty*. London: Routledge, 1952.

PAUL, G. A. 'Democracy.' *Chambers's Encyclopaedia, Vol. IV*, pp. 430–31. New edn. London: Newnes, 1955.

PEARS, D. F. *Incompatibilities of Colours*. In FLEW (2).

PETERS, R. S. See BENN.

PETERS, R. S., and TAJFEL, H. 'Hobbes and Hull—Metaphysicians of Behaviour.' *BJPS*, VIII (1957), pp. 30–44.

POPPER, K. R. (1) *Logik der Forschung*. Vienna: Springer, 1935; English tr. (*The Logic of Scientific Discovery*), with additions. London: Hutchinson, 1959.

(2) 'What can Logic Do for Philosophy?' *PAS*, SV, XXII (1948), pp. 141–54.

(3) *The Poverty of Historicism*. London: Routledge, 1957.

(4) *Conjectures and Refutations*. London: Routledge, 1963.

PRICE, H. H. (1) *Perception*. London: Methuen, 1932.

(2) *Truth and Corrigibility*. Oxford: Clarendon Press, 1936.

(3) 'Image Thinking'. *PAS*, LII (1952), pp. 135–66.

PRICHARD, H. A. *Moral Obligation*. Oxford: Clarendon Press, 1949.

PRIOR, A. N. (1) 'Can Religion be Discussed?' *Australasian Journal of Philosophy*, XX (1942), pp. 141–51; reprinted in F-M.

(2) 'Is Necessary Existence Possible?' *PPR*, XV (1955), pp. 545–47.

(3) *Time and Modality*. Oxford: Clarendon Press, 1957.

(4) 'Thank Goodness That's Over.' *Phil.*, XXIV (1959), pp. 12–17.

QUINE, W. V. (1) 'Two Dogmas of Empiricism.' *PR*, LX (1951), pp. 20–43; reprinted in QUINE (3).

(2) 'Mr Strawson on Logical Theory.' *Mind*, LXII (1953), pp. 433–51.

(3) *From a Logical Point of View*. Cambridge, Mass.: Harvard, 1953.

(4) *Word and Object*. Massachusetts Institute of Technology, 1960.

QUINTON, A. M. 'The Problem of Perception.' *Mind*, LXIV (1955), pp. 28–51.

RAINER, A. C. A. 'Necessity and God.' *Mind*, LVIII (1949), pp. 75–7; reprinted in F-M.

RAMSEY, F. P. *The Foundations of Mathematics*. London: Kegan Paul, 1931.

RAMSEY, I. T. *Religious Language*. London: SCM Press, 1957.

REICHENBACH, H. *Experience and Prediction*. University of Chicago Press, 1947.

ROBINSON, R. 'Necessary Propositions.' *Mind*, LXVII (1958), pp. 289–384.

ROSS, W. D. (1) *The Right and the Good*. Oxford: Clarendon Press, 1930.

(2) *Foundations of Ethics*. Oxford: Clarendon Press, 1939.

RUNCIMAN, W. G. See LASLETT.

RUSSELL, B. A. W. (1) 'On Denoting.' *Mind*, XIV (1905), pp. 479–93; reprinted in RUSSELL (7).

(2) *The Problems of Philosophy*. London: Williams and Norgate, 1912.

(3) *Our Knowledge of the External World*. London: Open Court, 1914.

(4) 'The Philosophy of Logical Atomism.' *The Monist* (1918–19); reprinted in RUSSELL (7).

(5) *Inquiry into Meaning and Truth*. London: Allen and Unwin, 1940.

(6) *Human Knowledge: Its Scope and Limits*. London: Allen and Unwin, 1948.

(7) *Logic and Knowledge*. Ed. R. C. Marsh. London: Allen and Unwin, 1956.

RUSSELL, B. A. W., and WHITEHEAD, A. N. *Principia Mathematica*. 2nd edn. Cambridge Univ. Press, 1925–7.

RYLE, G. (1) 'Systematically Misleading Expressions.' *PAS*, XXXII (1932), pp. 139–70; reprinted in FLEW (1).

(2) *The Concept of Mind*. London: Hutchinson, 1949.

(3) (Ed. and Introduction). *The Revolution in Philosophy*. London: Macmillan, 1957.

SARTRE, J-P. *L'Imaginaire*. Paris: Gallimard, 1948. English tr. (*Imagination*) by F. Williams, University of Michigan,1962.

SCHAFF, A. 'Sur le Marxisme et l'Existentialisme.' *Les Temps Modernes*, 1960.

SCHILLP, P. A. (ed.) *The Philosophy of G. E. Moore*. Chicago: N.W. University, 1942.

SCHLICK, M. (1) *Allgemeine Erkenntnislehre*. Berlin: Springer, 1918.

(2) Über das Fundament der Erkenntnis.' *Erkenntnis*, 1934; English tr. ('On the Foundations of Knowledge') in AYER (7).

SEARLE, J. R. 'Meaning and Speech Acts.' *PR*, LXXI (1962), pp. 423–32.

SHORTER, J. M. 'Imagination'. *Mind*, LXI (1952), pp. 528–42.

SINGER, M. G. *Generalization in Ethics*. London: Eyre and Spottiswoode, 1963.

SMART, J. J. C. (1) *Metaphysics, Logic and Theology*. In F-M.

(2) *The Existence of God*. In F-M.

STACE, W. T. *Mysticism and Philosophy*. London: Macmillan, 1960.

STEVENSON, C. L. (1) 'The Emotive Meaning of Ethical Terms.' *Mind*, XLVI (1937), pp. 14–31.

(2) 'Ethical Judgements and Avoidability.' *Mind*, XLVII (1938), pp. 45–57.

(3) 'Persuasive Definitions.' *Mind*, XLVII (1938), pp. 331–50.

(4) *Ethics and Language*. London: Oxford Univ. Press, 1953.

STRAWSON, P. F. (1) 'Truth.' *Analysis*, IX (1948), pp. 83–97.

(2) 'On Referring.' *Mind*, LIX (1950), pp. 320–44.

(3) 'Truth.' *PAS*, SV, XXIV (1950), pp. 129–56.

(4) *Introduction to Logical Theory*. London: Methuen, 1952.

(5) *Individuals*. London: Methuen, 1959.

TAJFEL, H. See PETERS.

TAYLOR, C. M. 'Review of CRP IV.' *PR*, LXXIII (1964), pp. 132–5.

TEALE, A. E. 'Moral Assurance.' *PAS*, SV, XXXI (1957), pp. 1–42.

TITCHENER, E. B. *Lectures on the Experimental Psychology of the Thought Processes*. New York: Macmillan, 1909.

TOULMIN, S. E. (1) *The Place of Reason in Ethics*. Cambridge Univ. Press, 1950.

(2) *The Uses of Argument*. Cambridge Univ. Press, 1958.

See also HEPBURN, R. W.

TOYNBEE, A. J. *A Study of History*. London: Oxford Univ. Press, 1934–61.

UNDERHILL, E. *Mysticism*. London: Methuen, 4th ed., 1912.

VIVAS, E., and KRIEGER, M. (eds.). *The Problems of Aesthetics*. New York: Rinehart, 1953.

WAISMANN, F. (1) 'Analytic-Synthetic.' *Analysis*, X (1949), pp. 25–40; *Analysis*, XIII (1952), pp. 1–14 and 73–89.

(2) 'Language Strata.' In FLEW (2).

WARNOCK, G. J. *Berkeley*. London: Pelican Books, 1953.

WARNOCK, H. M. (1) 'The Justification of Emotions.' *PAS*, SV, XXXI (1957), pp. 43–58.

(2) *Ethics Since 1900*. Oxford Univ. Press, 1960.

WATKINS, J. W. N. 'When Are Statements Empirical?' *BJPS*, X (1960), pp. 287–308.

WELDON, T. D. *The Vocabulary of Politics*. London: Pelican Books, 1953.

WHEWELL, W. *The Philosophy of the Inductive Sciences*. London: Parker, 1840.

WHITEHEAD, A. N. See RUSSELL.

WILLEY, B. *Nineteenth Century Studies*. Cambridge Univ. Press, 1949.

WITTGENSTEIN, L. (1) *Notebooks 1914–18*. Eds. G. H. von Wright and G. E. M. Anscombe. Oxford: Blackwell, 1961.

(2) *Tractatus Logico-Philosophicus* (Logisch-Philosophische Abhandlung). London: Kegan Paul, 1922.

(3) *The Blue and Brown Books*. Oxford: Blackwell, 1958.

(4) *Philosophical Investigations*. Oxford: Blackwell, 1953.

(5) *Remarks on the Foundations of Mathematics*. Oxford: Blackwell, 1956.

WOLLHEIM, R. A. (1) 'Philosophie Analytique et Pensée Politique.' *Revue Française de Science Politique*, II (1961).

(2) 'How Can One Person Represent Another?' *PAS*, SV, XXXIV (1960), pp. 209–24.

VON WRIGHT, G. H. *A Treatise on Induction and Probability*. London: Routledge, 1951.

INDEX

International
Library of Philosophy
& Scientific Method

Editor: Ted Honderich
Advisory Editor: Bernard Williams

List of titles, page two

International
Library of Psychology
Philosophy &
Scientific Method

Editor: C K Ogden

List of titles, page six

ROUTLEDGE AND KEGAN PAUL LTD
68 Carter Lane London EC4

International Library of Philosophy and Scientific Method
(Demy 8vo)

Allen, R. E. (Ed.)
Studies in Plato's Metaphysics
Contributors: J. L. Ackrill, R. E. Allen, R. S. Bluck, H. F. Cherniss, F. M.
Cornford, R. C. Cross, P. T. Geach, R. Hackforth, W. F. Hicken, A. C. Lloyd,
G. R. Morrow, G. E. L. Owen, G. Ryle, W. G. Runciman, G. Vlastos
464 pp. 1965. (2nd Impression 1967.) 70s.

Armstrong, D. M.
Perception and the Physical World
208 pp. 1961. (3rd Impression 1966.) 25s.

A Materialist Theory of the Mind
376 pp. 1967. about 45s.

Bambrough, Renford (Ed.)
New Essays on Plato and Aristotle
Contributors: J. L. Ackrill, G. E. M. Anscombe, Renford Bambrough,
R. M. Hare, D. M. MacKinnon, G. E. L. Owen, G. Ryle, G. Vlastos
184 pp. 1965. (2nd Impression 1967.) 28s.

Barry, Brian
Political Argument
382 pp. 1965. 50s.

Bird, Graham
Kant's Theory of Knowledge:
An Outline of One Central Argument in the *Critique of Pure Reason*
220 pp. 1962. (2nd Impression 1965.) 28s.

Brentano, Franz
The True and the Evident
Edited and narrated by Professor R. Chisholm
218 pp. 1965. 40s.

Broad, C. D.
Lectures on Psychical Research
Incorporating the Perrott Lectures given in Cambridge University in 1959
and 1960
461 pp. 1962. (2nd Impression 1966.) 56s.

Crombie, I. M.
An Examination of Plato's Doctrine
I. Plato on Man and Society
408 pp. 1962. (2nd Impression 1966.) 42s.
II. Plato on Knowledge and Reality
583 pp. 1963. (2nd Impression 1967.) 63s.

Day, John Patrick
Inductive Probability
352 pp. 1961. 40s.

International Library of Philosophy and Scientific Method
(Demy 8vo)

Edel, Abraham
Method in Ethical Theory
379 pp. 1963. 32s.

Flew, Anthony
Hume's Philosophy of Belief
A Study of his First "Inquiry"
296 pp. 1961. (2nd Impression 1966.) 30s.

Fogelin, Robert J.
Evidence and Meaning
Studies in Analytical Philosophy
200 pp. 1967. 25s.

Gale, Richard
The Language of Time
256 pp. 1967. about 30s.

Goldman, Lucien
The Hidden God
A Study of Tragic Vision in the *Pensées* of Pascal and the Tragedies of
Racine. Translated from the French by Philip Thody
424 pp. 1964. 70s.

Hamlyn, D. W.
Sensation and Perception
A History of the Philosophy of Perception
222 pp. 1961. (3rd Impression 1967.) 25s.

Kemp, J.
Reason, Action and Morality
216 pp. 1964. 30s.

Körner, Stephan
Experience and Theory
An Essay in the Philosophy of Science
272 pp. 1966. 45s.

Lazerowitz, Morris
Studies in Metaphilosophy
276 pp. 1964. 35s.

Linsky, Leonard
Referring
152 pp. 1967. about 28s.

Merleau-Ponty, M.
Phenomenology of Perception
Translated from the French by Colin Smith
487 pp. 1962. (4th Impression 1967.) 56s.

3

International Library of Philosophy and Scientific Method
(Demy 8vo)

Perelman, Chaim
The Idea of Justice and the Problem of Argument
Introduction by H. L. A. Hart. Translated from the French by John Petrie
224 pp. 1963. 28s.

Ross, Alf
Directives, Norms and their Logic
192 pp. 1967. about 25s.

Schlesinger, G.
Method in the Physical Sciences
148 pp. 1963. 21s.

Sellars, W. F.
Science, Perception and Reality
374 pp. 1963. (2nd Impression 1966.) 50s.

Shwayder, D. S.
The Stratification of Behaviour
A System of Definitions Propounded and Defended
428 pp. 1965. 56s.

Skolimowski, Henryk
Polish Analytical Philosophy
288 pp. 1967. 40s.

Smart, J. J. C.
Philosophy and Scientific Realism
168 pp. 1963. (3rd Impression 1967.) 25s.

Smythies, J. R. (Ed.)
Brain and Mind
Contributors: Lord Brain, John Beloff, C. J. Ducasse, Antony Flew, Hartwig Kuhlenbeck, D. M. MacKay, H. H. Price, Anthony Quinton and J. R. Smythies
288 pp. 1965. 40s.

Science and E.S.P.
Contributors: Gilbert Murray, H. H. Price, Rosalind Heywood, Cyril Burt, C. D. Broad, Francis Huxley and John Beloff
320 pp. about 40s.

Taylor, Charles
The Explanation of Behaviour
288 pp. 1964. (2nd Impression 1965.) 40s.

Williams, Bernard, and Montefiore, Alan
British Analytical Philosophy
352 pp. 1965. (2nd Impression 1967.) 45s.

International Library of Philosophy and Scientific Method
(Demy 8vo)

Wittgenstein, Ludwig
Tractatus Logico-Philosophicus
The German text of the *Logisch-Philosophische Abhandlung* with a new
translation by D. F. Pears and B. F. McGuinness. Introduction by Bertrand
Russell
188 pp. 1961. (3rd Impression 1966.) 21s.

Wright, Georg Henrik Von
Norm and Action
A Logical Enquiry. The Gifford Lectures
232 pp. 1963. (2nd Impression 1964.) 32s.

The Varieties of Goodness
The Gifford Lectures
236 pp. 1963. (3rd Impression 1966.) 28s.

Zinkernagel, Peter
Conditions for Description
Translated from the Danish by Olaf Lindum
272 pp. 1962. 37s. 6d.

International Library of Psychology, Philosophy, and Scientific Method
(Demy 8vo)

PHILOSOPHY

Anton, John Peter
Aristotle's Theory of Contrariety
276 pp. 1957. 25s.

Bentham, J.
The Theory of Fictions
Introduction by C. K. Ogden
214 pp. 1932. 30s.

Black, Max
The Nature of Mathematics
A Critical Survey
242 pp. 1933. (5th Impression 1965.) 28s.

Bluck, R. S.
Plato's Phaedo
A Translation with Introduction, Notes and Appendices
226 pp. 1955. 21s.

Broad, C. D.
Scientific Thought
556 pp. 1923. (4th Impression 1952.) 40s.

Five Types of Ethical Theory
322 pp. 1930. (9th Impression 1967.) 30s.

The Mind and Its Place in Nature
694 pp. 1925. (7th Impression 1962.) 55s. See also Lean, Martin

Buchler, Justus (Ed.)
The Philosophy of Peirce
Selected Writings
412 pp. 1940. (3rd Impression 1956.) 35s.

Burtt, E. A.
The Metaphysical Foundations of Modern Physical Science
A Historical and Critical Essay
364 pp. 2nd (revised) edition 1932. (5th Impression 1964.) 35s.

6

International Library of Psychology, Philosophy, and Scientific Method
(Demy 8vo)

Carnap, Rudolf
The Logical Syntax of Language
Translated from the German by Amethe Smeaton
376 pp. 1937. (7th Impression 1967.) 40s.

Chwistek, Leon
The Limits of Science
Outline of Logic and of the Methodology of the Exact Sciences
With Introduction and Appendix by Helen Charlotte Brodie
414 pp. 2nd edition 1949. 32s.

Cornford, F. M.
Plato's Theory of Knowledge
The Theaetetus and Sophist of Plato
Translated with a running commentary
358 pp. 1935. (7th Impression 1967.) 28s.

Plato's Cosmology
The Timaeus of Plato
Translated with a running commentary
402 pp. Frontispiece. 1937. (5th Impression 1966.) 45s.

Plato and Parmenides
Parmenides' *Way of Truth* and Plato's *Parmenides*
Translated with a running commentary
280 pp 1939 (5th Impression 1964.) 32s.

Crawshay-Williams, Rupert
Methods and Criteria of Reasoning
An Inquiry into the Structure of Controversy
312 pp. 1957. 32s.

Fritz, Charles A.
Bertrand Russell's Construction of the External World
252 pp. 1952. 30s.

Hulme, T. E.
Speculations
Essays on Humanism and the Philosophy of Art
Edited by Herbert Read. Foreword and Frontispiece by Jacob Epstein
296 pp. 2nd edition 1936. (6th Impression 1965.) 32s.

Lange, Frederick Albert
The History of Materialism
And Criticism of its Present Importance
With an Introduction by Bertrand Russell, F.R.S. Translated from the German
by Ernest Chester Thomas
1,146 pp. 1925. (3rd Impression 1957.) 70s.

8

International Library of Psychology, Philosophy, and Scientific Method
(Demy 8vo)

Smart, Ninian
Reasons and Faiths
An Investigation of Religious Discourse, Christian and Non-Christian
230 pp. 1958. (2nd Impression 1965.) 28s.

Vaihinger, H.
The Philosophy of As If
A System of the Theoretical, Practical and Religious Fictions of Mankind
Translated by C. K. Ogden
428 pp. 2nd edition 1935. (4th Impression 1965.) 45s.

Wittgenstein, Ludwig
Tractatus Logico-Philosophicus
With an Introduction by Bertrand Russell, F.R.S., German text with an English translation en regard
216 pp. 1922. (9th Impression 1962.) 21s.
For the Pears-McGuinness translation—*see page 5*

Wright, Georg Henrik von
Logical Studies
214 pp. 1957. (2nd Impression 1967.) 28s.

Zeller, Eduard
Outlines of the History of Greek Philosophy
Revised by Dr. Wilhelm Nestle. Translated from the German by L. R. Palmer
248 pp. 13th (revised) edition 1931. (5th Impression 1963.) 28s.

PSYCHOLOGY

Adler, Alfred
The Practice and Theory of Individual Psychology
Translated by P. Radin
368 pp. 2nd (revised) edition 1929. (8th Impression 1964.) 30s.

Eng, Helga
The Psychology of Children's Drawings
From the First Stroke to the Coloured Drawing
240 pp. 8 colour plates. 139 figures. 2nd edition 1954. (3rd Impression 1966.) 40s.

Jung, C. G.
Psychological Types
or The Psychology of Individuation
Translated from the German and with a Preface by H. Godwin Baynes
696 pp. 1923. (12th Impression 1964.) 45s.

International Library of Psychology, Philosophy, and Scientific Method
(Demy 8vo)

Koffka, Kurt
The Growth of the Mind
An Introduction to Child-Psychology
Translated from the German by Robert Morris Ogden
456 pp. 16 figures. 2nd edition (revised) 1928. (6th Impression 1965.) 45s.
Principles of Gestalt Psychology
740 pp. 112 figures. 39 tables. 1935. (5th Impression 1962.) 60s.

Malinowski, Bronislaw
Crime and Custom in Savage Society
152 pp. 6 plates. 1926. (8th Impression 1966.) 21s.
Sex and Repression in Savage Society
290 pp. 1927. (4th Impression 1953.) 28s.
See also Ogden, C. K.

Murphy, Gardner
An Historical Introduction to Modern Psychology
488 pp. 5th edition (revised) 1949. (6th Impression 1967.) 40s.

Paget, R.
Human Speech
Some Observations, Experiments, and Conclusions as to the Nature, Origin, Purpose and Possible Improvement of Human Speech
374 pp. 5 plates. 1930. (2nd Impression 1963.) 42s.

Petermann, Bruno
The Gestalt Theory and the Problem of Configuration
Translated from the German by Meyer Fortes
364 pp. 20 figures. 1932. (2nd Impression 1950.) 25s.

Piaget, Jean
The Language and Thought of the Child
Preface by E. Claparède. Translated from the French by Marjorie Gabain
220 pp. 3rd edition (revised and enlarged) 1959. (3rd Impression 1966.) 30s.

Judgment and Reasoning in the Child
Translated from the French by Marjorie Warden
276 pp. 1928 (4th Impression 1966.) 28s.

The Child's Conception of the World
Translated from the French by Joan and Andrew Tomlinson
408 pp. 1929. (4th Impression 1964.) 40s.

867 PRINTED BY HEADLEY BROTHERS LTD 109 KINGSWAY LONDON WC2 AND ASHFORD KENT